University of London Historical Studies

XXXVI

PALMERSTON, GUIZOT
AND THE COLLAPSE OF THE
ENTENTE CORDIALE

This volume is published with the help of
grants from the late Miss Isobel Thornley's
Bequest to the University of London
and from the Twenty-Seven Foundation

PALMERSTON, GUIZOT AND THE COLLAPSE OF THE ENTENTE CORDIALE

by
ROGER BULLEN

UNIVERSITY OF LONDON
THE ATHLONE PRESS
1974

Published by
THE ATHLONE PRESS
UNIVERSITY OF LONDON
at 4 *Gower Street London* WC1
Distributed by Tiptree Book Services Ltd
Tiptree, Essex
USA and Canada
Humanities Press Inc
New York

© *Roger Bullen* 1974

ISBN 0 485 13136 6

Printed in Great Britain by
WESTERN PRINTING SERVICES LTD
Bristol

To my Mother and Father

PREFACE

Like most books on diplomatic history, this is a study in conflict. Its purpose is to examine the collapse in 1846 of the first *entente cordiale* and the effect of that collapse on the foreign policies of England and France. This takes the story to February 1848 when it ends abruptly with the February revolution in France. The establishment of a Republic in France, and the subsequent revolutionary upheavals in Italy and Germany, changed completely the problems facing the policy makers of England and France. The prolonged conflict between Palmerston and Guizot over the Spanish succession fizzled out almost overnight.

Very soon after I began my research into the disintegration of the *entente cordiale* I became convinced that it could not be properly understood unless it was set firmly in the broader context of Anglo-French relations between 1830 and 1846. In the first place, the *entente cordiale* was not of Palmerston's making. It was established by Guizot and Aberdeen. It seemed to me that in order to understand why the *entente* failed, it was necessary to know in what circumstances it was created, what it had been designed to achieve and how it had worked before Palmerston returned to office. Moreover, it seemed essential to examine Palmerston's attitude to the *entente* whilst he was in opposition: his assumptions about it and his criticisms of it. My enquiries into the origins of the *entente cordiale* led me to the conclusion that the ideas, hopes and fears upon which it was based were the consequence of the near eastern crisis of 1839–41, when relations between England and France degenerated almost to the point of war, and of the failure of the 'liberal alliance' of the 1830s. In all these developments Lord Palmerston and the Whig party had played a crucial rôle; the Whigs were the party in power and it was they who put forward the idea that the establishment of good relations with Orleanist France was a necessary and worthwhile aim of

British foreign policy. For all these reasons Chapters I and II, which trace the development of Anglo-French relations from 1830 to 1846, seem to me an indispensable part of the story.

I have tried to show that between 1830 and 1846 Anglo-French relations fall into two distinct phases. The first period from 1830 to 1841 saw the rise and fall of the 'liberal alliance', the second period from 1841 to 1846 saw the rise and fall of the *entente cordiale*. This distinction between the 'liberal alliance' of the 1830s and the *entente cordiale* of the 1840s is not always made. André Guyot in his pioneering study, *La Première Entente Cordiale* of 1926, treated the history of England's relations with the Orleans Monarchy as the story of one *entente*. I have avoided this approach as it seems to me that the two periods of friendship were quite different. Both Guizot and Aberdeen were conscious of pursuing new policies; they prided themselves that the *entente cordiale* was pitched in a lower key than the 'liberal alliance'.

The limits of this book are the ideas, attitudes and actions of statesmen and the reactions of Parliaments, the press and public opinion to the vicissitudes of Anglo-French relations. It is a study of ideas, personalities and policies in conflict. The book does not take economic, social or cultural factors into account except in so far as they directly affected the actions of statesmen. Except for a few individuals, none of whom was concerned with policy making, there was very little desire on either side of the Channel to foster economic, social and cultural contacts between the two countries in order to create solid and lasting bonds of friendship. In these spheres, as in political matters, rivalry and marked divergences of opinion were more powerful than sympathy and understanding. In both the 1830s and the 1840s several attempts were made to put Anglo-French economic relations on a new basis. They all failed. The British believed that the French were jealous of the commercial power of England and that French industry needed to be protected against British competition. The French believed that any commercial treaty acceptable to Great Britain would be to the disadvantage of French industry. In fact it was much easier for the statesmen to conjure up old fears and old prejudices than to encourage sympathy and understanding. On both sides of the Channel the notion that the two states were hereditary enemies was much stronger than the belief that England and France could co-operate to their mutual benefit.

I should like first to acknowledge the gracious permission of Her Majesty the Queen to make use of material from the Royal Archives at Windsor Castle. Other owners kindly allowed me to consult manuscripts in their possession. They are the Trustees of the Broadlands Archives, Brigadier and Mrs Bulwer-Long, the Earl of Clarendon, the Marquess of Normanby, Dr Marc Schlumberger, and the Editor of *The Times*. To them and the many archivists and librarians in England and France who have helped me I offer my sincere thanks. I acknowledge with gratitude the financial support of the Central Research Funds of the University of London which enabled me to carry out research in Paris. I should also like to thank the Trustees of the Twenty-Seven Foundation and of the Isobel Thornley Bequest for their generous grants to assist publication. Parts of Chapter x are drawn from my article in the *English Historical Review* (July 1971) with the kind permission of the Editor.

Many friends and colleagues have helped me in the preparation of this book. I should like to thank Dr Kenneth Bourne, Professor A. G. Dickens, Professor R. M. Hatton, Professor H. Hearder and Professor W. N. Medlicott for their advice and encouragement. Mr J. P. T. Bury was the first to stimulate my interest in Anglo-French relations in the nineteenth century. His advice and guidance at an early stage in my researches was most valuable. I would also like to thank Douglas Johnson for all the help he has so generously given me. To James Joll I am deeply grateful for his guidance and encouragement at every stage in the preparation of this book. My greatest debt is to Felicity Ranger. Her assistance has been so varied and so constant that it almost amounts to collaboration. As I cannot adequately thank her I can only say that without her never-failing help and encouragement this book would never have been written.

The London School of Economics   Roger Bullen
   and Political Science
June 1973

CONTENTS

	Abbreviations	xii
I	The Liberal Alliance, 1830–41	1
II	Lord Palmerston and Anglo-French relations, 1841–6	25
III	The Whigs return	50
IV	The Spanish Marriages, July–August 1846	82
V	The first reaction, September–October 1846	120
VI	The struggle continues, October 1846–March 1847	148
VII	Currents of thought	184
VIII	Iberian problems, October 1846–February 1847	213
IX	Iberian problems, March 1847–February 1848	246
X	The *Sonderbund* crisis, 1847–8	293
XI	England and the fall of the Orleans monarchy	322
XII	Conclusion	332
	Select Bibliography	339
	Index	344

ABBREVIATIONS

A.A.E.C.P.	Archives du Ministère des Affaires Etrangères: Correspondance Politique
A.A.E. M. and D.	Archives du Ministère des Affaires Etrangères: Mémoires et Documents
B.M. Add. MSS.	British Museum Additional Manuscripts
B.M.M.	British Museum Microfilm
B.P.	Broadlands Papers
Clar. Dep.	Clarendon Deposit
F.O.	Foreign Office
G.P.	Guizot Papers
P.R.O.	Public Record Office
R.A.	Royal Archives

CHAPTER I

The Liberal Alliance, 1830–41

In November 1830 Lord Palmerston became Foreign Secretary in the Whig government of Lord Grey. His appointment occasioned some surprise. He was a Whig neither by background nor by conviction; indeed, he had served for eighteen years, between 1809 and 1828, as Secretary at War in five successive Tory administrations. His interest in foreign affairs was of recent origin, and to many of the Whig leaders he was virtually unknown. In his attitude to foreign policy he was an avowed Canningite. In 1828 he had resigned from the Duke of Wellington's government because he believed that Wellington was betraying the principles on which Canning's policy was based. For Palmerston the legacy of Canning meant two things: firstly he believed that it had been distinguished by the attempt to 'inspire' other states 'with a proper sense of the power of Great Britain' and by a preoccupation with the defence and the development of the legitimate interests of England; secondly he thought that in the execution of his policy Canning had shown great vision and courage. His legacy was not a sterile one: it lent itself to addition and development. Between his resignation from Wellington's cabinet and his entry into Grey's, Palmerston adjusted his interpretation of Canning's heritage to new circumstances both at home and abroad.

For Palmerston the essence of pragmatic Toryism was recognition of the political implications of social and economic change and the attempt to control them. By 1830 he was convinced that reform from above was the best antidote to revolution from below. At home he believed that a modicum of parliamentary reform and an extension of the franchise were necessary to prevent a violent struggle between the aristocracy and the middle classes. This was to be avoided at all costs. In foreign affairs, too, Palmerston opposed reactionary governments; he believed that it was in the best interests of England

and of political stability in Europe to encourage constitutional reforms in states where such changes seemed possible and desirable. He was convinced that reactionary governments in states where the forces of change were powerful were a source of perpetual danger: they were liable to succumb to revolution, and being too weak to reassert their own authority they appealed to the conservative great powers for support against their disaffected subjects. The intervention of great powers in the internal affairs of small states tended to disturb the European equilibrium, and in western Europe directly threatened the interests of England. As the patron of reform in Europe England would promote political stability and thereby increase her influence. Moreover, reform would bring progress, and progress meant increased wealth and trade, from which England, as the greatest trading nation, must benefit. Between 1828 and 1830 Palmerston thus developed Canning's pragmatic Toryism into a doctrine of reform and concession both at home and abroad. This intensified his opposition to Wellington's brand of unbending Toryism and disposed him to co-operate with his former rivals, the Whigs. The merger in 1830 of the Whigs and the Canningites under Lord Grey was the logical outcome of the development by the Canningites of the ideas of their master. By 1830 the similarities between the two groups seemed more marked than their differences; Lord John Russell wrote that the Whigs in 1830 proclaimed 'their principle in the toast "the cause of civil and religious liberty all over the world" ', and that 'Lord Palmerston in joining the Whigs thoroughly adopted this sentiment.'[1] This was true, but the fact remained that for the Whigs 'the cause of civil and religious liberty' was an almost sacred principle derived from Fox,[2] whereas for Palmerston it was a necessary extension of the doctrines of Canning. In their attitude to Europe and to British foreign policy the Whigs held beliefs which Palmerston did not share. The union of November 1830 undoubtedly contained the seeds of future discord.

Between 1792 and 1830 the Whigs had been bitter critics of

[1] *The Early Correspondence of Lord John Russell 1805–1840*, ed. Rollo Russell (London, 1913), i, 317.
[2] L. G. Mitchell, *Charles James Fox and the Disintegration of the Whig Party 1782–1794* (Oxford, 1971), ch. vii.

Tory foreign policy. Fox claimed that England in 1793 had allied herself with arbitrary and aggressive governments whose aims had been to exploit the French revolution in order to complete the dismemberment of Poland and to deny the French people their inalienable right to choose their own form of government. According to Fox, the French had become aggressive and expansionist only after they had been provoked by the despotic coalition against them.[3] The Whigs believed that the defeat of France in 1815 strengthened 'the conspiracy against liberty'; the peace-makers of 1815 had done nothing more than enslave the peoples of Europe to arbitrary monarchs.[4] In their view international relations between 1815 and 1830 were dominated by the rule of tyranny. They condemned Castlereagh for co-operating with a league of despots, and Canning for his ostentatious displays of power and his lack of concern for nations oppressed by arbitrary governments.[5] They looked forward to the day when the principles of Fox would guide the foreign policy of England, making her the promoter and protector of liberty instead of the collaborator of the aggressive despotisms of eastern Europe.[6] The attitude of the Foxite Whigs to foreign policy was dominated by intense suspicion of the eastern powers, particularly of Russia, and almost limitless enthusiasm for France, whose love of liberty and natural political development they saw as having been thwarted by the reactionary forces in Europe. For the followers of Charles James Fox these were long-cherished beliefs. When they took office in 1830 the Foxite Whigs believed that the events of that year confirmed the validity of these beliefs: in July the French people had defeated a European conspiracy to strengthen Bourbon despotism.[7]

[3] Lord John Russell [Earl Russell], *The Foreign Policy of England 1570–1870. An Historical Essay* (London, 1871), 56–7.
[4] Macintosh's famous indictment of the peace settlement of 1815 is printed in *Britain and Europe 1793–1950*, ed. James Joll (London, 1950), 60–8.
[5] See for example Grey's comments on Canning's foreign policy. Grey to Princess Lieven, 27 Jan. 1827. *The Correspondence of Princess Lieven and Earl Grey*, ed. G. Le Strange (London, 1890), i, 34.
[6] Lord John Russell, *A Letter to the Right Honourable Lord Holland on Foreign Politics* (London, 1819). It is not without significance that this pamphlet was republished with a new introduction in 1831.
[7] Holland believed that Wellington was implicated in the 'European conspiracy' to undermine the Charter of 1814. Holland to Grey, 5 Mar. 1830. Holland House Papers, British Museum [hereafter B.M.] Add. MS. 51548.

Charles X and his minister Polignac were overthrown and exiled, and a constitutional monarchy, established under the Duke of Orleans, proclaimed Louis Philippe King of the French. The Whigs believed that the French had set an example which the rest of Europe could follow;[8] with constitutionalism triumphant in France and the party of reform in office in England, a new era in the history of Europe was about to begin, which would at last vindicate the principles of Charles James Fox. 'I hope', declared Grey in the House of Lords in November 1830, 'that by the union of the two countries holding their liberties by the same means and on the same principles the peace of Europe will be maintained.'[9] Lord Holland, the nephew of Charles James Fox, immediately informed Palmerston that Russia, with her ambitious designs on her neighbours, posed the greatest danger to peace, and that 'nothing but a cordial understanding between France and England' could restrain her.[10] The Foxite Whigs in the Grey cabinet, Holland, Lansdowne, Althorp and Russell, regarded the establishment of intimate and cordial relations with the Orleans monarchy as the most urgent task facing British foreign policy. They anticipated formidable opposition, from the Tories at home, who harboured a bitter and irrational hatred of France, and from Russia who would endeavour to keep England and France apart and suspicious of one another.[11] These obstacles must, however, be overcome; 'for everything good in Europe', wrote Holland, 'a thorough cordiality with France is necessary'.[12] The French government had already made clear its wish to be on the best possible terms with England, and with the Whigs in particular; the Foxites therefore argued that friendly overtures would meet with an enthusiastic response in Paris.[13] Palmerston and other members of the cabinet, however,

---

[8] See Lord Lansdowne's speech in the House of Lords, 3 Nov. 1830. *Hansard's Parliamentary Debates* [hereafter *Hansard*], 3rd series, i, 246.

[9] *Hansard*, 3rd series, i, 38.

[10] Holland to Palmerston, 26 Dec. 1830. Broadlands Papers [hereafter B.P.] GC/HO/65.

[11] William Russell to Holland, 30 Jan. 1830. Holland House Papers, B.M. Add. MS. 51599.

[12] Holland to Palmerston, 27 Feb. 1831. B.P. GC/HO/66.

[13] Russell to Holland, 13 Sept. 1830. Holland House Papers, B.M. Add. MS. 51677. Russell was in Paris and had an interview with Louis Philippe.

had a different set of priorities. They regarded securities against the possibility of French aggression as more important than close friendship with France.

In July 1830 Palmerston had welcomed the revolution in France with enthusiasm,[14] but his attitude to the new régime when he came into office became more cautious and suspicious. He regarded France, under whatever government, as the main enemy of England, and he believed that the maintenance of the European balance of power and the containment of France within her 1815 borders should be the main objectives of British foreign policy. A number of his colleagues shared this view: Grey and Melbourne, Goderich and Graham, the other three Canningites in the cabinet. In Palmerston's opinion England had nothing to gain and much to lose by concessions to France and the abandonment of her tried and trusted allies. There could be no doubt, Palmerston informed Holland, that '...the best security for peace consists in the cordial good understanding of the other four powers, in the unfitness of the French army as yet to take up the field against Europe and in the dread which the French feel of a maritime contest with England', and that the Treaty of Vienna, 'however objectionable in some of the details of its arrangement, is yet with its accessories of Paris and Aix-la-Chapelle the great security of Europe against the inveterately enervating spirit of France'.[15] Holland was bitterly disappointed by Palmerston's refusal to abandon the Tory legacy in foreign policy, and accused him of being hidebound by obsolete and mistaken assumptions.[16] Palmerston was unmoved by the appeals of the Foxites; in 1830 and 1831 nothing could shake his profound distrust of France.[17]

The Belgian question in the spring and summer of 1831 emphasised the differences which had emerged in late 1830 and

---

[14] 'This event', wrote Palmerston, 'is decisive of the ascendancy of Liberal Principles throughout Europe; the evil spirit has been put down and will be trodden under foot. The reign of Metternich is over...' Mabell, Countess of Airlie, *Lady Palmerston and her Times* (London, 1922), i, 173.

[15] Palmerston to Holland, 9 Apr. 1831. Holland House Papers, B.M. Add. MS. 51599.

[16] Holland to Russell, 27 Jan. 1831. *The Early Correspondence of Lord John Russell 1805–1840*, ed. Rollo Russell, ii, 11.

[17] See Palmerston to Holland, 21 May 1831. Holland House Papers, B.M. Add. MS. 51599.

early 1831 between Palmerston and his Francophile colleagues. When the Flemish and Walloon subjects of the King of Holland rose in revolt against their Dutch masters in late 1830, the French invoked the doctrine of non-intervention, thus effectively preventing the conservative powers from intervening to help the King of Holland to suppress the revolt.[18] The most pressing danger raised by the Belgian question, in Palmerston's view, was that France might exploit the situation either to extend her northern borders or to create a new client state. In the spring of 1831 Palmerston therefore took the initiative: he announced that Great Britain would support the establishment of a new state of Belgium, and he called a conference of the powers in London to arrange the separation of Belgium and Holland. This policy brought him into conflict both with the eastern powers and with France, since the former wished to restore Dutch authority in the southern provinces, while the latter desired a revision of the 1815 settlement in her own favour. Palmerston's response was to use the spectre of French expansion to frighten the eastern powers, and the threat of isolation to cajole France. The Francophiles disapproved of this shifting policy; they thought complete and straightforward co-operation with France more sensible, and did not think that England's interests would be seriously endangered if France were to make some small gains on her northern borders: 'it is better', Holland informed Russell, 'to be outreached by a man whose main interest coincides with your own, than to foil him in some little artifice or design and thereby expose both his and your interests to entire discomfiture'. Once again he warned Palmerston that the real danger to peace and liberty lay in Russian aggression and expansion.[19] Palmerston strongly disagreed:

Russia it is true has added large tracts of country to her dominions but these additions are less important to the nations of Europe than the conquests which France might make because they do not in the same manner or degree affect the interests and independence of the

---

[18] For a full account of the Belgian revolt and Palmerston's settlement of the Belgian question, see C. K. Webster, *The Foreign Policy of Palmerston 1830–1841* [hereafter Webster, *Palmerston*] (new impression, London, 1969), i, ch. ii.

[19] Holland to Russell, 27 Jan. 1831. *The Early Correspondence of Lord John Russell 1805–1840*, ed. Rollo Russell, ii, 11. See also Holland to Palmerston, 21 May 1831. B.P. GC/HO/68.

nations of Europe. Whether Russia possesses a degree or two of latitude more or less in the Caucasus cannot be of the same importance to England, Prussia, Austria or Spain as any smaller variations in the territory and resources of France because the former adds but little to the means of Russia to attack the rest of Europe, while the latter might materially increase the offensive faculties of France.[20]

By the summer of 1831 Anglo-French relations had reached one of their lowest points since 1815. In order to force the Dutch to evacuate Belgium, French troops had entered the country to act in conjunction with a British squadron off Antwerp. When the French used this opportunity to renew their proposals for partition, Palmerston warned them that war would be the consequence of refusal to withdraw their troops unconditionally from Belgium.[21] For a few days Palmerston expected war, but the French agreed to withdraw after five of the barrier fortresses on her northern border had been transferred from Belgium to France.

The retreat of the French and their acceptance of an independent Belgium under Prince Leopold of Saxe-Coburg brought about a marked improvement in Anglo-French relations which coincided with a deterioration in England's relations with the eastern powers. The encouragement given in late 1831 and early 1832 by the northern Courts to the King of Holland in his intransigent refusal to recognise Belgian independence led Palmerston to co-operate increasingly with France in order to outmanœuvre them; he soon became convinced that only the union of England and France could preserve peace and stability in western Europe. In 1832 Palmerston began to speak publicly of 'a cordial good understanding' or *entente* between England and France.[22] For him, unlike his Francophile colleagues, its basis was not belief, but practice. Like the Foxites, he saw the union of the two powers as a security against the despotism and aggression of the eastern powers. For Palmerston, however, it was also a means whereby England could contain France, forcing her to accept a secondary

[20] Palmerston to Holland, 21 May 1831. Holland House Papers, B.M. Add. MS. 51599.
[21] Palmerston to Granville, 16 Aug. 1831. B.P. GC/GR/1341.
[22] K. Bourne, *The Foreign Policy of Victorian England 1830–1902* (Oxford, 1970), 32.

rôle particularly in western Europe. Palmerston saw the *entente* as an unequal relationship, England leading and France following. He rightly deduced that the hostility of the eastern powers to the Orleans monarchy meant that France must either work with England on England's terms, or accept isolation. For the French an *entente* on this basis was far from ideal but preferable for the moment to isolation, and there were French politicians like Broglie who hoped that it could be transformed into an equal and mutually beneficial relationship. By 1832 therefore Palmerston had done what the Foxites wanted: he had begun to work closely with France and he was becoming increasingly suspicious of the eastern powers. The Foxites could no longer criticise him for his refusal to co-operate with France. They warned him, however, that he should attempt to put Anglo-French relations on a basis of equality; the French could not be expected, wrote Holland, to practise 'for any long time...the self denial of obtaining neither strength nor glory at home and abroad'.[23]

'I quite concur in all you say about the necessity of being really on good terms with France', Palmerston assured Holland in January 1833,[24] and during 1833 and 1834 he made strenuous efforts to strengthen the *entente*, developing and extending the Anglo-French understanding to cover and serve almost every aspect of British foreign policy. As an ideological union he used it as a defence against and a challenge to the absolutist powers in Europe and the Tories at home; as a means of defence for British preponderance over the smaller states of western Europe it was extended from Belgium to the Iberian peninsula. To these original purposes of the *entente* Palmerston added another: the defence of British interests in the near east against Russian encroachment. The rapid deterioration in Anglo-Russian relations in 1833 played a very large part in prompting Palmerston to try to improve Anglo-French relations. By late 1833 he had come to share Whig assumptions about the character of Russian government and foreign policy, seeing in her the blind and obstinate champion of reaction, the greatest

---

[23] Holland to Palmerston, [?] Oct. 1831. B.P. GC/HO/76.
[24] Palmerston to Holland, 2 Jan. 1833. Holland House Papers, B.M. Add. MS. 51599.

threat to the peace of Europe.[25] Palmerston believed that Russia had in the near east conscious schemes of expansion which directly threatened British communications with India and which would ultimately destroy the European equilibrium. By 1834 Russia had, in his view, replaced France as the main enemy of England; 'there is', he wrote, 'the same principle of repulsion between Russia and us that there was between us and Buonaparte'.[26] He no longer maintained that Russian expansion outside Europe was of no consequence to the other European powers.

Palmerston's first attempt to deal with the eastern question was unsuccessful. He greatly underestimated the significance of the crisis confronting the Turkish Empire in 1832. As a result of Mehemet Ali's attacks on the Turkish position in Syria and the British refusal to assist the Porte, the Sultan, in desperation, turned to Russia for help.[27] In July 1833 the Turks and the Russians signed the defensive treaty of Unkiar Skelessi. Palmerston regarded this as a potentially dangerous development; its result, he wrote, was that 'the Russian Ambassador becomes chief Cabinet Minister of the Sultan'.[28] The Convention of Münchengrätz, concluded between Russia and Austria in September 1833,[29] added to his fears; he believed it was an agreement for the eventual partition of the Ottoman Empire. By the end of 1833 Palmerston was convinced that a war in the eastern Mediterranean to prevent the dismemberment of Turkey by Russia would sooner or later be inevitable.

The new situation in the near east raised, as Palmerston recognised, two vital questions: how was Russia to be restrained, and what support could Great Britain rely on in the event of war

---

[25] 'The military organization of her political fabric renders encroachment upon her neighbours almost a necessary condition of her existence', wrote Palmerston to Bligh, 26 Feb. 1834. Bligh Papers, B.M. Add. MS. 41285.
[26] Ibid.
[27] For an account of the near eastern crisis of 1832–3 see Webster, *Palmerston*, i, chs. iv and v, and M. S. Anderson, *The Eastern Question 1774–1923* (London, 1966), 77–93. For an account of Russian policy towards Turkey in the 1830s, see G. H. Bolsover, 'Nicholas I and the Partition of Turkey', *Slavonic and East European Review*, 1948–9, xxvii, 115–45.
[28] Webster, *Palmerston*, i, 305.
[29] For the texts of both these agreements, see M.S. Anderson, *The Great Powers and the Near East 1774–1923* (London, 1970), 42–5.

with Russia? Palmerston concluded that 'the danger will be best guarded against by a friendly union with France'.[30] His colleagues agreed: 'Russia will draw back if she sees we [England and France] are firm', Lansdowne confidently assured Holland.[31] From 1834 onwards therefore Palmerston regarded the *entente* with France as a diplomatic counterbalance to Russian influence at Constantinople, and he hoped that, should the necessity arise, it could be transformed into a wartime alliance to resist Russian aggression. By the beginning of 1834 Palmerston was convinced that the *entente*, publicly affirmed as the policy of the Whigs and the policy of peace, was firmly established: 'the common interests of England and France form too strong a bond of union' to be easily broken and Russia, he declared, would fail in any attempt to make France 'jealous of us'.[32] This belief had some basis in fact; the French had been as alarmed as the British by Unkiar Skelessi and Münchengrätz, and moreover they would not abandon the *entente* for isolation. Anglo-French co-operation in the near east, however, was no guarantee against Anglo-French differences elsewhere.

In the spring of 1834 Palmerston, deaf to Holland's warning that 'you cannot hope to have for ever a French Government ready to accommodate itself to every proposal you may bring forward...',[33] again encountered resistance when he tried to force France to play a subordinate rôle to England in western Europe. Palmerston's belief that constitutional monarchies ensured stable governments naturally inclined to England led him in 1831 and 1832 to support the cause of Queen Dona Maria of Portugal against her absolutist uncle, Dom Miguel, who claimed the throne on the grounds that Dona Maria was excluded by the Salic Law. The succession struggle completely divided Portuguese society: the liberals supported Dona Maria while the reactionary and clerical forces rallied to Dom Miguel.[34] By the end of 1831 Portugal was in the throes of a

[30] Palmerston to Holland, 25 Jan. 1834. Holland House Papers, B.M. Add. MS. 51556.
[31] Lansdowne to Holland, 24 Oct. 1834. Holland House Papers, B.M. Add. MS. 51688.
[32] Palmerston to Bligh, 26 Feb. 1834. Bligh Papers, B.M. Add. MS. 41285.
[33] Holland to Palmerston, 11 Nov. 1833. B.P. GC/HO/77.
[34] See H. V. Livermore, *A New History of Portugal* (Cambridge, 1969), 268–79.

bitter and bloody civil war. The European powers immediately took sides: Spain and the northern Courts supported Miguel, the British and French supported Dona Maria and the Constitutionalists. Palmerston was determined to prevent outside intervention in Portugal; he hoped that if Great Britain held the ring, the Constitutionalists would soon overcome the Miguelites. By 1833 his ability to prevent intervention in Portugal by any other power could be maintained only by increasing involvement in the cause of the Constitutionalists. In September 1833 the death of Ferdinand VII of Spain dramatically transformed the political situation in the Peninsula. Before his death Ferdinand had introduced a new law of succession so that his daughter Isabella could succeed him. Ferdinand's brother Don Carlos, who would have succeeded under the old Pragmatic Sanction of Philip V, took up arms against his niece and, like Miguel in Portugal, gained the support of the reactionary and clerical elements.[35] This forced the Queen Regent, Queen Christina, into an alliance with the liberal constitutionalists in both Spain and Portugal, which linked the fortunes of the two young queens and of the liberals in the Peninsula. The civil wars in Spain and Portugal were also linked to struggles between the great powers.[36] The eastern powers wanted a triumph for absolutism, the British and French knew that the victory of reaction, a setback for their principles wherever it occurred, would be particularly humiliating in western Europe. The political crisis in Spain also revealed a conflict of interests between England and France. Palmerston was intensely jealous of French influence at Madrid, and suspected the French of a desire to extend it to Portugal; if successful, they might one day be in a position to interrupt British communications with the Mediterranean and India. France feared that the British would attempt to exclude her from all influence in the Peninsula, and relegate her to the rank of a secondary power. Palmerston was well aware of the ambiguity of Anglo-French relations in the Peninsula. Immediately after the death of Ferdinand VII he

[35] Raymond Carr, *Spain 1808–1939* (Oxford, 1966), 155–68.
[36] As early as Sept. 1832 Palmerston described the conflict in Portugal as 'a struggle between the opposing principles which are in conflict all over Europe, between arbitrary power with all its concomitant abuses and rational government tempered by freedom and justice'. Draft article for *The Globe*. B.P. PRE/B/23.

began to stress their identity of outlook, but he also made it clear that he expected the French to take no action in Spain except 'in concert with us'.[37]

In January 1834 Palmerston first mentioned the existence of a 'Western union' of 'liberal and improving powers', comprising England, France, Spain and Portugal. For Palmerston, the significance of this 'new confederacy' was the effect it would have on international relations in Europe: 'The Triple League of the despotic governments...in the East will now be counterbalanced by a Quadruple Alliance in the West.'[38] Palmerston saw it as another barrier against Russian aggression, another security for peace and the European balance of power. Whereas in Europe the 'Western union' was directed against Russia, in the Peninsula itself it was designed to contain France. Palmerston hoped that in the long term constitutional Spain would draw closer to constitutional Portugal, and that both would look to England for guidance and support. In the short term his object was more specific. In Portugal the position of the young Queen was desperate. In January 1834 both Palmerston and Grey thought that the British government ought to intervene in Portugal, but the cabinet rejected their plan of intervention.[39] Palmerston hoped that the Spaniards would do what his colleagues would not allow England to do. The Spaniards, however, were unwilling to act alone and Miraflores, the Spanish minister in London, suggested to Palmerston that England and Spain should intervene jointly.[40] Acting on this suggestion, Palmerston immediately set about drafting a treaty for joint Anglo-Spanish intervention in Portugal to defeat and expel Dom Miguel. He wished France to be associated with the project of intervention, but to take no active part in it. This would have the dual advantage of keeping France out of the Peninsula while at the same time parading the unity of the four western powers in Europe. 'I am convinced that such a treaty would tell as far as Constantinople and the shores of the Euxine', Palmerston informed the British ambassador in Paris.[41]

[37] Palmerston to Holland, 9 Oct. 1833. Holland House Papers, B.M. Add. MS. 51599.
[38] Draft article for *The Globe*, 24 Jan. 1834. B.P. PRE/B/94.
[39] Webster, *Palmerston*, i, 388–9.   [40] Ibid., i, 392–3.
[41] Palmerston to Granville, 11 Apr. 1834. B.P. GC/GR/1517.

Granville was to inform the French government that 'England and France stand in different situations in this matter. England is bound by treaties to Portugal...France has not the same motive for being a party concerned and I think it would be more agreeable to many parties that the treaty should be confined to Spain, England and Portugal.'[42]

When Palmerston called Talleyrand to the Foreign Office in April to communicate the terms of the proposed Triple Treaty and invite French accession to it, the French ambassador declared that the British proposal was an insult to the dignity of France. France, stated Talleyrand, could only accede to the treaty as an equal partner. Palmerston agreed to raise this objection with his colleagues and with the Portuguese and Spanish ministers.[43] He preferred France becoming a full contracting member to the treaty to her complete exclusion from it. French absence from the league of liberal powers would mean that Palmerston would be denied his 'European counterbalance', and moreover it would give France the opportunity to intrigue against England in the Peninsula. The solution Palmerston proposed therefore was that France should have equal status with England in the treaty but not in the actual intervention. This Talleyrand accepted. The final drafting of the Quadruple Alliance between England, France, Spain and Portugal involved endless wrangling between Palmerston and Talleyrand. Palmerston complained that Talleyrand behaved as if 'he was conferring a favour upon us instead of our doing a favour by volunteering to let him in'.[44] If Palmerston found the French more difficult to satisfy than he had expected, they were scarcely delighted by the agreement. Talleyrand described it as an 'alliance Palmerston' rather than an 'alliance anglaise', and in France there were influential forces in and around the government who thought that France should assert her independence of and equality with England and pursue an independent policy in the Peninsula.[45] Palmerston, however, considered the treaty a great triumph: by it Miguel was expelled from Portugal and France was kept out of the Peninsula. In

---

[42] Palmerston to Granville, 10 Apr. 1834. B.P. GC/GR/1516.
[43] Palmerston to Granville, 14 Apr. 1834. B.P. GC/GR/1518.
[44] Webster, *Palmerston*, i, 396.   [45] Ibid., i, 409.

Europe there could be no doubt, declared Palmerston, that 'the Western Confederacy may now be looked upon as firmly established'.[46] In fact the most significant development of the first four years of Palmerston's second tenure of the Foreign Office was the decline of the *entente*.[47]

During 1833 and 1834 Palmerston constantly pressed the French government to reduce its high tariffs and conclude a trade agreement with England. The opposition these proposals met in Paris greatly disappointed him;[48] he believed that more than good commercial relations were at stake. He wanted to extend and strengthen political co-operation, and argued that a reduction in French tariffs would make the *entente* popular with the radicals in Parliament and the manufacturing classes in the country.[49] Great importance has been attached to the failure of the commercial negotiations as contributory to the progressive decline of the *entente*.[50] Its real significance lay in the fact that it revived Palmerston's suspicions about the good faith of Louis Philippe and French politicians. He began to think that the Orleans monarchy was as jealous of the greatness and prosperity of England as previous French governments had been, and that the constitutional monarchy could no more be trusted to act with sincerity and disinterestedness than its predecessors. As early as May 1834 Palmerston admitted to Granville that on some issues he thought that 'Louis Philippe is against us'.[51] It was, however, the conduct of the French towards Spain between 1835 and 1838 that transformed his suspicions into unshakeable convictions.

The intervention of England and Spain under the terms of the Quadruple Alliance ended the civil war in Portugal. In Spain, however, conflict between the Carlists and the Constitutionalists only began in earnest in late 1834. The Carlists received not

[46] Palmerston to Minto, 23 Sept. 1834. B.P. GC/MI/573.
[47] In Dec. 1834 the Whigs went out of office and Peel formed his first government. In Apr. 1835 the Whigs returned to power and Palmerston to the Foreign Office.
[48] Palmerston to Granville, 18 June 1833. B.P. GC/GR/1478.
[49] Palmerston to Granville, 3 Mar. 1834. B.P. GC/GR/1510.
[50] See A. Guyot, *La Première Entente Cordiale* (Paris, 1926), 251–2, and Charles Pouthas, 'Sur les rapports de la France et de l'Angleterre pendant la Monarchie de Juillet', *Revue d'Histoire Moderne*, Dec. 1927, xii, 455–68.
[51] Palmerston to Granville, 23 May 1834. B.P. GC/GR/1526.

THE LIBERAL ALLIANCE, 1830-41

only money but also large supplies of arms from the three northern Courts and from the lesser reactionary powers,[52] either over the Pyrenees or through the northern ports of Spain. Palmerston believed that the Quadruple Alliance bound England and France unreservedly to the Constitutional cause, and was therefore shocked to find that the French government was making no effort to block the supply of arms to the Carlists over the Pyrenees. It was clear to him that France cared little for her treaty obligations, and he soon began to have serious doubts about her adherence to the cause of liberalism in Spain.[53] By 1835 it was no longer possible to conceal the significant divergences between English and French policy towards Spain, and Palmerston began to accuse the French of wanting a Carlist victory.[54] By the summer of 1835 the position of the Constitutionalists was desperate, and the Queen Regent appealed to Britain and France for help, under the spirit although not the terms of the Quadruple Alliance. Palmerston responded immediately with loans on the London money market, arms, and parliamentary authority for the raising of a British legion of 10,000 men. The French, by contrast, were reluctant to help Queen Christina; their desultory efforts on her behalf were designed to be ineffective. At the end of 1835 the Whig press was bitterly attacking the Spanish policy of the French government,[55] and Palmerston regretfully admitted that Spain 'must give up all hope of real assistance' from France, because the French regarded 'the changes from despotism to free institutions as unfavourable to French ascendancy at Madrid...They see Spain fast slipping out of their hands and becoming instead of a satellite of France, an independent ally of England.'[56] Palmerston did not appreciate that the French might find just cause for alarm in the exclusive position which Villiers, the British minister at Madrid, had established in

---

[52] Webster, *Palmerston*, i, 423. See also Philip E. Moseley, 'Intervention and Non-Intervention in Spain 1838–1839', *Journal of Modern History*, June 1941, xiii, 195–217.
[53] Palmerston to Granville, 24 Nov. 1835. B.P. GC/GR/1578.
[54] Palmerston to Granville, 8 Dec. 1835. B.P. GC/GR/1582.
[55] Webster, *Palmerston*, i, 435.
[56] Palmerston to Granville, 24 Nov. 1835. B.P. GC/GR/1578. Palmerston to Granville, 27 Sept. 1836. B.P. GC/GR/1631.

the counsels of the Spanish government and in the British attempt to negotiate a 'most favoured nation' commercial treaty with Spain. His determination to deny France any independent rôle in the Peninsula, and the French determination to resist their exclusion led to a progressively marked deterioration in Anglo-French relations in western Europe. The fall of Broglie in February 1836 removed the only French politician wholeheartedly committed to co-operation with England. Palmerston made no secret of the fact that he regarded Thiers and Molé, Broglie's successors, as enemies of England.[57] Under them a policy of non-co-operation deteriorated into one of active and bitter rivalry over Spain; the two powers began to work with opposing factions within the Constitutionalists, the British patronising the more democratic Progresista party, the French the more aristocratic Moderados.

Palmerston did not conceal his exasperation with the French. In 1837 for the first time in five years the speech from the throne at the opening of the new parliamentary session contained no friendly reference to France or to the *entente*.[58] Holland[59] seconded a request from the French government for some indication that the relations of the two countries remained cordial and close,[60] and the result was a passing mention of the *entente* in the course of a debate.[61] This satisfied both the French and the Foxites, enabling the former to claim that they were not isolated in Europe and the latter to assert that the cherished principle of good relations with France remained the pivot of Whig foreign policy. In practice, however, this lukewarm reaffirmation of the *entente* on both sides of the Channel in 1837 made no difference to Anglo-French relations: their rivalry continued unabated in

[57] Palmerston to Granville, 9 Feb. 1836. B.P. GC/GR/1595. By Sept. 1836 Palmerston asserted that Molé and Thiers were both so hostile to England that whatever changes of ministry took place in France 'no other government could be worse for our policy'. Palmerston to Granville, 20 Sept. 1836. B.P. GC/GR/1628.
[58] Palmerston informed Granville that 'We can say nothing in praise [of the French] and therefore silence is the most complimentary thing we can bestow upon them.' 27 Jan. 1837. B.P. GC/GR/1655.
[59] Holland to Palmerston, 14 Feb. 1837. B.P. GC/HO/107.
[60] Palmerston thought the request 'a little unreasonable...They forget that their speech was highly affronting to us.' Palmerston to Granville, 7 Feb. 1837. B.P. GC/GR/1657.
[61] Palmerston to Granville, 14 Mar. 1837. B.P. GC/GR/1668.

THE LIBERAL ALLIANCE, 1830-41

Spain and was extended to Portugal, Belgium and Greece, establishing a pattern of conflict between the two powers which was to last until the fall of the Orleans monarchy.[62] Although the decline of the Anglo-French *entente* was apparent to both, neither the French nor the British government was prepared openly to admit its failure. The French wanted to hold on to it until they found an alternative alignment, and they could always appeal to its ideological basis if domestic or international circumstances required a parade of liberal principles. Although the *entente* no longer carried any force in western Europe, for Palmerston it remained a security against Russian aggression in the near east. For this reason Palmerston told Granville that he was not 'prepared to break with France'.[63]

Between 1834 and 1838 Palmerston's near eastern policy, which aimed at strengthening Turkey so that she might resist pressure either from Russia or from Egypt,[64] had met with only limited success, with the result that in 1838 he was as hostile to the Russians and Egyptians and as apprehensive about affairs in the eastern Mediterranean as he had been in 1834.[65] In May 1838 Mehemet Ali announced his intention to proclaim himself an independent ruler. This inaugurated a crisis in the near east which lasted until the summer of 1841 and which had profound repercussions on Anglo-French relations. Palmerston's first reaction to Mehemet Ali's declaration was to propose:

a short convention between England and France on the one hand and Turkey on the other by which the two former should bind themselves for a limited time, say eight or ten years, to afford to the other naval assistance...to protect his territory against attack... [by] either Russia or Mehemet Ali.[66]

---

[62] In Oct. 1837 Palmerston claimed that 'jealousy of the commercial prosperity of England' was 'very much the leading principle of French policy in all countries'. Palmerston to Howard de Walden, 7 Oct. 1837. Howard de Walden Papers, B.M. Add. MS. 45176.
[63] Palmerston to Granville, 24 Nov. 1835. B.P. GC/GR/1578.
[64] In the mid-1830s Palmerston believed that 'no man can doubt that there already exists the most complete understanding between Russia and Mehemet Ali, for purposes hostile to the Sultan and to our interests in the Levant'. Palmerston to Holland, 10 Feb. 1836. Holland House Papers, B.M. Add. MS. 51599.
[65] For accounts of the near eastern crisis of 1838 see Anderson, *The Eastern Question*, and Webster, *Palmerston*, ii.
[66] Palmerston to Granville, 8 June 1838. B.P. GC/GR/1729.

When France rejected his proposal outright, Palmerston turned instead to a 'concert' between the five powers to force Mehemet Ali to respect the *status quo* in the near east.[67] The concert was established, and succeeded in inducing Mehemet Ali to withdraw his declaration of independence. The minor crisis in the summer of 1838 revealed three important facts: that the French were not prepared to conclude an alliance with the British for the defence of Turkey, that France was the least hostile of all the great powers to Mehemet Ali, and that Russia was prepared to co-operate with England to defend the *status quo* in the near east. Palmerston's previous assumption that England and France would find themselves acting in close concert against Russia was proved mistaken, and the intensification of the crisis in 1839 widened still further the breach between British and French foreign policy.

In April 1839 Sultan Mahmud sent a Turkish army into Mehemet Ali's territories, and a new Turco-Egyptian war began. In June the Turks were defeated, Mahmud died and was succeeded by a sixteen-year-old boy, and the Turkish navy defected to the Egyptians. The Ottoman Empire seemed on the point of collapse. On 22 August the Porte asked the great powers to negotiate a settlement with Mehemet Ali. For the next year the emphasis was on diplomacy in Europe rather than on the actual conflict in the near east. Of the five great powers, the French were most favourable to Egypt; Mehemet employed French officers and technical experts, and France regarded her influence over Egypt as a valuable counterpoise to British dominance in the eastern Mediterranean. She was therefore unwilling to take a strongly anti-Egyptian line, and argued that concessions by the Sultan to Mehemet Ali in the Levant should be the basis for a settlement. Palmerston, however, was determined to evict Mehemet Ali from Syria, since control of Syria would enable the Egyptians to invade Mesopotamia, which would constitute a permanent threat to Turkey and also ensure to Mehemet Ali control of the Suez, Red Sea and overland routes to India. He could not understand the French enthusiasm for Mehemet Ali: 'France must and ought to wish to support the Sultan, but the Sultan and Mehemet Ali cannot

[67] Palmerston to Granville, 6 July 1838. B.P. GC/GR/1734.

exist as two powers. To make a power of Mehemet Ali is to destroy the Sultan and throw what would then remain of Turkey into the hands of Russia.'[68] By the summer of 1839 the divergences between British and French attitudes towards Mehemet Ali were so great that even Holland was forced to admit that France would be 'a much less handy weapon' to assist in the pacification of the near east 'than we at first hoped'.[69] Palmerston believed that French objections to a settlement which would deprive Mehemet Ali of Syria could only be overcome by a revival of the five-power concert of July 1838. If the other four powers showed their determination to act together, Palmerston hoped that France would follow them, as an arrangement 'made by the four powers without her participation would wear too much the appearance of a renewal of the alliance of 1813 and 1814'.[70] By the late summer of 1839 Palmerston recognised that the *entente* had failed in the near east as in western Europe. He was not, however, ready to acknowledge its failure publicly, but held it in reserve in case any independent action by Russia were again to unite England and France. The best way to settle the near eastern question seemed to Palmerston in the summer of 1839 to lie in Anglo-Austrian co-operation. At this juncture an important development occurred. In September Brunnow, a Russian diplomat, came to London to negotiate on the eastern question with the British government. The Russians knew that it would be impossible to renew the treaty of Unkiar Skelessi when it expired in 1841, and their depleted finances would not allow the Imperial government to pursue an independent policy in the near east. They believed that their major objective—to ensure that the Straits were closed in peace-time to ships of war—could best be realised by co-operation with Great Britain. This course had the added attraction to Nicholas I and his chancellor, Nesselrode, that it was likely to drive the two western powers farther apart. Palmerston responded immediately and positively to the Russian overtures, accepting the suggestion that the British government should regard the closure of the Straits as a principle

---

[68] Palmerston to Granville, 9 Aug. 1839. B.P. GC/GR/1774.
[69] Holland to Palmerston, 8 Sept. 1839. B.P. GC/HO/118.
[70] Palmerston to Melbourne, 19 Sept. 1839. Melbourne Papers, 12/10.

of the public law of Europe in return for the non-renewal of Unkiar Skelessi. The Francophiles in the cabinet were alarmed; they saw the Russian proposals as part of a plan whereby Russia would first separate England and France, and then abandon England to pursue her own ambitions in the near east.[71] Holland urged Palmerston to end the negotiations with Russia and base his policy on concessions to Mehemet Ali in order to satisfy the French and maintain and strengthen the *entente*. The fact is, Holland contended, hostility to Russia and friendship with France are the first principles of Whig foreign policy; their reversal would be 'a desperate bad exchange'.[72] Holland called for immediate action to show that the British government still attached the highest value to the *entente*.[73]

Palmerston heeded neither the appeals nor the arguments of his Francophile colleagues, but continued to negotiate with Brunnow. On 5 January 1840 he concluded an agreement confining Mehemet Ali to Egypt, in which Austria and Prussia also concurred. He refused to retreat from this position: 'France', he informed Granville, 'cannot be allowed to dictate to the rest of Europe; and we cannot sacrifice the interests of Europe...to gratify either Louis Philippe, the French press or the Chamber of Deputies.'[74] The increasing bellicosity of the French press and the French government's rejection of the January agreement did not alarm Palmerston: 'The French may talk big, but cannot make war for such a cause' was his confident judgment.[75] Some of his colleagues, however, were alarmed. Holland thought the time had come to alert the cabinet to the dangers inherent in Palmerston's policy of co-operation with Russia, and circulated a series of memoranda arguing that collaboration with Russia would bring only short-term gains and would certainly 'not advance the work of peace' and the progress of liberty.[76]

---

[71] 'The vast Empire with which Providence has entrusted' Nicholas of Russia, wrote Holland, 'becomes strangely enough a second rate power and he cannot resume his natural station and predominance among nations, unless the ancient jealousy between the two great maritime and popular monarchies be happily re-established'. Holland to Palmerston, 17 Oct. 1839. B.P. GC/HO/120.   [72] Ibid.
[73] Holland to Palmerston, 18 Oct. 1839. B.P. GC/HO/121.
[74] Palmerston to Granville, 7 Jan. 1840. B.P. GC/GR/1785.
[75] Palmerston to Granville, 11 Feb. 1840. B.P. GC/GR/1789.
[76] Holland's remarks on Lord Clanricarde's confidential despatch no. 125. B.P. GC/HO/138.

Clarendon, who had entered the cabinet on his return from Spain, agreed with Holland[77] but felt that his close relationship with Palmerston precluded his leading the opposition to his policy. He therefore suggested that Edward Ellice, Grey's son-in-law, whose extensive French contacts and antipathy to Palmerston were well known, should 'exert [his] influence' to canvass support for a pro-French line.[78] Although Ellice acted immediately, the pro-French party in the cabinet made little headway during the spring of 1840: their policy was both too late, in that the cabinet could not reverse the agreement of January, and too early, because it was impossible to refuse to join Russia in coercive measures against Mehemet Ali until such a proposal was actually made. Moreover, the fall of Soult left the Francophiles uncertain whether the concessions to Mehemet Ali which they advocated would be acceptable to the new government of Thiers. It was not until July and August 1840 that Palmerston had to face simultaneously the possibility of war with France and a bitter conflict with his colleagues.

On 15 July 1840 England, Austria, Prussia and Russia concluded a convention for the settlement of the near east. Palmerston claimed to have given the French 'full warning' that he would proceed without them,[79] but they bitterly condemned the agreement even though it stipulated that if Mehemet Ali submitted within ten days to the Sultan he could rule Egypt and southern Syria for his own lifetime. Palmerston threatened his resignation if the cabinet rejected the convention. The July agreement caused bitter division in the Whig cabinet. The majority accepted it, some enthusiastically, others with reluctance. Holland and Clarendon refused to accept it, but minuted their objections rather than resign.[80] They continued

[77] Clarendon to Holland, 5 Mar. 1840. Holland House Papers, B.M. Add. MS. 51617. Clarendon, who claimed to 'have abundant means of access to the French press', wondered whether 'to use them to deny our predilection for Russia over France'. Clarendon to Holland, 30 Jan. 1840. Holland House Papers, B.M. Add. MS. 51617.
[78] Clarendon to Ellice, 5 Mar. 1840. Ellice Papers, E56/65–6.
[79] Palmerston to Hobhouse, 27 July 1843. Hobhouse Papers, B.M. Add. MS. 36471. In this long letter Palmerston attempted to justify to Hobhouse his conduct towards France in 1840.
[80] For the text of the Cabinet Minute to the Queen with Record of Dissent by Lords Clarendon and Holland, 8–9 July 1840, see H. W. V. Temperley, *England*

to organise opposition to Palmerston's policy within the cabinet, and this division in the government soon became the subject of public and press discussion on both sides of the Channel. The execution of the July convention in the autumn of 1840 was thus conducted against a background of loud public and private recriminations and abuse between members of the Whig cabinet.

In August and September a new danger appeared. After the uncompromising rejection by Thiers of the four-power arrangement of July, the French press adopted a bellicose attitude which the French government proceeded to exploit. The imminent danger of war with France prompted the Francophiles again to plead for concessions that would calm the war fever by enabling the French government to claim that its honour had been satisfied.[81] Holland and Clarendon won over Russell and Duncannon to this opinion,[82] to which Grey and Spencer, the two elder statesmen of the Whig party, lent additional weight from their retirement.[83] Palmerston resolutely rejected their suggestion; he believed that Thiers' threat of war was a mere pose suggested to him 'by letters from London...which led him to think that bully and bravado would succeed'.[84] The fall of Thiers in October 1840 ended the threat of war but not the demands of the Francophiles, who suggested that Guizot, Thiers' successor,[85] should have his peace policy strengthened by small concessions. Palmerston remained firm. He claimed that it was the responsibility of the French government, not of

and the *Near East* (new impression, London, 1964), Appendix ii, 486–8. See also Holland's Circular to Cabinet Ministers, 8 July 1840. B.P. GC/HO/127.

[81] Clarendon to Melbourne, 31 Aug. 1840. Melbourne Papers, 3/11. Howden said that the British government should make it clear that any concession they made should not be 'to a barbarian Viceroy but to the spirit of this restless nation [France]'. Howden to Holland, 20 Sept. 1840. Holland House Papers, B.M. Add. MS. 51614.

[82] Duncannon to Ellice, n.d. Ellice Papers, E44/177–8; Russell to Melbourne, 28 Sept. 1840. B.P. MEL/RU/123.

[83] Holland to Melbourne, 17 Sept. 1840. Melbourne Papers, 7/27; Spencer to Melbourne, 7 Aug. 1840, enclosure Palmerston to Melbourne, 8 Aug. 1840. B.P. GC/ME/409; Grey to Princess Lieven, 1 Dec. 1840. *The Correspondence of Princess Lieven and Earl Grey*, ed. G. Le Strange, ii, 328–9.

[84] Palmerston to Beauvale, 15 Aug. 1840. Beauvale Papers, Box 10.

[85] Marshal Soult was the titular head of the ministry; Guizot, although only Foreign Minister, was recognised to be the real head of the government.

England, to calm the bellicose mood of the French people. There was, moreover, in his opinion nothing the great powers could do for France since her interests were not affected by the coercion of Mehemet Ali.[86] The possibility of French intervention on behalf of Mehemet Ali and of war in Europe was ended by the fall of Acre and the submission by Mehemet Ali to the terms proposed by the four powers. Palmerston's triumph over the French and over his Francophile colleagues was complete. The settlement in the near east and the death in October 1840 of Holland, the principal champion of France in the Whig cabinet, did not, however, end the debate on Anglo-French relations within the cabinet. In 1841 the Francophiles argued that, with the near eastern question settled, the best course would be to extend the olive branch to France and revive the *entente*, in Lansdowne's words, 'to smooth the ruffled feathers, which will require some care and attention, for after all it is an immense object to restore amicable feelings as well as amicable relations with [the French]'.[87] It was, however, Metternich, not Palmerston, who took the initiative in persuading the French to re-enter the concert on the near east in 1841 and sign the Straits Convention of July. Palmerston saw no point in making friendly overtures to the Guizot government or reviving the *entente*, since events had proved that 'France is much too knavish to be depended upon', and Guizot was unlikely to overcome 'the rooted hostility towards England which animates all the subordinate agents in Paris and elsewhere by whose means he will have to act'.[88] Palmerston believed the maintenance of peace to depend, not on the revival of the *entente*, but on a close union between England and the three northern Courts. 'It is evident', he informed Beauvale, the British ambassador at

[86] Palmerston to Beauvale, 5 Oct. 1840. Beauvale Papers, Box 10. It is vain, wrote Greville to Reeve, 'for the peace party here to carry any point in the cabinet, when the execution is left to P[almerston] who is resolved to proceed in his own violent course and to thwart all who oppose it'. Greville to Reeve, 9 Oct. 1840. Greville–Reeve Correspondence, B.M. Add. MS. 41184.

[87] Lansdowne to Palmerston, 19 Nov. 1840. B.P. GC/LA/60.

[88] Palmerston to Howard de Walden, 31 Oct. 1840. Howard de Walden Papers, B.M. Add. MS. 45176. Palmerston was more inclined to offer the French insults than a basis for reconciliation. In June 1841 in an election address at Tiverton, and subsequently in press articles, he violently denounced the conduct of French troops in Algiers. In a draft article for *The Globe*, 26 July 1841, he wrote: 'The French went

Vienna, 'that we shall have no peace in Europe unless we build up a strong barrier against French aggression.'[89] Of the northern Courts, Palmerston believed Russia to be 'the safest ally' of England; Austria was 'too timid and changeable'.[90] By 1841 Palmerston's outlook on foreign affairs had been transformed: Russia and France had changed positions. Russia was now England's potential ally, while France constituted the major threat to English interests and the peace of Europe. The increased defence expenditure which the French government proposed in late 1841 seemed to Palmerston to indicate their intentions:

> It is evident that Louis Philippe means to get up a large army and a large navy and a great quantity of warlike stores, not for the specific purpose of going to war with us or with Germany or Spain, but for the purpose generally of being able to give law to Europe and to carry in succession all his objects of aggression and aggrandizement by saying to every power which may object to his proceedings, 'If you do not let me have my own way you must fight me'. In short to effect upon twenty other matters...that which from default of means he failed to do this year about the Turkish question; namely to bully all the world into submission to his will.

He was, moreover, convinced that England would have to bear the brunt of opposing France:

> England is the power with which France will have most points of difference because she will be wanting to do things...which we shall not like and which will make a great outcry in this country.[91]

By no means all the Whigs agreed with Palmerston; many still believed that it was worth making sacrifices to be on good terms with France. On leaving office in 1841 the Whig government was as divided over Anglo-French relations as on entering office in 1830.

---

to Algiers with the pretence of introducing civilization and of putting an end to piracy and violence and crime; and yet they are every day committing more barbarous acts than the Algerian pirates themselves. The only difference is that what the Algerians did by sea and on a small scale, the French do by land and on a much larger scale.' B.P. PRE/B/135.

[89] Palmerston to Beauvale, 26 Dec. 1840. Beauvale Papers, Box 10.
[90] Palmerston to Beauvale, 9 Mar. 1841. Beauvale Papers, Box 10.
[91] Palmerston to Clarendon, 21 Dec. 1840. B.P. GC/CL/1359.

CHAPTER II

Lord Palmerston and Anglo-French Relations, 1841–6

'A tolerably quiet and fair understanding' between England and France was, in the opinion of one British diplomat in 1841, 'in the nature of things' and he was confident that 'we shall gradually and surely relapse into it if we adopt a steady and amicable bearing'.[1] This viewpoint was shared by many Whigs and by Palmerston's Tory successor at the Foreign Office, the Earl of Aberdeen. During the 1830s the Tories had condemned the close connection between England and France, the high Tories for its ideological basis, the moderate Tories because of its exclusive character. They believed that the object of British policy should be the establishment of good relations with all the great powers, not with France alone. The collapse of the liberal alliance during the near eastern crisis and England's improved relations with the eastern powers met with Tory approval, although they regretted the complete estrangement of England and France. When they came into office in 1841, Peel and his cabinet in part accepted and in part rejected Palmerston's legacy: they intended to strengthen the contacts he had established with the northern Courts, but they discarded his assumption that good relations with France were impossible on terms acceptable to England. A marked improvement in Anglo-French relations would, in their view, remove the main source of tension in international affairs, thus enabling the new government to concentrate its energies on domestic problems. This was what Peel wanted, and what he thought the country needed. The establishment of cordial relations with France would also emphasise the difference between the policies of Palmerston and Aberdeen, the aim of the latter, according to an influential Tory journal, being to 'steer his course by the wrecks of his

[1] Bulwer to Clarendon, 8 July 1841. Clar. Dep. C525.

predecessor'.[2] It was, moreover, a policy directed towards the maintenance of peace, and Aberdeen regarded himself as, above all else, a man of peace. From the outset, however, the Tories made it clear that they attached no ideological significance to friendship with France: 'You know', wrote Aberdeen to Princess Lieven, 'that I am no friend to what has been called the French alliance, or the union of England and France to the alienation and exclusion of the rest of the world.'[3] Aberdeen's aim in seeking a *rapprochement* with France was essentially negative: the avoidance of war in western Europe through the promotion of understanding and mutual trust.[4]

The new spirit of compromise and tact which Aberdeen brought to Anglo-French relations was greatly appreciated in Paris. It was in marked contrast to Palmerston's rancour and his indifference to Guizot's assurances that he was a minister of peace who earnestly desired a reconciliation with England.[5] Where Palmerston had been indifferent to Guizot and hostile towards Louis Philippe, Aberdeen was prepared to make great efforts to keep Guizot in office and regarded Louis Philippe as a security for peace.[6] Guizot also felt able to respond to Aberdeen because his general outlook on foreign policy was almost identical.[7] Like the Tory Foreign Secretary, Guizot had no wish to revive the 'liberal alliance'; his aims too were the preservation of peace and of good relations with all the powers.[8] Their

[2] *Quarterly Review*, Sept. 1841, lxviii, 517–18.

[3] Aberdeen to Princess Lieven, 9 Nov. 1840. *The Correspondence of Lord Aberdeen and Princess Lieven 1832–1854*, ed. E. Jones Parry [hereafter *Aberdeen–Lieven*] (London, 1938), i, 150–2.

[4] The best account of the foreign policy of Aberdeen is Muriel Chamberlain, 'The Character of the Foreign Policy of the Earl of Aberdeen 1841–1846', unpublished Oxford D.Phil. thesis, 1960. Bodleian Library. I am grateful to Dr Chamberlain for allowing me to consult her thesis.

[5] When Hobhouse visited Paris in 1843 'Guizot complained' to him that Palmerston had not 'cordially supported his government in its infant struggle'. Hobhouse to Palmerston, 4 Aug. 1843. B.P. GC/BR/130.

[6] Aberdeen to Princess Lieven, 12 Dec. 1840. *Aberdeen–Lieven*, i, 155–7.

[7] The best modern accounts of Guizot's foreign policy are Douglas Johnson, *Guizot, Aspects of French History 1787–1874* (London, 1963) and the same author's 'The Foreign Policy of Guizot, 1840–8', *University of Birmingham Historical Journal*, vi, no. 1, 62–87. See also Salvo Mastellone, *La Politica Estera del Guizot* (Florence, 1957) and E. Jones Parry, 'A Review of the Relations between Guizot and Lord Aberdeen 1840–52', *History*, 1938, xxiii, 25–36.

[8] In a speech in the Chamber of Deputies on 19 Jan. 1842 Guizot declared, 'The

similar outlook was strengthened by mutual admiration. Aberdeen respected Guizot's claim to be, like him, a minister of peace, and Guizot appreciated Aberdeen's efforts to understand the domestic difficulties he faced. The two men had met when Guizot was in London as French ambassador, and their mutual regard was encouraged by Princess Lieven, the friend and correspondent of Aberdeen and the confidant of Guizot.[9] Throughout their official relationship the Princess acted as a channel of communication between them. They did not, however, rely exclusively on her good offices for private contact; they wrote directly to one another, believing it a great virtue to by-pass the official channels of diplomacy.[10] Thus Aberdeen and Guizot brought not only a new spirit but also a new style to the conduct of Anglo-French relations. Their emphasis on personal contact culminated in three meetings between Queen Victoria, Louis Philippe and their Foreign Ministers in 1843, 1844 and 1845.

The new mood in Anglo-French relations was discernible almost immediately after the Tories returned to office, but practical effects were slower in being felt. In part this reflected the deliberate policy of Guizot and Aberdeen, neither of whom wished to rush into a close relationship. Their initial overtures were tentative and modest. Moreover, each knew that he could expect formidable opposition in any attempt to reach agreement on certain issues. Guizot in particular was acutely conscious of the still strong anti-English feeling in the Chambers and the country, and had no wish to endanger the stability of his government by adopting measures that would give the opposition an opportunity to accuse him of subservience to England. At first, therefore, Guizot and Aberdeen favoured private

intimate alliance with England has the disadvantage of linking closely three powers against us. The policy of isolation binds four against us. The only policy is that of neither—a policy of independence yet of good understanding with all.' *Morning Chronicle*, 24 Jan. 1842.

[9] The official relations of Aberdeen and Guizot from 1841 to 1846 can be closely followed from their private correspondence with Princess Lieven. See *Aberdeen–Lieven*, i, and *Lettres de François Guizot et de la Princesse de Lieven*, ed. Jacques Naville [hereafter *Guizot–Lieven*] (Paris, 1963–4), iii.

[10] Guizot believed that one of his and Aberdeen's greatest achievements was to have dealt with everything 'privately and confidentially'. Guizot to Jarnac, 22 Sept. 1846. Guizot Papers [hereafter G.P.], 42/AP/7.

reassurances of good intentions rather than public acts of reconciliation. Throughout 1842 relations between the two countries were marked by strains and disputes which neither statesman had anticipated. Guizot offended his English admirers by refusing to bring before the Chambers for ratification a Right of Search treaty which would empower each country to search ships belonging to the other which were suspected of carrying slaves, because he feared the reaction of the Anglophobe groups.[11] Peel was particularly disappointed by Guizot's timidity on this issue. The Slave Trade treaty was a popular question which was a source of public embarrassment to both Guizot and Aberdeen. Equally embarrassing, though less publicly so, was the fact that many of their subordinates did not share the new spirit in which relations between the two countries were being conducted. The rivalry of British and French diplomats in Spain, Portugal, Greece and the near east continued to be as active as it had been in the 1830s.[12] Although both regretted these difficulties, neither Aberdeen nor Guizot took any positive steps to alter the situation. Cordiality and understanding were therefore very much restricted to their personal relations; from the outset the new *entente* rested on a very narrow basis of support.

In the early 1840s, as in the 1830s, the relations between the two great west European powers turned on the course of Spanish politics. Aberdeen admitted that Spain was 'the chief, or indeed the only ground for apprehending a quarrel between us'.[13] When Palmerston left office Espartero, in uneasy alliance with the Progresistas, held power at Madrid, and he looked to England for support against the pro-French Moderados. During late 1841 and 1842 relations between the French government and the Espartero régime became strained; the Spanish government claimed that the French were party to the intrigues of the exiled Queen Christina in Paris and of the Moderados to overthrow Espartero. In 1843 he fell and in 1844 the Moderados returned to power. Although he regretted the loss of Espartero,

[11] See Johnson, *Guizot*, 287–90.
[12] One British diplomat commented that he thought Guizot's choice of diplomats 'was just the best calculated to embroil the two countries'. Howden to Bulwer, 20 Dec. 1844. Bulwer Papers, S/28.
[13] Aberdeen to Princess Lieven, 27 Dec. 1842. *Aberdeen–Lieven*, i, 211.

Aberdeen did not think it worthwhile to continue to support the Progresista party or to challenge French ascendancy at Madrid.[14] By early 1844 Anglo-French relations were on a new basis: in the Peninsula the two powers stood on an equal footing, British influence was predominant at Lisbon and French at Madrid, while in London and Paris each government proclaimed its faith in the necessity and the existence of a good understanding between them.[15]

The French opposition, led by Thiers, promptly claimed that the *entente* of Guizot and Aberdeen was a betrayal of the interests and honour of France; they launched a vigorous campaign against it in the hope of bringing down the government. The Whig opposition in England did not expect the Peel government to fall quickly, and certainly not on an issue of foreign policy. In fact, Aberdeen's new approach to Anglo-French relations kept alive old divisions and debates, and created new problems within the Whig party. Russell, who led the party in the Commons and was Melbourne's acknowledged heir as party leader, did not consider that foreign policy should play a large part in the Whig platform. What they needed, he informed Palmerston, was 'distinct ground for party union', and there was in domestic affairs 'sufficient matter' for this.[16] Palmerston did not agree; he believed that the Whigs ought to take a strong public stand on foreign policy and to give it a prominent part in their programme of opposition. Before he left office, he had tried to ensure that the *Morning Chronicle* would remain loyal to the Whigs,[17] thus providing him with a means

---

[14] '...it is on principle that I do not seek [exclusive influence] believing that, in the end, it is more likely to lead to evil than good.' Ibid.

[15] When he opened the new session of the Chambers on 27 Dec. 1843 Louis Philippe mentioned the existence of an 'entente cordiale'. This was the first time he had made a special mention of England in the speech from the throne since 1836. P. Thureau-Dangin, *Histoire de la Monarchie de Juillet* (Paris, 1880–94), v, 219. There was a friendly reference to France in Queen Victoria's speech from the throne in Jan. 1844. *The Letters of Queen Victoria 1837–1861*, 1st series, ed. A. C. Benson and Viscount Esher [hereafter *Q.V.L.*] (London, 1907), ii, 6.

[16] Russell to Palmerston, 4 Oct. 1841. B.P. GC/RU/60.

[17] 'The Chronicle', wrote Palmerston to Melbourne on 16 Aug. 1841, 'is the only morning paper we have or are likely to get; we shall want a paper when out of office even more than we did when in...' He suggested that Melbourne should recommend Easthope, the proprietor of the *Chronicle*, 'for a baronetcy. If you nail Easthope you will have a hold over the paper...' Melbourne Papers, Box 13/27.

of disseminating his views on foreign affairs to the widest possible audience. He informed Beauvale that he expected Aberdeen's 'submissive habits of mind' to lead to disastrous mistakes in foreign policy which he would feel bound to oppose.[18] If the Tory government failed to defend the interests and honour of England, he argued to Russell, it was the duty of the Whigs to condemn them. They therefore needed to take a close and consistent interest in foreign policy, and Palmerston believed that his experience and knowledge made him their natural spokesman.[19] Almost from the outset the debate on foreign policy between the government and the opposition was conducted through the press rather than in Parliament. There were good reasons for this. Whereas Parliament discussed foreign affairs infrequently, press discussion could be both more regular and more sustained. Moreover, the editorial of a newspaper offered more scope for unrestrained comment than a speech in Parliament: Palmerston was able to attack Aberdeen through the *Morning Chronicle* and Aberdeen to reply in *The Times*[20] with a vehemence and acrimony that neither could have adopted in Parliament.

Palmerston did not wait for Aberdeen to proclaim the existence of an *entente* before launching an attack on the government's policy towards France. His first assault on the new course in Anglo-French relations came in January 1842. Palmerston concentrated on two lines of attack: firstly, he condemned Aberdeen's general attitude towards France, and secondly, his handling of the particular issues in which the two powers were involved. He saw Aberdeen's emphasis on trust and understanding as a means merely of 'dragging down England to the position of...acting in subserviency to the views of France'.[21] Aberdeen's assumption that England and France could work together in a spirit of forbearance and compromise he regarded as not only erroneous but dangerous in its consequences. It would result in the sacrifice of 'the future and permanent interests of the country' for no real gain except 'to purchase

[18] Palmerston to Beauvale, 15 Sept. 1841. Beauvale Papers, Box 10.
[19] Palmerston to Russell, 14 Nov. 1842. B.P. GC/RU/970.
[20] For the connection between Aberdeen and *The Times*, see *The History of The Times 1841–1884* (London, 1939), ch. v.
[21] *Morning Chronicle*, 22 Jan. 1842.

relief from momentary embarrassment'.[22] Furthermore, Palmerston argued that such a policy of weakness would encourage other states to demand even greater concessions; there would come a point when these demands would require to be resisted, and the most likely outcome would be war.[23] In Palmerston's opinion, therefore, Aberdeen had embarked on a shortsighted and perilous course. Why then did he pursue such a policy? Palmerston thought that Aberdeen had been thoroughly duped by Guizot and Louis Philippe; he put his faith in Guizot's assurances of good intentions and ignored his hostile acts, and 'he seems not to have discovered or mistrusted that universal and unconquerable habit of the French King to follow an aim and a policy of his own, independent of his ministers and without their knowledge'.[24] To Easthope, the proprietor of the *Morning Chronicle,* Palmerston suggested that Aberdeen did not realise that 'the experience we have had of [the French] since 1830 shews that England never can reckon on France as an ally in any system of common policy'.[25] Aberdeen could not properly be said, however, to have allied England and France 'for alliance implies some terms on both sides'; all he had done, according to Palmerston, was 'to fling himself at the feet of Louis Philippe'.[26] The practical result of this 'obsequiousness [which] passes Christian humility'[27] was that in Europe 'instead of standing in an independent position between France and the Absolutist powers being able to act arbiter and exercise salutary influence over both we are despised and hooted as the mere foot boys of France',[28] in north America the United States had exploited the feeble spirit of British policy to extort enormous boundary concessions in the Webster–Ashburton treaty,[29] and in western Europe Spain had been abandoned to France. The

[22] Palmerston to Russell, [?] Sept. 1842. Russell Papers, Public Record Office [hereafter P.R.O.] 30/22/4C.
[23] Palmerston to Doyle, 6 Mar. 1843. B.P. GC/DO/42.
[24] *Morning Chronicle,* 20 Jan. 1842.
[25] Palmerston to Easthope, 9 Sept. 1842. B.P. GC/EA/31.
[26] *Morning Chronicle,* 15 Mar. 1844.
[27] *Morning Chronicle,* 6 Jan. 1844.
[28] *Morning Chronicle,* 15 Mar. 1844.
[29] For Palmerston's opposition to the Webster–Ashburton treaty and Aberdeen's American policy generally, see Frederick Merk, *The Oregon Question* (Cambridge, Mass., 1967).

fall of Espartero was, in Palmerston's view, the responsibility of the French, whose policy in Spain he stigmatised as one of the most 'disgusting' sights Europe had witnessed for many years. He considered Aberdeen's complicity in the triumph of the French and the Moderados at Madrid the most lamentable mistake he had made.[30] Louis Philippe's object in Spain, he wrote to Clarendon, was 'political domination'. It was therefore impossible for England and France to collaborate at Madrid: they were of necessity rivals.[31]

Palmerston's attacks on Aberdeen's handling of Anglo-French relations in 1842 and 1843 were completely consistent with the conclusions he had reached in the late 1830s on the nature and aims of French foreign policy. He retained his conviction that France was the main danger to the peace of Europe and that only a vigorous policy of resistance would contain her. 'Let us remember', he adjured Easthope, that we shall not maintain peace 'by proclaiming that we are ready to make any sacrifice or concession in order to avoid war; and if it is dangerous to declare our willingness to make concessions to avoid war it is still more dangerous actually to make concessions'. England must remain 'stout and obstinate' if France were not to carry her points.[32] Palmerston was certain that resistance was less likely to produce war than concession: 'We have always beaten the French in battle by sea and by land by the simple process of standing our ground the longest and by the same means we can always carry our points against them in diplomacy.'[33] The French ought, in Palmerston's view, to be treated as an enemy rather than as a friend; this was the best way to defend England's interests, and such an attitude would only reciprocate the hostility of the French towards England.[34] Palmerston therefore recommended that the government should abandon its uncritical attachment to Guizot, adopt a firmer tone in negotiation with the French, and immediately launch an offensive in Spain, in co-operation with the Progresistas, with

[30] *Morning Chronicle*, 6 Jan. 1843. Palmerston to Doyle, 6 Mar. 1843. B.P. GC/DO/42.
[31] Palmerston to Clarendon, 19 Feb. 1843. Clar. Dep. C524.
[32] Palmerston to Easthope, 16 Sept. 1842. B.P. GC/EA/32.
[33] Palmerston to Easthope, 9 Sept. 1842. B.P. GC/EA/31.
[34] *Morning Chronicle*, 24 Jan. 1844.

the avowed intention of undermining French influence and restoring constitutional government.³⁵ Until Aberdeen adopted this course, Palmerston informed Russell, he would continue to expose the government's foreign policy to 'public animadversion'.³⁶

To some of the Whig leaders Palmerston's unbridled attack on Aberdeen's policy and the hostility of the *Chronicle* towards France were profoundly disquieting. There were those like Lord Howick, the son of Lord Grey, the former Prime Minister, who considered that foreign policy should not play a large part in the attack on the government.³⁷ Others resented Palmerston's exclusive direction of the *Chronicle*.³⁸ His critics realised, however, that these questions of opposition strategy and party leadership, although important, were secondary; their basic objection was that Palmerston and the *Chronicle* were damaging the image of the Whigs as the party of peace and friendship with France. The Whig Francophiles in fact adopted the arguments put forward by *The Times* in reply to Palmerston's attacks: that Palmerston was a warmonger, and that there could never be good relations with France when he was at the Foreign Office.³⁹ Clarendon, Lansdowne, Howick and Wood, supported by Ellice and the Duke of Bedford, Russell's brother, were the leading Whig critics of Palmerston and the *Chronicle*.⁴⁰ They regarded with approval Aberdeen's attempt to improve Anglo-French relations and to foster a spirit of trust and understanding between the two countries, and argued that it should be supported, not opposed. Clarendon and Lansdowne thought it their duty publicly to affirm their belief in the desirability of good relations with France, to calm public hostility towards France, and to avoid embarrassing the government by an attack in Parliament on the principles on which the *entente* was

---

³⁵ *Morning Chronicle*, 15 Mar. 1844.
³⁶ Palmerston to Russell, [?] Sept. 1842. Russell Papers, P.R.O. 30/22/4C.
³⁷ Howick to Russell, 20 Nov. 1841. Russell Papers, P.R.O. 30/22/4B.
³⁸ Some of the Whigs, wrote Greville to Reeve on 4 Oct. 1842, call Palmerston 'Viscount Chronicle'. Greville–Reeve Correspondence, B.M. Add. MS. 41184. See also Russell to Palmerston, 11 Nov. 1842. B.P. GC/RU/69.
³⁹ *The Times*, 12, 13 Nov. 1842.
⁴⁰ Charles Buller, a friend of Howick and Grey, wrote articles for *The Globe* under the signature of 'Pacificus'. Buller to Russell, 23 Oct. 1842. Russell Papers, P.R.O. 30/22/4C.

based.[41] The restraint they exercised in the House of Lords did not go unnoticed. Greville, writing in July 1846, observed that: 'Throughout Aberdeen's foreign administration, Clarendon has constantly acted in concert with him, and has made his position in the House of Lords a bed of roses.'[42] The fact that several Whig leaders were closer to Aberdeen than to Palmerston in their outlook on foreign affairs made inevitable a direct clash within the Whig leadership, the Francophiles contending that Palmerston manifested unnecessary animosity towards France and thus acquired for the Whig party a reputation for bellicosity and irresponsibility in foreign affairs.

Palmerston first aroused the misgivings of some of his colleagues by his attacks on the Webster–Ashburton treaty, a boundary settlement between Canada and the United States, and by his general 'system of irritation' in Anglo-French relations. A group of Whigs, including Spencer and Ellice, urged the Duke of Bedford with whom they were staying to write to Lord John Russell warning him of the dangers inherent in Palmerston's conduct. Bedford criticised Palmerston's behaviour on three grounds: firstly he was giving 'a direction to the party and to public opinion thru' the newspapers without previous concert', secondly the tone and content of his views would 'disgust the best of the old Whig party', and thirdly 'the public having no other means of judging consider the writings they see in our papers to be the language and the sentiments of the Whig party'.[43] The implication of this letter was clear: Russell should attempt to control Palmerston in the interests of party unity and to preserve the public image of the Whigs as the party of peace and of amity with France. The task was, however, more difficult than Bedford supposed. Russell's hold over the party was weak, and Palmerston was not an easy man to discipline; Greville thought that Russell would not like 'openly to oppose Palmerston'.[44] More important still was the fact that Russell knew that the party was genuinely divided in its attitude to Anglo-French relations. Palmerston had as many supporters

[41] Lansdowne to Clarendon, 12 Nov. 1844. Clar. Dep. C561.
[42] *The Greville Memoirs*, ed. Henry Reeve (new impression, London, 1910), v, 411.
[43] Duke of Bedford to Russell, 6 Nov. 1842. Russell Papers, P.R.O. 30/22/4C.
[44] Greville to Reeve, 25 Sept. 1842. Greville–Reeve Correspondence, B.M. Add. MS. 41184.

as the 'Old Whigs'. Russell himself stood somewhere between the two; he approved of Aberdeen's aim to improve relations with France but was increasingly of the opinion that the slight improvement discernible was bought at too high a price.[45] After Bedford's letter, Russell had no alternative but to inform Palmerston of the dissatisfaction felt by some of his colleagues over the line he had taken on foreign policy, although he admitted frankly that he thought Ellice largely responsible for organising the opposition to Palmerston in the party. It was, however, in Russell's view more than just another of Ellice's intrigues; the fear that the party would acquire a warmongering image was widespread. To Easthope he suggested that the *Chronicle* should not 'provoke or irritate' France, and he urged Palmerston to do the same, 'otherwise Ellice will have a great advantage and may even detach from us some of the party'.[46] By ascribing to Ellice a large share in the opposition, Russell ruined his chances of making any real impression on Palmerston, who replied that Ellice 'is always plotting against those who will not let him manage them'. Both he and Easthope, he claimed, had successfully resisted 'Ellice's attempt to manage them', and the opposition within the party was no more than another attempt by Ellice 'to get up a cabal to thwart me'.[47] Russell was not disposed to accept this as a full explanation of the differences within the party; he reminded Palmerston that the Whigs prided themselves on being the party of peace.[48] Palmerston agreed, but saw no reason why the *Chronicle* should be pressed to alter its tone or he to express his views less forcibly.

There has not for a great number of years been a time when war was less likely than it is now; for two things are requisite for a good war. First some sufficient grounds for serious quarrel, secondly at least one power prepared and willing for war. Now at present there is no nation, not even the French, ready or willing to make aggressive and unprovoked war, and therefore it seems to me, at the present moment, to be unreasonable, to say no more, to accuse people of holding warlike language merely because they find fault with a bad

[45] Russell to Palmerston, 19 Sept. 1842. B.P. GC/RU/64.
[46] Russell to Palmerston, 11 Nov. 1842. B.P. GC/RU/69.
[47] Palmerston to Russell, 14 Nov. 1842. B.P. GC/RU/970.
[48] Russell to Palmerston, 16 Nov. 1842. B.P. GC/RU/70.

treaty, or blame a needless confusion and object to an uncalled for surrender of a right here or an unnecessary sacrifice of an interest there. Such charges can only have one effect and that is to stifle free discussion of national interests, and I don't see why the pretended fears of some Liberals and the mistaken alarm of others should do that, which no government in this country has power to do, namely gag the mouth of every man who is disposed to find fault with the conduct of the Ministers of the Crown in the management of our Foreign Affairs.[49]

Russell's attempt to persuade Palmerston and the *Chronicle* to moderate their language thus met with no success. Palmerston assured Easthope that criticism within the Whig party of the line taken by the *Chronicle* on foreign affairs was nothing but a 'petty intrigue' of Ellice, which 'may safely be despised'.[50] In fact, the only effect of Russell's action was that Palmerston broadened the basis of his attack, pointing out the deficiencies in the views of his colleagues as well as Aberdeen's. His attack was relentless:

I think it might be worthwhile to give again in the Chronicle the enclosed passage which I quoted from Mr. Fox's speech on the address on 5th December 1782 as it contains a strong justification of the language held by the Chronicle and found fault with by some of the old Foxites.[51]

The *Chronicle* faithfully followed Palmerston's instructions and defended itself and its mentor against their critics:

We shall not be deterred from insisting on the necessity of showing spirit in our foreign relations by the common outcry that an independent tone leads to war, or that we are a war party...We shall therefore not cease to protest against the debonnaire system of foreign policy which consists in diplomatising by bows and smiles... We do not want to make this a party question or to say that

[49] Palmerston to Russell, 18 Nov. 1842. B.P. GC/RU/971.
[50] Palmerston to Easthope, 13 Nov. 1842. B.P. GC/EA/36.
[51] Palmerston to Doyle, 3 May 1843. B.P. GC/DO/45. The passage ran as follows: 'If you teach them [other governments] that war induces you to cession there is no doubt but they will go to war. The true policy therefore is to teach them that you will not gratify passion so pursued; that you know there is no economy in cession and that it is wiser and more for your interest to continue even expensive wars than by unwise and foolish concessions to purchase a temporary peace neither safe nor honourable.'

the Tories alone have been in this respect at fault. The Whigs tried the debonnaire system long enough. In the affairs of Spain and the Levant none went further than they in putting implicit trust in the sincerity and straightforwardness of the French Government. Events showed that the trust was ill-reposed and the consequence was a coolness and a breach which need not at all have taken place but for the previous excess of confidence and friendship.[52]

Palmerston was as unwilling to moderate his views in opposition as he had been to change his policies in office to suit his Francophile colleagues. He adamantly refused to treat 'national interests' as party questions; in his opinion the 'real war party in this country' were those who truckled to France.[53]

Aberdeen was undeterred by Palmerston's scorn from pursuing the policy of *entente*. What Palmerston stigmatised as timidity and unnecessary concessions, Aberdeen regarded as goodwill and unimportant sacrifices in the interests of peace. At the beginning of 1844 Aberdeen and Guizot were united in the view that the *entente* was already well established and augured well for the future. There was some justification for this confidence. In September 1843 Queen Victoria and Aberdeen had visited Louis Philippe and Guizot at the Château d'Eu. In the course of their meeting Guizot heaped extravagant praise on Aberdeen[54] and also drove a hard bargain on the question of the marriage of the Queen of Spain. The implicit assumption of the French proposals on this question was that French influence was dominant at Madrid and that the British government would not use the marriage negotiations to undermine it. Aberdeen agreed to the French proposal that Queen Isabella should 'select' her consort 'from the descendants of Philip V', stipulating only that the sons of Louis Philippe should be excluded from the list of eligible Bourbon candidates. Guizot was well pleased by the British acceptance of 'superior' French influence in Spain.[55] It

[52] *Morning Chronicle*, 2 Jan. 1844.
[53] Palmerston to Macaulay, 7 Jan. 1845. B.P. GC/MA/15.
[54] Guizot told Aberdeen, 'Vous et moi, nous sommes bien nécessaires l'un à l'autre; sans vous je puis empêcher du mal; ce n'est qu'avec vous que je puis faire du bien.' Chamberlain, 'The Character of the Foreign Policy of the Earl of Aberdeen 1841–1846', 96.
[55] A. B. Cunningham, 'Peel, Aberdeen and the Entente Cordiale', *Bulletin of the Institute of Historical Research*, Nov. 1957, xxx, 199.

was agreed at Eu that Louis Philippe should visit England in the autumn of 1844. It was in that year, however, that the extreme fragility rather than the strength of the *entente* was demonstrated. In August 1842 the French admiral, Dupetit-Thouars, commander of the French Pacific fleet, declared a French protectorate over the island of Tahiti.[56] Despite his reservations over the wisdom of this action, Guizot declined to disavow it for fear of exposing himself to the accusation of truckling to England. The French protectorate had been declared while Pritchard, the British consul and Protestant missionary, was absent in Australia; on his return to Tahiti Pritchard persuaded the native ruler, Queen Pomare, to apply for British assistance in resisting the French. In November 1843, before the application was officially made, Dupetit-Thouars deposed Queen Pomare and declared the island a French possession. When the news reached Europe in February 1844 it was strongly criticised in the British press and warmly applauded by the French. Both governments, however, were anxious to avoid a clash over so minor a question: 'It would be deplorable', wrote Aberdeen to Guizot, if 'you and I, two Ministers of Peace, should be condemned to quarrel about a set of naked savages at the other end of the world'.[57] Guizot acted firmly by disavowing Dupetit-Thouars' action of November 1843 and restoring Queen Pomare and the French protectorate. Aberdeen, too, was inclined to be conciliatory, and proposed to transfer Pritchard to the consulship of another group of Pacific islands. The concessions made by the two Foreign Ministers did not silence the British and French press, who refused to drop the matter. It was in the context of virulent public animosity that the Duke of Joinville, son of Louis Philippe, published his pamphlet, *Note sur l'état des forces navales de la France*, which discussed the unfitness of the French navy to engage in a war with the British.[58] In England the pamphlet was interpreted as a recommendation that the French navy be strengthened to enable it to meet the British on equal terms.

[56] For a full account of the Tahiti question, see J. R. Baldwin, 'England and the French Seizure of the Society Islands', *Journal of Modern History*, 1938, x, 212–31.
[57] Chamberlain, op. cit., 7.
[58] For a full discussion of the Joinville pamphlet, see C. J. Bartlett, *Great Britain and Sea Power 1815–1853* (Oxford, 1963), 155–64.

British fears of further French expansion along the north African coast from their base at Algiers were aroused in June 1844 when the possibility that French troops might have to enter Moroccan territory in pursuit of the Algerian rebel Abdel Kadir was mentioned. Aberdeen, however, accepted Guizot's assurances that Tangier would not be bombarded by the French fleet and that no part of Morocco would be permanently occupied. When Pritchard arrived in England in late July 1844, claiming that he had been arrested, imprisoned and finally expelled from Tahiti by the French naval authorities, the British press, including *The Times*, took up his demand for a full apology, and Peel described his treatment in the House of Commons as 'a gross outrage'. While deprecating the Francophobia of the press,[59] Aberdeen was unable to ignore the sympathy for Pritchard evinced by his cabinet colleagues. On 13 August 1844 Aberdeen formally demanded redress for Pritchard from the French government. A few days later Tangier was bombarded by a French fleet despite Guizot's assurances to the contrary. The reaction in England was extremely hostile. Jarnac, the French chargé d'affaires in London, informed Guizot that 'war is now generally regarded as inevitable'.[60] Guizot was slow to appreciate the situation; he hoped that complete inaction would allow the crisis to pass without his having to offer redress for Pritchard or to acknowledge publicly that his assurances to Aberdeen about Tangier had been broken. Jarnac warned him repeatedly of the dangers inherent in this course, and Guizot finally agreed that Pritchard should receive pecuniary compensation for the indignities he had suffered. Even Aberdeen thought this 'rather slender' satisfaction, but he accepted it in preference to prolonging the dispute. On 10 September, less than a week after the settlement of the Tahiti question, the French concluded a peace treaty with the Sultan and withdrew their troops from Morocco. To Aberdeen the peaceful settlement of the various disputes that had bedevilled Anglo-French relations in the first nine months of 1844 seemed

[59] Aberdeen regarded the Tahiti dispute as trivial, and had it not been for the press 'it would have been settled much earlier'. Aberdeen to Delane, 15 Jan. 1845 Printing House Square MSS., Delane Correspondence, vol. 2.
[60] J. Hall, *England and the Orleans Monarchy* (London, 1912), 363.

a triumph for the trust and understanding that existed between him and Guizot. He was prepared to overlook Guizot's slowness and unwillingness to meet him anything like half-way, and he almost completely ignored the unpopularity of the *entente* revealed by the reaction of both press and public.

The Tahiti and Moroccan disputes severely shook the faith of Peel, Wellington and other members of the Tory government in the honesty of Guizot and the possibility of maintaining good relations with France for very long.[61] From the outset Wellington had been a stern critic of Aberdeen's policy of conciliating France, but he had failed to gain support for a firmer policy within the cabinet. The crises of 1844 changed the situation: Peel, Graham, the Home Secretary, and Goulburn, the Chancellor of the Exchequer, joined Wellington, leaving Aberdeen virtually isolated in the cabinet. Those who advocated a firmer line with France argued that Guizot was untrustworthy and weak. In any future dispute he might easily be overwhelmed by the war party in France. The relations between the two countries were in such a state, wrote Peel to Aberdeen, that 'some act of violence for which the French Ministry is not strong enough to make reparation or disavowal may not only dissipate the shadow of the entente cordiale but may change our relations from peace to war'. Peel and Wellington saw only one way to deal with the situation: 'Let us be prepared for war...They [the French] are much more likely to presume upon our weakness than to take offence at our strength.'[62] In 1845 the Peel government introduced increased naval estimates, and throughout the year Wellington occupied himself with the problem of how best to defend the British Isles against a surprise attack by the French. Aberdeen opposed increased defence expenditure, claiming that it would make his task of preserving good relations with France all the more difficult. Guizot agreed,[63] but as Peel pointed out with some bitterness Guizot himself had in 1841 claimed that increased defence expenditure would enable the

[61] For full accounts of the differences within the British government on Anglo-French relations and national defence, see Lady Frances Balfour, *The Life of George, Fourth Earl of Aberdeen* (London, 1923), ii, ch. x, Bartlett, op. cit., and Cunningham, op. cit.
[62] Peel to Aberdeen, 21 Aug. 1844. Aberdeen Papers, B.M. Add. MS. 43063.
[63] Chamberlain, op. cit., 278.

French government to strengthen peace, not to destroy it. Why then could this argument not be applied to the British proposals?[64]

Throughout 1845 therefore there was a sharp cleavage within the Peel government on Anglo-French relations. Aberdeen persevered with his policy of *entente*. On the Spanish Marriage question he made further concessions to Guizot. He continued to support the Bourbon principle in connection with the marriage of the Queen of Spain, and he agreed that the Queen's sister, the Infanta Luisa Fernanda, should marry Louis Philippe's son, the Duke of Montpensier, once the Queen had married and had children. He hoped that 'things should go on quietly in Spain' and that the French would not flaunt their influence. It was important, he informed Bulwer, the British minister at Madrid, to hold no brief 'for any particular party'.[65] Although Aberdeen was convinced of the wisdom of his policy, he was also acutely conscious of his isolation in the cabinet. In September 1845 he offered Peel his resignation, which was refused. By the autumn of 1845 Peel was becoming increasingly preoccupied with domestic affairs; the differences within the cabinet on the Corn Law question were of far greater importance than those over Anglo-French relations. The foreign policy and defence debates within the government receded into the background. Aberdeen remained at the Foreign Office and retained his attachment to Guizot and the *entente*; he had the support of the Queen but not of his colleagues. In a sense therefore only the Irish crisis prevented the divisions within the cabinet on Anglo-French relations from becoming public and the *entente* from being officially declared moribund.

The Whig party was largely unaware of the disagreement within the Peel government over Anglo-French relations. Greville told Clarendon that Wellington had lost faith in Guizot as a result of the Tahiti crisis,[66] and Peel's defence of increased naval expenditure in the House of Commons suggested to Palmerston that at last some Tories had begun to see sense,[67]

[64] Peel to Aberdeen, 17 Oct. 1845. Aberdeen Papers, B.M. Add. MS. 43065.
[65] Aberdeen to Bulwer, 3 Feb. 1845. Bulwer Papers, S/2.
[66] Greville to Clarendon, 29 Aug. 1844. Clar. Dep. C520.
[67] Palmerston to William Temple, 15 Nov. 1845. B.P. GC/TE/310.

but the Whigs did not realise that many members of the Tory government had abandoned confidence in Guizot and the *entente*. The Whig debate on Anglo-French relations was therefore unaffected by the fact that it was paralleled in the Tory government. The crises of 1844 won converts to a stronger line towards France within the Whig party as they did in the Tory cabinet. Russell became convinced that Aberdeen's policy was more likely to lead to war than to avert it. 'In this view of our foreign affairs', he informed Palmerston, 'I quite agree with you that a large sum ought to be applied to strengthening our coastal defences.'[68] Even the more devoted adherents of good relations with France were shocked by French conduct in 1844: Clarendon was afraid that after Tahiti 'fresh acts of insolence and aggression will not long be wanting'.[69] Easthope and Palmerston were well pleased with the way the events of 1844 had vindicated their strictures on Aberdeen and confirmed the superior wisdom of the course they had consistently advocated. 'I very cordially congratulate Your Lordship on your triumph', wrote Easthope to Palmerston in October 1844; 'nothing can be more complete...those who have engaged in taunts against Your Lordship's policy as too belligerent must feel awkward under the severer taunts which their own mistakes and blunders have brought upon them'.[70] Palmerston more modestly admitted that 'a glimmering of light is coming over some of our friends'.[71] The process of conversion to a firmer line, however, was slow and incomplete. Despite privately expressed doubts, Clarendon did not attack the *entente* in the debate on the Tahiti crisis. When the new parliamentary session opened in 1845 Russell thought it prudent for the Whigs to be very cautious in their attacks on the government's handling of the Moroccan question. 'I do not think it would be wise', he informed Palmerston, 'to move an amendment as Ellice would hear of it and would cabal against it with some success.'[72] Minto, who shared Palmerston's views on foreign policy without reservation,

[68] Russell to Palmerston, 2 Jan. 1845. B.P. GC/RU/88.
[69] Clarendon to Lady Holland, 20 Sept. 1844. Holland House Papers, B.M. Add. MS. 51617.
[70] Easthope to Palmerston, 4 Oct. 1844. B.P. GC/EA/14.
[71] Palmerston to Doyle, 4 Dec. 1844. B.P. GC/DO/53.
[72] Russell to Palmerston, [?] Jan. 1845. B.P. GC/RU/89.

also urged him not to take too strong a line in Parliament because it would inevitably antagonise 'the temper and feelings of the great majority of our friends'.[73] Macaulay thought that the task of the Whig party was not only to refrain from a hostile attack on the government's policy towards France, but also to rid itself of the warmongering image it had acquired. 'Nobody I am sure', he assured Palmerston on 9 January 1845,

knows better than yourself that of all imputations which can be thrown on a body of politicians that of being a war party is, in the present temper of the public mind, the most damaging. If that be so, we ought, I think, seriously to consider by what means, compatible with the faithful discharge of our duty to our country, we can get rid of this imputation. And indeed to clear ourselves from unjust aspersions and to keep our friends united is a part, and not an unimportant part, of our duty to our country.[74]

Earlier in January Palmerston had told Macaulay that he had no intention of adopting the views of the 'many foolish and ignorant members of our party',[75] and his speech in the House of Commons during the debate on the Tahiti crisis in February 1845 reflected this resolve. His attack on the government's handling of the Pritchard dispute was markedly stronger than Russell's.[76] In the House of Lords Lansdowne expressed great anxiety lest the *entente* be jeopardised by the animosity aroused in both England and France, and encouraged Aberdeen to make every effort to repair the damage done by the Tahiti affair.[77] Palmerston's subsequent instructions to the *Chronicle* were in no way moderated by the advice he had received from Russell, Minto and Macaulay. On 17 January 1845 he advised Doyle, the editor, to point out again that 'in the existing state of things in Europe the chief danger of war arises from the ruthless ambition and aggressive character of the French...'[78] Russell's second attempt to induce Palmerston to moderate his public

[73] Minto to Palmerston, 1 Feb. 1845. B.P. GC/MI/457.
[74] Macaulay to Palmerston, 9 Jan. 1845. B.P. GC/MA/16.
[75] Ibid.
[76] *Hansard*, 3rd series, lxxvii: House of Commons, 4 Feb. 1845, 112–18.
[77] Ibid., House of Lords, 34–8.
[78] Palmerston to Doyle, 17 Jan. 1845. B.P. GC/DO/57. Palmerston's colleagues were not the only ones who wanted him to restrain his attack on Aberdeen's handling of the Tahiti question. In Jan. 1845 Thiers informed Lord Leveson, the

utterances on Anglo-French relations met with the same fate as the first: once again Palmerston placed the 'national interest' above party unity.

In 1845 public interest in foreign affairs, aroused by the Pritchard dispute, swiftly disappeared under the impact of domestic crises and in the absence of any new dispute with France. For the Whigs and the Tories alike, differences over the Corn Law question were of far greater significance than differences over Anglo-French relations. By November 1845 it was apparent that a major crisis in British politics was at hand; the resignation of Peel and a split in the Tory party were thought to be imminent. On 6 December, after his failure to persuade his cabinet to abandon protection, Peel resigned. Russell, who had relinquished support for the fixed duty on imported corn in his famous Edinburgh letter of 27 November, was asked by the Queen to form a government, and spent the next eight days in consultation with his colleagues. On 10 December Russell assured Palmerston that he would be expected 'to go to the Foreign Office'[79] if the attempt to form a government succeeded. Before making this offer, Russell does not appear to have consulted his colleagues; Palmerston was the obvious choice for the Foreign Office and there was therefore no need to discuss the question. On 13 December, however, Ellice wrote to Russell from the north that he anticipated that Howick, whom he had

son of Lord Granville, the British ambassador in Paris, that the French opposition was anxious 'that the Whigs should not attack Lord Aberdeen on the subject of his concession on Tahiti. That it was a bad question for the Whigs to moot, that it must strengthen the two conservative govts in France and England.' Leveson to Palmerston, 29 Jan. 1845. B.P. GC/GR/1827. Palmerston replied: '...you say that M. Thiers had called on you to express his strong wish that the opposition in our Parliament should not in the approaching session attack the government on the subject of Tahiti, because if we blame our government for having been too yielding on that matter, our arguments would strengthen Guizot against the attacks of the opposition in France who have blamed him for conceding too much to us. This is certainly a case in which each of the two governments finds arguments for its own defence in the censures cast upon the other; but it is not easy to avoid this and it would be as difficult for the English opposition to admit that the result of the Tahiti affair has been satisfactory to England as it was for the French opposition to refrain from making that matter a ground of charge against the Govt of France. Each country has upon this point its peculiar interests and its national feeling and there are things which the popular party in Parliament cannot overlook.' Palmerston to Leveson, 2 Feb. 1845. B.P. GC/GR/1924.

[79] Palmerston to William Temple, 26 Jan. 1846. B.P. GC/TE/311.

seen, would 'be difficult about some arrangements at the Foreign Office'.[80] On the following day the Duke of Bedford informed his brother 'that the feeling against Palmerston is almost universal'; he himself recognised that Palmerston's 'return to the F[oreign] O[ffice] admits of no question' but advised that 'it will behove you to keep a steady and constant watch upon him and not to leave him to himself as Melbourne did'.[81] Russell must have expected opposition from a section of the party to Palmerston's return to the Foreign Office, but had no reason to think it insuperable so long as he were to give an assurance that Palmerston would be closely supervised.

Palmerston himself was more worried by the hostile reaction in France to the news of his impending return to the Foreign Office. The French press stated that this would be a calamity for the *entente* and claimed that Louis Philippe had written to Queen Victoria asking her to save the *entente* by appointing someone other than Palmerston to the Foreign Office.[82] In an attempt to reassure the French government he asked Easthope, who was in Paris, to inform Guizot 'that the new Govt if it does come in will be just as desirous of maintaining the most friendly relations with France as the late Govt can have been and you may remind them that the Whigs are their old friends and the Tories their new ones'.[83] Guizot was not inclined to place much confidence in Palmerston's overnight conversion to a policy he had spent four years condemning. Moreover, on the same day as Easthope delivered Palmerston's assurances, Jarnac reported that 'il m'est revenu que Lady Palmerston avait dit qu'il ne faudrait pas moins de deux ans pour remettre un peu d'ordre dans les relations extérieures'.[84] Guizot agreed with Desages, the permanent head of the French Foreign Office, that Palmerston's character and his approach to diplomacy alone boded ill for the *entente*: 'Je crains le tour d'esprit de l'homme qui se préoccupe passionnément de l'affaire spéciale du moment et oublie la politique générale, et encore plus le tour de son caractère qui

[80] Ellice to Russell, 13 Dec. 1845. Russell Papers, P.R.O. 30/22/4E.
[81] Duke of Bedford to Russell, 14 Dec. 1845. Russell Papers, P.R.O. 30/22/4E.
[82] Easthope to Palmerston, 15 Dec. 1845. B.P. GC/EA/19.
[83] Palmerston to Easthope, 15 Dec. 1845. B.P. GC/EA/41.
[84] Jarnac to Guizot, 18 Dec. 1845. G.P. 42/AP/69.

ne laisse tomber aucun sujet de discussion et de querelle.'[85] Most of all Guizot feared Palmerston's effect on the Spanish Marriages negotiations. His advice to Bresson, the French ambassador at Madrid, was: 'Profitez des moments; pressez les solutions. Plus il y aura, au début de notre nouveau compte, de faits accomplis, mieux cela vaudra.'[86]

In London Russell was preoccupied with the parliamentary difficulties that would confront any government he formed rather than with potential opposition to Palmerston's return to the Foreign Office.[87] On 15 December Russell saw Lord Grey and Ellice. His account of the interview suggested that both were in favour of taking office and that neither mentioned any objection to Palmerston's return to the Foreign Office.[88] During a conversation on 17 December with Sidney Herbert, a member of Peel's government, Grey expressed his desire for the maintenance of peace with France and his wish that 'we could keep Lord Aberdeen', as in his opinion Palmerston was 'a dangerous man'.[89] On 18 December the Whig leaders agreed to form a government and to undertake the task of repealing the Corn Laws despite their lack of a majority in the House of Commons. On the following day, however, Grey informed Russell that he could not serve in a government in which Palmerston was Foreign Secretary, since he believed that:

...justly or unjustly both friends and opponents regarded with considerable apprehension the prospect of his return to the Foreign Office and the existence of such a feeling was in my mind no slight objection to the appointment. But further when he formerly held the office events occurred which are by no means yet forgotten which have created feelings of apparent alienation between him and some of the chief statesmen and diplomatists of foreign countries more especially of France. Hence there is now undeniably on their part

---

[85] Guizot to Bresson, 20 Dec. 1845. G.P. 42/AP/8. See also Desages to Piscatory, 19 Dec. 1845. Desages Papers, vol. 25.

[86] Guizot to Bresson, 13 Dec. 1845. G.P. 42/AP/8.

[87] For an account of the internal political situation in Dec. 1845, see F. Dreyer, 'The Whigs and the Political Crisis of 1845', *English Historical Review*, July 1965, lxxx, 514–37.

[88] Russell's diary, 15 Dec. 1845. Russell Papers, P.R.O. 30/22/4E.

[89] Note by Sidney Herbert of a conversation with Lord Grey on 17 Dec. 1845. Royal Archives [hereafter R.A.] C/44/91.

a predisposition to view with jealousy whatever may be done by him...[90]

Russell declined to ask Palmerston to take any department other than the Foreign Office, but Grey remained adamant despite Ellice's supposed attempt to persuade him to change his mind. Russell therefore informed the Queen that he was unable to form a government since he could dispense with neither Grey nor Palmerston.[91] The Queen had no alternative but to ask Peel to return to office.

On reflection most of the Whig leaders believed that the party had done the right thing for the wrong reasons, that they should not have formed a government, but that their refusal to do so should have been ascribed to parliamentary rather than personal difficulties.[92] Grey was publicly criticised for having disgraced the party. In private, however, some of his colleagues admitted that he had saved them from an embarrassing situation.[93] Palmerston had no hesitation in attributing responsibility for what had happened:

I have found by various information which I have since received from many quarters that Ellice was the secret instigator of the whole thing and that Grey was his tool. Ellice acted from long cherished malice against me; from his general love of doing mischief and very likely from the effect of liberal grants of secret service money from Louis Philippe who hates the notion of a Whig government and of an English Secretary of State who would not be what Aberdeen is, Under Secretary of State to Guizot.[94]

Palmerston did not regret the decision either on party or on personal grounds, believing that his position had been strengthened by Grey's conduct: he claimed that even Peel admitted 'that whatever some of the Whigs might choose to think of my foreign policy', it had been 'enterprising and successful and done Melbourne's government great credit'.[95] The crisis of December 1845 showed, moreover, that opposition to Palmerston within the party had diminished appreciably, since none of the other

[90] Grey to Russell, 19 Dec. 1845. Russell Papers, P.R.O. 30/22/4E.
[91] Memorandum by Prince Albert, 20 Dec. 1845. R.A. C/44/76.
[92] Bessborough to Russell, 23 Dec. 1845. Russell Papers, P.R.O. 30/22/4E.
[93] Clarendon to G. C. Lewis, 21 Dec. 1845. Clar. Dep. C532.
[94] Palmerston to William Temple, 26 Jan. 1846. B.P. GC/TE/311. [95] Ibid.

Whig leaders supported Grey. Clarendon, for example, thought that '...energy such as Palmerston's is at this moment greatly needed at the Foreign Office and that it would tend far more than the present system to an entente really cordial between us and France'.[96] The Radical as well as the Whig press rallied to the defence of Palmerston. *The Examiner* deprecated Grey's conduct on the grounds that his action amounted to an admission that 'the appointments in our Government' should be 'regulated by the jealousies and personal antipathies of Foreign Powers'.[97] In Paris, however, the failure of the Whigs to form a government was a great relief. 'Here there is great joy at having Palmerston set aside', wrote Hervey to Clarendon, 'which they consider as a sort of homage to France.'[98] There can be no doubt that the crisis of December 1845 affirmed Palmerston's strength in the party and showed how isolated and few his opponents had become. Were Russell ever again asked to form a government, Palmerston would certainly return to the Foreign Office. As far as Anglo-French relations were concerned, all Grey had done was to gain a temporary reprieve for the *entente* of Guizot and Aberdeen.

During his last six months at the Foreign Office Aberdeen was unable to strengthen the *entente*. As before, the two Foreign Ministers exchanged numerous expressions of good faith and good intentions, but neither made any great effort to give them practical effect. Over the Spanish Marriages, the divergence of the policies of Guizot and Aberdeen became unmistakable: Guizot was increasingly anxious for a triumph at Madrid and increasingly irritated by his obligations to the British government. He was, moreover, acutely aware that Palmerston would return to the Foreign Office in the near future. He therefore wanted what he had urged Bresson to secure in December 1845, 'des faits accomplis'. Aberdeen too was conscious that his diplomacy would soon be subject to the close scrutiny of Palmerston, and he wanted to endow the final acts of his Spanish policy with the appearance of the qualities Palmerston

---

[96] Clarendon to Panizzi, 23 Dec. 1845. L. Fagan, *The Life of Anthony Panizzi* (London, 1880), i, 205–6.
[97] *Morning Chronicle*, 30 Dec. 1845. *The Examiner*, 3 Jan. 1846.
[98] Hervey to Clarendon, 26 Dec. 1845. Clar. Dep. C529.

claimed it lacked: firmness of purpose, resistance to French encroachment, and a respect for Spanish independence. As a consequence of his attempt to demonstrate these qualities, Aberdeen's policy during 1846 on the question of the Spanish Marriages became dangerously ambiguous.[99]

Whilst Aberdeen and Guizot were trying to prolong the life of the crumbling *entente*, Palmerston was striving to prove the friendliness of his disposition towards France. In April 1846 he visited Paris in what he described as an attempt 'to convince the French by ocular demonstration that I have not cloven feet and a tail'.[100] Easthope prepared the ground, and Palmerston was received by Louis Philippe, Guizot and Thiers. The visit appeared to him a great success:

> All the Liberal Party, who as you know, attach great importance to a good understanding between England and France are delighted at our good reception because it removes an unfounded apprehension which Ellice and some other low intriguers have contrived industriously to spread that if I returned to the Foreign Office there would be an immediate quarrel with France.[101]

The French were not as impressed by Palmerston as he believed. Desages commented that Palmerston 'est venu travailler ici à se rendre possible à Londres'.[102] Guizot explained to Palmerston that he and Aberdeen had worked together to maintain the *entente*: 'parce que nous ne sommes jamais laissés entraîner à oublier l'intérêt supérieur en présence de tel ou tel intérêt secondaire, parce que nous avons constamment placé notre politique générale de paix et de bonne intelligence au-dessus de toutes les questions spéciales'. Guizot clearly did not think that Palmerston could act in this spirit: '...en France, pour les hommes sérieux, lord Palmerston a paru, au fond, toujours le même, avec les mêmes dispositions, le même tour de caractère et d'esprit'.[103] Palmerston's visit to Paris thus only served to strengthen Guizot's misgivings as to the future of the *entente*.

[99] For a full account of Aberdeen's Spanish policy, Jan.–June 1846, see below, Chapter IV, pp. 84–91.
[100] Palmerston to William Temple, 10 Apr. 1846. B.P. GC/TE/314.
[101] Palmerston to William Temple, 13 May 1846. B.P. GC/TE/315.
[102] Desages to Piscatory, 20 Apr. 1846. Desages Papers, vol. 25.
[103] Guizot to Aberdeen, 28 Apr. 1846. *Lettres de Monsieur Guizot à sa famille et à ses amis*, ed. Madame de Witt (Paris, 1884), 239–42.

CHAPTER III

The Whigs Return

On 28 June 1846 Peel resigned. Queen Victoria, Louis Philippe and Guizot were desolate, but there was nothing they could do but bow to the inevitable and exchange sad letters of farewell with Peel and Aberdeen. The Tory disaster reflected no Whig triumph; it was, as Princess Lieven wrote, 'des pommes de terre malades'[1] which had brought down the government and split the Tory party. For the second time Queen Victoria sent for Lord John Russell. This time Russell acted with speed and determination; by 30 June he was able to inform the Queen that he had formed a government. Palmerston was back at the Foreign Office, 'the abode of his bliss' as Greville called it.[2] Although his return was regretted by some,[3] his claim to the Foreign Office was questioned by none. With the Oregon question recently settled[4] and the European situation calm, Palmerston's return attracted little attention in England. It was domestic issues which occupied the public mind: how long could the new government last, given that the Whig party was in a minority in the House of Commons? what measures would the government propose for the relief of famine in Ireland? These were the questions discussed in the press in July 1846; only the *Morning Chronicle* welcomed Palmerston back to the Foreign Office.[5]

In some respects the Palmerston who returned to office in 1846 was very different from the Palmerston who had left office in 1841: his position within the Whig party and in British politics was stronger than it had ever been. In the crisis of

---

[1] *Aberdeen–Lieven*, i, 259.
[2] *The Greville Memoirs*, ed. H. Reeve, v, 251–2.
[3] The Bishop of Oxford wrote to Anson, Prince Albert's Private Secretary, on 29 June 1846, 'Already there are whispers of Palmerston and War . . .' *Q.V.L.*, 1st series, ii, 98.
[4] See Frederick Merk, *The Oregon Question* (Cambridge, Mass., 1967).
[5] *Morning Chronicle*, 2 July 1846.

December 1845 Russell had made it clear that he regarded Palmerston's presence in a Whig government as indispensable and that if he wanted the seals of the Foreign Office he should have them. Grey's opposition had weakened not Palmerston but himself; in June 1846 Russell only included Grey in his cabinet under pressure whereas Palmerston's place in the Whig party in the House of Commons was second only to Russell's. The fact that some of his colleagues were among Palmerston's sternest critics imposed more strains on Russell's leadership than threats to Palmerston's position, which was more secure than that of the majority of his Whig critics. He possessed great administrative talents, he was industrious, he was popular with the Whig rank and file, and he was well known in the country. His vigour and vitality were astonishing. At the age of sixty-two he was accounted a coming man; Lord Palmerston, wrote *Fraser's Magazine* in March 1846, 'has begun where most men end'.[6]

It was in the governments of Grey and Melbourne that Palmerston had demonstrated his outstanding administrative gifts. Even his critics acknowledged his capacity for hard work, his mastery of the business of his department, and his political courage, although they considered that he sometimes carried them to excess.[7] Palmerston alone was exempt from the public contempt in which the Whig ministers were held just before the fall of the Melbourne government.[8] It was in opposition that he achieved popularity in the party. In the 1830s his heavy departmental duties had limited his attendance at the House except when foreign affairs were being discussed. Out of office, Palmerston had more time for the House of Commons; he took a leading part in the Whig attacks on the Peel government and invariably took Russell's place during his frequent absences.[9] His enthusiasm for the parliamentary struggle was unbounded, and he never lost confidence in the ability of the Whigs to displace the Tories.[10] In the House Palmerston spoke often and

[6] *Fraser's Magazine*, Mar. 1846, 317.
[7] Edward Ellice to Lord Holland, 1 Jan. 1836. Holland House Papers, B.M. Add. MS. 51587.
[8] *The Greville Memoirs*, ed. H. Reeve, iv, 345.
[9] Sir Spencer Walpole, *The Life of Lord John Russell* (London, 1891), i, 399.
[10] In 1843 Palmerston informed his brother that although he expected 'no change at present', two or three years more would 'alter the feelings of the country'.

on a variety of subjects, although most of his major speeches were on foreign affairs. He was not a brilliant parliamentarian, but he acquired a reputation as a competent one. Frequent attendance at the House brought him into contact with the party backbenchers, and his easy manner, his unpretentiousness and his energy won him a great measure of personal popularity. Palmerston had none of Russell's stiffness or touchiness, nor indeed any of his high-mindedness. His apparent ordinariness made him approachable and likeable. Palmerston, wrote Bagehot, 'was not a common man, but a common man might have been cut out of him'.[11] Throughout his third tenure of the Foreign Office from June 1846 to December 1851 Palmerston was therefore able to count on considerable support from the backbenchers.[12] He had put the years in opposition to good use; it was during that period that he laid the foundations of his later ascendancy over the Whig party.

By 1846 Palmerston had also begun to reap the social and political benefits of his marriage to Lady Cowper which had taken place in 1839. Lady Palmerston, the sister of Lord Melbourne and Lord Beauvale, was her husband's most powerful partisan in the inner sanctums of the Whig establishment, and her *salon* at Gloucester House was of great service to his political career. The *salon* remained an important social and political centre as long as the Whigs held the key to both society and politics. The death of Lord Holland in 1840 and the consequent decline of Holland House as the centre of Whig society left a vacuum which Lady Palmerston's *salon* filled. She and Lord Palmerston were brilliant hosts; Lord and Lady John Russell, both poorer and less sociable, could never rival them. Outside the Foreign Office and the cabinet Palmerston's manner was faultless; he had, Lord Normanby wrote, 'no conversational brilliancy whatever, therefore the stranger whom he

Palmerston to William Temple, 29 May 1843. Sir H. Bulwer (Lord Dalling), *Life of Viscount Palmerston (to 1846)* (London, 1870–6), iii, 125.

[11] *Bagehot's Historical Essays*, ed. N. St John-Stevas (New York, 1965), 216.

[12] In a debate in the House of Commons on 5 June 1848 Edward Shiel said, 'taking him [Palmerston] for all in all, there is no man intellectually and morally better qualified to encounter great emergencies—that he is fit to cope with mighty hazards—and that England may be sure of him, whenever there shall be need of great talents and great sagacity, and when tranquil courage and indomitable determination shall be required'. *Hansard*, 3rd series, 1848, xcix, 372.

cordially receives [is] pleased with his social familiarity, never humbled by his intellectual superiority, probably gratified that a great man of whom he has heard so much should shew himself in all respects so like the rest of the world'.[13] The Gloucester House *salon* was primarily a meeting place for Whigs, but it was by no means either socially or politically exclusive; Whig aristocrats mingled with middle-class Liberals, journalists and diplomats.[14] For all these reasons, when the Russell government was formed in 1846 Palmerston was both more of a party man and a more popular man than he had been when the Melbourne administration fell.

If in some respects Palmerston was a new man in 1846, in others he was unchanged. In foreign affairs nothing done by Aberdeen and nothing that had happened in Europe since he left office in 1841 had led him to change his outlook. Until the events of 1848, which had a profound impact on Palmerston and substantially modified his view of European politics, it was his experience of the late 1830s that determined his attitude. His approach had always been pragmatic; he acted on what existed, not on what he thought should be. The failure of the 'liberal alliance' greatly affected Palmerston's outlook on foreign affairs. In his opinion England had no permanent enemies but neither could she rely on any state for constant support or regular friendship. In 1838 Palmerston wrote to Sir Frederick Lamb, the British ambassador at Vienna:

My doctrine is that we should reckon upon ourselves; pursue a policy of our own; aim at objects of our own, and act upon principles of our own; use other Governments as we can, when we want them and find them willing to serve us; but never place ourselves in the wake of any of them. Lead when and where we can; but follow never.[15]

Palmerston did not regard this as a harsh doctrine or the basis

[13] Lord Normanby: Review of Lord Palmerston's Policy. Normanby Papers, Box P, bundle 18.
[14] Palmerston himself wrote that the Gloucester House *salon* was 'neutral ground where distinguished Persons of all political Parties whether Foreign or Domestic meet for social intercourse forgetting for the moment their political differences'. Palmerston to the editor of *The Globe*, 9 July 1849. Quoted *Manuscripts and Men* (London, 1969), 99.
[15] Palmerston to Lamb, 21 Mar. 1838. Beauvale Papers, Box 13.

for a pessimistic outlook. Although he saw ambition and conflict as the dominant characteristics of international society, he believed this to be a natural state of affairs. He was in fact an optimist who maintained an undimmed confidence in the power and strength of England. Palmerston never sought war nor relished the prospect of it, but neither did he share Aberdeen's dread of it. He often wrote of the inevitability of war, in the early 1830s with Russia, in the late 1830s with France, but he never doubted that England had the resources and ability to emerge victorious. He frequently complained about the poor state of the national defences but he never believed that their inadequacy presented more than a temporary danger. Palmerston's unswerving belief in the greatness and power of England was perhaps the most distinctive characteristic of his foreign policy; none of his successors at the Foreign Office has entertained it with such assurance and confidence.

Palmerston was convinced that England's power was the result of her progress. He therefore believed that it was her duty to act where and when she could as the agent of progress, 'to maintain the liberties and independence of all other nations' and 'to throw her moral weight into the scale of any people who are spontaneously striving for freedom, by which I mean rational government; and to extend as far and as fast as possible civilization all over the world'.[16] The vigour with which Palmerston promoted this doctrine, his hectoring and insulting condemnation of repressive systems of government, have been frequently criticised. The greatest defect of his gospel of progress was not the way it was expressed but its insularity and the naïvety of its premises. Depite Palmerston's extensive knowledge of European affairs, he had little understanding of any society other than that in which he lived.[17] He was convinced that what was good for England could be achieved by others and would prove equally good for them. He had no real conception of the continuous political development of any society other than

[16] Ibid.

[17] Normanby wrote to Granville on his appointment to the Foreign Office: 'You have...that personal knowledge of the continent in all its bearings which is generally the great deficiency of our statesmen, and singularly the misfortune of your predecessor...' Normanby to Granville, 28 Dec. 1851. Normanby Papers, Box P, bundle 17.

England; constitutional government, if not 'pure' in the way he thought English constitutionalism to be, was to him not constitutionalism at all. Thus his policies towards Greece, Spain and Portugal, with their insistence on pure constitutionalism, invited failure; these countries would always fall short of his expectations.[18]

Equally distinctive was Palmerston's approach to negotiation and the conduct of foreign policy. He believed that firmness of purpose, determination and a willingness to take risks were as important as clear objectives. He practised what would now be called 'negotiation from strength'. In 1847 and early 1848 he repeatedly warned his colleagues that failure to strengthen the national defences would weaken Great Britain's negotiating position.[19] Palmerston also believed in the efficacy of the well-timed menace. In September 1846, when he was attempting to prevent the marriage of the Duke of Montpensier and the Infanta Luisa of Spain, he suggested that a British squadron be stationed off the Spanish coast:

> This sort of demonstration often tells upon a negotiation; and it would do no harm at the Tuileries if any orders about fitting out line of battleships could be given in our dockyards, and mentioned in the newspapers, even if no active or real steps were taken to carry them into effect. Louis Philippe's letter to the Queen was marked by the twaddling of age, and by the consciousness of being in the wrong, and a little demonstration on our part not amounting to a threat, and committing us to nothing, might have its effect upon a mind in that condition.[20]

In negotiation Palmerston's objective was a limited one: to secure an immediate and particular end. How he got it depended upon the willingness or reluctance of other parties to concede it. By contrast, Aberdeen believed that the general relations of England with other countries mattered more than particular points of dispute. Aberdeen was therefore prepared

---

[18] The Queen and Prince Albert frequently told Palmerston this. Prince Albert had a very different view of the development of political society, and he considered Palmerston's to be both narrow and insular. See *Letters of the Prince Consort 1831–1861*, ed. K. Jagow (London, 1938), 124.
[19] Palmerston to Russell, 15 Jan. 1848. B.P. GC/RU/1037.
[20] Palmerston to Russell, 27 Sept. 1846. Russell Papers, P.R.O. 30/22/5C.

to concede small points to promote an atmosphere of friendship and co-operation. In Palmerston's view nothing was so worthless as to justify concession:

> It must perpetually happen that the particular object or interest, to defend which a country stands out to resist an aggressive war, may in its separate and intrinsic value not be worth the expenses that must be incurred to defend it. But any nation which were to act upon the principle of yielding to every demand made upon it, if each separate demand could be shown not to involve directly and immediately a vital interest, would at no distant period find itself progressively stripped of the means of defending its vital interests, when those interests came at last to be attacked.[21]

This belief alone, however, does not explain his conduct in negotiation. Palmerston was intensely combative; he enjoyed a battle, and above all he enjoyed winning. Some found his manner offensive and insulting and could not work with him. The Duke of Broglie, after six months as French ambassador in London, returned to Paris openly refusing to return on the grounds that he was unable to work with Palmerston.[22] His most severe critics claimed that all Palmerston sought in his constant affrays was cheap victories:

> The object of almost every one of Lord Palmerston's affairs seems not to have been its ultimate end but when the desired Parliamentary question was placed in the hands of some admiring satellite that [the] answer should round a telling point in a speech and that his dispatches should not sleep within the countless pages of a big Blue Book but should contain specific paragraphs to be extracted under his own auspices by some friendly editor to furnish an article in a convenient organ for his glorification. The purpose once effected in all probability the affair was never again heard of.[23]

Fraser's Magazine, in a generally favourable article, condemned Palmerston for his constant attempt to capture 'the

---

[21] Palmerston to Russell, 29 Sept. 1840. B.P. GC/RU/961.
[22] Normanby to Palmerston, 6 Jan. 1848. B.P. GC/NO/95.
[23] Lord Normanby: Review of Lord Palmerston's Policy. Normanby Papers, Box P, bundle 18. Normanby wrote: 'He is too much of a political prize fighter, his blows are all for victory, his scars but the natural result of his calling. He has as little of passion as of principle though he can as easily assume the one as he can loudly boast the other. With him political reputation is merely so much stock in trade...it has a marketable value; the acquirement and maintenance of place.'

THE WHIGS RETURN

popular feeling of the hour'.[24] Palmerston not only enjoyed winning his battles, he also wanted his victories known and appreciated. For Palmerston the connection between publicity and diplomacy was fundamental; an unsung triumph was only half a triumph. His emphasis on publicity had initially been defensive. In the early 1830s his policy had been frequently and bitterly attacked in the press and in Parliament, and he had felt it necessary to reply in kind. He therefore established close and frequent contact with some newspaper owners, editors and journalists. He gave them his patronage and supplied them with information, and they in turn noticed his activities and supported his policies. Palmerston was quick to appreciate the enormous power wielded by the press and soon began to exploit it to his own advantage. By the late 1830s the 'Palmerston Press' had created an image of Palmerston as the vigorous defender of English interests, the man in whom the country could place its trust. This was achieved both by direct panegyrics and indirectly by attacks on his opponents; foreign statesmen were condemned for their ambition, repression and unscrupulousness; domestic enemies, both Tory and Whig, were dismissed as intriguers and fools.[25] Palmerston's attempts to keep his merits and achievements in the public eye were only partially successful. He complained frequently of the indifference of the public to foreign policy[26] until the great events on the continent in 1848 brought foreign affairs to the forefront.[27] For the most part, and especially as far as Anglo-French

[24] *Fraser's Magazine*, Mar. 1846, 320.
[25] See for example the *Morning Chronicle*, 24 Jan. 1844, where Guizot and Louis Philippe were described as the plunderers and murderers of Spain, and 15 Apr. 1844 where Aberdeen was described as having the stupid gravity of a menial. Palmerston was sometimes reprimanded for these attacks. On 11 Oct. 1846 *La Presse* wrote that the language of the *Morning Chronicle* 'donne à l'Europe civilisée une étrange idée du ton de la société officielle en Angleterre et des passions qui agitent Lord Palmerston'. Lansdowne wrote to Russell on 30 Nov. 1846, 'I could wish there was a little less asperity of tone of vindictive feeling displayed in the M[orning] Chronicle articles which is unnecessary.' *The Later Correspondence of Lord John Russell*, ed. G. P. Gooch (London, 1925), i, 130.
[26] Palmerston to Normanby, 5 Mar. 1847. Normanby Papers, Box P, bundle 19.
[27] G. M. Young wrote, 'From 1815 to the Revolutions of '48 foreign affairs had engaged but a small share of the public attention...But from 1850 onwards the focus of interest is overseas...' *Early Victorian England*, ed. G. M. Young (London, 1934), ii, 482.

relations were concerned, the press debates on foreign policy, following a pattern of attack and counter-attack, were merely another dimension of diplomacy. Guizot knew that the *Morning Chronicle* was Palmerston's mouthpiece and Palmerston knew that the *Journal des Débats* was Guizot's. In these newspapers each could say things about the other that the conventions of diplomacy would never have allowed them to have said in despatches or speeches. In the first week of July 1846, however, the *Journal des Débats* launched no attack on Palmerston, claiming, like Guizot, to be giving him the benefit of the doubt.

Although the English public evinced little interest in Palmerston's return to the Foreign Office, amongst political circles in London and Paris it aroused much speculation. Despite efforts to appear calm, Louis Philippe and Guizot failed to conceal their anxiety.[28] In London Jarnac declined to discuss the reaction of the French government to Palmerston's return, but was keen to gather the views of others.[29] All speculation revolved round one question: would Palmerston strive to maintain the *entente cordiale*? There were as many answers to this as there were estimates of Palmerston, ranging from cautious optimism[30] to extreme pessimism.[31] More surprising than these divergences of view was the absence of any discussion of the actual state of Anglo-French relations. The assertion of Aberdeen and Guizot that the *entente* was flourishing was generally accepted. In fact it had been undermined from both within and without, and its basis had been progressively narrowed. In their letters of farewell Aberdeen and Guizot dwelt exclusively on their good intentions and their successes, both claiming to have achieved some good and averted much evil.[32]

[28] Hervey to Clarendon, 29 June 1846. Clar. Dep. C529.
[29] Jarnac to Guizot, 4 July 1846. G.P. 42/AP/69.
[30] Aberdeen told Jarnac that Russell 'veillera sur notre entente intime par goût et par sa disposition naturelle. Palmerston la maintiendra par nécessité.' Jarnac to Guizot, 15 July 1846. G.P. 42/AP/69.
[31] Desages thought that Palmerston would abandon the *entente* at the earliest opportunity. Desages to Bourqueney, 30 June 1846. Bourqueney Papers A.E. France 1900.
[32] Guizot wrote of 'la bonne et rare politique que nous avons fait triompher pendant cinq ans'. Quoted in Lady Frances Balfour, *The Life of George, Fourth Earl of Aberdeen* (London, 1922), ii, 143. Aberdeen to Guizot, 30 June 1846. G.P. 42/AP/7.

It would have been better for Palmerston had Aberdeen been more conscious of his failures. Palmerston and the Whigs did not know that for the last twelve months of the Peel government Aberdeen had maintained the *entente cordiale* almost in defiance of his colleagues. Neither did they know that Guizot and Aberdeen had come near to deadlock over the question of the Spanish Marriages, and that during the previous six months their Spanish policies had gradually drifted apart. Aberdeen exaggerated the value of his legacy to Palmerston both in public and in private, and it was in French interests to confirm this impression rather than to admit that the *entente* had already been vitally undermined. Palmerston was thus confronted with the task of co-operating with France when co-operation had ceased. The truth was that the *entente* needed to be revived rather than preserved.

The future of the *entente*, however, did not depend on Palmerston alone. Although he would undoubtedly play a major rôle in the formulation of policy, he would have to consult his colleagues and the Queen. How did they view Anglo-French relations? What did they think Palmerston ought to do? Had they the strength to control him if they thought that his policy endangered good relations with France? Palmerston would also have to rely on his subordinates to implement his policy. Were they the sort of men to execute his instructions faithfully? Were they capable of cordial co-operation with French diplomatic representatives? Equally important were the reactions of Guizot and the French government, and the attitude of French diplomats. Would they respond favourably to the new Whig government, give a full account of their policies, and make suggestions for active co-operation, or would they wait for Palmerston to reveal his policies, expecting them to be hostile, secretly hoping that he would make a false move?

On leaving office Peel and Aberdeen assured the first secretary of the French embassy in London, Count Jarnac, that his government could count on Lord John Russell as a sincere friend of France and a champion of the *entente cordiale*. He could be relied on to watch Palmerston and to prevent him from giving needless offence to France.[33] This view was shared by

[33] Jarnac to Guizot, 15 July 1846. G.P. 42/AP/69.

some members of the new Whig cabinet, who hoped that under Russell Palmerston would not be his own master as he had been under Melbourne.[34] Wood, the Chancellor of the Exchequer, informed Russell that the cabinet expected from him a day-by-day supervision of the affairs of the Foreign Office, 'no easy matter' as he admitted.[35] In July 1846 therefore Russell seemed to many the one man who could ensure the maintenance of good relations with France. 'Lord John Russell avait trop de sagesse pour se laisser entraîner par la violence de son collègue', wrote Flahaut, the French ambassador at Vienna and a friend of several of the Whig leaders, to Guizot.[36] In fact, however, Russell's position and his outlook on foreign affairs made him unlikely to play such a rôle.

Russell became Prime Minister at a very difficult moment. His hold over his party was unsure. Greville told Clarendon in 1848 that Russell had always been 'considered weak and indifferent as a leader'.[37] In the House of Commons he was dependent on the support of the Irish party and the Peelites for his majority,[38] and was constantly harassed by the radical wing of his own party. The Irish question, which was the main problem facing his new government, added greatly to his difficulties. Any solution must not only meet the needs of the Irish situation but also respect the powerful vested interests of the English aristocracy in Ireland. This almost impossible task consumed most of Russell's time and energy. He was not a strong man, and the burden of office undoubtedly undermined his health. The premiership 'nearly killed Peel by the time he left office', Greville informed Clarendon, and he 'is naturally far more robust than John'.[39] Russell was therefore unlikely to maintain a close watch over the conduct of foreign affairs. Although he did not share Palmerston's hostility to Orleanist France, it was wrong to assume that Russell's outlook on foreign

---

[34] Lord Normanby: Review of Lord Palmerston's Policy. Normanby Papers, Box P, bundle 18.
[35] Wood to Russell, 18 Sept. 1846. Russell Papers, P.R.O. 30/22/5C.
[36] Flahaut to Guizot, 5 Aug. 1846. G.P. 42/AP/68.
[37] Greville to Clarendon, 3 June 1848. Clar. Dep. C521.
[38] See J. B. Conacher, 'Peel and the Peelites, 1846–1850', *English Historical Review*, July 1958, lxxiv, 431–52.
[39] Greville to Clarendon, 6 Mar. 1848. Clar. Dep. C521.

THE WHIGS RETURN

policy was significantly different from that of Palmerston. The wish to maintain good relations with France was not the decisive factor; the important question was the price Russell was prepared to pay to remain on good terms with her. Russell's price was likely to be nearer Palmerston's than Aberdeen's. He had never objected to the principles on which Palmerston had founded his attacks on Aberdeen's foreign policy; he had merely regretted the vehemence of some of the onslaughts. Russell himself had been a fairly severe critic of Aberdeen; not long after the Whigs came into office Russell voiced the opinion that Aberdeen had 'committed himself much too far' to Guizot on the question of the Spanish Marriages.[40] He was no advocate of concession and compromise; he was as determined as Palmerston to defend the vital interests of Great Britain. Neither did he share Aberdeen's concern for appearances. In August 1846 he saw no cogent reason for the government to allude to its good relations with France at the end of the parliamentary session,[41] and he favoured telling the French bluntly that the British government could not co-operate with them over Spanish affairs whilst they maintained such a dictatorial attitude.[42] The possibility of serious disagreement between Palmerston and Russell was slight; they were on good terms, and until 1848 worked in almost complete harmony. The attempt of Guizot and Jarnac to separate them was sharply rebuffed by Russell.[43]

All Palmerston's colleagues theoretically favoured the maintenance of good relations with France, and the majority had at one time or another publicly expressed belief in its necessity. Jarnac was convinced that if the will of the cabinet were to determine foreign policy the *entente* would go from strength to strength.[44] An Anglo-French accord was, said Thiers, a fundamental article of Whig faith[45] and Clarendon called it one of their favourite hobby-horses.[46] The party was more cosmo-

---

[40] Russell to Palmerston, 13 Aug. 1846. B.P. GC/RU/104.
[41] 'I do not see how it is possible to say anything complimentary to France in the Speech.' Russell to Palmerston, 23 Aug. 1846. B.P. GC/RU/108.
[42] Russell to Palmerston, 28 Aug. 1846. B.P. GC/RU/109.
[43] Russell to Jarnac, 26 Oct. 1846. Russell Papers, P.R.O. 30/22/5D.
[44] Jarnac to Guizot, 18 Aug. 1846. G.P. 42/AP/69.
[45] Speech in the Chamber of Deputies, 14 Jan. 1847. *Le Constitutionnel*, 15 Jan. 1847.
[46] Sainte Aulaire to Guizot, 19 Sept. 1846. G.P. 42/AP/66.

politan than its Tory predecessor, and several members of the
Russell government had close contacts with French political and
diplomatic circles. Lord Lansdowne, Lord President of the
Council, was related to Flahaut, the French ambassador at
Vienna, and was also a close friend of the Duke of Broglie. Lord
Clarendon, President of the Board of Trade, had a number of
contacts inside and around the French government, and he even
claimed to know what went on in the meetings of the French
cabinet.[47] Lord Minto, the Lord Privy Seal, corresponded
regularly with Bresson, the French ambassador at Madrid.
Neither the friendly disposition of the new cabinet towards
France nor the close personal contacts of some of its members
with French diplomatic circles was a real insurance against coolness or even an open rupture. None of the cabinet members
most interested in foreign affairs—Clarendon, Lansdowne,
Minto and Auckland, the First Lord of the Admiralty—
believed in peace at any price; all had at different times been
severe critics of Guizot's foreign policy. Clarendon returned to
office convinced that Great Britain ought actively to counteract
French influence at Madrid, and both Palmerston and Bulwer
looked to him for advice on Spanish affairs.[48] In the early
1840s Minto had watched with growing alarm French expansion
along the coast of North Africa and the increase of French naval
power in the Mediterranean.[49] In Melbourne's ministry Lord
Auckland had been a warm supporter of Palmerston's policies;[50]
on his return to office in 1846 his major concern was the
inadequacy of the navy and the coastal defences, and he was no
more an advocate of concession than he had been in the 1830s.
Three members of the Russell administration, Clarendon,
Minto and Clanricarde, had served under Palmerston in the
diplomatic service in the 1830s,[51] the latter two at Courts where
the Orleans monarchy was viewed with suspicion. Although

[47] Clarendon to Palmerston, 8 Oct. 1847. B.P. GC/CL/477.
[48] 'Remember I look much to your consideration, advice and assistance in all
Spanish matters.' Bulwer to Clarendon, 14 Aug. 1846. Clar. Dep. C525. Palmerston
consulted Clarendon on Spanish affairs throughout July and August 1846. See
below, pp. 96–9.
[49] Minto to Russell, 15 Nov. 1844. Russell Papers, P.R.O. 30/22/4D.
[50] See Webster, *Palmerston*, i, 39–40.
[51] Clarendon at Madrid, Minto at Berlin, Clanricarde at St Petersburg.

neither had shared to the full the Prussian and Russian distrust of France, both had laboured to improve England's relations with the northern Courts. The suspicion and ignorance of the northern Courts which had led some of the Whig leaders in the 1830s to look exclusively to France was therefore likely to be tempered in the Russell government.

Lord Grey, the Secretary for War and the Colonies, and Sir Charles Wood, the Chancellor of the Exchequer, were the two cabinet ministers thought to be most hostile to Palmerston.[52] Their hostility was based on the contention that Palmerston's policies were generally quarrelsome, and that he was consequently viewed with suspicion and mistrust abroad. Both were accounted Francophiles because of their opposition to Palmerston and their close association with Edward Ellice, although neither was particularly well known in France or in close contact with French statesmen. They were isolated in the cabinet, Grey in particular being identified with the more radical wing of the party. Their presence in the government could not ensure the maintenance of good relations with France, neither could they do Palmerston much serious harm. Neither Grey nor Wood was well informed on matters of foreign policy,[53] and their views were unlikely to gain much cabinet support, especially as their criticisms of Palmerston were usually negative; they often complained of what he did but rarely suggested what he should do instead. Grey and Wood were themselves aware of their inability to prevent Palmerston from implementing what they considered objectionable courses of action. 'The mischief is done before we hear of anything', wrote Wood to Russell.[54] Moreover, they felt that the cabinet was an ineffective instrument of control: a body that met infrequently could hardly determine the daily affairs of one department, about which its members received inadequate information. 'A cabinet is too cumbersome a machine for such a work', declared Wood.[55] The only significant result of Grey's and Wood's opposition to Palmerston was to increase Russell's difficulties, and as Russell felt that he

---

[52] Jarnac to Louis Philippe, 29 July 1846. G.P. 42/AP/69.
[53] Ibid.
[54] Wood to Russell, 18 Sept. 1846. Russell Papers, P.R.O. 30/22/5C.
[55] Ibid.

could dispense with neither Grey nor Palmerston[56] he tried to accommodate both. It was only after 1848 that this became an almost impossible task. Between 1846 and 1848 the major disputes between Palmerston and the Grey faction concerned the national defences, not foreign policy.[57] The absence of strong and constructive cabinet opposition to his policy, Palmerston's ability to present his case to the cabinet with skill and persuasiveness, and the basic agreement of his more influential colleagues with his aims, meant that between 1846 and 1848 Palmerston received more active support and co-operation than opposition from his colleagues.

In part this harmony resulted from Palmerston's careful concealment from his colleagues of much of what he was doing. Although he was prepared to seek the advice or solicit the support of individuals if it seemed expedient, he had little faith in the judgment of most of his colleagues or of the cabinet as a whole on foreign affairs. 'None but the men who are actually engaged in the conduct of an affair can justly understand all the bearings of the circumstances and the full value of all the separate incidents of which it consists', Palmerston once informed Normanby.[58] He assumed that as he knew more about foreign affairs than his colleagues, his opinion must necessarily be superior to theirs. This assumption justified his increasingly common habit of failing to consult them. After his quarrel with Palmerston in 1851 Normanby accused him of bringing 'permanently into action that intolerable pretension that he should have the exclusive direction of measures of which others had to share the subsequent responsibility'.[59] When Russell suggested that the despatch to the three eastern powers on the suppression of the free state of Cracow should be submitted to the cabinet before it was sent, Palmerston replied, 'I thought your judgement would be sufficient in regard to this dispatch'; he saw 'no reason for submitting it to [the] cabinet'.[60]

---

[56] Palmerston was indispensable in the cabinet and in the Commons, Grey in the House of Lords where the Whig front benches were weak.
[57] See Palmerston to Wood, 24 Dec. 1846. B.P. GC/WO/186; and Wood to Palmerston, 26 Dec. 1846. B.P. GC/WO/20.
[58] Palmerston to Normanby, 5 Mar. 1847. Normanby Papers, Box P, bundle 19.
[59] Lord Normanby: Review of Lord Palmerston's Policy. Normanby Papers, Box P, bundle 18. [60] Palmerston to Russell, 14 Nov. 1846. B.P. GC/RU/1006.

THE WHIGS RETURN

For a long time members of the cabinet were unaware that they were not being properly consulted and that the information they received on foreign affairs was highly selective. Incoming despatches were circulated to the cabinet but they were frequently written so as to conceal the real policy of Palmerston and his agents. In November 1847 Palmerston wrote to Bulwer:

> Continue to do as you did by [the] last messenger, that is to say, in your dispatches confine yourself to stating events and their Spanish or foreign causes, but do not go into any explanation of the share which you may have had in bringing them about, except in very general terms. We must deal with men as we find them, and people who are engrossed with other matters and only take up a dispatch from a Foreign Minister now and then, on their return from the country, or in a lull of their own office business, fancy that Madrid is like London and Spain like England and the proper and legitimate endeavour of our minister at Madrid to counteract and defeat French intrigues, are [sic] just as if a foreign minister in London was to try to oust John Russell. Nevertheless go on exerting yourself to the utmost, only put your reports of your private communications on such matters into your private letters.[61]

Palmerston himself admitted that the private letters which passed between him and his diplomatic agents were more important than public despatches.[62] Communication by private letter had originally been a means of preventing confidential information and interim views from being published in a parliamentary Blue Book; Palmerston used his private correspondence as a means of conducting foreign policy behind the backs of his colleagues. Despatches rarely afforded any real insight into policy. Normanby stated frankly after reading Bulwer's official correspondence, 'there is nothing in his dispatches which would be worth carrying across the street, even if it had not already been in the newspapers'.[63] Palmerston rarely circulated outgoing despatches to the cabinet until after they had been sent. Lansdowne complained to Russell that 'dispatches involving important consequences should not be sent without the cabinet having an opportunity of forming a previous

[61] Palmerston to Bulwer, 17 Nov. 1847. Bulwer Papers, S/15.
[62] Palmerston to Seymour, 6 Feb. 1849. B.P. GC/SE/426.
[63] Normanby to Palmerston, 3 Aug. 1847. Normanby Papers, Box P, bundle 13.

judgement'.⁶⁴ Palmerston used his incoming private correspondence to suit his own purposes. If a letter contained information which he wished to be generally known he would send copies to some of his colleagues and to the Queen.⁶⁵ After the rupture with France in the autumn of 1846 he often circulated letters which gave accounts of French intrigue and duplicity. Palmerston did not, however, disclose the contents of his outgoing private letters.⁶⁶ Those of his colleagues who did not receive the occasional copy of a private letter were no better informed than the Palmerston press.⁶⁷ For a long time Palmerston's policy of careful control of the information which his colleagues received paid good dividends; it afforded him the free hand he wanted, and when cabinet exasperation did manifest itself it was Russell rather than Palmerston who bore its brunt.

Palmerston's treatment of the Queen was not dissimilar to his treatment of his colleagues. He expected grateful acceptance of the information he vouchsafed and her loyal support when he wanted it. His view of the rôle of the Crown was as much an underestimate of what it should be as the Queen's and Prince Albert's was an exaggeration. The Queen and the Prince had no intention of being the docile instruments of Palmerston. They had decided views of their own on foreign policy. In July 1846 their major preoccupation in foreign affairs was the maintenance of the *entente cordiale*, which they believed to be in the best interests of both England and France. This, however, is not an adequate explanation of their attachment to the *entente*. For the Queen good relations with France were part of an emotional commitment to Louis Philippe, and a visible expression of the influence and unity of the various branches of the Coburg

⁶⁴ Lansdowne to Russell, n.d. [1847/8]. Russell Papers, P.R.O. 30/22/6H.
⁶⁵ Palmerston sent some private letters he had received from Lord Howard de Walden, the British minister at Lisbon, to the Queen, as he thought it 'desirable that Your Majesty should see as much as possible what passes in the minds of Your Majesty's Ministers abroad, as well as what is contained in their formal and official dispatches'. Palmerston to the Queen, 5 Aug. 1846. R.A. C/25/73.
⁶⁶ Lansdowne informed Russell that 'Palmerston is very obliging in sending me a good deal of the private information which he receives, but very seldom the private instructions which he sends.' Lansdowne to Russell, n.d. [1847?]. Russell Papers, P.R.O. 30/22/6H.
⁶⁷ The contents of despatches were sometimes communicated to the press before they were seen by the cabinet. Greville to Clarendon, 2 June 1848. Clar. Dep. C521.

family.⁶⁸ Even under Aberdeen there had been two *ententes,* one royal, one governmental. They were linked, but the royal *entente* had never been able to save the governmental *entente* from vicissitudes and dangers. With Palmerston in office royal solidarity would have even less chance of overcoming intergovernmental friction. The Queen's ability to prevail over Palmerston depended on her ability to divide Russell and Palmerston. She knew when she was beaten: in August 1846 she withdrew her request for a friendly reference to France in the speech at the closing of the session when both Russell and Palmerston made it clear that they considered it inappropriate.⁶⁹ Moreover, even if the Queen were able to prevail over Palmerston there could be no guarantee that Louis Philippe could prevail over Guizot. The assurance of good intentions exchanged by Queen Victoria and Louis Philippe, and their mutual resolve to stand vigil over the *entente*⁷⁰ were of small value outside the closed circle of royalty. In fact neither sovereign was altogether frank with the other: Louis Philippe concealed from Queen Victoria his determination at all costs to marry his son, the Duke of Montpensier, to the Infanta Luisa of Spain; and Queen Victoria was equally reticent about her wish to effect a marriage between Prince Leopold of Coburg and Queen Isabella of Spain. A basic conflict of interests vitiated the close links between the Coburg and the Orleans families.⁷¹

The attachment of the Queen to Louis Philippe did not, however, blind her to what she regarded as unfortunate aspects of French diplomacy. She was no uncritical admirer of Guizot and his foreign policy,⁷² and there was no doubt where her sympathies would lie in a clash between British and French interests. The Queen had a clear conception of England's dignity and honour, and she was not prepared to countenance a slight on either. After the rupture over the Spanish Marriages the Queen

⁶⁸ Two of Queen Victoria's Coburg cousins were married to children of Louis Philippe.
⁶⁹ The Queen to Russell, 22 Aug. 1846. R.A. C/7/19. Russell to Palmerston, 23 Aug. 1846. B.P. GC/RU/108.
⁷⁰ Louis Philippe to Queen Victoria, 28 Aug. 1846. R.A. Y/48/69.
⁷¹ Guizot was also highly suspicious of Queen Victoria and the Coburgs. See Guizot to Princess Lieven, 3 Aug. 1846. *Guizot–Lieven,* iii, 241.
⁷² She had strongly condemned Guizot's policy during the Tahiti crisis. Queen Victoria to the King of the Belgians, 27 Aug. 1844. *Q.V.L.,* 1st series, ii, 24.

and the Prince gave Palmerston the support he wanted, while he fed their indignation against France and played upon the Queen's personal resentment of Louis Philippe's display of bad faith. It was on the Portuguese question rather than over Anglo-French differences that the Queen and Palmerston parted company.[73] Palmerston encountered considerably less royal opposition between 1846 and 1848 than he did later. The confident expectation of Louis Philippe and Guizot that Queen Victoria could be relied on to champion their cause was a dangerous mistake: the Queen was neither willing nor able to do so.

Palmerston's return to office in 1846 brought about a discernible change of mood in the British diplomatic corps.[74] The majority of British diplomats did not regret Aberdeen, who had gained neither the admiration nor the confidence of many of his subordinates overseas, and whose dealings with some had been marked by mutual exasperation. In certain respects Aberdeen had been unfortunate in his diplomatic establishment: he had been unable to find many men for diplomatic posts who shared his outlook on foreign affairs. In 1841 the Tories had intended to sweep away 'all the diplomatic Palmerston rubbish'.[75] An almost complete change of personnel usually accompanied a change of government, partly because foreign secretaries preferred to be served by party colleagues whom they knew and trusted, partly because diplomatic posts were a valuable source of patronage. Peel and Aberdeen were, however, unable to find enough competent, let alone talented, Tories to replace the Whig diplomats. Many of Palmerston's protégés therefore remained at their posts, and some were even promoted by Aberdeen. The dearth of diplomatic talent among the Tories pleased the Palmerstons[76] and annoyed Guizot, who complained

---

[73] For the correspondence on the Portuguese question, see B. Connell, *Regina v. Palmerston* (London, 1962), ch. ii.

[74] See for example Bulwer to Palmerston, 8 July 1846. B.P. GC/BU/254; and Lyons to Palmerston, 21 July 1846. B.P. GC/LY/347.

[75] Lord William Russell to Lord John Russell, 10 Sept. 1841. Russell Papers, P.R.O. 30/22/4B.

[76] In 1843 when Aberdeen appointed Bulwer to be British minister at Madrid Lady Palmerston wrote to Bulwer, 'It is very flattering to you and to the Whig party that Lord Aberdeen should be obliged to come to our side for good appointments. Lord Palmerston is delighted that our interests in Spain should be placed in

bitterly that in his diplomatic appointments Aberdeen was 'trop fidèle à l'héritage de Lord Palmerston'.[77] Aberdeen did not find it easy to work with diplomats trained under Palmerston. He found them headstrong, difficult to control and not entirely trustworthy, ill-suited to the passive rôle he generally expected them to play. The majority were vigorous and ambitious men, to whom inactivity was both unaccustomed and uncongenial. Aberdeen regretted their reluctance to discard habits and attitudes acquired under Palmerston.[78] Above all he, like Guizot, lamented the mutual suspicion and jealousy that prevented the majority of British diplomats from working with their French counterparts. Aberdeen's efforts to persuade his subordinates to co-operate with their French colleagues, as he did with Guizot, were unavailing. They felt constrained by the *entente cordiale*, which prevented them from defending the interests of England as and when they thought necessary. Some, notably Bulwer at Madrid and Lyons at Athens, felt unjustly betrayed by Aberdeen in the interests of good relations with Guizot. Palmerston's return to the Foreign Office unleashed the accumulated resentment of the British diplomatic corps against the *entente*. Only a few days after Russell formed his government Lord William Hervey, the first secretary of the British embassy in Paris, complained to Clarendon of the way British diplomats had been treated by Aberdeen:

It is a very pretty effect of the entente cordiale and only the natural consequence of the system which has sprung up of doing all business through the agents of France instead of through our own, of giving credit to all they say and believing nothing that we write and showing us up to Guizot whenever we do or say anything not intended to meet his eye or ear. The result of it is that our agents become first cowed, then angry and then indifferent and indolent, and end by being cyphers. Those of France become active and

such safe and good hands.' Lady Palmerston to Bulwer, 23 Oct. 1843. Bulwer Papers, S/1.

[77] E. Jones Parry, 'A Review of the Relations between Guizot and Lord Aberdeen 1840–52', *History*, 1938, xxiii, 29.

[78] 'You are by no means singular', Aberdeen wrote to one of his diplomats, 'amongst British agents, in a tendency to entertain suspicion and unnecessarily to attribute bad motives to the conduct of those foreign agents with whom they act.' Aberdeen to Colonel Rose, 4 July 1846. Aberdeen Papers, B.M. Add. MS. 43294.

arrogant; they are supported in all they do, complain of our agents if they thwart them in anything and their complaints are listened to. It is impossible for any man, whatever talent he may possess, to be an efficient servant upon terms such as these. If one is not safe in the confidential communications which one makes to one's own Government it is impossible to write anything worth reading.[79]

Palmerston was known to treat his diplomats differently. Lord Normanby, in his hostile 'Review of Lord Palmerston's Policy', admitted that Palmerston inspired great attachment in his subordinates because 'if any agent will give himself up body and soul to execute his will he will gallantly defend him to the last'.[80] Palmerston argued that complaints from foreign governments against his agents merely proved that they were doing their duty.[81] British diplomats appreciated the fact that Palmerston's loyalty afforded them much greater security from attack than they had enjoyed under Aberdeen.[82] Moreover, Palmerston demanded from his subordinates what they were prepared to give. He expected them to be 'imbued with British feelings and British principles',[83] and to defend with vigour British influence in any quarter, whenever it was under attack. Unlike Aberdeen, he never dealt exclusively with foreign diplomats in London or corresponded directly with foreign heads of government, believing it to be proper for the British Foreign Secretary to communicate with foreign governments through British representatives.[84] This alone would inevitably affect Anglo-French relations. Guizot and Aberdeen had frequently by-passed Cowley,[85] and transacted most business themselves or with the help of Sainte Aulaire and Jarnac. Before the Whigs resumed office, Hervey warned Clarendon that if important business continued to be transacted in London 'the ambassador here

[79] Hervey to Clarendon, 3 July 1846. Clar. Dep. C529.
[80] Lord Normanby: Review of Lord Palmerston's Policy. Normanby Papers, Box P, bundle 18.
[81] Palmerston to Prince Albert, 31 Dec. 1847. B.P. RC/HH/2.
[82] Wellesley to Lyons, 17 Sept. 1846. Cowley Papers, F.O. 519/141.
[83] Palmerston to Prince Albert, 31 Dec. 1847. B.P. RC/HH/2.
[84] Palmerston to Granville, 7 Oct. 1834. B.P. GC/GR/1539.
[85] Hervey to Clarendon, 3 July 1846. Clar. Dep. C529. Aberdeen had begun the practice of by-passing Cowley because of his incompetence. Peel wished that Aberdeen would replace Cowley with 'a really good man'. Peel to Aberdeen, 28 Dec. 1842. Aberdeen Papers, B.M. Add. MS. 43062.

THE WHIGS RETURN

immediately becomes a cypher, which is just what this [the French] Government likes because it relieves them from the eye of a person who is able to watch their proceedings...'[86] On his arrival in Paris, Lord Normanby immediately complained to Palmerston of:

> the very irregular manner in which of late years much of the international business between France and England has been transacted ...I have been told there remains no authentic record here of what has been done. Many of the connecting links in the affair having remained in the private pockets of Aberdeen and Guizot.

Normanby warned Palmerston that he would not tolerate this, but expected to be fully informed of all that passed.[87] Desages, the permanent head of the French Foreign Office, was therefore not exaggerating when he warned French diplomats to expect more assertive and aggressive conduct from British agents now that Palmerston was their master.[88]

Russell and Palmerston were agreed that those diplomats who were willing to serve the new government and who were 'fit and doing well' should remain at their posts.[89] Only two major changes were made in the diplomatic establishment: Lord Cowley, the British ambassador at Paris since 1841, was replaced by the Marquess of Normanby, and at Vienna Lord Ponsonby succeeded Sir Robert Gordon, the brother of Lord Aberdeen. These changes were important for Anglo-French relations. Cowley and Gordon were practically the only two diplomats of Aberdeen's who shared his outlook on foreign affairs. Guizot genuinely regretted the recall of Cowley, who was a sincere friend of France and of the *entente cordiale*.[90]

As in the eighteenth century, the Paris embassy was regarded as the most important post in the British diplomatic service. It 'is the keystone of our foreign relations', Palmerston informed Normanby.[91] Clarendon regarded its tenure as equal in im-

---

[86] Hervey to Clarendon, 22 June 1846. Clar. Dep. C529.
[87] Normanby to Palmerston, 27 Aug. 1846. Normanby Papers, Box P, bundle 12.
[88] Desages to Piscatory, 30 June 1846. Desages Papers, vol. 25; Desages to Bourqueney, 30 June 1846. Bourqueney Papers A.E. France 1900.
[89] Palmerston to Russell, 20 Aug. 1846. Russell Papers, P.R.O. 30/22/5B.
[90] Guizot to Jarnac, 20 July 1846. G.P. 42/AP/7.
[91] Palmerston to Normanby, 2 June 1848. Normanby Papers, Box P, bundle 20.

portance and prestige to a seat in the cabinet.[92] Lord Normanby claimed that he went as ambassador to Paris because his health would not stand up to cabinet office.[93] Normanby's lack of diplomatic experience, his ignorance of French politics and his indifferent French[94] were not regarded as serious drawbacks; his appointment rested on his high standing in the Whig party and the royal favour enjoyed by his family. Normanby was a talented man and an able politician, certainly superior in ability to his immediate predecessors, Granville and Cowley.[95]

It was Russell rather than Palmerston who suggested Normanby's appointment to Paris.[96] After his quarrel with Palmerston in 1851 Normanby claimed that Russell nominated him because he felt 'that the medium of communication with the French Government should be someone whose known opinions should tend to soften the prejudice felt against the departmental chief'.[97] This seems improbable. Normanby had no 'known opinions' on foreign policy; he had neither spoken on the subject in Parliament nor evinced a particular interest in it when he was in the cabinet.[98] The French regarded him as an unknown quantity.[99] His exaggerated sense of his own dignity made him scarcely the man to soften any prejudices. 'I trust we shall not be obliged to wear short breeches when we go and dine with him', was Lord Howden's comment when he heard of Normanby's appointment.[100] Moreover, Palmerston was hardly

[92] Russell to Normanby, 24 Feb. 1849. Normanby Papers, Box P, bundle 23.
[93] Lord Normanby: Review of Lord Palmerston's Policy. Normanby Papers, Box P, bundle 18.
[94] Howden told Clarendon that 'Normanby's French is execrable.' Howden to Clarendon, 15 Feb. 1847. Clar. Dep. C540.
[95] In his youth Normanby had travelled widely and written novels. In the early 1830s he was Lord Lieutenant of Ireland; in Melbourne's cabinet he had been first Colonial Secretary, then Home Secretary.
[96] 'Palmerston on our coming into office proposed to me Beauvale and Clarendon as the fittest persons for it [the Paris embassy]...Notwithstanding this, when I heard from Duncannon and yourself, that you wished for Paris, I proposed you to Palmerston and he, I must say, readily assented.' Russell to Normanby, 24 Feb. 1849. Normanby Papers, Box P, bundle 23.
[97] Lord Normanby: Review of Lord Palmerston's Policy. Normanby Papers, Box P, bundle 18.
[98] He does not seem to have taken much interest in the cabinet discussions on Palmerston's near eastern policy from 1839 to 1841. None of the principal participants in the debate either discussed his views or claimed to have his support.
[99] Guizot to Jarnac, 21 July 1846. G.P. 42/AP/69.
[100] Howden to Clarendon, 26 July 1846. Clar. Dep. C540.

likely to have acquiesced in the appointment had he thought Normanby's views on Anglo-French relations significantly different from his own. Palmerston undoubtedly approved of Normanby's appointment, and thought that his political experience would be an asset, that 'habits of debate are very useful to ambassadors'.[101] Moreover he did not want an ambassador in Paris who would be as easygoing with Guizot as Cowley had been. From the outset Palmerston and Normanby worked well together; their correspondence reveals mutual trust and respect.

Normanby was unlucky to arrive in Paris in late August 1846, only a few days before the rupture between England and France over the Spanish Marriages. He was, wrote Francis Baring to Clarendon, 'mal embarqué'.[102] Within a few days he was in dispute with Guizot, and by late September his position was very difficult. Guizot made no secret of his dislike of Normanby, and assisted by Princess Lieven made every effort to discredit him.[103] The French opposition tried to enlist Normanby's interest to discredit Guizot.[104] He could not avoid becoming a pawn in French domestic politics, and he took the *salon* gossip about himself far too seriously. Nevertheless there was no question of his recall; Palmerston gave him all the support he needed.

In addition to the ambassador, the Paris embassy was staffed by a first secretary and three or four unpaid attachés. Lord William Hervey, first secretary from 1843 to 1850, was a stern critic of both Aberdeen and Guizot. In July 1846 he was one of the few men to question Aberdeen's assertion that the *entente* was flourishing.[105] Hervey made little attempt to disguise his feelings. Greville, who visited Paris in January 1847, found him 'bitter, violent and open mouthed'.[106] Like Normanby,

---

[101] Palmerston to Normanby, 9 Oct. 1846. Normanby Papers, Box P, bundle 19.
[102] Baring to Clarendon, 18 Feb. 1847. Clar. Dep. C561.
[103] Normanby to Colonel Phipps, 8 Feb. 1847. R.A. J/47/53.
[104] King Leopold to Queen Victoria, 13 Mar. 1847. R.A. Y/73/33; Greville to Clarendon, 15 Jan. 1847. Clar. Dep. C520.
[105] 'Look at Spain, Greece, Syria and Montevideo, to say nothing of Tahiti, you will see enough in the state of these countries before you have been in office a fortnight to show that everything is not quite as bright as one could wish and that, in those quarters at least, our good understanding with France has not produced all the good results that might have been expected.' Hervey to Clarendon, 3 July 1846. Clar. Dep. C529. See also Hervey to Reeve, 3 July 1846. Hervey Papers, 941/61/1.
[106] Greville to Clarendon, 15 Jan. 1847. Clar. Dep. C520.

Hervey detested Guizot, who reciprocated his dislike. When Hervey was left as chargé d'affaires Guizot tried to avoid seeing him.[107] Hervey, who supervised the daily running of the embassy, had a low opinion of the attachés, three out of four of whom were lazy and 'rarely to be seen'.[108] The attachés in their turn complained that Hervey delegated only the most menial work to them.[109]

The refusal of Russell and Palmerston to recall the diplomats who had served under Aberdeen met with approval at home,[110] if not in Paris. Only within the diplomatic service, however, was it appreciated that Palmerston would evoke a very different response from many of Aberdeen's erstwhile agents. At Madrid Henry Bulwer, British minister to the Spanish Court since 1843 and one of Palmerston's most favoured disciples, was elated. Even before he went to Madrid he had been deeply suspicious of French foreign policy and French diplomats.[111] He considered it his duty to reduce their influence over the Spanish government, and was prepared to use any means at his disposal to accomplish this end. In June 1846 Guizot had suggested that Bulwer's conduct justified his recall, but Aberdeen had refused to take such an extreme step.[112] Bulwer had found Aberdeen's refusal to countenance a policy of vigorous opposition to French influence at Madrid both irksome and foolish and, whilst adhering to the letter of his instructions, he had always tried to keep open the options for an active policy. Bulwer's natural talent for intrigue was afforded ample scope by Spanish politics; he was deeply involved in their frequent political crises, and always ready to strike a blow at French influence at Madrid. The struggle was also a personal one between him and Bresson, the French ambassador. Behind a thin veil of politeness, the two men loathed one another: each delighted in the misfortunes, miscalculations and misdeeds of the other. Under

---

[107] Hervey to Clarendon, 24 May 1847. Clar. Dep. C529.
[108] Hervey to Clarendon, 5 June 1846. Clar. Dep. C529.
[109] Paget to Bulwer, 1 Apr. 1847. Bulwer Papers, S/8.
[110] *The Times*, 17 Aug. 1846.
[111] Bulwer had earlier been first secretary of the British embassy in Paris, and Palmerston had relied heavily on him, often preferring his reports and judgments to those of the ambassador, Lord Granville. His distrust of the French is seen for example in his despatch to Lord Aberdeen, 6 Sept. 1841. F.O. 27/628.
[112] See E. Jones Parry, *The Spanish Marriages* (London, 1936), 299.

THE WHIGS RETURN

Aberdeen their rivalry had been a constant source of petty irritation between the British and French governments. Palmerston's return to office altered the situation. Bulwer felt that he would have the confidence of his old master, and he began, with all the frenetic energy of which he was capable,[113] to reverse the policy of Aberdeen. He was an ambitious man, and his correspondence dwelt as much upon his personal rôle as upon the significance of the events in which he was involved. It was unfortunate for Anglo-French relations that both Guizot and Palmerston put so much trust in men who were anxious for spectacular personal success, and therefore lacked perspective in their outlook. Both Bresson and Bulwer assumed that Spanish affairs had the importance they attributed to them; they looked at Anglo-French relations not from the viewpoint of Paris or London, but from that of Madrid. Only in rare moments of reflection was Bulwer prepared to admit that this was a distortion.[114]

The rivalry of Bulwer and Bresson at Madrid was probably the most intense and persistent between British and French diplomats, but it was by no means exceptional. At Athens the British minister, Sir Edmund Lyons, was hardly on speaking terms with Piscatory, the French minister.[115] They were the patrons of rival Greek political parties and delighted in hurling personal insults at one another in the Greek press.[116] Aberdeen and Guizot had been unable to moderate or contain their mutual antipathy, and as instructions took several weeks to reach Athens from London and Paris, Lyons and Piscatory pursued highly personal policies. Like Bulwer, Lyons had begun his diplomatic career as a protégé of Palmerston, and it was generally expected that Palmerston would strengthen his position at Athens.[117]

---

[113] Bulwer suffered from bad headaches and frequent sickness. He was often incapable of transacting official business and sometimes took drugs before writing his despatches. Normanby to Palmerston, 3 Aug. 1847. Normanby Papers, Box P, bundle 13. Normanby to Colonel Phipps, 8 Feb. 1847. R.A. J/47/53.

[114] 'I think that an employee should always avoid committing the general policy of his government, of which he cannot know all the bearings in his particular sphere.' Bulwer to Clarendon, 16 Mar. 1844. Clar. Dep. C525.

[115] Lyons to Palmerston, 21 July 1846. B.P. GC/LY/347.

[116] Flahaut to Guizot, 15 July 1846. G.P. 42/AP/68.

[117] Wellesley to Lyons, 17 Sept. 1846. Cowley Papers, F.O. 519/141; Desages to Piscatory, 30 June 1846. Desages Papers, vol. 25.

At Paris and Vienna, where Sir Robert Gordon and the French ambassador, Flahaut, had worked well together, the appointment of Lord Ponsonby was received with dismay. He was known to be rabidly anti-French. Although *The Times* was lending its support to the new Whig government in July and August 1846, the foreign affairs leader writer, Henry Reeve, could not refrain from criticising Ponsonby's appointment. 'A more unfortunate nomination could not have been made', was his comment.[118] His Francophobia[119] made him bitterly disliked in France, and he went to Vienna with the avowed aim of establishing a close understanding between England and Austria.[120] He and Flahaut detested one another. 'C'est un homme sans principe', wrote Flahaut to Guizot, impossible to work with, a true disciple of Palmerston.[121]

Thus, despite attempts to argue the contrary, the fall of Aberdeen would undoubtedly alter Anglo-French relations. The fragile *entente* could not survive unchanged the termination of the official relationship of Guizot and Aberdeen, whose personal friendship it mirrored. The future, however, did not depend solely on Palmerston. Guizot bore equal responsibility for the maintenance of cordial relations, and his reaction to Palmerston and the extent to which he was willing to adjust French foreign policy to a new situation were crucial factors. Suspicion and fear of Palmerston might call for caution in dealing with him, but if good relations were to continue some friendly gesture, some frankness, was essential.

The fall of the Peel government was a hard blow for Guizot. 'They are sorry here for the change', wrote Hervey to Clarendon on 29 June, 'but I don't believe that they care twopence about Peel. If Aberdeen could continue at the F[oreign] O[ffice] they would not mind seeing anyone, Whig, Tory or Radical, prime minister.'[122] Guizot attached great importance to the personal

---

[118] *The Times*, 17 Aug. 1846.
[119] Ponsonby had been British ambassador at Constantinople from 1833 to 1841, where he had played a distinguished if eccentric rôle. The full strength of his Francophobia had been revealed during the Mehemet Ali crisis. See Webster, *Palmerston*, ii, ch. viii.
[120] Ponsonby to Palmerston, 6 Nov. 1846. B.P. GC/PO/539.
[121] Flahaut to Guizot, 22 Jan. 1847. G.P. 42/AP/68.
[122] Hervey to Clarendon, 29 June 1846. Clar. Dep. C529.

element in diplomacy.[123] He did not expect from Palmerston the forbearance and understanding he had received from Aberdeen, and was too much of a realist to anticipate the establishment of a similar relationship with Palmerston, whose character was totally different from Aberdeen's. As Desages observed, at Palmerston's age there was little likelihood of his changing.[124] There could never be, wrote Guizot, more than a 'mariage de raison' between himself and Palmerston.[125] Although far from ideal, this was not without its value; 'we must do our best', wrote Jarnac, first secretary of the French embassy in London, 'as every bad has its worse'.[126] Guizot's willingness to adjust to Palmerston, however, had definite limits. Palmerston's assurances of good intentions were not enough. He wanted practical proof of willingness to co-operate on terms acceptable to France, and until he received them he maintained an attitude of cautious reserve grounded in fear. 'Par instinct', he admitted to Jarnac, 'on craint Lord Palmerston.'[127] Guizot feared Palmerston in a number of ways. He shared the fear common to most Frenchmen of Palmerston as the implacable enemy of France, the man responsible for her isolation and humiliation in 1840. Throughout July and August 1846 the memory of 1840 was never far from Guizot's mind; he was determined that Palmerston should not dupe him as he had duped Thiers. Inherent in this attitude was the idea of revenge. Guizot was certainly aware that a tit for tat with Palmerston would afford great satisfaction to his countrymen. The personal knowledge of Palmerston he had gained when he was French ambassador in London meant that there was no chance of him underestimating Palmerston, whose skill in negotiation, tenacity and firmness of purpose he recognised. Above all, Guizot was worried by Palmerston's known contempt for Aberdeen's foreign policy.[128] He feared that Palmerston might attempt to

[123] For a discussion of this point, see Douglas Johnson, *Guizot: Aspects of French History, 1787–1874* (London, 1963), 275.
[124] Desages to Bourqueney, 7 Aug. 1846. Bourqueney Papers A.E. France 1900.
[125] Guizot to Princess Lieven, 19 July 1846. *Guizot–Lieven*, iii, 226.
[126] Jarnac to Aberdeen, 14 Aug. 1846. Aberdeen Papers, B.M. Add. MS. 43133.
[127] Guizot to Jarnac, 15 Oct. 1846. G.P. 42/AP/7.
[128] It also worried Princess Lieven: on 25 July 1846, after a discussion with Lord William Hervey on Anglo-French relations, she informed Guizot that Hervey had told her that the new Whig government thought that the conduct of Aberdeen had

undo the legacy of the past four and a half years, and launch an offensive against French influence wherever it had been extended since 1841.[129] This would make it difficult to maintain friendly relations between England and France, and would mean that there could be no security for French interests, no peace for Guizot at home, no calm for Europe.

Guizot recognised that the defence of French interests abroad against Palmerston's attacks would require his constant vigilance, and that the opposition would exploit his difficulties in the Chambers. Foreign policy would thus become for him an even greater source of anxiety than it already was. Aberdeen had never harassed Guizot by jealousy of France or unwillingness to see his point of view. For Guizot the basis of the *entente* had been Aberdeen's willing acceptance of the legitimate exercise and expansion of French influence in western Europe and the Mediterranean. He was determined that this basis should remain unchanged. Hervey thought that Aberdeen had allowed Guizot to demand too much and to give very little:

> The truth is, I fear, that they [the French] are too prone to attribute to ill-will anything that is not to be treated in the manner most agreeable to them. And they have been so long used to do as they like, have had to deal with so easy a man, and have calculated so confidently upon being able to secure the accomplishment of their purposes that they become irritated the moment they perceive a chance of being thwarted.

Hervey was sure that Guizot would not make enough effort to meet Palmerston half-way: 'I am far from easy as to the maintenance of an agreeable state of relations with the Court', he confessed to Clarendon.[130]

Guizot's fears over Palmerston's intentions manifested themselves in his anxiety about Spain. 'L'Espagne me préoccupe beaucoup', he confided to Princess Lieven.[131] Since the be-

---

been 'trop subservient to France'. Princess Lieven to Guizot, 25 July 1846. *Guizot–Lieven*, iii, 232.

[129] 'Le trait distinctif et nouveau de notre attitude mutuelle à Aberdeen et à moi, c'était l'abolition de l'esprit de rivalité nationale et d'amour-propre personnel. Palmerston les ressuscitera l'un et l'autre.' Guizot to Princess Lieven, 8 Aug. 1846. *Guizot–Lieven*, iii, 246.

[130] Hervey to Clarendon, 30 Aug. 1846. Clar. Dep. C529.

[131] Guizot to Princess Lieven, 14 July 1846. *Guizot–Lieven*, iii, 217.

ginning of 1846 he had become increasingly concerned about the question of the marriages of the Queen of Spain and her sister, the Infanta. The setbacks dealt by the Spanish government to his marriages policy had made him aware that a settlement favourable to France was by no means certain, and Palmerston's return to the Foreign Office increased the chances of failure. Guizot feared that Palmerston would attempt to use the issue of the Queen of Spain's marriage to undermine French preponderance at Madrid.[132] Guizot oscillated between extremes of optimism and pessimism, at one time believing that co-operation with Palmerston would be possible, at another that a rupture was imminent.

Exclusive preoccupation with Spanish affairs meant that it was reports from London and Madrid on the state of negotiations over the Queen of Spain's marriage that determined Guizot's mood. Other issues were brushed aside as of secondary importance.[133] Palmerston's initial silence on Spain and the views of his own advisers and subordinates contributed to Guizot's pessimism. Palmerston's return unleashed the latent Anglophobia of French diplomats who even in the heyday of the *entente* had not been particularly well disposed towards England. From Madrid Bresson painted in lurid colours the effect on Bulwer of the return of his former patron; he urged Guizot to give him freedom of action to combat Bulwer's schemes.[134] Flahaut in Vienna predicted a combined offensive by Palmerston and British diplomats against French influence wherever it was superior to that of Great Britain.[135] From Athens Piscatory, who 'made no secret...of his having been brought up in dislike and distrust of England or of his being no friend to l'alliance Anglo-Française',[136] warned that new offensives were being prepared by Lyons and the British party in Greece against the pro-French government of Colettis.[137] Desages was

[132] Guizot to Bresson, 5 July 1846. G.P. 42/AP/8.
[133] 'Palmerston me fait demander en effet ce que nous pensons des affaires de Rome...et ce qu'il doit dire et faire pour être, comme il veut, d'accord avec nous. Cela sera facile à Rome où il n'est rien, et nous ne tirerons pas grand profit. C'est à Madrid qu'il faudrait se mettre d'accord...' Guizot to Princess Lieven, 24 July 1846. *Guizot–Lieven*, iii, 229.   [134] Bresson to Guizot, 4 July 1846. G.P. 42/AP/65.
[135] Flahaut to Guizot, 15 July 1846. G.P. 42/AP/68.
[136] Lyons to Aberdeen, 12 Dec. 1844. Aberdeen Papers, B.M. Add. MS. 43137.
[137] Piscatory to Guizot, 20 Aug. 1846. G.P. 42/AP/7.

convinced that Palmerston was only awaiting a convenient opportunity to make a hostile move against France.[138] Jarnac, in charge of the London embassy during the absence of Sainte Aulaire, was almost the only diplomat to encourage Guizot to view the future with optimism, although even he was perturbed by Palmerston's delay in discussing Spanish affairs.[139]

Guizot's alternations between cautious optimism and pessimism gave rise to two entirely different possible courses of action. At times Guizot felt that all would be well if he offered Palmerston terms for co-operation the acceptance of which would indicate his willingness to recognise French dominance at Madrid.[140] This Guizot did at the end of the third week of July 1846. On the other hand, he believed in the necessity of preventive diplomacy: if Palmerston meditated an attack on the French position at Madrid, it was incumbent upon the French government to protect and if possible consolidate its interests in advance. Bresson had long favoured a solution to the Spanish Marriages question made without reference to England, and if necessary in defiance of England. In moments of despair Guizot had himself contemplated such a course, but Aberdeen's impeccable conduct had afforded no justification for it. Palmerston's return, however, provided both excuse and opportunity; Guizot began to hope that he could have a triumph in Spain at Palmerston's expense.

Guizot, watching with care the political crisis that led to Peel's resignation, believed that English politics were entering a period of instability in which anything could happen. He was aware that Russell's government lacked a clear parliamentary majority and was composed of many discordant elements. He knew too that in the immediate future Irish affairs would preoccupy both the government and the country.[141] From his knowledge of the Whig leaders he assumed a considerable difference between the outlook of Palmerston and Russell on foreign affairs, and that of the cabinet; Jarnac's reports corro-

[138] Desages to Bourqueney, 7 Aug. 1846. Bourqueney Papers A.E. France 1900.
[139] Jarnac to Guizot, 14 July 1846. Archives du Ministère des Affaires Etrangères: Correspondance Politique [hereafter A.A.E.C.P.] Angleterre 666.
[140] Guizot to Jarnac, 20 July 1846. G.P. 42/AP/7.
[141] Jarnac to Guizot, 14 July 1846. A.A.E.C.P. Angleterre 666; Guizot to Bresson, 5 July 1846. G.P. 42/AP/8.

borated this view.[142] Guizot believed that these differences could be exploited, and that Palmerston's colleagues were so suspicious of him that they would tend to blame him for any quarrel between England and France.[143] Further, Guizot assumed that no one in the English government except Palmerston was prepared to contemplate a permanent rupture between England and France, and that if he took independent action in Spain he would have at most a temporary coolness to contend with. Thirdly, Guizot believed that it would be impossible for Palmerston to whip up any public enthusiasm against France.[144] Even if he did succeed in drawing public attention to foreign affairs, it would redound to his own disadvantage: he would be accused of destroying the *entente*.[145] There were therefore two distinct currents of thought in France in July 1846. On the one hand, Guizot was prepared to work with Palmerston, but not at the expense of the essential interests of France. On the other hand, if Palmerston tried to undermine French influence in Spain, Guizot was prepared to act alone. In the first two weeks of July 1846 Palmerston's silence on Spain and Guizot's determination to achieve a resounding triumph for French diplomacy at Madrid augured ill for the future.

[142] 'Jarnac pense mal de la disposition de Lord Palmerston. Et par compensation mal aussi de sa position. Lord John s'en méfie, et dit beaucoup qu'il surveillera de très près. Le duc de Bedford surveille Lord John pour qu'il surveille Lord Palmerston.' Guizot to Princess Lieven, 8 Aug. 1846. *Guizot–Lieven*, iii, 246.
[143] Guizot to Bresson, 5 July 1846. G.P. 42/AP/8.
[144] 'Tout le monde veut la continuation de la politique de Lord Aberdeen...Il y a conspiration générale pour l'entente cordiale.' Guizot to Princess Lieven, 8 Aug. 1846. *Guizot–Lieven*, iii, 246.
[145] Guizot to Bresson, 5 July 1846. G.P. 42/AP/8. On 22 Aug. Guizot wrote to Bresson, 'Tenez pour certain que la paix et les bons rapports avec la France sont en fait de politique extérieure, la première idée, le premier vœu du peuple anglais, et qu'aucun cabinet anglais ne se risquerait aisément à blesser ce vœu public; le cabinet actuel moins qu'un autre car Lord Palmerston est suspect à l'endroit de la France. Ses principaux collègues, beaucoup de ses amis dans le Parlement, le public tout entier, se méfient de lui et le surveillent à cet égard.' Guizot to Bresson, 22 Aug. 1846. G.P. 42/AP/8.

CHAPTER IV

The Spanish Marriages, July–August 1846

In the 1830s Palmerston attempted to exclude French influence from the whole of the Iberian peninsula: his support of Spanish constitutionalism was as much anti-French as anti-absolutist. He believed that if constitutional government were firmly established in Spain, she would cease to be 'a satellite of France' and become 'an independent ally of England'.[1] French policy by contrast was designed to maintain the eighteenth-century system of balance in the Iberian peninsula, of French preponderance at Madrid and British preponderance at Lisbon, interrupted during the Revolutionary and Napoleonic Wars, but restored by Louis XVIII when he intervened in Spain in 1823. Louis Philippe was as determined as his predecessor to defend the legacy of Louis XIV.

In the mid-1830s the Anglo-French conflict was superimposed on the civil conflict between the Carlists and the Constitutionalists in Spain. Palmerston's unequivocal support of Spanish constitutionalism put the French government in a dilemma; they wished neither to betray the principles of 1830 nor to sacrifice the traditional interests of France. They therefore took up a middle position: by giving only equivocal support to the Constitutionalists and being only moderately anti-Carlist they hoped to avoid the danger of exclusion from Spanish affairs. In fact this danger was more apparent than real. Palmerston both overestimated the purity of Spanish constitutionalism and the strength of pro-English feeling among the Constitutionalists, and underestimated the strength of Spanish political traditions. His expectation of a complete break with the past was unfulfilled. The defeat of the Carlists in 1838 was a total victory neither

---

[1] For an account of Anglo-French rivalry in Spain in the 1830s, see Webster, *Palmerston*, i, chs. v and vi.

THE SPANISH MARRIAGES

for constitutionalism nor for British influence. Even before the end of the civil war a new pattern of Spanish politics had begun to emerge, and Anglo-French rivalry was immediately and inextricably involved in the new struggle for exclusive power in Spain. France became the patron of the more aristocratic Moderado party, while England supported the more liberal Progresista party.

The involvement of international rivalry over Spain with party rivalry within Spain lasted from 1838 to 1848. The Moderados were in power from 1838 to 1840, followed by a three-year period of Progresista ascendancy, and the reinstatement of the Moderados in 1844. Within these periods, however, ministries rose and fell or were reshuffled with alarming rapidity, and the Cortes was frequently dissolved.[2] Everyone agreed that stability was lacking. Some looked to the army to provide stability, but it was not politically homogeneous: Progresista generals and their troops vied for power and influence with Moderado generals and their troops.[3] Normally most Spaniards expected the Crown to provide stability.[4] Both Moderados and Progresistas therefore attached great importance to royal support. Each party sought to dismiss the other to the political wilderness, either with the support of the Court or, as in 1840 in the case of the Progresistas, by control of the Court. Thus in order to maintain themselves in, and their rivals out of, power, the support of the Crown was essential. The Progresistas found this especially difficult to secure. Although Queen Christina, the Queen Regent, was not prepared to be the docile instrument of either party—she had the prerogatives of the Crown and her personal interests to safeguard—she found the traditionalist Moderados more to her liking and more amenable than the Progresistas. The alliance

[2] Between 1835 and 1858 the Cortes was dissolved fourteen times. *Quarterly Review*, 1862, no. 221, 161.
[3] For the rôle of the Spanish army in politics, see E. Christiansen, *The Origins of Military Power in Spain, 1800–1854* (Oxford, 1967).
[4] 'Everything in Spain has depended upon the character of the Sovereign... New institutions may possibly in the course of time modify this peculiarity but at present it is not to be forgotten that on the throne of Spain, sits the destiny of Spain.' Bulwer to Aberdeen, 8 July 1846. F.O. 72/698. '...aucun ministère, aucun homme ne peut encore se soutenir ici contre et malgré la cour'. Bresson to Guizot, 25 July 1846. G.P. 42/AP/65.

of Christina and the Moderados, although never easy, was from 1840 onwards a basic factor in Spanish politics. The end of Christina's supremacy, however, was in sight. Once the young Queen began to discharge her political duties there would be new views and new men at Court. On one thing all were agreed: the rôle of the Queen's husband would be crucial, his influence at Court second to none.[5] Both parties therefore wanted, as a consort for the Queen, a partisan of their own cause, whose influence would ensure them supremacy. The question of the Spanish Marriages was not just one of finding a husband for the Queen of Spain; it was bound up with struggles for power within Spain and for influence over Spain.

When Palmerston left the Foreign Office in 1841 British influence was dominant in Spain. Palmerston supported the military dictatorship of General Espartero, in alliance with the Progresistas, because, although by no means constitutional, it was the only alternative to the absolutist system of Queen Christina and the Moderados. It was also anti-French. After Christina had been deprived of the regency by Espartero in 1840, she left Spain and lived in exile in Paris. In Palmerston's opinion, Paris became the centre of Spanish absolutism, with Christina and the Moderado exiles in constant communication with their French patrons. He believed that the British government should defend Espartero at all costs, and resolutely oppose French intrigues. Lord Aberdeen, returning to the Foreign Office in 1841, claimed that his Spanish policy was the same as Palmerston's. In fact it was not: Aberdeen supported the Espartero régime merely on the grounds that it existed, he did not think that it should be supported at all costs. Although he feared political upheaval in Spain as he did elsewhere, he did not share Palmerston's fear of Moderado rule and consequent exclusive French influence at Madrid. Aberdeen's was therefore

[5] 'The Queen...is a child of fifteen. No one but can perceive that the husband of a girl of that age will exercise over her a great authority. The question therefore as to who is to be her husband is one which the Spaniards with a natural instinct of their fate, feel to be of the utmost importance. It is of no use to talk to them of their liberties being protected by their laws, of their prosperity being advanced by their institutions, of the security they have in the Cortes, of the possibility that they may find a Minister of intelligence, they will reply to you that if superstition, ignorance and imbecility are to occupy the Palace, all the rest will be of no avail.' Bulwer to Aberdeen, 8 July 1846. F.O. 72/698.

a policy of passive rather than active support. When in 1843 Espartero fell, Aberdeen made no efforts to save him. By 1844 Queen Christina and the Moderados, backed by a large part of the army and with the blessing of the French government, were firmly reinstated in power at Madrid. The Progresistas were faced with the prospect of a long period of exclusion from power. Lord Palmerston's system had collapsed.

The French reacted enthusiastically to the triumph of the Court and the Moderados over Espartero and the Progresistas. Guizot believed that it was a triumph not only for France but for his foreign policy. Moreover, he thought that the system of government established by Christina, General Narvaez and the Moderado party was the one best suited to the needs of Spain.[6] He was consequently determined to support the new régime unreservedly.

It was in the context of renewed French predominance at Madrid that serious negotiations began over the marriage of the Queen of Spain.[7] From 1844 onwards the French government made the running on this issue. French policy depended on an assumption that they did not themselves believe but wished Great Britain to accept: that the only question was that of finding a consort for the Queen of Spain. British acceptance of this simplification would have three desirable consequences: firstly, it would mean that the British government agreed not to use the marriage question to challenge French influence at Madrid; secondly, it would enable the French to use the question to strengthen their own influence; thirdly, it would strengthen France in her attempt to prevent the Spanish government from playing the double game that a more active rôle by Britain would facilitate. In 1843, in order to consolidate their position on the marriage question, the French introduced into the negotiations the Bourbon principle which stipulated that the Queen of Spain could only marry a descendant of Philip V. This principle was designed to exclude any candidate hostile either to Moderado ascendancy at Madrid or to French

[6] Guizot to Bresson, 11 Apr. 1846. G.P. 42/AP/8.
[7] For an account of the negotiations on the Spanish marriages between 1844 and 1846, see E. Jones Parry, *The Spanish Marriages, 1841-1846* (London, 1936). My own account differs significantly from that of Jones Parry.

predominance in Spain. From the beginning the French attached immense importance to the marriage issue, and their attempts to insure against the success of any counter-influence made the question of the marriage of the Queen of Spain appear more French than Spanish.

Lord Aberdeen offered no real resistance to French dictation. He accepted the assumption that the only question involved was the marriage of the Queen of Spain and the Bourbon principle, insisting only on the obvious safeguards: that the sons of Louis Philippe should be excluded from the list of eligible Bourbon candidates, and that the young Queen and the Spanish government be given as much freedom of choice as possible within this limitation. In 1845 the French government attempted to strengthen its position still further by proposing a marriage between the Duke of Montpensier, fifth son of Louis Philippe, and the Infanta Luisa Fernanda, sister of Queen Isabella and heiress presumptive to the Spanish throne. Aberdeen once again only demanded safeguards. The French agreed to his request that the marriage should not take place until the Queen of Spain was married and had children,[8] although they never informed the Spanish government that they had accepted this condition. The French suggested the Montpensier marriage because of the difficulties in applying the Bourbon principle. Queen Christina wanted important alliances for both her daughters, not Bourbon nonentities. She would have liked a British connection for one daughter, and a French connection for the other. The French hoped that the promise of Montpensier for her younger daughter would induce Christina to accept an unspectacular Bourbon for Queen Isabella.

The year 1845 and early 1846 saw, not the fruition of French policy, but mounting opposition to it. Queen Christina continued to toy with the idea of a marriage between Queen Isabella and her own younger brother, the Neapolitan Count of Trapani, while at the same time pointing out the grave political and personal objections to the match: Spaniards would regard

---

[8] Guizot later claimed that Aberdeen said that the marriage should not take place until after the Queen had a child. Guizot to Jarnac, 22 Nov. 1846. *Correspondence relating to the Marriages of the Queen of Spain and Infanta of Spain. Accounts and Papers, 1847*, lxix.

a Neapolitan consort as an insult to their pride, and Trapani was in any case too unprepossessing to suit her headstrong daughter. Spanish evasiveness gave grounds for the fears inherent in French policy, which looked for conspiracies and appeared to find them. Guizot trusted Aberdeen, but not the British Court or Bulwer, the British minister in Spain since 1843. He was rightly convinced that Queen Victoria and Prince Albert resented 'French dictation', and favoured a marriage between Queen Isabella and Prince Leopold of Coburg, a member of the Catholic branch of the Coburg family and a brother of King Ferdinand of Portugal. Bulwer's inclinations were to favour and to participate in any scheme that might reduce French influence at Madrid. Above all the French feared duplicity by a combination of Queen Christina, Bulwer and the Coburgs. Guizot's fears were not only for French influence in Spain, but also for the effect a setback in Spain would have on the position of his government at home. If Queen Isabella married a Coburg instead of a Bourbon, the French government would lose prestige and the opposition charge that in its foreign policy the government was subservient to England would be confirmed.[9] Guizot wished to maintain good relations with England and he justified the *entente* as a mutually beneficial relationship of equals. But he also believed that French ascendancy in Spain and a triumph over the marriage question were indispensable; they would be proof of the equality of the relationship. The more elusive success appeared, the more frantic became the French search for a successful conclusion to the affair.

In the first six months of 1846 negotiations on the Spanish marriages entered a new phase. 'The question', wrote Hervey to Bulwer, 'is growing every day more important and pressing.'[10] There were a number of reasons for this: the French wanted a triumph, and they wanted it quickly, before the Peel government fell and Palmerston returned to the Foreign Office, a prospect which haunted the French government from January

[9] Louis Philippe told Lord Cowley that his acquiescence in the Coburg marriage 'would be considered as an abandonment of French interests and injurious to himself and his dynasty'. Cowley to Palmerston, 13 July 1846. F.O. 27/753.
[10] Hervey to Bulwer, 31 May 1846. Bulwer Papers, S/26.

to June 1846. Moreover, an unmistakable success over the marriages would improve the government's chances in the general elections to be held in the summer. It would serve to counteract the still vivid memory of the Tahiti incident and the 'surrender' over Pritchard, both kept alive by the opposition and opposition press.[11] The French government was also being pressed by the Spaniards and by Queen Isabella's desire to marry as soon as possible. In this new atmosphere of increased tension and urgency, the British and French governments discarded, not their basic policies, but some of the appearances in which they had been cloaked. The French considered jettisoning the procedural niceties which had given their policy of dictation a semblance of decency, and the British began to withdraw from a policy of complete acquiescence in French direction. Neither was fully aware of the implications of their retreat: Guizot began to think in terms of a unilateral solution but was convinced that the *entente* was strong enough to survive the inevitable storm; Aberdeen thought that he could please the Spanish government and pay public lip service to its independence without any adverse effect on the French government. Thus, between February and June 1846 the British and French governments drifted gradually but perceptibly apart in their policies over the Spanish marriages.

In February 1846 the French ambassador in London, Sainte Aulaire, presented Aberdeen with a memorandum on the Spanish marriages drawn up by Guizot. It was a curious document, more like an ultimatum than a basis for negotiation.[12] In effect it stated that if the British government did not accept the French view completely, and in particular if the French

---

[11] During the election campaign in July 1846 Cowley reported that 'the stupid cry against the Pritchardistes, as they are called, has not been without its effects'. Cowley to Palmerston, 17 July 1846. F.O. 27/753.

[12] F. Guizot, *Mémoires pour servir à l'histoire de mon temps* [hereafter Guizot, *Mémoires*] (Paris, 1856–67), viii, 251–3. Bulwer commented on the memorandum of Feb. 1846: 'You are to continue under the influence of and be guided with consideration to the obligations of our mutual engagement; but if we at any time see, or fancy that we see a probability of something happening though you may be entirely ignorant of our fears, why then we can consider our engagement over and we are at liberty to take you by surprise whenever and however we think proper.' Bulwer to Palmerston, 19 Jan. 1847. 'A General Review of occurrences connected with the marriage of Queen Isabella', Bulwer Papers, S/12.

government had reason to suspect that Britain supported a non-Bourbon candidate, France would feel free to act alone, without informing Great Britain, and disregarding all previous agreements. This memorandum was an attempt by 'shock tactics' to range Great Britain firmly behind France in order to deprive Spain of any opportunity to play off one against the other; the strength of its language indicated the extent of French apprehensions. Aberdeen appears to have recognised that it was not meant literally, and was therefore embarrassed rather than outraged by it. Instead of informing his colleagues, which would have involved rejecting the note and offending Guizot, he suppressed the memorandum. He took no copy of it, and never informed Palmerston of its existence; he later informed Peel that he 'did not attach much importance to it'.[13] The French, likewise, attached little importance to the literal meaning of the memorandum; its value lay in that it had tested the position of the British government. The most important development in French policy in the first six months of 1846 was that Guizot in his letters to Bresson, the French ambassador in Madrid, began seriously to discuss the advantages of decisive unilateral action, as a possible answer to dangerous contingencies such as concerted action by Christina and the Coburgs in favour of Prince Leopold. Bresson, pushing Guizot's thinking to its logical conclusion, argued that the French government should not be nice about means if it wished for a successful conclusion: dangerous situations justified some risks. It was not the continued presence of Aberdeen at the Foreign Office which restrained Guizot, but the conscience of Louis Philippe who refused to break his obligations to Queen Victoria.

The willingness of France to consider a *coup* on the marriage question was largely the result of their apprehensions over Spanish duplicity and intrigue. By 1846 the French government had lost all confidence in the probity of Christina and the Spanish government.[14] Christina was doing her utmost to avoid marrying her daughter to a Bourbon nonentity. She wanted

[13] Aberdeen to Peel, 17 Jan. 1847. Peel Papers, B.M. Add. MS. 40455.
[14] 'De ce côté', wrote Bresson from Madrid, 'nous avons tout à appréhender: faiblesse, trahison, aveuglement, calcul mal entendu, timidité, précipitation pour sortir d'un embarras présent, tout, tout est possible.' Bresson to Guizot, 24 May 1846. Jones Parry, *The Spanish Marriages*, 299.

Leopold of Coburg for Queen Isabella and the Duke of Montpensier for the Infanta, and thought her only chance of achieving this was by dividing the British and French governments. In this attempt she was encouraged and assisted by Bulwer, who believed that it was in the interests of Great Britain to undermine French influence in Spain. He was also anxious for a personal triumph. A Coburg marriage would secure these aims simultaneously. On 2 May 1846, with Bulwer's connivance, Christina wrote via Lisbon to the reigning Duke of Saxe-Coburg to suggest formally a marriage between Queen Isabella and Prince Leopold.[15] Bulwer was surprised by Aberdeen's hostile reaction to his involvement in the offer. Aberdeen realised that it would confirm the fears of the French. In an interview with Sainte Aulaire on 20 May he therefore informed the French government of the offer to the Coburgs and completely dissociated the British government from it. He hoped by doing this to prevent the incident from developing into a crisis. French fears were by no means completely allayed by Aberdeen's positive disavowal of the offer to the Coburgs. It afforded proof of what they had long suspected, that Christina was playing a double game, and that Bulwer was prepared to do the same. Moreover, the Peel government could not long survive, and Palmerston would then return to the Foreign Office. To French distrust of Christina and Bulwer would be added fear of Palmerston. The prospects for a successful French policy were therefore not very encouraging.

French uneasiness was increased by Aberdeen's note of 22 June 1846 to Sotomayor,[16] the Spanish ambassador in London, who had been instructed by his government to sound out the probable reaction of the British government should the Queen of Spain choose to marry outside the House of Bourbon. The question was ostensibly academic, but in fact derived from Queen Christina's wish to know whether her Coburg plans would meet with active opposition from Great Britain. Aberdeen's reply—that the Spanish government was free to choose whom it liked for the Queen of Spain—was influenced by two considerations. Firstly, he did not wish to insist that the

[15] Ibid., 287.
[16] *Accounts and Papers, 1847*, lxix.

Queen of Spain *must* marry a Bourbon, because this would afford public support for French dictation and give the Spanish government grounds for alleging that they were being denied their independence and freedom of action. Secondly, Aberdeen wished to convince Palmerston that his policy had been less subservient to France than it actually was. Lord William Hervey doubted whether Aberdeen would have 'expressed himself in favour of Spanish independence. . .if he. . .had not had the fear of Palmerston before his eyes'.[17] Aberdeen recognised that his last-minute attempts to please the Spaniards and deceive Palmerston were incompatible with his major objective throughout the negotiations of pleasing the French. He therefore gave a verbal summary only of his note to Sotomayor to Sainte Aulaire, who nevertheless 'appeared to be a good deal surprised'.[18] The French saw clearly that Aberdeen's reply to Sotomayor would provide Palmerston with a starting point for moving even further from Aberdeen's previous passive policy.

When Aberdeen left the Foreign Office, therefore, the question of the Spanish marriages was in confusion. Hervey was not alone when he confessed to Bulwer that he was 'quite unable to foresee what will be the solution of it'.[19] Everything seemed to depend on Palmerston's attitude: would he acquiesce in the French view that the only question involved was that of securing a suitable husband for the Queen of Spain, or would he use the issue to revive the struggle between England and France for influence over Spain?

During the first two weeks of July 1846 Palmerston made no pronouncements on the question of the Spanish marriages. He was not fully aware of its extreme urgency, and he needed time to acquaint himself with the details of the recent negotiations. His first discussions were with Aberdeen, who gave him a verbal account of his policy and copies of his more important public and private correspondence. Palmerston, unimpressed by Aberdeen's conduct of the negotiations, transmitted the correspondence to Russell with the comment: '. . .in general he has taken just and correct notions of what ought to be done but has

[17] Hervey to Clarendon, 6 July 1846. Clar. Dep. C529.
[18] Aberdeen to Bulwer, n.d. Aberdeen Papers, B.M. Add. MS. 43294.
[19] Hervey to Bulwer, 31 May 1846. Bulwer Papers, S/26.

been unable to persuade intriguing allies or contumacious agents to follow the right course, and in consequence allowed himself to be dragged on by both in a wrong one.'[20] Palmerston clearly intended to put British policy on 'the right course', but he did not define it or the changes it would involve. In his first interview with Sainte Aulaire Palmerston refused to discuss Spanish affairs in detail.[21] The new Foreign Secretary refused to be rushed.

Palmerston did not want for advice. He was bombarded with information, from Bulwer, from Lord Clarendon, who had maintained many of the contacts he had made when he was British minister in Spain, from the Spanish government, and from the Progresista exiles in London. Only the French government remained silent. They were anxious to know Palmerston's intentions, but felt that their own hopes and fears must remain concealed until Palmerston openly avowed his policy.

Bulwer immediately requested Palmerston 'to suspend your judgement on Spanish affairs, until I shall have had the opportunity of writing to you fully and confidentially upon them'.[22] He urged Palmerston to abandon all his preconceived notions about Spanish politics. Immense changes had taken place in Spain since 1841. The outlook and position of the political parties had altered almost beyond recognition, and any successful policy in Spain would depend upon skilful exploitation of the new circumstances. Bulwer was obviously confident that Palmerston's aims would be different from those of Aberdeen. He assumed that Palmerston would try to use the question of the Queen's marriage to effect the restoration of constitutional government in Spain:

> The great question is that of the marriage...since on that depends every other. A popular marriage must lead necessarily to a popular ministry and I do not think that it is presumptuous to say that in such a case, the prospects of the country...are upon the whole peaceful and prosperous.[23]

Bulwer was also convinced that Palmerston would want a

[20] Palmerston to Russell, 7 July 1846. B.P. GC/RU/981.
[21] Sainte Aulaire to Guizot, 9 July 1846. A.A.E.C.P. Angleterre 666.
[22] Bulwer to Palmerston, 8 July 1846. B.P. GC/BU/254.
[23] Bulwer to Palmerston, 8 July 1846. F.O. 72/698.

marriage alliance likely to diminish French influence in Spain. This was desirable for a number of reasons:

> I do consider a separation of the two families ruling in Spain and France, would make Spain more independent of the latter power, and consequently if times of war and danger should again arrive, less likely to join in carrying out the notions of conquest and ambition which that enterprising and warlike nation still entertains. This consideration is not unimportant...Our position on the Mediterranean has also undergone a change by the French colonization of the coast of Africa and the recent importance given to the Port of Algiers. It is impossible not to be aware that French sentiment points out, and the French policy universally and constantly, though not effectually, tends towards the domination of that sea...This much speaks in favour of an alliance without the Bourbon family.[24]

The only candidate outside the Bourbon family was Prince Leopold of Saxe-Coburg. British support for him would certainly elicit French opposition; this alliance would therefore need to be 'prepared secretly, and almost wear the aspect of intrigue, in order to avoid the effects of intrigue'.[25] Above all it—indeed, any successful policy—would require important tactical adjustments of British policy. The present régime in Spain, Bulwer informed Palmerston, could only be overthrown by undermining it from within. It was the subtlety of the tactics that was important. Success would depend on the recognition of three basic facts: the preponderant rôle of the Court in Spanish politics, exercised for the time being by Queen Christina; the ascendancy of the Moderados; and the virtual impotence of the Progresistas. Bulwer admitted that the policy he advocated involved certain dangers and sacrifices, particularly in the short term of principles to tactics, but he believed that the long-term costs would be minimal and the result—a constitutional and pro-British Spain—worthwhile. Like Guizot, he considered the *entente* strong enough to weather a temporary storm, and he was sure that the French would soon reconcile themselves to the loss of influence in Spain. He assured Palmerston that refusal to adopt the course he advocated could have only one result: France and Spain 'will make their peace and Count Trapani

[24] Bulwer to Palmerston, 19 July 1846. F.O. 72/698.
[25] Ibid.

will probably be tried at all hazards; the marriage being made by Narvaez who will be recalled and protected by a French army on the Spanish frontier'.[26] Clearly what Bulwer wanted was an active and anti-French policy.

Palmerston made no immediate response to Bulwer's letters and despatches of the first half of July 1846; indeed, he never answered them explicitly. Bulwer, left without instructions for three weeks, had an ideal opportunity for pursuing his own course. Time was running out, and he felt that he had no alternative but to promote the Coburg candidature without definitely committing his government. He hoped it would be persuaded to champion Prince Leopold officially in response to the expectations he had raised in Spain. The Spanish government, wrote Bulwer, was enthusiastic for the marriage; they were only waiting for an answer from the Duke of Saxe-Coburg. 'If that is favourable, I fancy the affair will go forward in spite of France and the devil.'[27] The French were well aware of the effect of Bulwer's encouragement on the Spanish government. Bresson informed Guizot that the Spanish government and press were convinced that the new Whig government in England would support the Coburg candidature.[28] French suspicions were confirmed by Christina's conduct: she was raising every possible objection to a Bourbon marriage, and then complaining that any alternative was prevented by the French government.[29]

Like Bulwer, Queen Victoria and Prince Albert expected some changes in Great Britain's Spanish marriages policy with Palmerston's return to the Foreign Office. Their own views were at variance with the spirit of Aberdeen's policy, but they were anxious to maintain one of its distinguishing characteristics, the willingness to consult and co-operate with France. They too favoured a marriage between Queen Isabella and Prince Leopold of Saxe-Coburg, but whereas Bulwer wanted it for its political consequences, the Queen and Prince Albert wanted it to be devoid of political consequences. They desired it as a good

---

[26] Bulwer to Palmerston, 8 July 1846. B.P. GC/BU/254.
[27] Bulwer to Aberdeen, 8 July 1846. Aberdeen Papers, B.M. Add. MS. 42294.
[28] Bresson to Guizot, 4 July 1846. A.A.E.C.P. Espagne 827.
[29] Bresson to Guizot, 4 July 1846. G.P. 42/AP/65.

dynastic connection, but not as the means of overthrowing the existing régime in Spain or the cause of coolness or conflict between England and France. Unlike Bulwer, who thought the Coburg match should be adopted immediately and in defiance of France, the Queen and the Prince wanted it to emerge gradually and with French support. Thus, despite Aberdeen's frequent assurances to France that the British government would not support Prince Leopold's candidature, the British Court hoped that the French would eventually realise that all the Bourbon candidates were unsuitable, and then accept Coburg. To achieve this would need time and careful handling of French susceptibilities. The Prince thought that Aberdeen's method of dealing with the French, not attempting 'to argue a question which admits of no argument',[30] was a wise one. He feared that Palmerston's return to the Foreign Office could lead to a 'chapter of accidents' which might result in the estrangement of England and France, and the destruction of all Prince Leopold's chances of marrying Queen Isabella. In a memorandum of 15 July he wrote:

There is no doubt that Lord Palmerston's return to office has given hopes to the Democratic Party in Spain, that there exist traditional connections between the Whig statesmen and the Progresistas, between the English Press and the constitutional party in Spain. There lies great danger, and that is increased if France tries to consolidate a party under her colours, which she will be inclined to do. The two parties once at war in Spain, they cannot fail to embroil England and France.[31]

Whereas Bulwer and the English Court feared that Palmerston's return might revive the connection between the party struggle within Spain and Anglo-French rivalry for influence over Spain, this was exactly what the Progresistas wanted. Unable to regain power unaided, they hoped that Palmerston would renew his former support. Espartero, who lived in exile in England, told Colonel Wylde, the former commander of the British volunteer force in Spain, that he hoped:

that the new Ministry would not follow such an apathetic policy towards Spain as the last, for if they did England would lose all her

[30] Memorandum by Prince Albert, 15 July 1846. R.A. J/44/14.   [31] Ibid.

influence there even with the Liberal Party, who now looked up to her as their natural support, and France would have it all her own way.³²

In July, therefore, there was a great increase in Progresista activity. It was the Progresista exiles in London and Brussels who took the initiative in making known to Palmerston their views and aspirations. Those who remained in Spain were neither numerous nor able, and they were additionally hampered because their representations to the British government had to be transmitted through Bulwer, who was not very sympathetic towards them.³³ In London Espartero had direct access to Palmerston.³⁴ Other important party leaders and Don Enrique, Duke of Seville, the only Progresista partisan in the Spanish royal family,³⁵ were in Brussels, and the two groups of exiles were in frequent contact with each other.³⁶

The Progresistas regarded Queen Christina as their major enemy in Spain, yet they were aware that, apart from insurrection, their future lay in some form of accommodation with the Court. As Queen Isabella was as yet politically unaligned, the solution seemed to lie in a Progresista husband for the Queen, one who would not only restore the Progresistas to power but also secure them the permanent and exclusive supremacy that they, like their rivals, sought. The only Progresista prince, Don Enrique, had identified himself so closely with the Spanish opposition to Christina and the Moderados that he had been forced into voluntary exile. The Progresista plan—that Don Enrique should marry the Queen and replace Queen Christina as the controlling influence at Court—was not only a simple

³² Memorandum by Col. Wylde of conversations with the Duke de la Victoria on 27 July, 1 and 3 Aug. 1846. R.A. J/44/16.
³³ Palmerston to Bulwer, 19 July 1846. B.P. GC/BU/508.
³⁴ Clarendon, however, sometimes acted as go-between. Clarendon to Palmerston, 28 July 1846. B.P. GC/CL/454.
³⁵ His father, Don Francisco de Paula, was a waverer. He kept in contact with the Progresista leaders, but his support could never be relied on.
³⁶ Olozaga was Don Enrique's chief adviser, and he corresponded with Lord Clarendon. In July Espartero sent one of his aides-de-camp to concert measures with the Brussels contingent. Seymour to Palmerston, 25 July 1846. F.O. 10/124. The French government expected the return of Lord Palmerston to lead to renewed Progresista activity. They were particularly anxious to prevent them using the Franco-Spanish frontier as a means of contacting the Progresistas who had remained in Spain. Duchâtel to Guizot, 7 July 1846. A.A.E.C.P. Espagne 827.

solution, it was also naïve. Christina and the Moderados, in whose hands the choice of a husband lay, would hardly connive at their own downfall. Moreover, besides being politically obnoxious, Don Enrique was unprepossessing[37] and said to be diseased.[38] The French government did not regard his candidature seriously; Louis Philippe told Lord Cowley that Don Enrique had ruined his own chances by his political views and activities. However, they did fear that he was plotting 'to push his fortunes as a partisan of the Progresistas' and that he would leave Brussels for London to concert measures with Espartero 'for the advancement of the projects of that Party'.[39] To the French and Spanish governments Don Enrique appeared a royal renegade, at best a nuisance, at worst a dangerous and intriguing opponent.[40]

By 14 July Palmerston had made up his mind on Spanish affairs. In an interview with Jarnac on that day he gave his personal opinions on the question of the Queen's marriage without committing the Queen and his colleagues, with whom he had not yet discussed it. Palmerston considered that it would be best for Queen Isabella to marry a Spanish prince, and that Don Enrique seemed the most suitable; there could, however, be no doubt that both Queen Christina and Queen Isabella preferred the Prince of Coburg. In reply to Jarnac's immediate response that his government could not permit a marriage outside the Bourbon family, Palmerston assured him that 'je ne vois aucun intérêt Anglais ni aucun avantage dans le succès du Prince de Coburg'.[41] Palmerston in fact regarded the Prince of Coburg as more closely connected with the French royal family than with the British. Both men agreed that joint action by England and France was the only satisfactory way to settle the question of the Queen's marriage.[42]

[37] 'As regards the Infant's looks they are not in his favour.' Seymour to Palmerston, 28 July 1846. B.P. GC/SE/236.
[38] 'I am told that the Queen and her mother have an insuperable aversion to Don Enrique, and that the Queen Mother declares she will never consent to the marriage of her daughter with a man who is diseased.' Hervey to Clarendon, 6 July 1846. Clar. Dep. C529.   [39] Cowley to Palmerston, 13 July 1846. F.O. 27/753.
[40] Bulwer warned Palmerston of his hopeless position from the outset. Bulwer to Palmerston, 8 July 1846. B.P. GC/BU/254.
[41] Jarnac to Guizot, 15 July 1846. G.P. 42/AP/69.
[42] Jarnac to Guizot, 14 July 1846. A.A.E.C.P. Angleterre 666.

Two days later Palmerston outlined his views on the Queen of Spain's marriage to Queen Victoria. He presented his policy not as a new initiative on his part but as the logical outcome of recent negotiations and of the principles laid down by the French government: 'The state of the matter seems, in a few words, to be...that the alternative now lies between Don Enrique and the Prince Leopold of Coburg.'[43] Of these two candidates, Don Enrique appeared the more suitable: he was a Spanish prince, a fact which appealed to 'a very large portion of the Spanish nation'; and he fell within the category of Bourbon princes descended from Philip V on which France insisted. Palmerston did, however, admit that an objection was: 'the aversion of the Queen Mother founded on her family differences with her late sister, and the apprehensions of the present Ministers in Spain, who would think their power endangered by the political connection between Don Enrique and the more Liberal Party'.[44] In his letter to the Queen Palmerston did not mention the question of the marriage of the Infanta, Luisa Fernanda. The next day, however, he expressed his views on this subject in a letter to Lord Clarendon: 'I intirely agree with you that the Montpensier marrying the Infanta would be worse, if possible, than his marrying the Queen, and that it would be highly important for the interests of this country, as well as of Europe, that such a marriage should not take place.'[45] If Montpensier were to marry the Infanta, 'he would be the centre of every kind of intrigue'[46] and the permanent head of the French party in Spain. To Clarendon, as to Bulwer,[47] Palmerston argued that it would be better for objections to the Montpensier marriage to 'originate in Spain

[43] Palmerston to the Queen, 16 July 1846. *Q.V.L.*, 1st series, ii, 106–7.
[44] Ibid.
[45] Palmerston to Clarendon, 17 July 1846. Clar. Dep. C524. Clarendon had already made known his objections to the Montpensier marriage to Hervey as well as to Palmerston. 'I am very glad to see that you are alive to the danger of Montpensier for the Queen's sister.' Hervey to Clarendon, 6 July 1846. Clar. Dep. C529. Palmerston informed Bulwer on 19 July that he had told Guizot when he was in Paris in the spring of 1846 that 'the marriage of Montpensier to the Infanta would seem to me nearly as objectionable as his marriage to the Queen and would be almost equally injurious to the friendly relations between England and Spain and England and France'. Palmerston to Bulwer, 19 July 1846. B.P. GC/BU/508.
[46] Hervey to Clarendon, 6 July 1846. Clar. Dep. C529.
[47] Palmerston to Bulwer, 19 July 1846. B.P. GC/BU/508.

and in Spanish feeling'.[48] He probably hoped that they would encourage their contacts to foment opposition to the Montpensier marriage in Spain.

Palmerston's policy on the Spanish marriages was a complete departure from Aberdeen's. Unlike Aberdeen, he expressed a strong preference for a particular candidate for the Queen's hand. He also wished to go back on the agreement with the French government about the eventual marriage of the Duke of Montpensier and the Infanta Luisa, but he realised that this would not be easy. More fundamentally, where Aberdeen had been content to allow existing conditions in Spain to continue without British strictures or opposition, Palmerston wished to overthrow the Spanish régime and to replace French by British influence at Madrid. Palmerston believed this policy to be a straightforward and disinterested response to the situation in Spain. 'All I want', he informed Bulwer, 'is that Spain should be free, tranquil and independent.'[49] This was what he had struggled for in the 1830s, and he clearly thought it necessary to do battle for it again. He was willing to help the Progresistas to do what they could not do alone.

Despite Bulwer's warnings that the question was very urgent, Palmerston believed that a gradual solution was possible, and he envisaged two stages in the marriage negotiations. Firstly the Queen was to be married, then opposition to the marriage of Montpensier and the Infanta was to be organised. If Isabella married Enrique, the second stage would be relatively easy. He therefore concentrated on bringing about the marriage of the Queen and Don Enrique. The preliminary step was to make public the views of the British government on the Queen's marriage, which he did in his famous despatch of 19 July 1846 to Bulwer. It was written not primarily as an instruction for Bulwer, but for the effect it would have on the French. Palmerston tried to make it appear as if the British government had no specific views on the question of the Queen's marriage: 'The British Government is not prepared to give any active support to the pretensions of any of the Persons who are now candidates for the Queen of Spain's hand, and does not feel

[48] Palmerston to Clarendon, 17 July 1846. Clar. Dep. C529.
[49] Palmerston to Bulwer, 19 July 1846. B.P. GC/BU/508.

itself called upon to make any objections to any of them.' He went on to name the three contenders left in the field: Prince Leopold of Saxe-Coburg and the two sons of Don Francisco de Paula, Don Francisco, Duke of Cadiz, and Don Enrique, Duke of Seville, and to express the hope that the Queen would choose 'the one who may be most likely to secure [her] happiness. . . and to promote the welfare of the Spanish nation'.[50] Palmerston was, however, convinced that Queen Isabella would reject Cadiz on personal grounds, and he knew that the French were resolutely opposed to Coburg. This left Don Enrique. The purpose of this despatch was clear: Palmerston had followed the advice of the Progresistas who told him 'that by alarming Louis Philippe as to a Coburg, that monarch would adopt the candidature of Prince Henry as a Bourbon'.[51] If England and France were united in favour of Enrique, Christina would have no alternative but to accept him. Palmerston then warned the French that they should not expect him to continue Aberdeen's passive policy towards Spain. He bitterly attacked the system which Christina and Narvaez had established in Spain under the patronage of France:

> That political condition must indeed be the subject of deep regret and concern to every well wisher to the Spanish people. After a struggle of now thirty four years duration for constitutional freedom Spain finds herself under a system of government almost as arbitrary in practice, whatever it may be in theory, as any which existed in any former period of her history.[52]

This system, declared Palmerston, if not substantially modified from above, would be overthrown from below. This diatribe against the despotism of Christina and the Moderados was mainly meant for French eyes. Bulwer was not instructed to convey these views directly to the Spanish government, merely 'not to conceal the fact that such opinions are entertained by the British Government'. Palmerston's tactics for bringing Christina and the Spanish government round to his policy were quite different. These were laid down in a private letter to Bulwer which accompanied his despatch. Christina must be persuaded

---

[50] *Accounts and Papers, 1847*, lxix.
[51] Bulwer in the *Quarterly Review*, 1868, no. 247, 135.
[52] Palmerston to Bulwer, 19 July 1846. *Accounts and Papers, 1847*, lxix.

JULY-AUGUST 1846

that the first task was not the marriage of the Queen but the modification of the present system of government. The first and most essential thing

> is to effect a reconciliation between Christina and the Progresistas; and this can be done only by removing from her mind all apprehensions that in the event of their again obtaining power in Spain, they would use that power hostilely towards her. There must be complete amnesty between them, and not only amnesty for the past but security for the future.[53]

Palmerston instructed Bulwer to take no part in effecting this reconciliation, but he did suggest that Bulwer should establish closer contacts with the Progresista party. Once the reconciliation between Christina and the Progresistas was under way, 'the next thing to be desired is that the Ministry should be modified by getting rid of some of the arbitrary power men, and filling their places by moderate Moderados, so as to get back to legal order and constitutional government'. Bulwer was also instructed to abstain from playing a leading rôle in this task. England could advise on what ought to be done and suggest that it must be done immediately, but the Spaniards themselves must actually do it. Palmerston believed that with France frightened and Christina chastened, the Spanish government would alter its ways of proceeding and choose Enrique as husband for the Queen; when he was established in the palace, it should not be difficult to prevent the Montpensier marriage, restore the Progresistas to power and undermine French influence.

On 21 July Palmerston gave Jarnac a copy of his despatch of 19 July to Bulwer. In reply to Jarnac's comment that his view of the question of the Queen's marriage differed widely from Aberdeen's, Palmerston replied that the three candidates were not of his choice but were those publicly known to be the most likely.[54]

Over the next few days Palmerston took a more definite stand both publicly and privately. On 24 July he changed his tactics towards the French government. Instead of supporting Don

---

[53] Palmerston to Bulwer, 19 July 1846. B.P. GC/BU/508.
[54] Jarnac to Guizot, 21 July 1846. G.P. 42/AP/69.

Enrique by implication only, he informed Jarnac that: 'on the marriage question we are passive officially...but my own opinion coincided with that which was entertained by Lord Aberdeen, that Don Enrique would be the best choice for the Queen'.[55] He believed that the French were reacting as he intended, and informed Bulwer that: 'the French Government are uneasy about the view which we may take of the marriage question and fear that we shall be inclined to support the Prince of Coburg'.[56] This encouraging development led Palmerston to reveal his policy in full:

> The best arrangement for all parties would I think be, that Enrique should marry the Queen and Prince Coburg the Infanta. Enrique would be a good Spanish husband for the Queen and Coburg married to the Infanta would be a perfect personification of the Quadruple Alliance and would centre in himself the ties of alliance between France, England, Spain and Portugal.[57]

This English double marriages plan was warmly supported by Espartero.[58]

By the end of July Palmerston's plans seemed a step nearer fruition. The Coburgs were all gathered in London, Duke Ernst on his way back to Germany from Lisbon, King Leopold of the Belgians on a private visit to Queen Victoria. After a long discussion and with Palmerston's advice[59] they decided that they had no alternative but to decline Christina's offer of her daughter's hand to Prince Leopold. Neither Queen Victoria and Prince Albert nor the King of the Belgians was prepared for the open hostility of France that acceptance at that stage would have aroused. The carefully worded letter of rejection did not reach Madrid until mid-August. However, the Coburgs still believed that the marriage between Queen Isabella and Prince

---

[55] Palmerston to Bulwer, 24 July 1846. F.O. 72/694.
[56] Palmerston to Bulwer, 24 July 1846. B.P. GC/BU/509.
[57] Palmerston thought that 'no foreign government would be entitled to feel jealous of either marriage, and if any government would gain by it any influence in Spain that government would be France, by virtue of the family connection already existing between Prince Leopold and the Orleans branch. But the great advantage of this would be, that a French Prince would not be placed next door to the Palace at Madrid...' Ibid.
[58] Memorandum by Col. Wylde of conversations with the Duke de la Victoria on 27 July, 1 and 3 Aug. 1846. R.A. J/44/16.
[59] Jones Parry, *The Spanish Marriages*, 316.

Leopold was possible if the objections of Louis Philippe could be overcome, and this, they thought, depended on the absolute confidence of France in British policy. They were therefore anxious about the effects of Palmerston's policy on the French government; King Leopold informed Aberdeen that he feared that 'new elements will be brought into play' and that Palmerston would raise 'political passions that had been dormant'.[60] Palmerston was satisfied with the Coburg position. Their rejection of Christina's formal offer would, he believed, make her more willing to accept Don Enrique. The fact that they still placed some hope in Leopold's candidature would make France uneasy and therefore the more anxious to support Enrique.[61]

Throughout July, whilst Palmerston was evolving a new policy, the British government was almost totally unaware of the activities of the French government. Bresson, with better contacts in the Spanish government, knew far more about Bulwer's conduct than Bulwer did of his, and Christina did not reveal to Bulwer the details of her private discussions with the French ambassador. She knew that both England and France were aware of her duplicity, but she hoped to conceal from each the details of her dealings with the other. Even had they desired it, no co-operation at Madrid between the English and French governments was possible until Palmerston's policy was known. The alternatives open to the French were either to wait until they knew what Palmerston proposed to do, or else to follow their own course. They chose to do the latter. It was in fact during late June and July that the French government laid the basis of the double marriages policy that came to fruition in late August. The information about Palmerston's intentions which the French government obtained in late July confirmed rather than created their suspicions, and it precipitated their pursuit of a policy which Guizot and Bresson were keen to adopt.

The policy over the Spanish marriages which France had

[60] King Leopold to Aberdeen, 29 July 1846. Aberdeen Papers, B.M. Add. MS. 43294.
[61] In early August Prince Albert sent his private secretary, Praetorius, on a mission to Prince Leopold to ascertain whether he still wanted to marry Queen Isabella. Jones Parry, op. cit., 316. The Orleans family could not fail to know of these new Coburg moves either through the Queen of the Belgians or through Louis Philippe's Coburg son-in-law and daughter-in-law.

begun to pursue even before Aberdeen's fall from office reflected the determination of Guizot and Louis Philippe to bring it to a triumphant conclusion. Perhaps the only important truthful remark of Jarnac to Palmerston during July was that his government considered 'les intérêts de la France sont plus grands, plus légitimes en Espagne que les vôtres'.[62] The news that Queen Christina had made a formal offer of the Queen's hand to Prince Leopold reminded the French how little they could trust Spaniards. Like Bulwer, they realised that success was only possible if they adopted some underhand ways of proceeding. Moreover, Bresson himself was a natural intriguer; he pushed Guizot along, committing his government without instructions, confident that he would not be disavowed.[63] Finally, Aberdeen's note to Sotomayor and the fall of Peel's government convinced the French that the question was about to enter a new phase. Guizot reflected to Bresson that 'Nous n'avons plus la loyauté de Lord Aberdeen pour nous révéler les pièges.'[64]

Bresson, however, had never placed much faith in the loyalty of Aberdeen; at Madrid Bulwer, not Aberdeen, had represented the spirit of British policy. He anticipated that Palmerston's resumption of control of foreign affairs would alter Bulwer's conduct, and he used this assumption to justify his own behaviour.[65] On 27 June Guizot informed Bresson that the fall of the Peel government was imminent; 'Dans ma prochaine lettre, je vous dirai tout ce que je pense de la nouvelle situation, de ses chances et de l'attitude que nous y prendrons.'[66] Bresson acted without waiting for this letter. Throughout May and early June, when the French government's reaction to Christina's Coburg offer had been to transfer their hopes to the Carlist, Count Montemolin,[67] Bresson had stressed that, if the opposition of Christina and Isabella to the sons of Don Francisco de Paula

---

[62] Jarnac to Guizot, 21 July 1846. G.P. 42/AP/69.
[63] Desages encouraged Bresson in this course: 'Votre conduite a d'ailleurs été parfaite, mon cher ami; le Roi et M. Guizot sont fort contents de vous. Continuez...' Desages to Bresson, 5 June 1846. Desages Papers, Espagne, vol. 2.
[64] Guizot to Bresson, 27 June 1846. G.P. 42/AP/8.
[65] Bresson to Guizot, 22 July 1846. G.P. 42/AP/65.
[66] Guizot to Bresson, 27 June 1846. G.P. 42/AP/8.
[67] Bresson to Guizot, 26 May and 20 June 1846. G.P. 42/AP/65.

could be overcome, a marriage to one of them would be easiest to arrange.[68] Louis Philippe, in a letter to Christina of 16 June, also recommended that Isabella must marry either Don Francisco or Don Enrique as the only possible solution.[69] Christina pointed out the grave political objections to Don Enrique in a letter to the Queen of the French, although she raised no such objections to Don Francisco.[70] On 28 June, during an interview with Bresson on the marriage question, Christina emphasised that she still wanted a spectacular marriage for Queen Isabella, and suggested that Montpensier should marry the Queen and Trapani the Infanta. When Bresson rejected this as an impossible combination, Christina's husband, Rianzares, suggested Don Francisco for the Queen and Montpensier for the Infanta. There were, however, said Queen Christina, two obstacles to the former marriage: the personal antipathy of the Queen to her cousin, and the rumour that he was impotent.[71] Bresson was uncertain whether Christina's and Rianzares' proposals constituted a serious offer or a delaying tactic to prolong negotiations with the French while she pursued her Coburg plans.[72] The latter seems more probable, since the Spanish government sent Miraflores on a mission to Paris to attempt to persuade Louis Philippe to regard a Coburg match more favourably[73] and, encouraged by Bulwer, made renewed, but this time indirect, overtures to the Coburgs.[74]

The French, however, had to treat the suggestion seriously. Guizot reacted swiftly to Bresson's letter announcing that Christina had reintroduced the name of Don Francisco, Duke of Cadiz, as a possible candidate. He wrote to Bresson on 5 July: 'Entrez donc sans hésiter dans la voie que le duc de Rianzares

[68] Bresson to Guizot, 31 May 1846. G.P. 42/AP/65.
[69] Louis Philippe to Queen Christina. *Revue Retrospective*, 50.
[70] Queen Christina to the Queen of the French. *Revue Retrospective*, 52.
[71] Bresson to Guizot, 28 June 1846. G.P. 42/AP/65.
[72] Bresson to Guizot, 4 July 1846. G.P. 42/AP/65. Glucksburg told Guizot that he thought that Christina had mentioned Cadiz's impotence as a way out if the Coburgs took up her offer. Guizot to Bresson, 5 July 1846. G.P. 42/AP/8.
[73] Jones Parry, *The Spanish Marriages*, 306–7.
[74] Rianzares wrote to Huth, who acted as intermediary between Christina and the Coburgs, that Christina 'is waiting anxiously for a resolution from your side, as her present position is not maintainable for long'. Rianzares to Huth, 6 July 1846. R.A. J/44/3.

nous a ouverte le 28 Juin: Cadix et Montpensier. En soi elle nous convient parfaitement. Dans l'état actuel des faits, c'est la plus facile, la plus prompte et la plus sûre.' In his decision to advocate this combination, Guizot was mainly influenced by Palmerston's return to the Foreign Office. 'Ce ne sera pas moi qui livrerai l'Espagne à Lord Palmerston.' He instructed Bresson to point out to Christina and Rianzares that: 'Ils n'auront jamais dans Lord Palmerston qu'un ennemi, car il ne sera jamais que le patron du parti progressiste, c'est-à-dire de leurs ennemis.' Guizot was convinced that on the marriage question Palmerston would declare himself in favour of either Coburg or Enrique, the two candidates inimical to the interests of France. Cadiz, however, was politically innocuous, and he could be combined with Montpensier in a way which would suit the French government. Bresson was instructed to urge this combination as forcefully as possible, and Guizot put 20,000 francs at his disposal to influence the Spanish press.[75]

Bresson felt that Guizot's instructions contained an element of ambiguity. There was no indication of the lengths to which he might go in his advocacy of Cadiz, in presenting an unattractive match in the most favourable light. Letters from Desages and Glucksburg (first secretary at the Madrid embassy on leave in Paris), which were commentaries on and developments of Guizot's letter of the 5th, left Bresson in no doubt that Guizot would sanction any offer to Christina to negotiate the marriages of the Queen and Cadiz and of the Infanta and Montpensier side by side.[76] Guizot had himself admitted to Bresson that the return of Palmerston to the Foreign Office enabled him to take more risks: 'J'ai avec Lord Palmerston cet avantage que, s'il survenait entre nous et Londres, quelque refroidissement, quelque embarras, ce serait à lui, et non à moi, qu'en France, en Angleterre, partout, on en imputerait la faute.'[77] As instructed by Guizot, Bresson pointed out to Christina on 10 July that she could expect nothing from Palmerston, who was the patron of the Progresistas. On the marriage question, he remarked: 'dans toute combinaison

[75] Guizot to Bresson, 5 July 1846. G.P. 42/AP/8.
[76] Bresson to Guizot, 12 July 1846. G.P. 42/AP/65.
[77] Guizot to Bresson, 5 July 1846. G.P. 42/AP/8.

Bourbon, le duc de Montpensier prît place à côté du mari de la reine, c'est-à-dire que les deux mariages, si l'un devait faciliter l'autre, se célébrassent ou fussent du moins déclarés simultanément.'[78] Christina reacted favourably to this offer, agreeing that of all the possible Bourbon matches, that with Cadiz would be easiest to arrange. It could be effected, wrote Bresson, 'sans trouble, sans opposition, sans commotion'.[79] Christina herself undertook the most difficult task, that of overcoming Queen Isabella's opposition to marriage with a man she disliked, and immediately recalled Cadiz to Madrid.[80] On the same day the editor of the *Heraldo*, a Moderado newspaper, promised to support the candidature of Cadiz.[81]

Guizot's 'thinking aloud' in his letter to Bresson and his more explicit conversations with Desages and Glucksburg on the possibility of a double arrangement were obviously deliberate. He was clearly anxious to settle the affair, and in a way to make it a clear triumph for France. The opposition election campaign in France had begun, and Guizot was once again being labelled as a Pritchardiste. Although Palmerston's policy was still unknown, Guizot was convinced that it would not be the same as Aberdeen's. At best it could only be a policy of limited co-operation with France, at worst it could be hostile to France. Whatever it proved to be, Guizot was anxious to forestall it. His determination to pursue a separate policy, and if necessary to abandon the obligations he had contracted on the question, was grounded in fear. He was above all anxious to avoid a repetition of the humiliation of France by Palmerston in 1840, and to a lesser extent he also wished to avenge 1840. Guizot's policy was therefore a combination of fear and determination. He was also caught in a trap of his own making: he had constantly said that the question was a vital issue of prestige, and because of this he could not afford failure. However, he could not express explicitly his views on the course he thought best because he had no authority to do so from either the cabinet or the King. Guizot appears to have hoped that Bresson would act on his hints, thus

[78] Bresson to Guizot, 12 July 1846. G.P. 42/AP/65.
[79] Bresson to Guizot, 12 July 1846. A.A.E.C.P. Espagne 827.
[80] Bresson to Guizot, 13 July 1846. G.P. 42/AP/65.
[81] Ibid. Narvaez told Louis Philippe that it would be easy to make Cadiz popular in Spain. Louis Philippe to Guizot, 17 July 1846. G.P. 42/AP/286.

enabling him to present his new policy to his colleagues and the King as already under way and in the logic of events. Louis Philippe, when he heard of the plan to associate the two marriages, assumed that Bresson had acted solely on his own initiative. The King immediately insisted on a formal retraction of the offer Bresson had made to Christina on 10 July.[82] Guizot was at his country house, Val Richer, preparing for the elections, and was thus in a better position deliberately to delay fulfilling the King's instructions than if he had been in Paris. He continued to encourage Bresson to press for the double arrangement, confident that the King's objections could be overcome.

At the same time as he was pressing the secret policy of the double arrangement, Guizot suggested to the British government that they should co-operate at Madrid in support of either of the two sons of Don Francisco de Paula, the choice being left to the Spanish government.[83] This was in fact no more than another version of the same policy. The only difference lay in the means by which it would be accomplished. Guizot knew that Enrique was unacceptable to Queen Christina, and that British co-operation on this basis would ensure eventual success to Cadiz. His motives were various. British agreement to his suggestion would enable him to accomplish his aims legitimately and within the framework of the *entente*, for there could be little doubt that if Cadiz married the Queen, Montpensier would marry the Infanta. Further, he hoped that a positive suggestion would elicit a positive British reaction on the question of the Queen's marriage, which he felt had been long enough deferred. Lastly, if the British government refused to collaborate and made a counter-suggestion in which Coburg figured, Guizot would have both a public defence for pursuing the unilateral policy of the double marriages and powerful arguments for overcoming the scruples of the King.

There was therefore a period in mid-July 1846 when there were sharp divisions among the policy makers in both England

[82] Louis Philippe to Guizot, 20 July 1846. G.P. 42/AP/286.
[83] Guizot to Jarnac, 20 July 1846. G.P. 42/AP/7. Hervey warned Clarendon on 19 July that the offer the French government was about to make for either of the sons of Don Francisco de Paula was nothing but a thinly disguised attempt to push Cadiz, and that its purpose was to conceal their real ambition, which was the marriage of Montpensier and the Infanta. Clar. Dep. C529.

and France on the question of the Spanish marriages. Bulwer was urging the Spanish government to press as hard as possible for the Coburg match while Palmerston was preparing to embark upon a quite different course. Bresson and Guizot were offering the Spanish government a solution which their sovereign considered impossible. For the first time since the negotiations had begun, Queen Christina had a free hand, and she was not prepared to commit herself either to Bresson's or to Bulwer's solution unless one proved either untenable or a certainty. Indeed, she probably hoped for a combination of both proposals.

This fluid state of affairs could not last long, and it was ended in the fourth week of July when Jarnac sent Guizot an account of his interview of 21 July with Palmerston and the copy which Palmerston had given him of his despatch of 19 July to Bulwer.[84] Guizot, Jarnac and Louis Philippe all construed this as British abandonment of the policy of *entente*.[85] They saw Palmerston's despatch for what it was, a revival of the struggle for influence in Spain between England and France. They were well aware that the despatch championed not Coburg but Espartero and Enrique, and it was this which they feared most. Guizot had anticipated this and was not surprised. His first reaction was to consider how best to exploit it. It meant, Guizot wrote, that the King was now at liberty to act as he pleased: 'Il n'aurait plus à tenir compte que des intérêts de la France et de l'honneur de sa couronne.'[86] To Bresson he wrote that Palmerston's despatch to Bulwer was 'raison de plus pour nous de poursuivre Cadix et Montpensier'. Guizot believed not only that Palmerston's despatch justified vigorous pursuit of the double arrangement, but also that it increased the chances of its success as, firstly, Christina would clearly perceive that Palmerston was determined to overthrow her and the Moderados,[87] and secondly, it would give Guizot the necessary arguments to overcome the scruples of the King.

At the end of July therefore Palmerston thought that the

[84] Jarnac to Guizot, 21 July 1846. G.P. 42/AP/69.
[85] Guizot to Jarnac, 24 July 1846. G.P. 42/AP/7; Louis Philippe to Guizot, 25 July 1846. G.P. 42/AP/286.
[86] Guizot to Jarnac, 24 July 1846. G.P. 42/AP/7.
[87] Guizot to Bresson, 24 July 1846. G.P. 42/AP/8.

question of the Spanish marriages was going as he intended; the French appeared to be reacting to his despatch of 19 July precisely as he expected. For his part, Guizot believed success to be imminent. In fact, however, the outcome depended on Queen Christina and the Spanish government.

At the beginning of July Bulwer had been in a stronger position than Bresson, able to exploit the coolness between the French and Spanish governments and to hold out to Christina the prospect of open support for the Coburg candidate by the new Whig government. By early August, however, their positions were reversed, and Bresson was more confident of success. He had something definite to offer the Spanish government, and authority to use whatever means he judged best to persuade them to accept the double marriage proposal. Bresson knew that his position was further strengthened by Bulwer's obvious difficulties.[88] Bulwer, by contrast, was in despair. Palmerston had ignored his advice, and had instructed him to pursue a policy which he knew to have no chance of success. Even prevarication had its dangers; Bulwer recognised that Christina would soon draw the inevitable conclusions if he ceased to press the Coburg match, and would turn to Bresson for an alternative.

In his correspondence, Bulwer became increasingly frantic. He warned Palmerston repeatedly that the only result of his advocacy of Don Enrique's candidature would be that Great Britain would 'entirely lose the confidence of the palace here' and that Spain would turn to France.[89] He even adduced the recent attempt on the life of Louis Philippe as further proof of the advisability of determined pursuit of the Coburg match.[90] To Stanley, Under Secretary at the Foreign Office, Bulwer wrote scathingly that what Palmerston demanded of Christina

[88] Bresson to Guizot, 1 Aug. 1846. G.P. 42/AP/65.
[89] Bulwer to Palmerston, 4 Aug. 1846. F.O. 72/698.
[90] 'The policy of maintaining good relations with France is a wise and great policy; but the excellence of everything must be measured by the chances of its duration. What would follow if King Louis Philippe died? The power of a great military country would be in the hands of three or four enterprising young men, burning for glory in their several careers. . .The policy of good relations with France then, I much fear, depends upon the life of a man of seventy four, and the well or ill directed aim of an assassin. God forbid that we should hasten such a calamity as war, which will come too soon whenever it does come; but we should be provided against its approach.' Ibid.

and the Moderados was like asking 'an army which has gained a battle [to lay] down its arms to the flying foe upon the condition that the lives of the unfortunate victors shall be spared and their noses and ears not cut off'.[91] To strengthen his argument, Bulwer also sent Palmerston a letter from Isturiz, in which the Spanish Prime Minister described the candidature of Don Enrique as: 'tout à fait impossible, sous les circonstances actuelles, à moins d'être imposée par une révolution triomphante'.[92] However, until Bulwer's letters and despatches of 4 August arrived in London on 11 August, Palmerston remained convinced that his chosen course was the right one. 'Upon the marriage question our opinion becomes confirmed by reflection', he informed Bulwer on 3 August.[93] Stanley wrote even more explicitly: 'You will find that Lord Palmerston is sincerely opposed to a Coburg marriage, and feels that such an alliance would, far from improving our position or giving us additional influence in Spain, only give us the semblance without the reality of power.'[94]

At the end of July Hervey warned Clarendon that the French were alarmed by Palmerston's despatch of 19 July and that, when he saw Guizot at Princess Lieven's, 'hints were given about France remaining isolée and pursuing her own objects by herself'.[95] This left Palmerston unperturbed.[96] He was, however, disconcerted by Bulwer's blunt letter of 4 August. He immediately informed Russell of Bulwer's arguments in favour of adopting Coburg. It was clear, however, that he was not convinced that they were compelling or that a Coburg marriage would result either in the necessary changes in Spanish politics or the prevention of the Montpensier marriage. Palmerston feared that Prince Leopold's personal shortcomings would render him inadequate to the task he would face in Spain, and that once Christina had achieved her aims through British support for Coburg she would attempt to placate Louis Philippe

[91] Bulwer to Stanley, 3 Aug. 1846. Bulwer Papers, S/44.
[92] Isturiz to Bulwer, 12 Aug. 1846, enclosure Bulwer to Palmerston, 14 Aug. 1846. B.P. GC/BU/260.   [93] Palmerston to Bulwer, 3 Aug. 1846. F.O. 72/694.
[94] Stanley to Bulwer, 3 Aug. 1846. Bulwer Papers, S/40.
[95] Hervey to Clarendon, 31 July 1846. Clar. Dep. C529. Clarendon passed this letter on to Palmerston with Hervey's approval. Hervey to Clarendon, 7 Aug. 1846. Clar. Dep. C529.   [96] Stanley to Bulwer, 3 Aug. 1846. Bulwer Papers, S/40.

by marrying the Infanta to Montpensier.[97] Russell was even less keen to resort to so bold a move: 'I think it will not do to encourage Bulwer in his wild notions...We should be required very soon to support Spain against France.'[98]

Palmerston accepted Russell's judgment, admitting to Bulwer that 'it is very difficult to satisfy oneself that any given course upon the marriage question is the best'. He nevertheless remained optimistic about the chances of success for his policy, believing that the French were sufficiently worried to be willing to agree to one of the sons of Don Francisco de Paula, and that as Cadiz was 'personally ridiculous and politically a nonentity' Isabella would choose Enrique. Moreover, once opposition to the marriage of Montpensier and the Infanta had emerged in Spain, Palmerston believed that there would be 'no difficulty in coming to an understanding with the French Government that it shall not take place'. Above all, he thought that the British government must remain 'free to follow the course which we think best, unfettered by any engagements towards France'.[99] Bulwer was not alone in his dissatisfaction with Palmerston's policy. By mid-August the Queen and Prince Albert were convinced that it would damage Anglo-French relations. It was clear, the Queen wrote to Russell on 17 August, that Palmerston's intention was to undermine French influence in Spain; this was both impractical and wrong in spirit.[100] Clearly the Queen and Prince Albert feared that the introduction of political issues into the marriage question would decrease the chances of persuading Louis Philippe that the Coburg marriage could be a-political. Both Palmerston and Russell vigorously defended their policy.[101] The Court was therefore forced into silent disapproval. The warnings of Bulwer and Queen Victoria thus

[97] Palmerston to Russell, 11 Aug. 1846. Russell Papers, P.R.O. 30/22/5B.
[98] Russell to Palmerston, 13 Aug. 1846. B.P. GC/RU/104.
[99] Palmerston to Bulwer, 16 Aug. 1846. B.P. GC/BU/511.
[100] The Queen to Russell, 17 Aug. 1846. Q.V.L., 1st series, ii, 113–14. She asked Russell to pass on her letter to Palmerston. The Queen to Palmerston, 17 Aug. 1846. B.P. RC/F/268. King Leopold of the Belgians had forwarded a letter to Queen Victoria which he had received from Madrid which stated that 'Don Enrique is the Progresista candidate and the Progresistas mean revolution.' Marnix to Van Praet, 14 Aug. 1846. R.A. J/44/32.
[101] Palmerston to the Queen, 19 Aug. 1846. Q.V.L., 1st series, ii, 115–17. Russell to the Queen, 19 Aug. 1846. R.A. J/44/21.

had little discernible result. Palmerston continued to advocate the same policy although with diminished confidence, and Bulwer remained powerless to retrieve the situation at Madrid. Palmerston's cautious optimism proved unfounded. At Madrid the position was tending increasingly to favour France. Christina was losing her freedom of action. British support for Coburg, which Bulwer had encouraged her to expect, was not forthcoming; she construed the reply from the reigning Duke of Saxe-Coburg to her offer of May as a polite refusal.[102] All that remained of Christina's Coburg aspirations were Bulwer's hints that the British government might still be persuaded to support a Coburg match and the anticipated report on the private disposition of the Coburgs to be brought within a few days by Rianzares' brother, Muñoz. Moreover, the French government had informed Christina and the Spanish ministers of Palmerston's strictures on their system of government in his despatch of 19 July. Christina apprehended a direct attack on the political *status quo* in Spain: 'les anglais et la révolution nous menacent', she informed Mon on 8 August.[103] Bresson heightened her hysteria by supplying her with the reports of the French police on the subversive activities of the Progresista exiles.[104] Christina was determined to save herself and the Moderados. On 9 August she declared herself in favour of Cadiz if the Montpensier marriage were associated with it. Bresson raised no objection to this, but said that various points arising out of the double arrangement would need settling.[105] The next day a letter from Guizot authorised Bresson to continue the negotiations,[106] in the belief that Palmerston's opposition to the Montpensier marriage would convince the King that it was essential to conclude the double arrangement immediately.

The middle of August 1846 witnessed crucial developments in both Spain and France. In Spain the newspapers in the pay of Bresson greeted with enthusiasm the arrival in Madrid of Cadiz, and Christina began her attempts to overcome Isabella's resistance to marriage with her cousin.[107] In France Louis Philippe,

[102] Bresson to Guizot, 17, 18 Aug. 1846. G.P. 42/AP/65.
[103] Bresson to Guizot, 8 Aug. 1846. G.P. 42/AP/65.
[104] Bresson to Guizot, 9 Aug. 1846. G.P. 42/AP/65.   [105] Ibid.
[106] Guizot to Bresson, 10 Aug. 1846. G.P. 42/AP/8.
[107] Bresson to Guizot, 16 Aug. 1846. A.A.E.C.P. Espagne 828.

on holiday at the Château d'Eu, discussed Spanish affairs on 14 August with his family: Montpensier, Guizot informed Bresson, will do whatever the King approves.[108] Louis Philippe returned to Paris the following day for discussions with Guizot, and finally consented to approve the double arrangement of Cadiz and Montpensier.[109] In his change of mind he was influenced by Palmerston's attack on the Moderado régime, Bresson's reports of ministerial instability at Madrid,[110] and the English government's opposition to the marriage of Montpensier and the Infanta. He yielded to Guizot's argument that only by conceding some of Christina's wishes about the marriages could the *status quo* in Spain be maintained.

Christina was trapped, but Guizot still did not trust her. He therefore drew up a scheme for the arrangement of the marriages which would eliminate any risk of last-minute deceit on her part. The French government, he informed Bresson, would agree to the association of the two marriages, but not until Louis Philippe had heard from Christina that Isabella agreed to marry Cadiz, and Cadiz agreed to marry Isabella. Once this was agreed, the Queen should be married immediately; the marriage of the Infanta and Montpensier could follow later. Guizot knew that once the arrangement became public, the government must be prepared for considerable opposition. With this in mind, he advocated the return to Spain of Narvaez, who after quarrelling with Christina had left Spain for France, as the best means of ensuring firm and resolute action at Madrid. If any mention was made during the negotiations of the rights of the Infanta to the throne, and particularly if the renunciation of her succession rights was suggested, Bresson was instructed: 'n'acceptez pas, ni ne repoussez de prime abord'.[111]

On 18 August Bresson, now in daily contact with Christina and Rianzares, was informed by Christina that she hoped the Queen's marriage could be settled within a week, the Cortes convoked in fifteen days, and the arrangement of the two

---

[108] Guizot to Bresson, 15 Aug. 1846. G.P. 42/AP/8.
[109] Guizot to Bresson, 17 Aug. 1846. G.P. 42/AP/8.
[110] On 8 Aug. Bresson informed Guizot that a change of ministry in Spain was quite possible and that he would find it very difficult to prevent the formation of a ministry favourable to the Coburg candidature. Bresson to Guizot, 8 Aug. 1846. G.P. 42/AP/65.   [111] Guizot to Bresson, 17 Aug. 1846. G.P. 42/AP/8.

marriages announced.¹¹² On 20 August Bresson drafted a provisional agreement closely based on Guizot's instructions of the 17th. This, he informed Guizot, Christina approved without exception.¹¹³ The French negotiations therefore seemed to be approaching their conclusion.

Meanwhile, Bulwer made a final attempt to convert Palmerston to the Coburg match. In a despatch of 20 August he warned Palmerston that everything would be lost unless his next despatch came out openly in favour of Coburg; he predicted that Queen Isabella would marry Cadiz, and that the marriage of Montpensier and the Infanta would follow.¹¹⁴ Two days later he informed Palmerston that Isturiz and Rianzares had agreed to do nothing for five days; if within that time the British government proclaimed their support for Coburg, Rianzares believed that the Spanish government could be persuaded to accept him.¹¹⁵ Beyond that time they would promise nothing. It is probable that this offer of Isturiz and Rianzares was only half-hearted. Isturiz, who had compromised himself hopelessly throughout the negotiations of July and August, was no more than the tool of Christina. Rianzares, the morganatic husband of Christina, had never enjoyed the favour of her Bourbon relations; he probably hoped to thwart the plans of Louis Philippe. In any case five days were of little value to Bulwer, whose despatches took a week between Madrid and London.

Unknown to Bulwer, Palmerston was again having doubts as to the wisdom of his policy. To Russell he confessed that recent communications from Bulwer 'make me doubt very much our success in persuading Christina to adopt Enrique; and it would not probably be wise to pledge ourselves too much in his favour'. He drafted fresh instructions, stating a preference for Don Enrique but also 'an avowed and declared opinion that the Queen had a perfect right to choose Coburg if she pleases'. If the Spanish government were to opt for Coburg, Palmerston was convinced that 'Louis Philippe's resentment would yield to his

---

¹¹² Bresson to Guizot, 18 Aug. 1846. G.P. 42/AP/65.
¹¹³ Bresson to Guizot, 20 Aug. 1846. G.P. 42/AP/65.
¹¹⁴ Bulwer to Palmerston, 20 Aug. 1846. F.O. 72/698.
¹¹⁵ Bulwer to Palmerston, 22 Aug. 1846. F.O. 72/698.

better judgement'.[116] Russell, although aware of 'the dangers and mischiefs of every course other than a Coburg marriage', advised against its open espousal. He thought the British government could only point out 'the advantages of the marriage with Don Enrique'. To champion Coburg would be too drastic a change of policy. It would go 'beyond the line of the late Government' and would arouse the inevitable opposition of Louis Philippe; and 'we shall then be asked for support against the ill humour of France'. However, his reply ended on an ambiguous note: 'It may be as well to refer Bulwer to Lord Aberdeen's note to M. Sotomayor as the ground on which we stand.'[117] (In this note Aberdeen had declared that the Spanish government had perfect freedom to choose whom they thought best for the Queen and for Spain.) Palmerston accepted Russell's views, and sent a redrafted despatch to Windsor for the Queen's approval.[118] He did so, however, with misgivings, fearing 'that Christina if hopelessly thwarted as to the Coburg marriage may turn round suddenly and in a pet adopt Cadiz for the Queen and Montpensier for the Infanta'.[119] Having rejected the possibility of a complete change from Enrique to Coburg, Palmerston decided on 23 August to answer officially the French proposal of 21 July for joint action in favour of one of the sons of Don Francisco de Paula. Normanby was instructed to inform Guizot that: 'the British government favoured Enrique, but there was no ground on which to object to Coburg and...[we] could object only to a French Prince'.[120] To Bulwer Palmerston wrote that the recommendation could not be joint 'because we must not place ourselves upon the same footing of authoritative dictation' as France.[121] Jarnac, when informed of Palmerston's reply, gave his opinion that 'the King and his Government will rejoice too much at the renewed prospect of acting with you in complete concert in our Spanish diffi-

[116] Palmerston to Russell, 22 Aug. 1846. Russell Papers, P.R.O. 30/22/5B.
[117] Russell to Palmerston, 23 Aug. 1846. B.P. GC/RU/108.
[118] 'I conclude that whatever we write to Bulwer on this must go down to the Queen before it is sent off.' Palmerston to Russell, 22 Aug. 1846. Russell Papers, P.R.O. 30/22/5B. The Queen did not return the despatches until 25 Aug. Palmerston to Russell, 25 Aug. 1846. Russell Papers, P.R.O. 30/22/5B.
[119] Palmerston to Russell, 23 Aug. 1846. B.P. GC/RU/985.
[120] Palmerston to Normanby, 25 Aug. 1846. Normanby Papers, Box P, bundle 19.
[121] Palmerston to Bulwer, 22 Aug. 1846. B.P. GC/BU/512.

culties...'¹²² As far as the French were concerned, there was no change in British policy on the marriage question. In his three despatches of 25 August to Bulwer, however, Palmerston significantly shifted his ground. In the first he came out clearly in favour of Don Enrique; the second opposed the marriage of Montpensier and the Infanta; the third stated that: 'H.M.'s Govt. see no reason to depart from the doctrines laid down in Lord Aberdeen's confidential note to the Duke of Sotomayor of the 22nd of June last.'¹²³ The substance of Palmerston's revised instructions was that, although the British government still preferred Enrique, they were prepared (as Russell wrote) to make 'the best of a situation we did not produce';¹²⁴ if the Court remained determined to support Leopold in spite of the hazards, and to present 'that match to the Coburg family as the unanimous wish of the Court, the Govt., the Cortes and the nation',¹²⁵ the British government would not oppose it. This revision represented no fundamental change; indeed, it reflected the consistency of Palmerston's aims. He favoured Enrique not only because of his political connections with the Progresistas but also as a means of preventing the marriage of Montpensier and the Infanta, thus frustrating both present and future French influence. When this proved impracticable Palmerston had to weigh his priorities more carefully. He thought that it was in British interests to concentrate on preventing the Montpensier marriage. To Normanby he admitted that: 'I own I think it more important to prevent that marriage than to carry any particular marriage for Isabella.'¹²⁶ However, the British government did not feel able openly to espouse the Coburg candidature. The Coburgs themselves did not want a marriage if it caused a rupture with France, and Russell did not feel that his government could go back on Aberdeen's promise that Great Britain would not actively support the Coburg match.¹²⁷ All Palmerston could say, therefore, was that the British govern-

---

¹²² Jarnac to Palmerston, 27 Aug. 1846. G.P. 42/AP/69.
¹²³ Palmerston to Bulwer, 25 Aug. 1846. F.O. 72/694, nos. 21, 22 and 23.
¹²⁴ Russell to Palmerston, 23 Aug. 1846. B.P. GC/RU/108.
¹²⁵ Palmerston to Bulwer, 22 Aug. 1846. B.P. GC/BU/512.
¹²⁶ Palmerston to Normanby, 25 Aug. 1846. Normanby Papers, Box P, bundle 19.
¹²⁷ Russell to Palmerston, 23 Aug. 1846. B.P. GC/RU/108. Palmerston thought differently: 'You may say in reply to Guizot's assertions of a sort of agreement by

ment would not oppose a Coburg match. He may have hoped that his despatches of 25 August would afford Bulwer and Christina an opening to revive the Coburg negotiations, and that fresh initiatives might lead Russell to reconsider the question. This seems likely in view of the fact that neither Palmerston nor Russell expected an immediate solution to the marriage question.[128] Palmerston's despatches of the 25th, throwing the initiative back on Christina and Bulwer, arrived in Paris on 27 August. Hervey sent them on by the overland route to Bulwer, fearing that 'they will arrive rather late'.[129] His fears were well grounded; the question had already been settled.

By 22 August Queen Isabella's continued refusal to marry Cadiz was the sole obstacle to the formal conclusion of the provisional agreement drawn up by Bresson and approved by Queen Christina. Bresson told Isturiz that Bulwer had sent a courier to London to inform Palmerston of the Franco-Spanish negotiations; this made an immediate settlement essential, before Bulwer had time to whip up opposition.[130] Guizot was also counselling a speedy conclusion. He urged Bresson to assure the Spanish government that, whatever protests and opposition came from London, 'nous soutiendrons ce que l'Espagne aura fait de concert avec nous'.[131] On 23 August Bresson told Rianzares that 'chaque heure perdue est irréparable'.[132] At the same time he tried to impel the Spanish government into action by handing them further and more alarming French police reports on the activities of the Progresista exiles.[133] Nevertheless,

Aberdeen to prevent Coburg, that no trace of any such agreement appears in any records of my office, where on the contrary I find opinions hardly consistent with such an agreement, and that I certainly heard nothing to that effect from Aberdeen when he explained to me verbally the state of our affairs in different parts of the world. That which stands on record is that Coburg is not an English candidate, and that the Queen of Spain has a full right to choose him if she likes. But be all this as it may, no such agreement made by Aberdeen can be binding on us, and we cannot adopt it.' Palmerston to Normanby, 25 Aug. 1846. Normanby Papers, Box P, bundle 19.

[128] Palmerston to Bulwer, 22 Aug. 1846. B.P. GC/BU/512; Russell to the Queen, 24 Aug. 1846. R.A. J/44/30.
[129] Hervey to Bulwer, 27 Aug. 1846. Bulwer Papers, S/26.
[130] Bresson to Guizot, 22 Aug. 1846. G.P. 42/AP/65.
[131] Guizot to Bresson, 22 and 23 Aug. 1846. G.P. 42/AP/8.
[132] Bresson to Rianzares, 23 Aug. 1846. G.P. 42/AP/65.
[133] Bresson to Guizot, 23 Aug. 1846. A.A.E.C.P. Espagne 828.

Bresson was optimistic; the Queen had shown no signs of invincible repugnance to Cadiz, and he felt therefore that her acceptance could not be long delayed. Meanwhile in Paris, while the French government anxiously awaited news from Madrid, Normanby presented his letters of credence to Louis Philippe on 24 August. The King assured him that he would be treated as an 'ambassadeur de famille',[134] and on the same day wrote to Queen Victoria that he would always make great efforts 'pour la continuation de l'accord si heureusement établi entre nos deux Gouvernements'.[135]

For two days there was little progress at Madrid, and Bresson even feared setbacks. The Queen remained unwilling to marry her cousin,[136] and Isturiz was alarmed at the prospect of Palmerston's opposition to the Montpensier marriage.[137] Bresson began to panic, and he increased the pressure on Christina and Rianzares to induce the Queen to accept Cadiz, no easy assignment, he admitted, as she was a true daughter of Ferdinand VII.[138] On the night of 27 August Queen Isabella finally consented to marry Cadiz. Within minutes Bresson formally asked for the hand of the Infanta for the Duke of Montpensier, and a contract which officially associated the marriages without stipulating that they should be celebrated simultaneously, was signed the next day.[139] On 29 August Bulwer wrote to inform Palmerston of the arrangement of the two marriages: 'I know no case which more justifies an armed struggle for Spanish independence, than that which the French Government have now contrived to bring about.'[140] Bulwer was convinced that Palmerston would agree with him, and that the British government would meet the French actions with determined resistance.[141] Guizot, however, thought differently: 'Le Cabinet Anglais n'ira pas loin dans son humeur.'[142]

[134] Normanby to Palmerston, 24 Aug. 1846. Normanby Papers, Box P, bundle 12.
[135] Louis Philippe to Queen Victoria, 24 Aug. 1846. R.A. Y/48/68.
[136] Bresson to Guizot, 26 Aug. 1846. G.P. 42/AP/65.
[137] Bresson to Guizot, 25 Aug. 1846. G.P. 42/AP/65.
[138] Bresson to Guizot, 27 Aug. 1846. G.P. 42/AP/65.
[139] Bresson to Guizot, 28 Aug. 1846. G.P. 42/AP/65.
[140] Bulwer to Palmerston, 29 Aug. 1846. F.O. 72/698.
[141] Bulwer to Clarendon, 30 Aug. 1846. Clar. Dep. C525.
[142] Guizot to Bresson, 22 Aug. 1846. G.P. 42/AP/8.

CHAPTER V

The First Reaction, September–October 1846

On 31 August 1846 Palmerston left London to act as minister in attendance on the Queen during her yachting holiday off the west of England, instructing Addington, the Permanent Under Secretary at the Foreign Office, to go to Russell 'if anything should occur to require speedy decision'.[1] Palmerston also granted Normanby permission to spend a fortnight out of Paris. The prevention of the marriage of the Duke of Montpensier and the Infanta Luisa was the only important matter to be dealt with, wrote Palmerston, but 'the time is not yet come for broaching that subject'.[2] He remained confident that his plans would come to maturity. Unknown to him, however, Guizot was enjoying the first flush of his triumph.

Guizot and Bresson greeted with relief, astonishment and pleasure Queen Christina's agreement to the marriages of Queen Isabella to the Duke of Cadiz and of the Infanta Luisa to the Duke of Montpensier. They were relieved that they had defeated Palmerston's attempt to use the marriage question to overthrow French influence at Madrid, astonished that Christina's continual evasion and duplicity had ended in her consent, and pleased that their resolution and willingness to take risks had been rewarded. Both Guizot and Bresson regarded the arrangement of the marriages as a great personal triumph. Bresson believed his tactical skill to have been primarily responsible for the French success, and Guizot regarded the negotiations at Madrid towards the end of August as a triumph for the unity and direction he had given to French foreign policy; the King had followed his lead and Bresson had executed his instructions.

[1] Palmerston to Russell, 30 Aug. 1846. B.P. GC/RU/986.
[2] Palmerston to Normanby, 31 Aug. 1846. Normanby Papers, Box P, bundle 19.

For Guizot the triumph in Spain was well timed; he believed that, combined with his recent electoral victory,[3] it would give him a commanding position when the new session of the Chambers opened. The depleted opposition would be hard pressed to make a convincing case against his foreign policy, and would undoubtedly have to abandon the charge of subservience to England. Although Guizot expected the arrangement of the marriages to strengthen him at home, he did not anticipate any great or permanent changes abroad. As far as Spain was concerned, he regarded the position as unaltered: French influence had been safeguarded rather than extended. He hoped that his vigorous defence of French interests would have convinced the British government that his government regarded predominance at Madrid as vital to French prestige. Russell and the majority of the Whig cabinet, if not Palmerston, would be forced to realise that any attempt by Britain to undermine French predominance at Madrid would inevitably have adverse effects on Anglo-French relations. Guizot hoped that Palmerston's colleagues would compel him to respect French interests and to treat her as an equal. Initially Guizot expected that Palmerston would fulminate against French ambition and duplicity, but he anticipated indifference from the English public and strong opposition to any diplomatic offensive from Palmerston's cabinet colleagues. He therefore expected no real breach, only a short period of coolness.

Guizot knew that the way in which he broke the news of the arrangement of the marriages would be of great importance. If he claimed it as a French triumph Palmerston would be able to exaggerate English indignation. He therefore began by underplaying the significance of the marriages. The *Journal des Débats*, Guizot's unofficial organ and the first newspaper to carry news of the marriages, stressed the fact that the Queen of Spain was to marry a Spanish prince, and described the Montpensier match as a family arrangement.[4] Guizot next informed the British ambassador, Normanby, of the conclusion of the

---

[3] The opposition parties lost forty-nine seats to the Conservative party. Guizot expected to have a majority of about a hundred in the new Chambers. Guizot to Princess Lieven, 7 Aug. 1846. *Guizot–Lieven*, iii, 244–5.

[4] *Journal des Débats*, 1 Sept. 1846.

negotiations.⁵ It was during this interview with Normanby on 1 September 1846 that Guizot first encountered the difficulty of publicly defending his conduct. He did not feel able to avow openly the real motive behind his decision to seek a unilateral solution to the question of the Spanish marriages—the preservation of French predominance at Madrid. This would alienate the sympathy he hoped to gain in England. Moreover, justification of his conduct on these grounds would represent the Spanish government as the tool of France, thus confirming all the accusations of Bulwer and the Spanish opposition against the Moderado régime. Guizot therefore needed a spurious justification of his conduct for public consumption, and he turned to the memorandum of 27 February 1846 which Sainte Aulaire had read to Aberdeen.⁶ In this memorandum the French government had asserted that it would resume full liberty of action if the British government were to propose Prince Leopold of Coburg as a candidate for the Queen of Spain's hand. In his interview with Normanby Guizot alleged that, in his despatch of 19 July 1846 to Bulwer, Palmerston had championed Prince Leopold. Guizot's case was a weak one. Aberdeen had never formally accepted the February memorandum, although he had not categorically rejected it. There was no copy of it in the Foreign Office, and Palmerston was totally ignorant of its existence. The position of the memorandum was very irregular.

Even had the memorandum been known to and accepted by Palmerston, Guizot's case would still have been bad. In his despatch of 19 July Palmerston had mentioned Prince Leopold only as one of the candidates, and as a fact for which the Spanish government and not he was responsible. Far from naming Prince Leopold as the British candidate, Palmerston had even stated the objections to his candidature. Moreover, after 19 July Palmerston had not only given specific assurances to Jarnac that the British government did not support the Prince of Coburg,⁷ but had also come out explicitly in favour of the Duke of Seville. This was, however, the only case Guizot

---

⁵ Normanby to Palmerston, 1 Sept. 1846. B.P. GC/NO/19.
⁶ See Chapter IV above, pp. 88–9.
⁷ For example on 13 Aug. 1846. Jarnac to Guizot, 13 Aug. 1846. G.P. 42/AP/69.

could devise with even a semblance of plausibility, and he had to make the best of it. He further justified his actions by reference to the unreasonable delay of over a month before Palmerston had replied to his offer of co-operation in favour of one of the sons of Don Francisco de Paula. Guizot's interview with Normanby was a difficult one. He was disconcerted by the ease with which Normanby refuted the arguments he advanced for the first time to defend his conduct.[8] Moreover, the negotiations with the Spanish government were not yet complete: Guizot and Louis Philippe had still not agreed to the Spanish demand for the simultaneous celebration of the marriages in October. In reply to Normanby's question when the Montpensier marriage would take place, Guizot replied that it would be celebrated after the Queen's marriage. This was later construed as a deliberate deception, and Palmerston exploited it skilfully to discredit Guizot.[9] Normanby concluded the interview by predicting that the French action at Madrid would 'excite very unpleasant feelings' in England; Guizot replied that 'he trusted nothing that would last'.[10]

Guizot was not unduly perturbed by Normanby's hostile reaction to the news of the arrangement of the marriages; he did not regard Normanby's attitude as particularly important. He was waiting for the reaction of Queen Victoria, Russell and the British press, confident of their sympathy. He instructed Jarnac to inform Russell that the Montpensier match was 'une affaire de famille', and to state that it was Palmerston's advocacy of the Coburg candidate that had precipitated unilateral French action.[11] Russell was dismayed: he thought the news convincing proof of what Palmerston had always argued, that 'no promise of the French Court is binding'. Until he had consulted Palmerston, however, he was not prepared to commit himself or to discuss the matter with the French government. He advised Normanby to be 'as reserved and cautious as possible till you

[8] Normanby to Palmerston, 1 Sept. 1846. B.P. GC/NO/19.
[9] Palmerston thought it 'unrivalled as a quibble. There is not a blackleg on the turf who would not be ashamed of such equivocation; perhaps a second rate country horse dealer might think it allowable.' Palmerston to Clarendon, 28 Sept. 1846. Clar. Dep. C524.
[10] Normanby to Palmerston, 1 Sept. 1846. F.O. 27/754.
[11] Guizot to Jarnac, 1 Sept. 1846. G.P. 42/AP/7.

get Palmerston's instructions'.[12] Russell's silence and the absence of the Queen and Palmerston meant that no immediate reaction was forthcoming from the British government. *The Times*, however, recently urged by Greville to adopt a more friendly attitude towards French policy in Spain,[13] assumed that the British government was party to the arrangement of the marriages,[14] and commented favourably on them.[15] Jarnac was elated,[16] and Guizot shared his view that the article in *The Times* was an excellent augury. He immediately informed Bresson that the reaction of London was calm: 'ni le public, ni la Couronne ne prendront feu. Du bruit, de l'humeur, de la froideur, des essais de revanche; rien de plus grave.'[17] Guizot was persuaded by the official silence and the warm approval of *The Times* that there would be even less indignation in England than he had expected. In the first week of September he believed that the matter would be quickly forgotten,[18] and was anxious to promote so favourable a development. The *Journal des Débats* continued to play down the importance of the marriages; it welcomed the impartiality and justice shown by *The Times* and expressed confidence that its view would be shared by most Englishmen.[19]

While Guizot awaited the reaction of Palmerston and Queen Victoria he was committing his government still further in Spain. The agreement signed in Madrid on 28 August had associated the two marriages but stipulated that the Montpensier marriage should take place after that of the Queen and Cadiz. No precise interval was specified but it was generally assumed that it would be several months. Both the French and the Spanish governments were agreed that the Queen's marriage should take place as soon as possible. Immediately the agreement was signed, Queen Christina pressed Bresson to urge his

[12] Russell to Normanby, 2 Sept. 1846. Normanby Papers, Box P, bundle 23.
[13] Greville to Dasent, n.d. [Aug. 1846]. Printing House Square MSS., Delane Correspondence, vol. 2.
[14] Greville to Reeve, 9 Sept. 1846. *The Letters of Charles Greville and Henry Reeve*, ed. A. H. Johnson (London, 1924), 150–1.
[15] *The Times*, 3 Sept. 1846.
[16] Jarnac to Guizot, 3 Sept. 1846. G.P. 42/AP/69.
[17] Guizot to Bresson, 4 Sept. 1846. G.P. 42/AP/8.
[18] Guizot to Flahaut, 5 Sept. 1846. A.A.E.C.P. Autriche 433.
[19] *Journal des Débats*, 5 Sept. 1846.

government to agree that the marriages should be celebrated on the same day and as soon as possible.[20] She assured him that she anticipated no difficulty in gaining the assent of the Cortes, and consequently that no impediments should prevent the immediate completion of the arrangements.[21] Christina's motives were obvious. Although she was never prepared to compromise with opposition either to her rule or to her policies, she greatly feared it. She believed that to delay the Montpensier marriage would favour its opponents—Bulwer and the Progresistas condemned it as soon as it was announced[22]—and give them time to whip up popular enthusiasm against it. She rightly assumed that the opposition would be dispirited and weakened if the marriages took place immediately. Christina also feared that British opposition might undermine French resolve, and that if the Montpensier marriage were delayed it might never take place, leaving her with only the less satisfactory marriage alliance. Bresson supported Christina's demand for an early and simultaneous conclusion of the marriages, and put strong pressure on Guizot.[23] Guizot and Louis Philippe did not long withstand her request; on 4 September they agreed to both marriages taking place on 10 October.[24] Guizot's motives were variants of Christina's. Bresson had already warned him that Bulwer was putting pressure on members of the Spanish government in an attempt to prevent the Montpensier marriage.[25] Guizot feared that any signs of weakness or hesitation on the part of the French government would have disastrous results in Spain. He also believed that the best way to frustrate Palmerston's opposition to the Montpensier marriage would be by leaving no openings which he and Bulwer might exploit. He shared Christina's belief that the sooner the arrangement was accomplished the sooner it would be forgotten. If the marriages were celebrated promptly, and the Infanta and Montpensier lived in Paris, as

[20] Bresson to Guizot, 28 Aug. 1846. G.P. 42/AP/65.
[21] Bresson to Guizot, 29 Aug. 1846. G.P. 42/AP/65.
[22] Bresson to Guizot, 2 Sept. 1846. A.A.E.C.P. Espagne 828. *El Español*, the press organ of the Progresista party, denounced the Montpensier marriage on 31 Aug. Hervey to Palmerston, 7 Sept. 1846. F.O. 27/755.
[23] Bresson to Guizot, 2 Sept. 1846. G.P. 42/AP/65.
[24] Guizot to Bresson, 4 Sept. 1846. G.P. 42/AP/8.
[25] Bresson to Guizot, 2 Sept. 1846. A.A.E.C.P. Espagne 828.

Louis Philippe and Guizot stipulated they should,[26] Palmerston would have no opportunity to claim that the French were attempting to organise a party around either the Infanta or Montpensier at Madrid. Thus when Palmerston and the Queen returned to London, the negotiations at Madrid had advanced to an extent which the French had initially neither desired nor expected. The agreement that the marriages should take place in a month's time and on the same day seriously impaired the chances of a sympathetic reaction in London to the French case even amongst the traditionally pro-French. On 1 September Guizot had informed Normanby that the Montpensier marriage would take place after the Queen's; it was therefore easy for Palmerston to represent French policy as unscrupulous and ambitious, and Guizot as a liar and deliberate deceiver. Whatever credibility Guizot's word had had in England vanished overnight.[27]

Palmerston, like Russell, was dismayed when the news of the arrangement of the marriages reached him through a messenger sent by Russell to Penzance. He wrote to Jarnac stating that if the Montpensier marriage took place it would be a 'very bad augury for the future relations between England and France' and convincing proof that the French government attached no value to the *entente cordiale*.[28] He did not, however, consider the situation sufficiently urgent to require his immediate presence in London, and he continued with the royal yachting party. Even before Palmerston returned to feed their indignation, his cabinet colleagues began their bitter denunciations of Guizot's conduct. Lansdowne informed Russell that he 'knew enough to be certain the French case must be very bad, but its rottenness and duplicity when it comes to be looked at as a whole far exceeds what I expected'.[29] Clarendon was amazed 'at the treachery of Louis Philippe' and asserted that nothing equalled the conduct of Guizot 'since the most insolent days of Napoleon'.[30]

[26] Guizot to Bresson, 22 Aug. 1846. G.P. 42/AP/8.
[27] Hervey informed Palmerston of the agreement to celebrate the marriages on the same day on 4 Sept. The *Journal des Débats* announced on 4 Sept. that the marriages would take place in October. Hervey to Palmerston, 4 Sept. 1846. F.O. 27/754.   [28] Palmerston to Jarnac, 6 Sept. 1846. F.O. 27/764.
[29] Lansdowne to Russell, 7 Sept. 1846. Russell Papers, P.R.O. 30/22/5C.
[30] Clarendon to Russell, 8 Sept. 1846. Russell Papers, P.R.O. 30/22/5C.

Russell's anger increased with reflection; he told Clarendon that he was convinced that the French government had 'been trying to get up a cause of quarrel ever since the Whig government came in'.[31] Outside the cabinet, condemnation of the French was equally strong. Even Edward Ellice thought that Louis Philippe had acted too boldly 'and may yet finish his career in trouble'.[32] On 7 September *The Times*, now aware of the way in which the marriages had been arranged, launched a series of rabidly anti-French leaders, warning the French government that nature had created the Pyrenees as a barrier between France and Spain and 'is apt to avenge any violence done to her laws'.[33] Thus before Palmerston and the Queen returned to London many of those on whom Guizot had counted for a sympathetic reaction had already strongly condemned the conduct of France. The first thing Palmerston did was to exploit this general feeling of indignation.

Palmerston was willing to admit that the situation was in part the result of the shortcomings of the Spanish policy he had pursued in July and August.[34] These had been tactical mistakes, but the fundamental error of the Whig government had been one of assumptions, not tactics. The truth was, he informed Clarendon, that:

the whole Whig party [has] been cowed by France, and [we] have attached an infinitely too great importance to keeping the French Government in good humour, forgetting that their good humour is a means and not an end; and that if we sacrifice permanent interests for the temporary convenience we inflict injury on our country.[35]

[31] Clarendon to Palmerston, 8 Sept. 1846. B.P. GC/CL/457.
[32] Ellice to Russell, 7 Sept. 1846. Russell Papers, P.R.O. 30/22/5C.
[33] *The Times*, 7 Sept. 1846.
[34] The French, wrote Palmerston to Clarendon, 'gained over us the advantage which boldness, decision and promptness must ever have over timidity, wavering and delay. We have been cowed by France and I fear a little bamboozled by some of the Progresistas. The thing came suddenly upon us before we had got fairly into the saddle. It had in some degree been maimed by our predecessors, and it has been spoilt by ourselves, and I include myself fully as sharer in the mistake. But in a complicated matter of this sort it is difficult to take up the game towards the end and play it successfully; one acts at a disadvantage if one is comparatively ignorant of what has gone before, and if at least one has not had the conduct of the preceding transactions.' Palmerston to Clarendon, 10 Sept. 1846. Clar. Dep. C524.
[35] Ibid.

To Russell Palmerston reflected how foolish it was to 'have stood more in awe of France than France has stood in awe of us'.[36] Palmerston certainly derived some satisfaction from the fact that the recent transactions of the French in Spain completely vindicated his low view of French foreign policy. Once again he had been right, his colleagues wrong. He was determined to transform a diplomatic setback into a domestic success, to vindicate his past conduct and to ensure his future freedom of action. To the Queen, whom he perhaps suspected of still entertaining some lingering sympathy for Louis Philippe, Palmerston sent a devastating indictment of Guizot's conduct, emphasising that a reconciliation was impossible if the Montpensier marriage took place. It afforded, he claimed, manifest 'proof of diverging policy, if not of the contemplation of contingent hostility on the part of France'.[37] The Queen shared Palmerston's anger to the full. She considered that Guizot had acted 'very unhandsomely and unfairly',[38] she was astonished at Louis Philippe's duplicity,[39] and she was aggrieved to find her Coburg plans thwarted. Prince Albert was equally indignant that Louis Philippe should stoop so low as 'to dupe a friend',[40] and he admitted to Aberdeen that as a result of the French conduct 'the entente cordiale is virtually buried'.[41]

By the end of the second week of September many of Guizot's expectations concerning the reactions of the English government and public had proved to be vain. Even Aberdeen condemned Guizot's conduct and found no real fault with that of Palmerston.[42] Guizot had expected the bitter and violent polemics of the *Morning Chronicle,* launched after Palmerston's return to London,[43] but he was dismayed when *The Times* joined the attack,[44] and by the universal condemnation of his conduct in

[36] Palmerston to Russell, 10 Sept. 1846. Russell Papers, P.R.O. 30/22/5C.
[37] Palmerston to the Queen, 12 Sept. 1846. R.A. J/44/48.
[38] The Queen to Palmerston, 10 Sept. 1846. B.P. RC/F/271.
[39] The Queen to the King of the Belgians, 14 Sept. 1846. Q.V.L., 1st series, ii, 121–3.
[40] Prince Albert to Peel, 12 Sept. 1846. Peel Papers, B.M. Add. MS. 40441.
[41] Prince Albert to Aberdeen, 9 Sept. 1846. R.A. J/44/42.
[42] Aberdeen to Guizot, 14 Sept. 1846. Aberdeen Papers, B.M. Add. MS. 43134.
[43] *Morning Chronicle,* 12, 13, 14 Sept. 1846.
[44] Guizot to Bresson, 11 Sept. 1846. G.P. 42/AP/8.

London.[45] His hopes of controlling the situation and minimising discussion of the marriages were dashed: 'il y a évidemment à Londres et ici, un travail pour tout grossir et tout enflammer', he complained to Jarnac.[46]

A war between the government and opposition press began in France in the first week of September. Initially the opposition press dismissed the marriages contemptuously as a purely dynastic matter, of no significance to France.[47] The government press retaliated by claiming that the arrangement of the marriages was a triumph for French foreign policy in the tradition of Louis XIV.[48] In rejoinder, influenced by the hostility of *The Times* and the *Morning Chronicle*, the opposition press changed tactics; they began to attack the arrangement of the marriages as a mean act, accomplished at the price of the destruction of the *entente cordiale*, bringing neither advantage to France nor credit to her government.[49] Thiers' paper, *Le Constitutionnel*, made skilful and frequent use of the attacks on Guizot in the English press. The *Journal des Débats* fell back on an appeal to patriotism; it demanded the support of all Frenchmen for the government's bold and triumphant foreign policy, and pointed out that whereas in 1840 Palmerston had defeated Thiers, in 1846 Guizot had outwitted Palmerston.[50] This confirmed the suspicion in London that what Guizot wanted was 'the appearance of a triumph over England, and especially over Lord Palmerston'.[51] Guizot's motives thus appeared as ignoble as his conduct had been deceitful.

Although the almost unanimously hostile reaction to the marriages in London took Guizot unawares, he had expected that Palmerston and Bulwer would try to prevent or delay the Montpensier marriage.[52] The grounds on which the British

---

[45] 'La Reine, tout le monde partage le ressentiment.' Jarnac to Guizot, 11 Sept. 1846. G.P. 42/AP/69.   [46] Guizot to Jarnac, 21 Sept. 1846. G.P. 42/AP/7.
[47] This was the opinion of *Le Constitutionnel*, which supported Thiers and the left centre, and *Le Siècle*, which supported Odilon Barrot and the constitutional left. See *Le Constitutionnel*, 3 and 4 Sept. 1846, and *Le Siècle*, 4 and 5 Sept. 1846. *La Presse*, which followed Molé and the centre right, supported the marriages because they considered them a triumph at the expense of England. *La Presse*, 4 Sept. 1846.
[48] *Journal des Débats*, 10 Sept. 1846.   [49] *Le Constitutionnel*, 12, 13 Sept. 1846.
[50] *Journal des Débats*, 16, 19 Sept. 1846.
[51] Prince Albert to Aberdeen, 9 Sept. 1846. R.A. J/44/42.
[52] Guizot to Jarnac, 10 Sept. 1846. G.P. 42/AP/7.

based their objection to the Montpensier marriage did, however, surprise him. Guizot had at no stage in the negotiations considered with care the effect the Montpensier marriage would have on Franco-Spanish relations apart from the consolidation of French influence at Madrid. Palmerston's attempt to replace French by British influence at Madrid had created an atmosphere of panic in which Guizot had thought solely of the immediate objective, the defence of French interests. He expected others to recognise that his motive was defensive only; he did not expect his policy to be interpreted as an attempt to bring Spain completely under French tutelage. Nor did he expect the succession rights of the Infanta to become a major issue of debate and conflict between England and France. The accusation that the impotence of the Duke of Cadiz[53] was the reason for marrying him to the Queen, and that the French were trying to ensure the eventual succession of the Infanta and Montpensier, must remain unproven.[54] In the first place it was Christina who introduced the matter of Cadiz's impotence at a comparatively late stage in the negotiations. The French sincerely believed that her motive was to provide a loophole should a more attractive candidate present himself.[55] Cadiz was proposed for the Queen not because of his impotence but for his political insignificance. Moreover, his conjectured impotence was no barrier to the Queen having children. The morals of the Spanish Court were lax, and the French had no means of preventing the young Queen from finding consolation elsewhere if

[53] Cadiz was not in fact impotent. 'King Louis Philippe said to Lord Normanby that he had taken pains to ascertain the truth and he found his incapacity not to be incurable, an operation would set all to rights.' Prince Albert to Peel, 12 Sept. 1846. Peel Papers, B.M. Add. MS. 40441.
[54] This was believed by practically every member of the British government and the British diplomatic service. See Palmerston to Bulwer, 27 Sept. 1846. B.P. GC/BU/515. Russell described it as 'an attempt to annexe the Crown of Spain to that of France'. Russell to Normanby, 2 Oct. 1846. Normanby Papers, Box P, bundle 23. Bulwer and Hervey were convinced that the French would do all they could to gain the Crown for the Infanta and Montpensier as soon as possible. Hervey to Reeve, 7 Dec. 1846. Hervey Papers, 941/61/1. Bulwer to Palmerston, 19 Jan. 1847. Bulwer Papers, S/12. The rumours of Cadiz's supposed impotence soon became public. 'What is the state of affairs Louis Philippe is founding at Madrid? In a few years a French Prince...will, it is said, most probably be the husband of the Queen.' *The Times*, 2 Oct. 1846.
[55] Guizot to Bresson, 5 July 1846. G.P. 42/AP/8.

her husband proved unsatisfactory.[56] In their view in September 1846 the question of the succession presented a temporary uncertainty which would naturally solve itself when the Queen had children. The French had, however, cogent reasons for refusing to countenance the renunciation by the Infanta of her rights to the throne. In the first place Guizot and Louis Philippe regarded the maintenance of her succession rights as a matter of prestige:[57] their renunciation would give the impression that the French government had succumbed to British protests and pressure. The French were also aware that Queen Christina had fought a civil war to defend the rights conferred on both her daughters by the will of Ferdinand VII; even to appease the wrath of Lord Palmerston she would never voluntarily renounce half of what she had fought for. Moreover, if the Infanta were removed from the line of succession the French position at Madrid would be weakened: it would be construed by the Spanish government as revealing a lack of courage, and would give the British an opportunity to create a rival court party around the family of Don Francisco de Paula who followed the Infanta in the line of succession.[58] The objections to renunciation were strong and the problems it would raise greater than those it would solve; to Guizot the very suggestion was frivolous.[59]

From the moment the arrangement of the marriages was announced, Bulwer had assumed that Palmerston would want to prevent, or at least to delay, the Montpensier marriage.[60] He received no instructions whatever for over a fortnight after the announcement,[61] but nevertheless began immediately to foment

[56] The Queen Mother had for years carried on a disreputable private life, and even at sixteen Queen Isabella had a roving eye. Bulwer thought that as the Queen was being forced to marry a man she detested, it was inevitable 'that her Court will soon present a series of scandalous and discreditable intrigues'. Bulwer to Palmerston, 30 Aug. 1846. B.P. GC/BU/263.
[57] Guizot to Bresson, 8 Sept. 1846. G.P. 42/AP/8.
[58] The order of succession was established by the constitution of 1837, and confirmed in the new constitution of 1845 which excluded Don Carlos and his descendants from the line of succession. See Palmerston to Normanby, 22 Sept. 1846, F.O. 27/746, for a full discussion of acts and laws governing the succession to the Spanish Crown.
[59] Guizot to Bresson, 8 Sept. 1846. G.P. 42/AP/8; Bresson to Guizot, 2 Sept. 1846. A.A.E.C.P. Espagne 828.
[60] Bulwer to Palmerston, 30 Aug. 1846. B.P. GC/BU/263.
[61] Palmerston's first instructions to Bulwer and Hervey left London on 14 Sept.

and organise opposition to the marriages within Spain, justifying himself on the grounds that the task could not be left to the Progresistas alone 'since these people want courage if they are not backed by a foreign power of importance'.[62] Bulwer's first object was to persuade the Progresistas to come out strongly against the French marriage. This was easy: the Progresistas were prepared to condemn anything resembling subservience to France, and the Progresista press was willing to accept any secret service money which Bulwer could dispense. The day following the announcement of the marriages brought bitter denunciations of the Montpensier marriage by the two opposition papers published in Madrid, the *Español* and the *Clamor Publico*, which both voiced the hope that the Infanta would still marry a Spanish prince.[63] Bulwer's next aim was to broaden the basis of the opposition, to unite Progresistas and liberal Moderados in a national, rather than a party, outcry against the Montpensier marriage.[64] He hoped that widespread opposition to the marriage in Spain would force the Spanish government to have second thoughts. Constitutional opposition within Spain, however, would not be sufficient. Bulwer thought the situation serious and urgent enough to justify a direct assault on the Spanish government. On 31 August he wrote a strong letter of protest to Isturiz, the Spanish Prime Minister, stressing the injurious effect the Montpensier marriage would inevitably have on relations between England and Spain.[65] On the same day he wrote to Rianzares urging him to use his influence over Queen Christina to postpone the Montpensier marriage until Queen Isabella had children.[66] To Clarendon, Bulwer wrote that he would engage the Spanish government 'in a correspondence which shall be as terrifying and as little compromising as

Hervey complained bitterly of the absence of instructions, Hervey to Bulwer, 13 Sept. 1846. Bulwer Papers, S/26. Bulwer informed Palmerston that he must have instructions before the Cortes met to discuss the marriages on 14 Sept. Bulwer to Palmerston, 2 Sept. 1846. F.O. 72/699. Russell rebuked Palmerston on 13 Sept. for having 'delayed rather too long in sending a messenger to Bulwer'. Russell to Palmerston, 13 Sept. 1846. B.P. GC/RU/111.

[62] Bulwer to Palmerston, 30 Aug. 1846. B.P. GC/BU/264.
[63] Bulwer to Palmerston, 2 Sept. 1846. F.O. 72/699.
[64] Bulwer to Palmerston, 30 Aug. 1846. B.P. GC/BU/264.
[65] Bulwer to Isturiz, 31 Aug. 1846. Copy, F.O. 72/699.
[66] Bulwer to Rianzares, 31 Aug. 1846. Copy, B.P. GC/BU/266/4.

possible... This keeps up the spirit of our folks, damps theirs and may possibly introduce division into the Government itself.'[67] To reinforce his own protests, Bulwer urged Palmerston to send strong remonstrances to the French and Spanish governments,[68] and to ensure that the British press should express unabated indignation about the Montpensier marriage.[69] Everything must be done, wrote Bulwer, to weaken the resolve of the Spanish government and to rally sufficient opposition to induce the Cortes to reject the marriages.[70] If the Spanish government did not yield to pressure within Spain and from England and withdraw its consent to the marriage, there were constitutional and legal impediments that could be advanced.

The Infanta, as heiress presumptive, had to secure the consent of the Cortes to her marriage.[71] Bulwer claimed that it was possible to buy votes in the Cortes;[72] if this was impracticable, objections could be raised to the Infanta marrying a prince of the House of Orleans since in 1713 the Duke of Orleans, grandson of Louis XIV, had renounced for himself and his heirs their succession rights to the throne of Spain. The Spanish constitutions of 1837 and 1845 forbade those in line to the throne to marry anyone excluded from the succession.[73] The Progresista press had already begun to raise objections based on the provisions of the Treaty of Utrecht,[74] and Bulwer hoped that if

[67] Bulwer to Clarendon, 6 Sept. 1846. Clar. Dep. C525.
[68] Bulwer to Palmerston, 2 Sept. 1846. F.O. 72/699.
[69] Bulwer to Palmerston, 2 Sept. 1846. B.P. GC/BU/265.
[70] Bulwer to Clarendon, 6 Sept. 1846. Clar. Dep. C525.
[71] Article 47 of the constitution of 1845 stated: 'The King, before he contracts a marriage, shall apprize the Cortes of his intention, and submit to their approbation the stipulations and matrimonial contracts which must be the subject of a law. The same shall be observed with regard to the marriage of the immediate successor to the Crown. Neither the King nor the next heir to the throne can marry a person which, by the law, is excluded from the succession to the Crown.' Enclosure, Bulwer to Palmerston, 2 Sept. 1846. B.P. GC/BU/268.
[72] Bulwer to Palmerston, 9 Sept. 1846. F.O. 72/699.
[73] As soon as this objection was raised the Spanish government claimed that article 47 of the 1845 constitution only prevented the Queen and the Infanta from marrying Carlist princes and not Orleanist princes. Hervey to Clarendon, 7 Sept. 1846. Clar. Dep. C529.
[74] The *Clamor Publico* and the *Español* first raised these objections on 31 Aug. 1846. Within a week *The Times* supported this case and the French press began to argue against it. *The Times*, 7 Sept. 1846. *La Presse*, 6 Sept. 1846. Hervey sent extracts from the Spanish and French press on this question to Palmerston. Hervey to Palmerston, 7 Sept. 1846. F.O. 27/755.

the British government raised similar objections and impressed them upon as many members of the Cortes as possible, they might become a decisive factor in preventing the marriage.[75] Apart from these legitimate and constitutional ways of exerting pressure, there was only one other way to stop the Montpensier marriage—'resistance by open force'—which many Progresistas favoured.[76] At first Bulwer favoured constitutional resistance, but his enthusiasm for it faded as its chances of success became more remote. On 6 September he wrote to Palmerston:

> The Cortes...is composed of persons so easily influenced by illegitimate means that no reliance is to be placed upon it; and if matters are decided by its vote, we shall possibly get the worst of it. It is well therefore to look out for every chance, and though I am no insurrectionist I would prefer an insurrection with its many but short evils, to foreign domination with its perpetual ones.[77]

Bulwer appealed to Clarendon to exert in favour of resistance 'by all and every means' the influence over his cabinet colleagues which his specialised knowledge of Spanish affairs gave him. If sufficient money and energy were devoted to the task, Bulwer assured Clarendon that a revolution could be well under way 'by this time next week'.[78]

The Progresista exiles also favoured a revolution. Olozaga told Hervey that a localised revolt in Madrid would be sufficient 'to compel the Court to abandon their iniquitous schemes',[79] and Espartero asked Clarendon to urge the British government to support any violent action undertaken by the Progresistas.[80] In the absence of instructions from London, however, even Bulwer had doubts about committing his government to support for violent resistance. In any case, the chances of a successful revolution were small; the Moderado régime was better at organising repression than the Progresistas were at organising revolution. The Spanish government immediately took measures to forestall insurrection,[81] and the Moderado press, reinforced

[75] Bulwer to Palmerston, 2 Sept. 1846. B.P. GC/BU/268.
[76] Bulwer to Palmerston, 2 Sept. 1846. F.O. 72/699.
[77] Bulwer to Palmerston, 6 Sept. 1846. B.P. GC/BU/269.
[78] Bulwer to Clarendon, 6 Sept. 1846. Clar. Dep. C525.
[79] Hervey to Clarendon, 4 Sept. 1846. Clar. Dep. C529.
[80] Clarendon to Russell, 8 Sept. 1846. Russell Papers, P.R.O. 30/22/5C.
[81] Bresson to Guizot, 6 Sept. 1846. G.P. 42/AP/65.

by French secret service money,[82] began to issue powerful counterblasts to the Progresista opposition to the Montpensier marriage.[83] Bulwer himself admitted that at least £100,000 would be needed to launch a revolution,[84] and that it would inevitably fail if it did not attract the support of some Moderado generals and their troops.[85] Revolution was therefore never a practical possibility; the fact that the Progresistas and Bulwer contemplated it only reveals the ineffectiveness of constitutional opposition and the hopelessness of their position. Although he talked and wrote of revolution, Bulwer had to rely on legitimate opposition which he knew was certain to fail. Nevertheless he did not relax his efforts: 'energy here', he informed Clarendon, 'shall not be wanting'.[86] He continued to dispense secret service money to the Spanish press, and he redoubled his efforts to unite Progresista and Moderado opposition to the marriage. He even tried to secure the support of the Duke of Cadiz, and to persuade him and his father that a marriage between the Infanta and Don Enrique could still be arranged if the Montpensier marriage could be stopped.[87] Soon, however, Bulwer began tacitly to admit failure. He complained bitterly that the favourable tone of the early articles in *The Times* had convinced the Spaniards that England would not seriously oppose the Montpensier

[82] Bresson to Guizot, 7 Sept. 1846. G.P. 42/AP/65.

[83] By 19 Sept. Louis Philippe thought their success complete. Louis Philippe to Guizot, 19 Sept. 1846. G.P. 42/AP/286. On 29 Sept. Decazes informed Guizot that the Spanish opposition was completely disheartened: 'il est certain que, sans les articles des journaux anglais, et sans l'appui de M. Bulwer, la coterie serait déjà réduite au silence'. Decazes to Guizot, 29 Sept. 1846. A.A.E.C.P. Espagne 828.

[84] Bulwer thought, however, that disturbances at Madrid could be organised for as little as £5,000. Bulwer to Palmerston, 2 Sept. 1846. B.P. GC/BU/265. It was not just a question of money. 'What we want are two things, money, and that that money should be properly spent. This is necessary not only to put things in motion but when in motion to keep them from running into confusion. The money got, and you must help to get it, should be placed under the control of a small committee, and the object of its expenditure should be clearly defined, so that it should take place in favour of our great attempt, and not be dribbled away in small and petty ones.' Bulwer to Clarendon, 6 Sept. 1846. Clar. Dep. C525.

[85] 'If an insurrection is attempted...nothing should be done to give it the effect of a purely Progresista movement.' Bulwer to Palmerston, 30 Aug. 1846. B.P. GC/BU/264.

[86] Bulwer to Clarendon, 6 Sept. 1846. Clar. Dep. C525.

[87] Bulwer to Palmerston, 30 Aug. 1846. B.P. GC/BU/263; Bulwer to Palmerston 9 Sept. 1846. F.O. 72/699.

marriage. By 9 September Bulwer had come to place his hopes of preventing or delaying the marriage on the effect a strong and immediate protest from Palmerston would have on the Spanish and French governments. For the first time Bulwer admitted to Palmerston that he thought there would be a majority in the Cortes in favour of the marriage.[88] As far as Bulwer was concerned, the situation was desperate; everything therefore depended on swift and decisive action by Palmerston.

In early September 1846 Palmerston believed that the arrangement of the Montpensier marriage was only tentative, and that as a consequence there was a good chance of either preventing or delaying it until Queen Isabella had a child. To Russell he wrote on 3 September: 'Guizot is trying a little diplomacy upon us and wants to see whether a supposed fait accompli will not go down better than an announced intention.'[89] Even when the date of the two marriages was announced Palmerston hoped that skilful and determined opposition from the British government would force the French and Spanish governments to retreat. 'While there is life there is hope,' wrote Palmerston to Russell, 'and till the marriage is actually solemnised we ought not to relax our efforts to prevent it.'[90] It was characteristic of Palmerston that he was not prepared to concede defeat until the very last minute.

Palmerston had a number of reasons for wishing to prevent the Montpensier marriage, not least his desire to deprive Guizot of a triumph at his expense. What Palmerston wanted was a triumph at Guizot's expense; this was what he would have had if Don Enrique had married the Queen, and the prevention of the Montpensier marriage would achieve the same result. It would damage Guizot's reputation in France and French prestige in Europe. Guizot was therefore not mistaken in detecting an element of *amour-propre* in the campaign waged by Palmerston against the Montpensier marriage.[91] Palmerston also realised that if the Montpensier marriage took place his own Spanish policy would suffer a grave setback. It would be

---

[88] Bulwer to Palmerston, 9 Sept. 1846. B.P. GC/BU/270.
[89] Palmerston to Russell, 3 Sept. 1846. Russell Papers, P.R.O. 30/22/5C.
[90] Palmerston to Russell, 10 Sept. 1846. Russell Papers, P.R.O. 30/22/5C.
[91] Guizot to Jarnac, 17 Sept. 1846. G.P. 42/AP/7.

far more difficult to restore the Progresistas to power and to reduce French influence at Madrid with a French prince married to the heiress presumptive to the Spanish throne. Important as these considerations were, Palmerston could not acknowledge them openly or base his attempt to prevent the Montpensier marriage on them; he needed a case against the marriage that was both convincing and suitable for public consumption. His first reaction was to resort to the cry of broken engagements, accusing the French of having wilfully disregarded the agreement made with Queen Victoria and Aberdeen at the Château d'Eu in 1845 not to marry Montpensier to the Infanta until Queen Isabella had children. Palmerston could easily demonstrate that he had not departed from the letter of Aberdeen's policy, and that he had faithfully adhered to the Bourbon principle laid down by France. Although in England this was a powerful argument which enabled Palmerston to discredit Guizot and Louis Philippe, it was of no use in preventing the Montpensier marriage as Guizot clung tenaciously to the argument that Palmerston's conduct released him from his promise to Aberdeen and he was unlikely to admit the charge of misconduct. Moreover, the debate on *procédés*, as Guizot called it, restricted the question to the English and French governments, whereas Palmerston decided as a matter of tactics to make opposition to the marriage as widespread as possible; he not only expected support from within Spain,[92] but also hoped to secure active opposition from the northern Courts.[93] If the prevention of the marriage was to be made into a Spanish and European question, then Spanish and European objections had to be raised against it.

Palmerston relied at first on his own ingenuity in devising a case against the marriage. In the first protest which he sent to Bulwer for presentation to the Spanish government, Palmerston contended that the projected marriage was 'a political measure of the highest importance; seriously affecting the balance of power in Europe; deeply concerning the interests of other states; and against which the Governments of those countries whose interests would be thus prejudiced, would have an

[92] Palmerston to Clarendon, 10 Sept. 1846. Clar. Dep. C524.
[93] Palmerston to Russell, 10 Sept. 1846. Russell Papers, P.R.O. 30/22/5C.

indisputable right of urging the strongest remonstrance'. The marriage would tend 'to place the political independence of Spain in a danger, perhaps as great as any with which in former periods it has been threatened by the open force of arms'.[94]

Palmerston hoped to rally many Spaniards to the cry that the independence of Spain was in jeopardy, and he expected that the eastern powers would view with dismay a marriage likely to upset the European balance of power. He used the same arguments in conversations with Jarnac and Dumon, the French Minister of Public Works who visited England in mid-September,[95] holding out the prospect of a diplomatic revolution, perhaps even of war, should the Montpensier marriage take place. England would be forced in this contingency to 'seek alliances and intimacy with foreign powers...calculated with the view of obtaining for Great Britain a counter balance for the accession of political, military and naval strength which is the evident object of this projected marriage to secure to France on the side of Spain'.[96] Palmerston warned them that French persistence in the marriage and the attempt to subjugate Spain to France would arouse national resistance in Spain; and if British assistance were called for, there would be 'another Peninsular War'.[97] The warning was clear: if France persisted in her attempt to upset the balance of power, she would soon find the balance of power turned against her.

Palmerston returned to London on 10 September, and on 14

[94] Draft of note to be presented by Bulwer to the Spanish government. Enclosure, Palmerston to Bulwer, 14 Sept. 1846. *Accounts and Papers, 1847*, lxix, 276–8.

[95] Palmerston invited Dumon and Jarnac to Broadlands to discuss the Montpensier marriage and the effect it would have on Anglo-French relations. Palmerston to Jarnac, 13 Sept. 1846. Copy, R.A. J/44/55. Before going to Broadlands Dumon was the guest of Clarendon, who was requested by Palmerston to employ strong language in his conversations with Dumon. Clarendon to Russell, 12 Sept. 1846. Russell Papers, P.R.O. 30/22/5C.

[96] Palmerston gave the Queen a long account of his first interview with Jarnac on 11 Sept. Palmerston to the Queen, 12 Sept. 1846. B.P. RC/FF/6. Jarnac's account to Guizot of this conversation is much shorter and much less explicit. Jarnac to Guizot, 13 Sept. 1846. G.P. 42/AP/69. Palmerston informed Russell that he had had a friendly conversation with Jarnac, and had spoken in a 'high tone, not of menace but of displeasure, with a strong anticipation of the grave though undefined effects which it [the marriage] must have on the relations between the two countries'. Palmerston to Russell, 12 Sept. 1846. Russell Papers, P.R.O. 30/22/5C.

[97] Palmerston to the Queen, 12 Sept. 1846. B.P. RC/FF/6.

September the first protest for Bulwer to deliver to the Spanish government was despatched. The protest and the accompanying instructions were of little comfort to Bulwer. Russell and the Queen[98] had both rejected Bulwer's suggestion that he be upgraded to the rank of ambassador to be on a par with Bresson and to entitle him to claim direct access to the Queen,[99] although initially it had Palmerston's support; both recoiled from the prospect of a diplomatic *guerre à l'outrance* between Bulwer and Bresson. Bulwer's request that almost unlimited sums of secret service money be put at his disposal was also rejected by Russell,[100] who made it quite clear to Palmerston that Bulwer must be instructed not to encourage or participate in any projected insurrection.[101] Palmerston was not completely faithful to Russell's ruling: he instructed Bulwer to 'take good care not to be mixed up with any schemes for insurrection' but advised him that:

you need not interfere to overrule those who from knowledge of their own may think that they will obtain sufficient national support to make any attempt of this kind worth risking...You may do anything you can to excite a flame against France. We are entirely freed from all delicacy on this score.[102]

The ambiguity of Palmerston's instructions afforded Bulwer little real assistance; as he had pointed out, it was not the will to insurrection that was lacking, but money and direction, neither of which he was permitted to give.

On the same day as Palmerston sent off his protest, which would take almost a week to reach Bulwer, the Cortes met in Madrid and consented by a substantial majority to both marriages. Bulwer and *The Times* dismissed the result as the vote of a packed and servile assembly,[103] Guizot and the *Journal des Débats* regarded it as the true reflection of the will of

---

[98] Russell to the Queen, 14 Sept. 1846. Copy, Russell Papers, P.R.O. 30/22/5C; the Queen to Palmerston, 14 Sept. 1846. B.P. RC/F/273.
[99] Bulwer to Palmerston, 6 Sept. 1846. B.P. GC/BU/269.
[100] Russell to the Queen, 14 Sept. 1846. Copy, Russell Papers, P.R.O. 30/22/5C.
[101] Russell to Palmerston, 13 Sept. 1846. B.P. GC/RU/111.
[102] Palmerston to Bulwer, 16 Sept. 1846. B.P. GC/BU/514.
[103] Bulwer to Palmerston, 17 Sept. 1846. B.P. GC/BU/274; *The Times*, 19 Sept. 1846.

the Spanish nation.[104] Whatever its real significance in Spain, the vote certainly reflected the determination of the French and Spanish governments to go ahead with the marriages, and from 14 September onwards Palmerston's attempt to prevent the Montpensier marriage was a race against time. Neither the Queen nor Russell believed that the Montpensier marriage could be postponed, let alone prevented;[105] only Hervey, Bulwer and the *Morning Chronicle* shared Palmerston's optimism.[106]

Ever since the announcement of the marriages both Hervey and Bulwer had urged Palmerston not merely to protest against the Montpensier marriage but also to use the legal arguments against it advanced by the Progresistas and their newspapers:[107] firstly that the projected union was prohibited by the Spanish constitution, and secondly that any issue of the marriage would be debarred from the succession by the Treaty of Utrecht. These arguments, hastily contrived by Spanish journalists, were ingenious and complex, and during the latter months of 1846 they were endlessly debated and refined by the statesmen of Europe. The basis for both arguments was the renunciation by the Duke of Orleans on 10 September 1712 for himself and his descendants of all rights to the Spanish throne.[108] The purpose of the renunciation, incorporated into the Treaty of Utrecht of 13 July 1713, was to allay the fears of the maritime powers in the coalition against Louis XIV that the crowns of Spain and France might devolve on the same head. As the Duke of Montpensier was a direct descendant of the Duke of Orleans, grandson of Louis XIV, the Progresista press claimed that he was excluded from the Spanish succession; if the Infanta married him she would thereby contravene article 47 of the constitution of 1845 which forbade the sovereign and the

---

[104] Guizot to Bresson, 19 Sept. 1846. G.P. 42/AP/8; *Journal des Débats*, 17 Sept. 1846.
[105] Russell to Palmerston, 13 Sept. 1846. B.P. GC/RU/111.
[106] Bulwer to Palmerston, 18 Sept. 1846. B.P. GC/BU/275; Hervey to Clarendon, 18 Sept. 1846. Clar. Dep. C529.
[107] Bulwer to Palmerston, 2 Sept. 1846. B.P. GC/BU/268; Hervey to Palmerston, 7 Sept. 1846. F.O. 27/755.
[108] The renunciation is printed in 'Treaty of Utrecht: Appendix to the correspondence relating to the marriages of the Queen and Infanta of Spain', *Accounts and Papers, 1847*, lxix, 375–436.

next heir to marry anyone excluded from the succession. By contracting a prohibited marriage, the Progresistas claimed that the Infanta would remove herself from the line of succession, and any issue of her marriage with the Duke of Montpensier would, as members of the House of Orleans, be excluded by the renunciation of 1712.[109]

Palmerston's first protest to the Spanish government contained no reference to these arguments. In the third week of September, however, he took them up with enthusiasm.[110] An appeal to the provisions of the Treaty of Utrecht made the opposition to the marriages a matter of 'the public law of Europe',[111] and Palmerston hoped that this would induce the eastern powers to take the British side in the dispute. In his first remonstrance of 22 September to the French government, Palmerston combined his original argument based on the balance of power with those based on the Treaty of Utrecht which he described as 'strong and conclusive'.[112] The war of notes between Palmerston and Guizot, which was to last until January 1847, had begun. Palmerston also made his first attempt to involve the eastern powers in opposition to the marriage by sending copies of his despatch to the British representatives at Vienna, Berlin and St Petersburg, instructing them to discuss the question with the governments to which they were accredited.[113] He felt confident that opposition from three fronts, from England, from within Spain, and from the eastern powers, would weaken the resolve of the French who would try

[109] Hervey to Clarendon, 18 Sept. 1846. Clar. Dep. C529.

[110] On 18 Sept. Clarendon sent Palmerston a letter from Hervey on the Treaty of Utrecht 'in case you should mean to make use of that weapon, which seems to me an important one in any protest against the Montpensier marriage'. Clarendon to Palmerston, 18 Sept. 1846. B.P. GC/CL/459. Palmerston first mentioned the Utrecht arguments in a despatch to Normanby of 22 Sept. 1846. F.O. 27/746.

[111] Palmerston to Normanby, 22 Sept. 1846. F.O. 27/746.

[112] Palmerston to Normanby, 22 Sept. 1846. *Accounts and Papers, 1847,* lxix, 278–83.

[113] Palmerston minuted on the draft despatch to Normanby that copies were to be sent to Gordon at Vienna, Westmorland at Berlin and Buchanan at St Petersburg. They were to read the despatch to the ministers of the three Courts but not to present them with copies, 'and to ask those ministers whether their respective Courts do not feel the force of the objections which have been urged against the marriage of the Duke of Montpensier and whether they will not deem it right to take some official steps upon the subject'. Minute by Palmerston, 21 Sept. 1846. F.O. 27/746.

to strike a bargain with the British government by offering to postpone the Montpensier marriage until Queen Isabella had children. Although this compromise would be far from satisfactory, Palmerston informed Bulwer that he would be disposed to accept it unless it was clear that there was sufficient Spanish opposition to prevent the marriage altogether.[114]

Guizot's reaction to the British attempt to prevent or postpone the marriage belied Palmerston's expectations. His decision to go ahead with the marriages simultaneously had been hasty but not, he believed, ill-advised, and he had committed his government too far to retreat without disastrous loss of prestige. Moreover, he firmly believed that once again Palmerston could be defeated. If Palmerston thought that he could excite opposition in Spain and amongst the eastern powers to the policy of France, Guizot would ensure that this opposition would be both limited and ineffectual. If Palmerston thought he could make Guizot lose face in France, Guizot would ensure that Palmerston was discredited in England. As soon as Palmerston's plan of campaign became clear, Guizot began a counter-offensive.

Guizot's task was easiest in Spain where Bulwer and the Progresistas were rapidly losing hope in the efficacy of their own efforts to prevent the marriage. Bulwer attributed the slackening of the opposition to the inertia and inconsistency of the Progresistas, the Progresistas complained of Bulwer's broken promises of support, and all blamed the repressive measures of the Moderado government.[115] By the last week in September both Louis Philippe and Guizot were convinced that the marriages met with the full approval of the Spanish nation.[116] On 30 September the Duke of Montpensier left Paris for Madrid. The French government took extra precautions to guard against disturbances by Progresista exiles on the frontier,[117] and the Spanish government sent a detachment of infantry to meet him.[118] The latter no longer feared that the French would back down. From the end of September Bulwer and the Progresistas

---

[114] Palmerston to Bulwer, 27 Sept. 1846. B.P. GC/BU/515.
[115] Bulwer to Palmerston, 23 Sept. 1846. B.P. GC/BU/274.
[116] Louis Philippe to Guizot, 29 Sept. 1846. G.P. 42/AP/286; Guizot to Jarnac, 28 Sept. 1846. G.P. 42/AP/7.
[117] Guizot to Martinez de la Rosa, 23 Sept. 1846. A.A.E.C.P. Espagne 828.
[118] Bresson to Guizot, 27 Sept. 1846. G.P. 42/AP/65.

could only watch what they were powerless to stop. Bulwer's assertion to Palmerston that even if the marriage did take place 'all was not lost'[119] was in reality an admission of despair. Guizot found 'strange indeed' Palmerston's appeal to the Treaty of Utrecht in order to secure the opposition of the eastern powers to the Montpensier marriage.[120] Early in September 1846 he had himself begun to solicit the support of Metternich, hoping to offset the anticipated temporary estrangement from England by Austrian assistance.[121] On 5 September he instructed Flahaut to emphasise to Metternich that the Montpensier marriage was a family affair, and that Cadiz, a Spanish prince 'd'un esprit judicieux, d'opinion modérée, et d'un sincère amour de l'ordre' was a most suitable consort for the Queen.[122] Guizot knew that Metternich would be disappointed that his plan for a marriage between Queen Isabella and the Carlist Count of Montemolin had been thwarted. He was anxious therefore to present his own arrangements as favourably as possible, to persuade Metternich that, although not ideal, Cadiz presented fewer dangers to political stability in Spain than his revolutionary brother. Metternich's response to Guizot's overtures of early September was less favourable than Guizot and Flahaut had hoped: he rehearsed the familiar arguments on the evils of the will of Ferdinand VII, and for a few days Flahaut feared that he might associate himself with any policy that would leave open the door for Montemolin. But this alone would not satisfy Palmerston, and Flahaut therefore concluded that joint action by Metternich and Palmerston 'ne me parait donc pas probable'. In any case the French had no cause for immediate alarm. Speed was not a characteristic of Metternich's diplomacy; even if the eastern powers began to discuss Palmerston's protest at once, any decision they might reach could not be known in western Europe until after the solemnisation of the Montpensier marriage.[123] Moreover, Flahaut thought Metternich unlikely to take a positive stand in a dispute in which he had no direct

[119] Bulwer to Palmerston, 23 Sept. 1846. B.P. GC/BU/276.
[120] Guizot to Bresson, 19 Sept. 1846. G.P. 42/AP/8.
[121] P. Thureau-Dangin, 'La France et l'Europe à la veille de la révolution de 1848', *Revue d'Histoire Diplomatique*, 1892, 113–14.
[122] Guizot to Flahaut, 5 Sept. 1846. A.A.E.C.P. Autriche 433.
[123] Flahaut to Guizot, 22 Sept. 1846. G.P. 42/AP/68.

interest, especially since it would tend to weaken the *entente cordiale*, a combination he had always feared and disliked.[124]

For Guizot the most alarming aspect of the situation in late September 1846 was the almost unanimous disapproval of his conduct which was being voiced in England. 'Il est certain', wrote *Le National* on 24 September, 'que l'opposition de l'Angleterre devienne plus ferme chaque jour.' Guizot and Jarnac attributed this in part to the fact that both *The Times* and the *Morning Chronicle*, the two most powerful newspapers, took their cue from the Foreign Office.[125] Moreover, the conviction of the Queen that she had been personally deceived made it impossible for politicians of any party to defend the conduct of France without the appearance of disloyalty to their sovereign.[126] Guizot also thought that Palmerston had won over his cabinet colleagues and even some members of the opposition by giving a garbled version of the negotiations of July and August.[127] The obvious way to win over the Queen, Russell and the cabinet, Peel and Aberdeen, and if possible the press, was to expose Palmerston's misconduct in July and August, which had both occasioned and justified French unilateral action.

Guizot left Louis Philippe and the Orleans family to deal with Queen Victoria, whose curt and cold reply to the letter of the Queen of the French announcing the arrangement of the Montpensier marriage had surprised Louis Philippe.[128] His next approach was therefore indirect: he wrote justifying his conduct to his daughter, Queen Louise of the Belgians, and she passed his letters on to Queen Victoria, her niece by marriage.[129] Queen Victoria's replies to the Queen of the Belgians were

[124] Flahaut to Guizot, 5 Oct. 1846. G.P. 42/AP/68.
[125] Guizot to Jarnac, 1 Oct. 1846. G.P. 42/AP/69.
[126] Jarnac to Guizot, 1 Oct. 1846. G.P. 42/AP/69.
[127] Guizot to Jarnac, 21 Sept. 1846. G.P. 42/AP/69.
[128] Before Queen Victoria's reply to the letter of the Queen of the French was received, Louis Philippe informed Guizot that he and the Queen of the Belgians expected that 'le ton sera que le mariage Cadix est bon pour les deux pays, que celui de Montpensier n'est pas bon pour l'Angleterre mais qu'il doit être supporté'. Louis Philippe to Guizot, 8 Sept. 1846. G.P. 42/AP/286. For Queen Marie Amélie's letter and Queen Victoria's reply, see *Q.V.L.*, 1st series, ii, 119–20.
[129] Louis Philippe to the Queen of the Belgians, 14 Sept. 1846. R.A. J/45/10. The Queen of the Belgians to Queen Victoria, 14 Sept. 1846. R.A. J/44/62.

written in a tone of pain rather than of anger, but she resolutely refused to accept any justification for the misconduct of the French. She condemned Guizot more harshly than Louis Philippe, but this was mere form. Her real judgment was expressed to King Leopold: 'It is so sad—for dear Louise to whom one cannot say that her father has behaved dishonestly.'[130]

Once it became clear that Queen Victoria was unlikely to acquit the French of blame, Louis Philippe began, through King Leopold of the Belgians, to urge her to save the *entente cordiale*.[131] These efforts were futile: the Queen was incapable of prevailing over Palmerston and Russell. In any case, the Queen herself was disenchanted: the Montpensier marriage, wrote Greville, 'has been a great damper to the Queen's engouement for the House of Orleans'.[132]

The discussion of political matters in the correspondence of sovereigns and amongst members of related royal families was accepted practice which aroused neither comment nor indignation, but when Guizot attempted to discredit Palmerston amongst his cabinet colleagues and the opposition his action was bitterly resented in England. Guizot's assertion, repeated by Jarnac to Whig and Tory leaders, that Russell did not share Palmerston's opinion that the French had behaved dishonestly or that the Montpensier marriage was a cause for alarm[133] brought a sharp reproof from Russell. He dismissed the assertion as incorrect, and informed Jarnac that he thought it highly improper of Guizot to have made it.[134] Guizot realised that he had made a tactical error, and in an attempt to prevent the breach between the two governments from being widened he tried to move the discussion away from the proceedings of July

[130] Queen Victoria to the King of the Belgians, 21 Sept. 1846. *Q.V.L.*, 1st series, ii, 124-5.
[131] 'I must say the peace of Europe must not be compromised too much; it will be for you dearest Victoria to watch over this...' The King of the Belgians to Queen Victoria, 1 Oct. 1846. R.A. Y/73/9.
[132] *The Greville Memoirs*, v, 429.
[133] Guizot to Jarnac, 21 Sept. 1846. G.P. 42/AP/7.
[134] Russell also told Jarnac, 'Si l'on pense que l'on peut changer la politique de la France à l'égard de notre Cour et compter sur le préjugé public pour rendre Lord Palmerston responsable du fait et du conséquence [*sic*], on se trompe également. Je crois tous les hommes politiques et tout ce qui représente réellement le pays d'accord avec nous sur la question actuelle et sur le jugement que nous en avons porté.' Jarnac to Guizot, 4 Oct. 1846. G.P. 42/AP/69.

and August to the future of the *entente*. Would Russell, he asked, sacrifice the peace of the world and the civilising mission of England and France in order to prevent the unlikely contingency of the grandchildren of the King of the French occupying the throne of Spain?[135] Russell refused to be drawn.[136] Guizot's attempt to separate Russell and Palmerston not only assisted Palmerston's cause but damaged his own and greatly weakened Jarnac's position in London. The latter was sharply rebuked by Palmerston for the impropriety of his conduct, and thereafter the Palmerstons were able to dismiss him as an intriguer.[137] From October 1846 to January 1847 Palmerston profited greatly from the fact that statements emanating from the French embassy in London completely lacked credibility. Guizot's attempts to win over Peel and Aberdeen also failed.[138] Peel shared fully the resentment of the Whig government,[139] and Aberdeen did not consider that Guizot's rash conduct could be justified by the reasonable apprehensions he might have had as to Palmerston's intentions.[140] Aberdeen was, moreover, conscious of the ambiguity of his own Spanish marriages policy. He therefore neither criticised Palmerston's conduct publicly nor exerted influence over *The Times* to induce it to change its views.

Early in October 1846 Louis Philippe wrote to Guizot regretting the English reaction to the French triumph over the marriages: 'il me semble que la défection contre nous augmente en Angleterre, et cela m'afflige'.[141] The French government was

[135] Guizot to Jarnac, 15 Oct. 1846. G.P. 42/AP/7.
[136] Jarnac to Guizot, 18 Oct. 1846. G.P. 42/AP/69.
[137] Jarnac to Guizot, 15 Oct. 1846. G.P. 42/AP/69; Lady Palmerston to Beauvale, n.d. [? Oct. 1846]. *The Letters of Lady Palmerston*, ed. Tresham Lever (London, 1957), 284–6.
[138] Guizot wrote directly to Aberdeen to explain why he had acted as he did. Guizot to Aberdeen, 7 Sept. 1846. Aberdeen Papers, B.M. Add. MS. 43134. He instructed Jarnac to get in touch with Peel and show him Guizot's memorandum of 17 Sept. which justified his conduct. Guizot to Jarnac, 28 Sept. 1846. G.P. 42/AP/7.
[139] 'I think the worst act of Louis Philippe's life is this marriage of the Infanta to the Duke of Montpensier...I am utterly ashamed of the King and Guizot.' Peel to Aberdeen, 22 Sept. 1846. Aberdeen Papers, B.M. Add. MS. 43295.
[140] Aberdeen to Guizot, 14 Sept. 1846. Copy, Aberdeen Papers, B.M. Add. MS. 43134.
[141] Louis Philippe to Guizot, 5 Oct. 1846. G.P. 42/AP/286.

forced to watch Palmerston consolidate a domestic triumph and to bear the full brunt of the charge of the French opposition that they had wantonly destroyed the *entente cordiale*.

Even though the Spanish opposition had failed him and the eastern powers had as yet made no positive response to his despatch of 22 September, Palmerston was riding on the crest of a wave in England. The anti-French vituperations of the press were more frequent and more bitter than he could have hoped for. The Queen and his colleagues shared his indignation and resentment against France. Palmerston was not exaggerating when he informed Bulwer:

You may fearlessly say that there is but one opinion in England from the highest to the lowest among those who have paid any attention to the subject as to the conduct of the French Government in this affair and many who never before thought of foreign matters have taken much interest in this.[142]

It was against this background that the marriages took place in Madrid on 10 October 1846. Bulwer, who absented himself from the celebrations, reported that they had been a dismal affair, the only public enthusiasm having been paid for by French gold.[143] Bresson, by contrast, reported that Montpensier had been well received, and that the marriages had occasioned spontaneous outbursts of national joy.[144] The solemnisation of the Montpensier marriage was not to be the end of the affair, as Guizot had originally hoped. Palmerston had no intention of abandoning the struggle. He had virtually a free hand at home, there was no pressure from either the Queen or his colleagues to drop the matter and resume friendly relations with France. As soon as he realised the impossibility of preventing the Montpensier marriage, Palmerston turned his mind to future tactics. In Spain, he wrote to Bulwer, we shall 'keep quiet and wait for better times...In Europe we must endeavour to get Austria, Russia and Prussia to join us in declaring that the offspring of the marriage will not be acknowledged as entitled to succeed to the throne of Spain.'[145]

[142] Palmerston to Bulwer, 8 Oct. 1846. B.P. GC/BU/518.
[143] Bulwer to Palmerston, 11 Oct. 1846. F.O. 72/700.
[144] Bresson to Guizot, 11 Oct. 1846. G.P. 42/AP/65.
[145] Palmerston to Bulwer, 8 Oct. 1846. B.P. GC/BU/518.

CHAPTER VI

The Struggle Continues, October 1846–March 1847

After the solemnisation of the Montpensier marriage the struggle between Palmerston and Guizot intensified rather than abated. As late as February 1847 Flahaut told Metternich that the question of the Spanish succession was 'une guerre à mort entre M. Guizot et Lord Palmerston'.[1] Although it was Palmerston who began the struggle with his attempt to remove the Duchess of Montpensier and her descendants from the line of succession to the Spanish throne, Guizot was equally responsible for its bitterness and length. Neither controlled or concealed his hatred of the other, and neither was prepared to accept an inconclusive end to the contest. 'L'affaire', Palmerston warned Sainte Aulaire, 'ne sera finie que lorsqu'une certaine chose aura été faite.'[2] Palmerston and Guizot could join battle so fiercely and for so long because no effective restraints were imposed upon them. Guizot's colleagues and advisers rallied behind him in face of Palmerston's vindictiveness and the opportunistic attacks of the French opposition on the government's foreign policy. Although Louis Philippe, Duchâtel, the Minister of the Interior, and Broglie, whom Guizot frequently consulted on foreign affairs, were all anxious for the restoration of good relations with England,[3] neither they nor Guizot were prepared to submit to the humiliation of France, Palmerston's prerequisite for a *rapprochement*.[4] Palmerston could count on the full support of the Queen and his colleagues as a result of

[1] Flahaut to Guizot, 24 Feb. 1847. G.P. 42/AP/68.
[2] Sainte Aulaire to Guizot, 5 Nov. 1846. G.P. 42/AP/66.
[3] Normanby to Palmerston, 26 Oct. 1846. Normanby Papers, Box P, bundle 12.
[4] Guizot to Rayneval, 11 Nov. 1846. G.P. 42/AP/9. 'Tout ce que nous pensions de l'alliance anglaise nous le pensons encore. Mais nous n'avons jamais dit que là où les intérêts seraient opposés, la France devrait nécessairement se sacrifier, céder, toujours céder', wrote the *Journal des Débats*, 26 Oct. 1846.

Guizot's treachery in Spain and his and Jarnac's intrigues in England in September; even Wood applauded his efforts to deny the Duchess of Montpensier her rights to the Spanish throne.[5] Jarnac emphatically warned Guizot that the French government would be foolish to expect any assistance against Palmerston from the Queen or from former Francophiles.[6] As well as being long and fierce, the battle was waged on every front and with every available weapon. The major objective of both Palmerston and Guizot was to gain the support of Austria, Russia and Prussia, but some of the secondary powers were also asked for their opinions on the interpretation of the Treaty of Utrecht.[7] Each tried to weaken the other by enlisting the aid of his domestic opponents; by January 1847 the reception rooms of the British embassy in Paris had become one of the meeting places of the dynastic opposition,[8] and in London Jarnac and Sainte Aulaire made great efforts to secure the support of the Protectionists in the House of Commons,[9] and of Lord Aberdeen in the House of Lords.[10] The long and bitter polemic, as Guizot called it, was conducted by the direct exchange of notes, by carefully timed publications, and by a supporting press war which was sustained and uninhibited.

In France the collapse of the *entente* became a major issue in domestic politics. Thiers and the opposition believed that an attack on his foreign policy was the best way to discredit Guizot,[11] whereas Guizot believed that he could exploit his successes in foreign policy to consolidate his government in the

[5] Wood to Palmerston, 10 Oct. 1846. B.P. GC/WO/16.
[6] Jarnac to Desages, 22 Dec. 1846. G.P. 42/AP/69.
[7] Guizot sent copies of his despatch to Jarnac of 5 Oct. not only to Vienna, St Petersburg and Berlin, but also to The Hague, Frankfurt, Stuttgart, Munich, Turin and Florence. 'Il faut créer pour nous', he wrote, 'une opinion Européenne.' Guizot to Jarnac, 16 Oct. 1846. G.P. 42/AP/7.
[8] Guizot to Sainte Aulaire, 20 Feb. 1847. G.P. 42/AP/9. Lord Howden, who was in Paris in Jan. 1847, informed Aberdeen that Thiers came every day to the British embassy and Molé only a little less often. Howden to Aberdeen, 13 Jan. 1847. Aberdeen Papers, B.M. Add. MS. 43296.
[9] Jarnac to Desages, 5 Dec. 1846. G.P. 42/AP/69.
[10] Sainte Aulaire to Guizot, 18 Jan. 1847. G.P. 42/AP/66.
[11] Thiers told Greville that the opposition would try to use the debate on the Spanish marriages to 'damage Guizot as much as they can, and lay on his bad management the rupture with us...and that if Guizot had the worst of the encounter he would fall, not, however, by the desertion of the majority in the Chamber but by the King'. Greville to Clarendon, 11 Jan. 1847. Clar. Dep. C521.

Chambers and in the country.[12] Thus from late 1846 until his fall in February 1848 Guizot was defending his foreign policy both at home and abroad. Palmerston had an easier domestic situation to contend with than Guizot. The Peelites made no attempt to embarrass the government over Anglo-French relations; Peel considered that opposition to the Infanta's succession rights was a national, not a party, question,[13] and Aberdeen did not harass the government in the House of Lords. The Protectionists had no expert spokesman on foreign affairs; their random attacks on the government's foreign policy carried neither weight nor conviction. Palmerston did not, however, receive the extensive public support he anticipated; after the initial outburst of indignation in September Spanish issues received little public attention, and by the end of November 1846 the only newspaper with a wide circulation which continued regularly to attack Guizot was the *Morning Chronicle*. *The Times* deserted Lord Palmerston in late October when its editor, Delane, resumed contact with Lord Aberdeen.[14] Thereafter its attacks on Guizot were both infrequent and moderate in tone; their value to Palmerston was cancelled out by the strong condemnation of his methods and policies which Reeve resumed under Aberdeen's guidance.[15]

Although Palmerston's domestic circumstances were easier than Guizot's, in other respects his task was the harder. His policy was more ambitious and his case more difficult to argue than Guizot's; he also demanded much more in the way of co-operation from the eastern powers. He wanted them to join England in a declaration stating that the four powers considered that the Treaty of Utrecht debarred the Duchess of Montpensier and her descendants from inheriting the throne of Spain. For

---

[12] On 29 Dec. 1846 the *Journal des Débats* announced that debates on foreign policy would be the most important in the coming session.

[13] 'I quite concur in the opinion...that party considerations ought not to trap the judgement and influence the action of public men in a matter of such deep importance as that which arises out of the Spanish Marriages.' Peel to Prince Albert, 12 Nov. 1846. Draft, Peel Papers, B.M. Add. MS. 40441.

[14] Delane to Aberdeen, 24 Oct. 1846. Aberdeen Papers, B.M. Add. MS. 43295. Aberdeen was surprised by Delane's letter as he thought *The Times* had made some agreement with the Whigs, but he soon fell back into his old habit of writing regularly to Reeve and Delane on foreign affairs. See *The History of The Times* (London, 1939), ii, 102.   [15] See for example *The Times*, 14 Jan. 1847.

Palmerston this declaration would serve two purposes. It would give him the appearance of a triumph over Guizot and a basis of legality for any attempt to prevent the Duchess of Montpensier from ascending the throne of Spain should Queen Isabella die without issue—personal satisfaction for the present and a future safeguard for the balance of power. Guizot had an undoubted advantage over Palmerston in the fact that his policy was entirely negative: he wished to prevent the eastern powers from subscribing to the British declaration against the Duchess of Montpensier's succession rights, but he did not insist that they should explicitly recognise or affirm her rights. 'Je ne demande au Prince Metternich', wrote Guizot to Flahaut, 'que de rester neutre dans le différend.'[16]

Palmerston hoped to conceal from the French government his intention to approach the eastern powers until he had made his first overtures to the three Courts.[17] To begin with, therefore, he moved cautiously; he sent copies of the first and second British protests to the French government to the British representatives at Vienna, St Petersburg and Berlin, instructing them to ask the three Foreign Ministers to state whether they concurred with the opinions expressed by Palmerston on the Treaty of Utrecht and its bearing on the succession rights of the Duchess of Montpensier and her descendants.[18] This would enable him to drop the matter if the eastern powers immediately declined to be associated with the protest. Only if there appeared to be some chance of success was Palmerston prepared to pursue this plan. By mid-October the first reactions of the eastern powers had been received and Palmerston regarded them as favourable.

In an interview with Gordon on 5 October Metternich condemned the rapacious conduct of Louis Philippe towards Spain, which exposed 'the peace of Europe to imminent danger'. He refused, however, to commit his government to any definite attitude on the questions raised by Palmerston's despatches until he had consulted the Russian and Prussian governments,

[16] Guizot to Flahaut, 14 Nov. 1846. G.P. 42/AP/9.
[17] Palmerston to Bulwer, 8 Oct. 1846. B.P. GC/BU/518.
[18] Palmerston to Gordon, 29 Sept. 1846. F.O. 7/327; Palmerston to Buchanan, 29 Sept. 1846. F.O. 65/330; Palmerston to Westmorland, 29 Sept. 1846. F.O. 64/262.

for he believed that it was essential to preserve the unanimity of the three powers on Spanish affairs. Gordon, encouraged by Metternich's reaction, assured Palmerston 'that in the event of this marriage unfortunately becoming the cause at any future period of a rupture betwixt Great Britain and France, we shall have with us, not only the voice, but, if necessary, the arms of Austria'.[19] In Berlin too Frederick William IV expressed strong disapproval of French policy towards Spain,[20] and Canitz, the Prussian Foreign Minister, informed Howard, the British chargé d'affaires, that he would immediately investigate the issues arising out of Palmerston's despatches, but could not commit himself before consulting Metternich and Nesselrode.[21] The Russian response was similar, but Nesselrode gave Buchanan, the British chargé d'affaires, the distinct impression 'that the Imperial Cabinet will learn with satisfaction that Austria is prepared to recommend an expression of disapproval...of the alliance which is about to be contracted between the royal houses of France and Spain'.[22] Nesselrode also expressed approval of the strong terms in which Brunnow, the Russian ambassador in London, had condemned Louis Philippe and Guizot in a conversation with Russell, and the Russian Emperor did not conceal his hope that the dispute over the Montpensier marriage would 'greatly impair if not entirely destroy the cordial and good understanding' between England and France.[23] There could be no doubt, wrote Hervey to Clarendon, that the language of Russia was 'for the moment...more important' for England 'than that of Austria'.[24]

These reports convinced Palmerston that he stood a good chance of repeating successfully the tactics he had employed during the Mehemet Ali crisis. In 1839 and 1840 friendly overtures from Russia had led Britain into concert with the eastern powers and a subsequent triumph in the near east, which had left France under Thiers isolated and humiliated. Palmerston hoped to do the same to Guizot in 1846. The circumstances

[19] Gordon to Palmerston, 5 Oct. 1846. F.O. 7/329.
[20] Westmorland to Palmerston, 9 Oct. 1846. B.P. GC/WE/162.
[21] Howard to Palmerston, 5 Oct. 1846. F.O. 64/266.
[22] Buchanan to Palmerston, 8 Oct. 1846. F.O. 65/323.
[23] Buchanan to Palmerston, 13 Oct. 1846. F.O. 65/323.
[24] Hervey to Clarendon, 23 Oct. 1846. Clar. Dep. C529.

were propitious: Russia desired the permanent separation of England and France, Metternich was facing a serious situation in Italy where France was the traditional rival of Austria, and the King of Prussia was not only violently anti-French, but also desirous of giving the recently established intimacy between the British and Prussian royal families some political manifestation.[25] By raising the spectre of French aggression and basing his own policy on the maintenance of the balance of power,[26] Palmerston believed that he could secure the support of those powers who had joined with Great Britain in 1814 and 1815 in making the territorial order on which this equilibrium was based. He therefore began to prepare a despatch which would give the eastern powers a fuller account of his views on the Spanish succession and suggest possible joint action.

Before the new instructions were sent, Gordon's despatch of 10 October somewhat modified Palmerston's first impression of Metternich's views. In Metternich's opinion the refusal of the northern Courts to recognise the will of Ferdinand VII of Spain or the government of Queen Isabella[27] constituted a permanent protest against the female succession, and he felt that a special protest against the rights of the Infanta would weaken this position.[28] Metternich instructed Dietrichstein, the Austrian representative in London, to inform Palmerston of his belief that this objection constituted a very great difficulty in the way of any joint protest against the succession rights of the Duchess of Montpensier.[29] Palmerston, however, did not agree; he instructed Ponsonby to inform Metternich that the British government would find a way out of the difficulty.[30] By 22 October Palmerston had prepared instructions for Ponsonby which not only dealt with Metternich's reservations about a special protest but also contained the first proposals for joint action by the four powers.

[25] Palmerston to Westmorland, 23 Oct. 1846. Westmorland Papers, British Museum Microfilm [hereafter B.M.M.] 509.
[26] Palmerston to Ponsonby, 22 Oct. 1846. F.O. 7/327.
[27] For the attitude of the eastern powers to the Spanish succession in the 1830s, see Webster, *Palmerston*, i, ch. v, and P. E. Moseley, 'Intervention and Non-Intervention in Spain, 1838–39', *Journal of Modern History*, June 1941, xiii, 195–217.
[28] Gordon to Palmerston, 10 Oct. 1846. F.O. 7/329.
[29] Metternich to Dietrichstein, 16 Oct. 1846. Copy, R.A. J/46/2.
[30] Palmerston to Ponsonby, 22 Oct. 1846. F.O. 7/327.

Palmerston contended that Metternich was wrong to suggest that the will of Ferdinand VII constituted a departure from the order of succession established at Utrecht. The Pragmatic Act, on which the northern Courts based their objection to the female succession and the will of Ferdinand VII, had been introduced into Spain after the Treaty of Utrecht;[31] the will of Ferdinand VII therefore 'only restored the law of succession in Spain to precisely the same state in which it was at the time when the treaty of Utrecht was signed'.[32] Ponsonby was moreover to remind Metternich that the public law of Europe did not alter because of altered circumstances within one state: the object of Utrecht had been to safeguard the balance of power, not to regulate the internal affairs of Spain.[33] Palmerston considered these arguments incontrovertible, but even if Metternich disputed them he believed that there was sufficient common ground for a joint protest by the four powers. He suggested that they should issue a protocol stating that the descendants of the Duke of Montpensier, as descendants of the Duke of Orleans of 1712, could under no circumstances 'according to the public law of Europe' ascend the throne of Spain. All four powers could subscribe equally to this declaration because all acknowledged the validity of the Treaty of Utrecht. No mention need be made of the Infanta, about whose capacity to convey rights to her descendants they differed. Palmerston suggested, however, that the eastern powers should add a proviso to the proposed protocol stating that they considered that the Pragmatic Act of 1713 excluded the Duchess of Montpensier from the succession.[34]

In order to allay the fears expressed by Canitz that if Prussia joined Great Britain in a declaration on the Spanish succession she might be called on to become an active participant in the dispute between England and France,[35] Palmerston hastened to assure the powers that his intention was only to 'lay the foundation for something by and by which might much attenuate the dangerous effects of the Montpensier Marriage',

---

[31] This was, as Guizot pointed out to Jarnac, only a semi-Salic Law. Guizot to Jarnac, 5 Oct. 1846. *Accounts and Papers, 1847*, lxix, 302–12.
[32] Palmerston to Ponsonby, 22 Oct. 1846. F.O. 7/327.
[33] Ibid.
[34] Ibid.
[35] Howard to Palmerston, 12 Oct. 1846. F.O. 64/266.

not to bind anyone 'to any inconvenient action'.[36] He assured Bloomfield that it was only 'the sentiments of the Russian government upon the matter in question' that he desired.[37] Although, as Palmerston was well aware, it was Metternich who would formulate the views of the eastern powers on points of international law, he hoped that pressure from Russia and Prussia, the two powers who appeared to be most hostile to France, in favour of co-operation with Great Britain would help to remove any misgivings Metternich might have about committing himself quickly and definitely on a complex issue.[38] He instructed Westmorland and Bloomfield, the British ministers at Berlin and St Petersburg, to urge the Prussian and Russian governments to put in 'a good word to Metternich' for the British case,[39] and suggested to Bunsen, the Prussian minister in London, and to Brunnow that they should do the same.

By the end of September the French government was aware of Palmerston's approaches to the eastern powers.[40] Flahaut believed that Metternich would not commit himself to Palmerston's views on the Spanish succession but would remain a neutral observer, and that the French government therefore had nothing to fear. He wrote to Guizot: 'Je crois que l'on peut attribuer l'attitude et le rôle adoptés par la Court d'Autriche dans cette affaire à la grande confiance qu'elle place dans la sagesse du Roi et dans son ministre et à la méfiance au contraire que lui inspire Lord Palmerston.'[41] Despite Flahaut's confidence, Guizot was not prepared to leave anything to chance; he feared Palmerston as an opponent too much to ignore his moves. He therefore began a vigorous counter-offensive. 'Il faut être partout présent et actif', he wrote to Jarnac on 5 October, 'car on nous attaquera partout.'[42] Guizot's tactics were Palmerston's in reverse. He contended that the Treaty of Utrecht reaffirmed rather than invalidated the succession rights of the Duchess of Montpensier and her descendants, and he urged the eastern

---

[36] Palmerston to Westmorland, 23 Oct. 1846. Westmorland Papers, B.M.M. 509.
[37] Palmerston to Bloomfield, 23 Oct. 1846. B.P. GC/BL/219.
[38] Palmerston to Westmorland, 23 Oct. 1846. Westmorland Papers, B.M.M. 509.
[39] Ibid.; Palmerston to Bloomfield, 23 Oct. 1846. B.P. GC/BL/219.
[40] Flahaut to Guizot, 20 Sept. 1846. G.P. 42/AP/68.
[41] Flahaut to Guizot, 26 Sept. 1846. G.P. 42/AP/68.
[42] Guizot to Jarnac, 5 Oct. 1846. G.P. 42/AP/7.

powers to remain neutral (and thus implicitly to side with France) in the dispute over the Spanish succession. In his despatch of 5 October in reply to Palmerston's first protest of 22 September 1846, Guizot defined the French attitude towards the Treaty of Utrecht, and refused to recognise any validity or substance in Palmerston's protest. He argued that close scrutiny of Utrecht clearly showed that:

the twofold object of this Treaty, distinctly recognized and declared was,—
1. To secure the Crown of Spain to Philip V and his descendants.
2. To prevent the union of the Crowns of France and of Spain upon the same head being ever possible. . .By the marriage of the Infanta and the Duke of Montpensier, the Crown of Spain is secured from passing away from the House of Bourbon and from the descendants of Philip V, and at the same time the provisions against the possibility of an union of the two Crowns of France and of Spain remain in full vigour. The twofold object of the Treaty of Utrecht is therefore fulfilled.[43]

To give his case additional weight, Guizot pointed out that Utrecht had never 'been considered or appealed to as opposing an obstacle to marriages between the several branches of the Bourbons'. In the eighteenth century a number of Spanish princesses had married French princes,[44] and as the Pragmatic Act of 1713 had not totally excluded females from the Spanish succession but only placed them after all heirs male, these princesses had brought with them 'a contingent though positive right to the Crown of Spain', but there had been no protests against these marriages. Guizot concluded that Palmerston's protest lacked validity as it was not based on 'an anterior right'.[45]

Guizot and Palmerston approached Utrecht from completely different viewpoints and reached completely different con-

[43] Guizot to Jarnac, 5 Oct. 1846. *Accounts and Papers, 1847*, lxix, 302–12.
[44] Guizot cited the example of the Dauphin, son of Louis XV, who in 1745 married the daughter of Philip V of Spain. He regarded it as 'very remarkable, for it was the immediate heir to the Crown of France who married one of the heiresses of the Crown of Spain'. Guizot to Jarnac, 5 Oct. 1846. *Accounts and Papers, 1847*, lxix, 302–12.
[45] Ibid.

clusions: Guizot argued from the preambles and ignored the stipulations; Palmerston based his whole case on the stipulations and dismissed the preambles as irrelevant. Guizot appealed to precedent; Palmerston denied that the oversights of his predecessors could invalidate his protest.[46] Neither wished to establish common ground between their interpretations of Utrecht. A compromise solution was impossible—either the Duchess of Montpensier and her descendants had succession rights or they had not—but had a compromise been possible neither would have wanted it. Palmerston's attack on the succession rights of the Duchess of Montpensier in the autumn of 1846 was a means to an end, the real object of attack being French influence at Madrid and French prestige in Europe. If Queen Isabella had children, the purely contingent question of the succession rights of the Duchess of Montpensier would lose all importance except as an issue of principle; if she died without issue the question would have to be re-examined. Both Guizot and Palmerston knew that their extreme positions on the principles involved would not necessarily commit them to extreme action in the future. The tenacity with which each clung to his interpretation of Utrecht merely reflected his determination to win the battle of the moment.

In October 1846 Guizot took a calm view of the situation which faced France as a result of Palmerston's approaches to the eastern powers on the Spanish succession. He saw no need for the diplomacy of either bargain or menace. Although in September Metternich had suggested that France and Austria should unite to present a firm front to the Swiss radicals,[47] Guizot neither hurried to respond to this overture, nor did he attempt to connect Swiss and Spanish matters.[48] He issued no warning to the eastern powers about the consequences of any action which might isolate and humiliate France. All that Guizot believed the situation required was constant vigilance. 'Je n'ai pas besoin de vous dire que c'est sur ce point, et pour

---

[46] '...a Treaty is not annulled for one generation because another generation, under circumstances essentially different, may have allowed its stipulations to lie dormant.' Palmerston to Normanby, 31 Oct. 1846. *Accounts and Papers, 1847*, lxix, 318–27.
[47] Flahaut to Guizot, 19 Sept. 1846. A.A.E.C.P. Autriche 433.
[48] Guizot to Flahaut, 24 Oct. 1846. A.A.E.C.P. Autriche 433.

prévenir toute démarche semblable, toute union des trois Cours du Nord avec l'Angleterre dans une politique et une attitude commune, que vous devez diriger votre attention et tout votre effort', he wrote to Rayneval, the French chargé d'affaires at St Petersburg.[49]

Guizot instructed French diplomats at the northern Courts to emphasise that the dispute over the succession rights of the Duchess of Montpensier was an exclusively Anglo-French quarrel in which Austria, Russia and Prussia had no direct interest, and from which they had nothing to gain by active participation.[50] All he asked was that the eastern powers should not join Palmerston's proposed protest but should continue to adhere to the attitude to the Spanish succession they had first adopted in 1833. Unless the northern Courts were to endorse and actively support the French interpretation of Utrecht, which Guizot realised was unlikely, he thought that three attitudes among the great powers towards the Spanish succession were preferable to two. If the eastern powers persisted in their refusal to recognise the will of Ferdinand VII and in their adherence to the principle that the Pragmatic Act should be regarded as the basis of the law of Spanish Succession—by 1846 a totally unrealistic attitude—Guizot could for practical purposes ignore their views. Since the defeat of the Carlists, Austria, Russia and Prussia had ceased to play an active part in Spanish affairs and only took a passing interest in them. Guizot had no reason to expect that the eastern powers would make a sudden and major change in policy by supporting the British interpretation of Utrecht, which would be tantamount to a declaration of support for Great Britain in her rivalry with France over Spain. Guizot believed that Metternich was in no position to pursue a policy that would inevitably lead to an open rupture with France. Metternich himself admitted the probability that he would soon have to take stern measures against radical discontent in Italy and Switzerland; he would in that eventuality want as little opposition from France as possible. Palmerston was unlikely to give unreserved support for Metternich's conservative policies in Switzerland and Italy, and

[49] Guizot to Rayneval, 5 Oct. 1846. G.P. 42/AP/9.
[50] Guizot to Jarnac, 5 Oct. 1846. G.P. 42/AP/7.

even if he did his support would not be sufficient to counteract the anti-Austrian feeling which France could stimulate in these states. In Guizot's view Metternich had nothing to gain and much to lose by a hostile gesture to France; he therefore thought that the eastern powers would probably stand aloof from the dispute over the Spanish succession in the hope that the breach between England and France would widen.[51]

Flahaut's reports of his conversations with Metternich in early October 1846 seemed to confirm Guizot's analysis. On 5 October Metternich pledged Austria and her two allies to rigid adherence to their 1833 position: 'Si nous nous mêlions de l'affaire, notre protestation serait contre les droits de la Reine Isabelle et non contre son mariage. Quant à celui de sa sœur, il n'est autre chose à nos yeux que l'union d'une Infante d'Espagne avec le 5ᵉ fils du Roi des Français.' Metternich's only concern, reported Flahaut, was to ensure that the dispute did not endanger the peace of Europe, asserting that he would try to prevent Palmerston from going beyond pacific measures of protest. Flahaut was convinced that the fact that Metternich feared that Palmerston might push the dispute into war served the interests of France as it made Austrian support for the British protest even more unlikely.[52] On 10 October Metternich unequivocally informed Flahaut that the eastern powers could not judge between the British and French views of the Spanish succession: 'C'est comme si un Luthérien se trouvait avoir un différend religieux avec un Calviniste et venait demander à un Catholique de se prononcer entr'eux. Le Catholique n'aurait autre chose à dire si ce n'est: vous avez tort tous les deux.'[53]

Rayneval's reports of the Russian reaction to Palmerston's protest were equally satisfactory; he assured Guizot that a favourable response to the British overture was improbable, and that Nesselrode, the Imperial Chancellor, would almost certainly follow Metternich's lead.[54] Until the fourth week of October the only source of anxiety to the French government

[51] Guizot to Rayneval, 5 Oct. 1846. G.P. 42/AP/9.
[52] Flahaut to Guizot, 5 Oct. 1846. G.P. 42/AP/68.
[53] Flahaut to Guizot, 10 Oct. 1846. G.P. 42/AP/68.
[54] Guizot to Jarnac, 16 Oct. 1846. G.P. 42/AP/7.

was the report of Dalmatie, their minister in Berlin, that the Prussian government was disposed to accept the British interpretation of Utrecht and willing to sign Palmerston's proposed declaration.[55] The news from Berlin did not please Guizot,[56] but neither did it perturb him unduly. He rated Prussia as the least important of the three northern Courts, and thought it unlikely that she would act independently of her allies. Dalmatie shared this opinion.[57] On 16 October Guizot was able to inform Jarnac that Palmerston's attempts to secure the support of the eastern powers for his interpretation of Utrecht were meeting with no success; the attitudes of the eastern powers were 'en général bonnes'.[58]

On 21 October, however, Flahaut reported rumours current in Vienna that Metternich was prepared to collaborate with Palmerston over Spanish affairs if Britain would agree to the restoration of the Carlist Count of Montemolin to the line of succession.[59] Although Flahaut himself anticipated no change in Austria's position, he thought that these rumours could not be ignored altogether as Metternich had hinted at this possibility in an interview on 10 October.[60] Moreover, Flahaut believed that the British government would not necessarily reject such a proposition; Palmerston was unprincipled enough to abandon the Spanish Constitutionalists, and Ponsonby would countenance almost any sacrifice for a *rapprochement* between England and Austria.[61] Guizot, on the contrary, thought Palmerston unlikely to desert the Spanish Constitutionalists and unite with the Carlists, hitherto the object of his constant and bitter enmity. Such a change of allegiance would alter the whole basis of his policy in Spain; it would lose him the support of the Progresistas and would also complicate his position in Portugal where Guizot believed him determined to support the ultra-Liberals.[62]

[55] Dalmatie to Guizot, 12 Oct. 1846. G.P. 42/AP/80.
[56] Guizot to Jarnac, 16 Oct. 1846. G.P. 42/AP/7.
[57] Dalmatie to Guizot, 26 Oct. 1846. G.P. 42/AP/80.
[58] Guizot to Jarnac, 16 Oct. 1846. G.P. 42/AP/7.
[59] Flahaut to Guizot, 21 Oct. 1846. G.P. 42/AP/68.
[60] Flahaut to Guizot, 10 Oct. 1846. G.P. 42/AP/68.
[61] Flahaut to Guizot, 21 Oct. 1846. G.P. 42/AP/68.
[62] Guizot to Jarnac, 27 Oct. 1846. G.P. 42/AP/7.

At the end of October 1846, therefore, both Palmerston and Guizot felt reasonably confident of the support of the eastern powers. Palmerston had followed up the friendly responses to his preliminary overtures with a positive proposal for joint action; Guizot thought there was no danger of the northern Courts making so hostile a gesture to France as Palmerston demanded. While Palmerston may have been slightly overoptimistic and Guizot slightly too complacent, neither had adopted attitudes that were fundamentally at variance with the reports they had received from Vienna, St Petersburg and Berlin, and neither had reason to suppose that their diplomats had sent other than accurate accounts of their conversations with the foreign ministers of the three Courts. The fact was that Metternich in particular had suggested to both the British and French ambassadors that Austria was likely to adopt the interpretation of Utrecht supported by their governments. In principle his statements to the two ambassadors were perfectly consistent. Taking his stand on the Pragmatic Act of 1713, Metternich could inform Gordon and Ponsonby that Austria considered the Duchess of Montpensier to be excluded from the Spanish succession, and Flahaut that Austria's standing protest against the female succession rendered a separate protest against her rights both unnecessary and undesirable.[63] There can be no doubt, however, that Metternich was trying to mislead both the British and the French governments into expecting some Austrian support. His more general comments on the dispute between England and France confirm this. To Flahaut he expressed approval of Guizot's unilateral action of August and condemned Palmerston's policy as likely to lead to war; to Gordon he expressed astonishment at the bad faith shown by France towards England, and the fear that Louis Philippe would plunge Europe into war. Metternich was clearly trying to do more than simply prevent England and France from solving their differences and reviving the *entente cordiale*;[64] his object was

[63] Even so, Hervey detected a 'difference of tone in the communications made at Paris and London'. Hervey to Bulwer, 30 Oct. 1846. Bulwer Papers, S/26.
[64] The British and French diplomats who had little faith in Metternich thought that his diplomacy was both simple and short-sighted. 'The truth is', wrote Hervey to Bulwer, 'that the three powers are enchanted to see the entente cordiale at an end, and try to encourage both parties to persevere in their respective lines with the

more short-term and pressing.⁶⁵ By suggesting to both France and England that Austrian support would be forthcoming, and then introducing difficulties and doubts, Metternich hoped to make both Palmerston and Guizot apprehensive that he would support the other, and to prolong the discussion of a question which his straightforward answer to the original approaches of the British and French governments could have ended immediately. The clue to Metternich's motives lay in his announcement in early November 1846 that the northern Courts had agreed to the suppression of the free state of Cracow and its incorporation into the Austrian Empire; 'on est résolu', wrote Nesselrode, 'de profiter du moment actuel pour lancer la barque'.⁶⁶

The town of Cracow had become part of the Habsburg dominions by the third partition of Poland of 1795. In 1809 it was ceded by Francis I under pressure from Napoleon to the Grand Duchy of Warsaw. At Vienna in 1815 it was claimed by both Russia and Austria and, as neither power would agree to its annexation by the other, Cracow was created a separate state, and its independence was formally recognised by a treaty of 3 May 1815 between Austria, Russia and Prussia. This treaty reflected not only Austro-Russian rivalry but also the fear of the three powers that an independent Polish state, however small, might provide a refuge and a propaganda centre for Polish patriots and malcontents. Restrictions were imposed upon immigration into Cracow and the three powers reserved to themselves the right to pursue and apprehend fugitives from their own territories in Cracow; and the Cracovian government was forbidden to publish literature or to take any action hostile to the Austrian, Russian and Prussian governments. From its creation, therefore, Cracow was a client state; 'but a geographical atom placed between three great monarchies' was Metter-

view of preventing it from being renewed. This is natural, though not very wise, for if this should produce an open rupture the consequences to them, especially to Austria, may be infinitely more serious than the little *dérangement* of seeing England and France continue on friendly terms.' Ibid. Bresson made similar remarks in a letter to Guizot. Bresson to Guizot, 25 Oct. 1846. G.P. 42/AP/65.

⁶⁵ Nesselrode to Meyendorff, 26 Oct. 1846. Nesselrode, *Lettres et Papiers*, viii, 354–6.
⁶⁶ Ibid.

nich's description of it.⁶⁷ Its existence depended on the goodwill of its powerful neighbours. The treaty of 3 May 1813, the result of separate negotiations between Austria, Russia and Prussia, was incorporated into the General Act of the Congress of Vienna signed on 9 May 1815.⁶⁸ Almost immediately Cracow became the centre of discontent the three powers had feared. By the 1830s Cracow was regarded with suspicion and mistrust by the three powers with Polish territories, and they constantly invoked the treaty of 1815 in order to pursue refugees from their own territories and to interfere in the internal affairs of Cracow itself. Amongst the liberals of western Europe Cracow became an object of special regard as the last remnant of independent Poland and the potential nucleus of a reconstituted and free Poland. Its importance therefore was out of all proportion to its size.

In 1838, despite the protests of England and France, the three founding powers invaded and occupied Cracow, and only evacuated their troops in 1841. In 1846 the revolt in the Austrian province of Galicia spread to Cracow, where a radical régime replaced the conservative government.⁶⁹ In March 1846 Austrian troops, with the consent of both Russia and Prussia, invaded Cracow for the second time. Neither Aberdeen nor Guizot protested, but each expressed the hope that Austrian troops would leave once order was restored, and that no change would be made in the legal status of Cracow.⁷⁰ In August 1846 the eastern powers established a special and secret conference at Vienna to discuss common Polish problems. The Russian government proposed that Cracow be suppressed and incorporated into Austrian Galicia. Metternich appears to have been reluctant to agree to this solution at first, but he yielded to Russian pressure.⁷¹ Initially he feared that the traditional

⁶⁷ Metternich to Dietrichstein, 6 Nov. 1846. 'Papers relative to the Suppression of Cracow', *Accounts and Papers, 1847*, lxix, 153-4. ⁶⁸ Articles VI-X.
⁶⁹ C. A. Macartney, *The Habsburg Empire, 1790–1918* (London, 1969), 307-12.
⁷⁰ Aberdeen to Colonel du Plat, 25 June 1846. *Accounts and Papers, 1847*, lxix, 149. For Guizot's first statement on Cracow, see *Discours prononcé par M. Guizot dans la discussion du projet de loi relatif aux réfugiés étrangers*, 2 July 1846.
⁷¹ Both Ponsonby and Westmorland thought that Metternich was not the 'author of the arrangement' but that it was the result of Russian pressure. Ponsonby to Palmerston, 21 Nov. 1846. F.O. 7/329. Westmorland to Palmerston, 26 Nov. 1846. Westmorland Papers, B.M.M. 509.

pro-Polish sympathies of England and France, and their concern for the maintenance of the treaty structure of Europe, would be likely to unite them in a joint protest; this would provide a basis for the revival of the 'liberal alliance' of the 1830s. If Europe were again divided into two hostile ideological groupings, Metternich would be confronted with grave difficulties if he were forced to take repressive measures in Italy. On the other hand, the eastern powers had a unique opportunity to exploit to their own advantage the situation created by the rupture between England and France over the Spanish marriages and their simultaneous overtures to the governments of Austria, Russia and Prussia for support on the question of the Spanish succession. The suppression of Cracow while these conditions prevailed would, it was hoped at Vienna and St Petersburg, elicit totally different responses from England and France from those originally expected by Metternich. On 6 October Metternich therefore sent despatches to Dietrichstein in London and Apponyi in Paris to announce to the British and French governments the suppression of Cracow.[72] For justification of this act the eastern powers turned to the treaty of 3 May 1815; they claimed that Cracow had failed to comply with the conditions laid down for its independence. Since Cracow had been established by the three powers acting alone, the right to suppress it was likewise theirs alone.[73] The three eastern powers

[72] Metternich to Dietrichstein, 6 Nov. 1846. *Accounts and Papers, 1847*, lxix, 153–4. An identic despatch was sent to Apponyi.
[73] Metternich to Dietrichstein, 6 Nov. 1846. *Accounts and Papers, 1847*, lxix, 153–4. Canitz, in conversation with Westmorland, 'rested his case on the plea of necessity, and on the rights the three powers had acquired by the breach of neutrality by the state of Cracow to which it was also bound by treaty, and which it had violated both by its secret endeavours to produce disturbances and rebellion in the neighbouring states and lastly by open and armed aggression. He states that this constitutes both a violation of neutrality and a state of war, the result of which was the conquest of the territory and the annihilation of the independence of the state, and he conceives that the three powers whose forces took possession of it, and who had originally given it independence had, upon giving sufficient reason in the protection they were bound to afford to their own countries, a right to take it back.' Westmorland to Palmerston, 26 Nov. 1846. Westmorland Papers, B.M.M. 509. Metternich argued that the insertion of the treaty of 3 May 1815 in the General Act of the Congress of Vienna did not give to the signatories of the latter any 'rights belonging exclusively to the Contracting Parties to the Treaty of the 3rd May'. Metternich to Dietrichstein, 4 Jan. 1847. *Accounts and Papers, 1847*, lxix, 185–6.

thus chose to set aside as unimportant the fact that the independence of Cracow had been incorporated into the General Act of the Congress of Vienna, a treaty which both Great Britain and France had signed. The suppression of Cracow was more than a rebuff to England and France; it infringed the accepted usages of international law which required the consent of all the original parties to treaty alterations. The eastern powers had taken a calculated risk. They believed that the Anglo-French dispute over the Treaty of Utrecht of 1713 gave them an opportunity to infringe the Treaty of Vienna of 1815 without immediate danger to themselves or long-term repercussions in Europe.[74] Their action might, however, so outrage public opinion that the governments of England and France would overcome their differences to unite in a strong protest, and thereafter resolve to maintain a concerted vigilance over the liberties of peoples and the faith of treaties.

Just before the suppression of Cracow was announced, the French government learned that Palmerston had formally proposed that the eastern powers should join with England in a protocol denying the Duchess of Montpensier any right of succession to the Spanish throne. Guizot believed that it was the favourable attitude of Prussia that had led to this move,[75] and that stronger French pressure at Vienna and St Petersburg would force them to warn their German ally to end her flirtation with England. He therefore instructed Rayneval to remind Nesselrode that: 'On a besoin de nous partout. Le mal ou le bien, le trouble ou le repos en Europe, c'est surtout la France qui peut le donner.'[76] Flahaut was likewise instructed to inform Metternich that:

Je ne lui demande rien aujourd'hui, tandis que l'Angleterre veut l'entraîner à sa suite. Il saura distinguer, je l'espère, le ministre conservateur du ministre brouillon. Il se rappellera que le concours de la France, son bon vouloir, sa bonne conduite sont nécessaires en Suisse, en Italie, partout où les vrais intérêts de l'Autriche, de

---

[74] Metternich informed Flahaut that he thought Cracow would soon be forgotten and that there was no likelihood of its endangering the peace of Europe. Flahaut to Guizot, 18 Nov. 1846. G.P. 42/AP/68.
[75] Guizot to Dalmatie, 12 Nov. 1846. G.P. 42/AP/8.
[76] Guizot to Rayneval, 11 Nov. 1846. G.P. 42/AP/9.

l'Europe, ou les vrais intérêts de la paix du monde sont ou peuvent être en question. Il me retrouvera partout, toujours sur cette ligne de conservation, de politique ferme et tranquille qui me donne, je crois, quelques droits à la confiance des cabinets Européens, mais des droits aussi à leur neutralité tout au moins dans la circonstance présente. Cette neutralité est, pour nous, d'une grande importance, et, pour eux, la simple continuation d'une attitude prise depuis quatorze ans.[77]

In addition Guizot warned the Prussian government that they would be heavily compromised and incur untold future risks if they gave Palmerston more than the slight encouragement they had already given.[78]

No reactions to these warnings had been received from Vienna, St Petersburg and Berlin when news of the suppression of Cracow reached Paris. Public reaction was immediate and predictable. Every newspaper condemned the act. The *Journal des Débats* did so in measured and dignified language, but its disapproval was unequivocal.[79] The opposition press was violent in its denunciation of the oppressors of Poland and of the French government whom it considered largely responsible. It was, wrote *Le Constitutionnel*, Guizot's foolish Spanish policy that had destroyed the *entente cordiale* and given the eastern powers the opportunity to suppress finally the liberties and hopes of the Polish people.[80] Lamartine made similar accusations in *La Presse*.[81] Immediately the fate of Cracow was known, Guizot realised Metternich's motives in acting as he had over the Spanish succession. He informed Jarnac that Metternich was playing England and France off against one another; although not pleasing to behold, this at least had the merit of placing England and France in identical positions. Guizot saw no reason, however, why Metternich alone should profit from the situation. If properly handled it could be used to settle the problems in foreign relations which France faced.[82] Guizot pointed out that both he and Palmerston had recently used

[77] Guizot to Flahaut, 14 Nov. 1846. G.P. 42/AP/9.
[78] Guizot to Dalmatie, 12 Nov. 1846. G.P. 42/AP/8.
[79] *Journal des Débats*, 20 Nov. 1846.
[80] *Le Constitutionnel*, 23 Nov. 1846.
[81] *La Presse*, 27 Nov. 1846.
[82] Guizot to Jarnac, 19 Nov. 1846. G.P. 42/AP/7.

strong language about Cracow.[83] If Palmerston were consistent, and willing to act with France, this could provide the basis for a *rapprochement* between England and France. If, however,

il sera complaisant pour M. de Metternich, froid avec nous, et nous témoignera l'intention d'agir seul, selon sa seule convenance: ... nous serons plus libres, après avoir offert à Londres l'action commune, de limiter comme il nous conviendra, envers Vienne, Berlin et Petersbourg, notre action isolée. Voilà selon moi, le trait essentiel de la situation, par conséquent l'idée dirigeante de notre conduite, et ce qui rend convenable et utile dans toutes les hypothèses, l'initiative que nous prenons envers Londres.[84]

Guizot's offer to co-operate with Palmerston over the suppression of Cracow would not only result in his being able to give a clear direction to his foreign policy, something which he had not been able to do since the beginning of September; it would also ease his domestic position. The King and Guizot's Anglophile cabinet colleagues[85] would be pleased by the offer, and if he made the offer publicly known, which he intended to do, the opposition would not be able to accuse him of refusing to work with England. Guizot was convinced that Palmerston would be disposed to accept the French offer of a joint protest to the eastern powers, if only because Palmerston's cabinet colleagues and public opinion would want him to do so. Guizot therefore instructed Jarnac to make preliminary approaches to Palmerston on the question of Cracow, to ask him if his views on the matter coincided with those of the French government.[86]

[83] 'Lord Palmerston a, tout récemment, tenu sur Cracovie et la question Polonaise, un langage encore plus prononcé que le mien', wrote Guizot. He thought it would be difficult for Palmerston to make a mild protest as if he did the inconsistency of his language would be exposed. Ibid.
[84] Ibid.
[85] An unsigned report in the Royal Archives of 25 Nov. 1846 stated that Louis Philippe was anxious for a reconciliation with England. R.A. J/46/21. King Leopold of the Belgians, who was staying with his father-in-law in late October, was, wrote Guizot to Jarnac, trying to act as mediator between the French and British royal families with the full approval of Louis Philippe. Guizot to Jarnac, 1 Nov. 1846. G.P. 42/AP/7. Another report in the Royal Archives of 17 Dec. 1846 headed 'Conversation with Duchâtel', probably written by Lord Normanby, stated that Duchâtel was deeply grieved at the quarrel between England and France, and regretted that the two governments had not found a solution to their differences. R.A. J/46/42.
[86] Guizot to Jarnac, 19 Nov. 1846. A.A.E.C.P. Angleterre 667.

Palmerston received encouraging news from the eastern powers in early November 1846. Westmorland and Bloomfield reported that the Prussian and Russian governments were well disposed towards his proposed protocol,[87] and Ponsonby wrote that Metternich was 'anxious to confirm and preserve the closest relations of amity with you', only needing a little time 'to overcome the many difficulties...in the arrangement of the affair now in agitation'.[88] With the negotiations on the Spanish succession apparently in this favourable state, on 12 November Dietrichstein informed Palmerston in confidence that he was about to give him official notification of the suppression of Cracow.[89] Palmerston was dismayed; he regretted the disappearance of Cracow and he realised that it could easily compromise the negotiations on the Spanish succession. Great Britain would be forced to protest against the infringement of international law, and a prolonged dispute with Metternich over Cracow could not fail to embitter Anglo-Austrian relations. In his opinion the only way out of the difficulty was immediately to send to Vienna a despatch urging the Austrian government to withdraw its troops and restore the liberties of Cracow. He explained his reasoning to Russell:

I confess it seems to me that with a view to our relations with Austria it would be far better that we should state our opinions as bearing upon a question which we may officially assume to be yet undecided rather than that we should at once have to protest against a measure announced to us as taken. By the first course at least we gain time for the coming to some understanding about the Spanish question, by the latter course we are drawn at once into argumentative conflict with Austria, or we must leave unnoticed a measure which in Parliament we could not defend ourselves for not protesting against.[90]

Palmerston submitted a despatch drafted on these lines to the Queen and Russell for approval.[91] Russell refused to sanction

[87] Westmorland to Palmerston, 5 Nov. 1846. Westmorland Papers, B.M.M. 509; Bloomfield to Palmerston, 6 Nov. 1846. B.P. GC/BL/158.
[88] Ponsonby to Palmerston, 6 Nov. 1846. B.P. GC/PO/539.
[89] Palmerston to Russell, 13 Nov. 1846. Russell Papers, P.R.O. 30/22/5E.
[90] Ibid.
[91] In a covering letter to the Queen, Palmerston stated that he stood 'pledged to the House of Commons to address some communication of this kind to the three

this course of action, and informed Palmerston that no despatch on Cracow could be sent off until it had been discussed and approved by the cabinet. Palmerston retorted that he could see no reason for delay, since his draft despatch departed in no respect from the policy laid down 'by our party for many years on Polish questions both officially and in Parliament'.[92] Nevertheless Russell remained adamant and Palmerston was forced to yield. Russell also suggested that the draft should be revised to make it 'as void of offence as possible' and 'to avoid any slip which our crafty neighbour might take advantage of to say "We are as you are Conservatives; England wishes to promote Jacobinism and anarchy; it is your interest to join with us, and if we keep down revolution in Spain, you ought to be thankful to us." '[93] Thus, despite their differences over tactics, both Russell and Palmerston agreed that a protest against the suppression of Cracow must be made as inoffensive as possible to the eastern powers in order not to compromise the negotiations on the Spanish succession. More significantly, neither envisaged using the situation created by the Cracow incident as an opportunity for a reconciliation with France.

On 15 November, the same day as Dietrichstein communicated Metternich's despatch on the suppression of Cracow to Palmerston officially, Metternich himself made a new overture on the question of the Spanish succession in a letter to Ponsonby. His suggestion was that the three Courts should reaffirm their general position on the Spanish succession and explicitly condemn the setting aside of the Pragmatic Act; this would amount to a denial of the succession rights of the Duchess of Montpensier since her marriage infringed the principles upheld by the northern Courts.[94] Metternich's tactics were obvious: by making the proposal to the British government he appeared to suggest that Austria had more in common with England than with France, and that he was anxious to establish closer relations with England; if Palmerston accepted the proposal, Metternich

powers; he has hitherto delayed it chiefly in consequence of the intervening discussion about the Spanish Marriages'. Palmerston to the Queen, 13 Nov. 1846. R.A. B/10/48.

[92] Palmerston to Russell, 14 Nov. 1846. B.P. GC/RU/1006.
[93] Russell to Palmerston, 14 Nov. 1846. B.P. GC/RU/124.
[94] Metternich to Ponsonby, 15 Nov. 1846. F.O. 7/329.

could point out to France that by the declaration he had done precisely what Guizot asked, maintain the position on the Spanish succession he had adopted in 1833. In the long run, therefore, the proposal could not compromise Metternich in any way, and its opportune timing could greatly assist him in the short run. At this point, Jarnac approached Palmerston on 21 November to enquire whether the British government intended to consult France before making any communication on the suppression of Cracow to the eastern powers.[95] Jarnac's note was delivered to Palmerston while the cabinet was discussing the despatch to be sent to Vienna, St Petersburg and Berlin about Cracow.[96] He replied immediately that the British government had already prepared its protest, a copy of which would be communicated to the French government in due course.[97] The decision to act alone over Cracow which Russell and Palmerston made was warmly supported by British diplomats in Paris.[98] A day before the French offer of co-operation was officially made, Normanby warned Palmerston that it was imminent and was a 'trap', 'a means enabling Guizot to boast at the meeting of the Chambers that he has not only made the marriages but restored the entente cordiale'. He urged Palmerston to reject it outright, to avoid strengthening Guizot and making it difficult for the French opposition to attack the government's foreign policy at the beginning of the new session.[99] Normanby's warning was unnecessary: Palmerston was already convinced that Guizot's offer to co-operate over Cracow had two objectives, to compromise the negotiations between England and the eastern powers over the Spanish succession and to reduce Guizot's own

[95] Jarnac to Palmerston, 21 Nov. 1846. G.P. 42/AP/69.
[96] Jarnac to Guizot, 21 Nov. 1846. G.P. 42/AP/69.
[97] Palmerston to Jarnac, 21 Nov. 1846. G.P. 42/AP/69.
[98] Lord Howden, who was in Paris to consult with the French government on the affairs of the River Plate, was against co-operation with France on Cracow. He thought that Guizot made the offer as a way out of his domestic difficulties. 'There is a party here', he wrote to Lord Clarendon, 'that talks of "dignified isolation" as the proper state of France in her international or rather non-international relations. There is not a man of this party means what he says, and who is not frightened to death at the idea of standing alone in the world.' Howden to Clarendon, 20 Nov. 1846. Clar. Dep. C540. Hervey thought that Palmerston must reject Guizot's offer as 'what faith can be placed in any proposal he may make to us?' Hervey to Clarendon, 20 Nov. 1846. Clar. Dep. C529.
[99] Normanby to Palmerston, 20 Nov. 1846. Normanby Papers, Box P, bundle 12.

domestic difficulties. He believed that rejection of the offer would end in Guizot's dismissal—'a just punishment' was Palmerston's verdict to the proprietor of the *Morning Chronicle*.[100]

Jarnac was not surprised by Palmerston's rebuff. It was commonly said among the diplomatic corps in London, wrote Jarnac, that the mildest protest over Cracow would earn the support of the northern Courts over the Spanish succession.[101] Guizot was disappointed, but Palmerston's dismissal of his offer of co-operation had at least clarified the situation: he knew the ends to which he should now direct his policy.[102] However, his task was a difficult one: he would have to strike a delicate balance between conflicting objectives.[103] He had to satisfy 'the flame of indignation'[104] which had swept Paris after the announcement of the suppression of Cracow, but he was in no position to deliver a protest that would offend the eastern powers. Palmerston had an easier task; London, wrote Greville to Reeve, was quite indifferent to the disappearance of Cracow.[105]

Palmerston believed that a protest on the suppression of Cracow was unavoidable. He genuinely regretted the violation of the General Act of the Congress of Vienna, which he feared might inaugurate an era of lawlessness in Europe.[106] On the question of Poland Palmerston was a thorough-going Whig; his despatch on the disappearance of the last vestiges of Polish

[100] Palmerston to Easthope, 25 Nov. 1846. B.P. GC/EA/55.
[101] Jarnac to Guizot, 21 Nov. 1846. G.P. 42/AP/69.
[102] Guizot to Flahaut, 25 Nov. 1846. G.P. 42/AP/9.
[103] Guizot to Jarnac, 23 Nov. 1846. G.P. 42/AP/7.
[104] Greville to Reeve, 25 Nov. 1846. Clar. Dep. C520. Guizot wrote, 'Ici le mouvement public est vif, très vif, et très général. Les uns s'y livreront avec passion. Les autres exploiteront avec perfide.' Guizot to Flahaut, 25 Nov. 1846. G.P. 42/AP/9.
[105] Greville to Reeve, 25 Nov. 1846. Clar. Dep. C520.
[106] 'It is impossible', Palmerston wrote to Westmorland, 'for the 3 powers to maintain for an instant that they have any right to deal with Cracow in any manner inconsistent with the Treaty of Vienna, without the concurrence of the other powers who were partners to that treaty; and they are thus for a most trifling advantage, setting to Europe an example which cuts down from under Prussia, Austria, Bavaria, Sardinia and other powers the right of which they hold some of the territories which they value the most...The truth is that the 3 powers are about to throw Europe into a state of diplomatic anarchy; all the bonds by which treaties bind nations must henceforward be deemed to be dissolved; and the old German Law of the Middle Ages, the Faustrecht, or law of the strongest must henceforward be the law of nations in Europe.' Palmerston to Westmorland, 17 Nov. 1846. Westmorland Papers, B.M.M. 509.

liberty in 1846 reflected the concern the Whigs had shown for the fate of Poland ever since Fox had condemned the third partition of Poland in 1795. Palmerston's protest followed closely the statements on Cracow he and other Whig leaders had made in Parliament in the 1830s and in July 1846 at the end of the last parliamentary session; he was anxious to avoid any discrepancy of principle, even if there was one of tone, in his public statements on Cracow. These were the considerations which led Palmerston to protest, but it was his desire not to offend the eastern powers and thus compromise the negotiations on the Spanish succession which made his tone and language uncharacteristic. The protest contained neither direct threats nor abuse, and it avoided the hectoring tones he usually employed on such occasions. There was little that Metternich could object to either in its restrained language or its content. Palmerston argued that the General Act of the Congress of Vienna was the basis of the European territorial and political order, and that it could only be altered with the consent of all the contracting parties. Metternich was in fundamental agreement with this statement; the only difference lay in the fact that he regarded Cracow as an exception to the rule whereas Palmerston did not.[107] British diplomats at Vienna, St Petersburg and Berlin were instructed to stress the sacrifices Palmerston had made on the question of Cracow in making his protest as mild as possible and rejecting Guizot's offer of joint action.[108] In drafting his protest Palmerston had shown no concern for the arguments and tone Guizot was likely to adopt. He believed that the eastern powers were moving towards his view that France posed the greatest threat to the peace of Europe, and that consequently any protest from France would be unlikely to find favour at the northern Courts.[109] Moreover, Palmerston did not think it possible to make the British protest any milder.

[107] See Palmerston to Ponsonby, 23 Nov. 1846. *Accounts and Papers, 1847*, lxix, 169–71; and Metternich to Dietrichstein, 4 Jan. 1847. Ibid., 185–6.

[108] Palmerston to Bloomfield, 23 Nov. 1846. B.P. GC/BL/222; Palmerston to Ponsonby, 23 Nov. 1846. F.O. 7/327; Palmerston to Westmorland, 23 Nov. 1846. Westmorland Papers, B.M.M. 509.

[109] Normanby pointed out that the government which had violated the Treaty of Utrecht could hardly use strong language to the powers who had violated the Treaty of Vienna. Normanby to Palmerston, 28 Nov. 1846. Normanby Papers, Box P, bundle 12.

Guizot, by contrast, was acutely anxious to learn what the tone and arguments of the British protest would be. For a few days he feared that Palmerston and Ponsonby would react to Cracow with a mildness that pro-Polish opinion in France would make it difficult for him to match.[110] On 27 November, however, Guizot's fears were allayed when Normanby gave him a copy of the British protest.[111] He immediately began drafting his own protest which in tone closely resembled Palmerston's, since he also wished to avoid giving offence to the eastern powers. Guizot too deplored the breach of treaty and the extinction of a Polish state: the suppression of Cracow, he wrote, was neither necessary nor lawfully accomplished.[112] In a covering note he instructed Flahaut to explain to Metternich that the protest was as moderate as was possible given the state of French public opinion.[113] The French and British protests were rival ones, but could scarcely have been more alike had they been jointly prepared. The intention of both was to make the minimum fuss over Cracow so as not to prejudice their negotiations with the eastern powers over the Spanish succession. In this they were successful. In so far as Cracow became the subject of acrimonious debate, it was not between the governments of the western constitutional powers and the eastern absolutist powers, but between the government and opposition press in France.

In December 1846 neither Palmerston nor Guizot succeeded in eliciting a firm and unequivocal statement of views on the Spanish succession from the northern Courts. Metternich was deliberately evasive; until Cracow was completely forgotten he wished to keep them in suspense, and the disturbed state of Switzerland and Italy made him anxious to avoid committing himself or offending either Britain or France. He therefore continued the elaborate game he had begun in early October, appearing to be on the verge of committing himself to one view

[110] Guizot to Jarnac, 25 Nov. 1846. G.P. 42/AP/7.
[111] Normanby thought Guizot was very relieved when he read Palmerston's protest. Normanby to Palmerston, 28 Nov. 1846. Normanby Papers, Box P, bundle 12.
[112] Guizot to Flahaut, 3 Dec. 1846. *Documents communiqués aux Chambres sur Cracovie*, Jan. 1847.
[113] Guizot to Flahaut, 3 Dec. 1846. G.P. 42/AP/9.

of Utrecht and then moving towards the other. The effect of Metternich's diplomacy in December coupled with his offer to Ponsonby of late November was to convince Palmerston that an Austrian declaration in his favour was imminent, and Guizot that it was possible that the three powers would abandon their attitude of 1833 to the Spanish succession. In December, therefore, Palmerston remained optimistic whereas Guizot was somewhat dispirited.

The British protest on Cracow reached Vienna almost a fortnight before the French protest, since Guizot had waited to learn the line Palmerston would take before drafting his despatch. Guizot was clearly disconcerted by the favourable effect that Palmerston's despatch created at Vienna, and for a few days Louis Philippe genuinely feared that Palmerston's efforts to revive the Quadruple Alliance and isolate France would meet with success.[114] Metternich's unfavourable reaction to the hostility to the eastern powers evinced by the French press also gave rise to anxiety in Paris. In early December Flahaut despondently concluded that if Palmerston were to follow up his moderate despatch on Cracow with an overture that would open the way for the restoration of the Carlist Count of Montemolin to the Spanish succession, the eastern powers might well join Great Britain in a declaration against the succession rights of the Duchess of Montpensier.[115] Guizot's anxiety was increased by the reports of Dalmatie from Berlin, where the Prussian government appeared even more eager than in October to comply with Palmerston's requests.[116] As a countermeasure, Guizot redoubled his efforts to convince the eastern powers that he was making every possible sacrifice over Cracow;[117] he assured them of the conservative orientation of his foreign policy. This policy, he pointed out, was in marked contrast to Palmerston's support of every radical cause in Europe. The choice confronting the eastern powers, wrote Guizot, was clear: they could either lend their support to conservative France, or they could deliver themselves and

---

[114] Louis Philippe to Guizot, 28 Nov. 1846. G.P. 42/AP/286.
[115] Flahaut to Guizot, 3 Dec. 1846. G.P. 42/AP/68.
[116] Dalmatie to Guizot, 29 Nov. 1846. G.P. 42/AP/80.
[117] Guizot to Dalmatie, 5 Dec. 1846. G.P. 42/AP/8.

Europe into chaos and anarchy by supporting Palmerston.[118] The unresponsiveness of the northern Courts to the French overtures only served to increase Guizot's anxiety, and as a result he turned his mind once again to the only other alternative open to him, given that he, like most Frenchmen, dreaded isolation. Was there, despite Palmerston's rebuff on Cracow, still a chance of a reconciliation between England and France?

Guizot expected little from Palmerston himself; he knew that there was no likelihood of his voluntarily renouncing his attempt to remove the Duchess of Montpensier from the Spanish succession: 'c'est son défaut accoutumé de tout subordonner, de tout sacrifier à sa passion, à sa question spéciale et du moment', he wrote of Palmerston.[119] The reports of Jarnac and Sainte Aulaire from London, however, indicated that none of his colleagues felt anything like the same concern about the Spanish succession.[120] Guizot believed that they might yet do what he had anticipated in September, restrain Palmerston's Francophobia and insist that he work towards a reconciliation with France. Jarnac reported that some members of the British cabinet looked forward to an improvement in Anglo-French relations after the Spanish marriages had been debated in both the British Parliament and the French Chambers. He and Guizot agreed that the debates should be moderate and short, that feelings on both sides of the Channel should not be exacerbated by indulging in bitter recriminations and public abuse.[121] Moderation would show English Francophiles that goodwill towards England still existed in France, and thus enable them to overcome Palmerston's resistance to a *rapprochement*. At the end of December 1846 Guizot was therefore prepared to move either towards a *détente* with the eastern powers or back into some sort of alignment with England. The latter would be preferable; it would ease his domestic position and be a more appropriate grouping for France if the problems of 1847 were likely to arise, as Guizot anticipated, out of liberal and national discontent in central Europe.

[118] Guizot to Rayneval, 4 Dec. 1846. G.P. 42/AP/9.
[119] Guizot to Flahaut, 3 Dec. 1846. G.P. 42/AP/9.
[120] Jarnac to Guizot, 26 Nov. 1846. A.A.E.C.P. Angleterre 667; Sainte Aulaire to Guizot, 22 Dec. 1846. G.P. 42/AP/66.
[121] Jarnac to Desages, 22 Dec. 1846. G.P. 42/AP/69.

As far as Palmerston was concerned in December 1846 reconciliation with France was utterly inconceivable while the two powers remained fundamentally at variance over the Spanish succession.[122] Moreover, as Normanby pointed out, any gesture of friendship towards France would strengthen Guizot, and weaken Thiers and the opposition.[123] Greville discussed the possibility of a reconciliation with Russell, and informed Clarendon that 'John seems to me at present rather in Palmerston's view.'[124] There was no chance, therefore, of Palmerston abandoning his efforts to secure a four-power declaration on the Spanish succession in order to effect some improvement in Anglo-French relations. At the beginning of December he rejected Metternich's proposal that the northern Courts could establish their identity of outlook with Great Britain by reaffirming the principles they had adopted in 1833; he pointed out that this would be as inoffensive to France as it would be unsatisfactory for Great Britain. He therefore reiterated his original suggestion of a four-power protocol.[125] The Prussians continued to express enthusiastic support;[126] Nesselrode, when pressed by Bloomfield to discuss the matter, reaffirmed that he would follow the line Vienna laid down. Metternich continued to prevaricate. He assured Ponsonby of his relief and gratitude that the *entente cordiale* had not been revived over Cracow and denied any Austro-French agreement on the Spanish succession, but he still refused to take the steps that would identify him with the British view. In fact, the only positive step Metternich and Nesselrode took was to impress upon the Prussians the folly of committing the three powers to either Great Britain or France.[127]

In mid-December Palmerston tried to revive the question of the Spanish succession. He warned Metternich that Guizot, anxious to avoid French isolation, had approached the British government as well as the eastern powers; it was clear that

[122] Palmerston to Ponsonby, 19 Dec. 1846. B.P. GC/PO/796.
[123] Normanby to Palmerston, 11 Dec. 1846. Normanby Papers, Box P, bundle 12.
[124] Greville to Clarendon, 31 Dec. 1846. Clar. Dep. C520.
[125] Palmerston to Ponsonby, 7 Dec. 1846. F.O. 7/327.
[126] Westmorland to Palmerston, 7 Dec. 1846. F.O. 64/266.
[127] Nesselrode to Meyendorff, 30 Nov. 1846. Nesselrode, *Lettres et Papiers*, viii, 358.

neither offer of co-operation was sincere. Palmerston realised, however, that he was more likely to gain the support of the northern Courts by trying to establish common ground between them and England than he was by attempting to discredit Guizot. He therefore began to consider the re-establishment of the Salic Law in Spain; if the British government advanced this as its policy on the Spanish succession, he hoped the eastern powers would meet him half-way by recognising Queen Isabella on condition that females were debarred from the succession after her death.[128] This scheme had the additional advantage that if Queen Isabella had male heirs the succession would remain unaltered in practice if not in principle; if however she had no sons, by Salic Law the succession would pass to Don Francisco de Paula and his sons; in either eventuality, the Duchess of Montpensier would be excluded. Palmerston recognised, however, that such a step could not be taken by Great Britain and the eastern powers alone. If the Spanish constitution and the law of succession were to be altered, it would be necessary to create within Spain a party in favour of these changes, and to bring it to power. He authorised Clarendon,

[128] In Nov. 1846 Montemolin, who was staying in London, was visited by Palmerston. This visit to the Pretender to the Spanish throne was adversely commented on in the Madrid press. Bulwer to Palmerston, 27 Dec. 1846. Bulwer Papers, S/11. Palmerston explained to the Queen that his meeting with Montemolin was 'only an attention which he thought due to a Prince of [the] Royal Family of Spain'. Palmerston to the Queen, 25 Nov. 1846. R.A. B/10/60. Palmerston also informed the Queen that he 'was very agreeably surprised by the appearance, manner and intelligence of the Prince'. Palmerston to the Queen, 26 Nov. 1846. R.A. J/46/66. 'As far as professions go', Palmerston wrote to Normanby, Montemolin 'is quite liberal in his political opinions'. Palmerston to Normanby, 27 Nov. 1846. Normanby Papers, Box P, bundle 23. Palmerston was obviously trying to make an assessment of Montemolin's character and his willingness to fall in with whatever plans Palmerston might evolve for the re-ordering of the line of succession. Palmerston was anxious to associate Montemolin with his Progresista cousins by a marriage between Montemolin and a daughter of Don Francisco de Paula. Palmerston to Bulwer, 26 Nov. 1846. B.P. GC/BU/528. No doubt Palmerston also hoped that a visit to Montemolin would encourage the eastern powers to think that he was favourably disposed towards him, and thus make them more anxious to declare against the rights of the Duchess of Montpensier and her descendants in order to reach some understanding with Palmerston which would restore Montemolin to the succession. Given that Palmerston wrote to Bulwer on 26 Nov. 1846 that the restoration of Montemolin to the line of succession was only 'something to think of' (B.P. GC/BU/528), the short-term tactical consideration seems to have been uppermost in his mind.

with whom he had discussed the possibility of re-introducing the Salic Law, to sound Olozaga, one of the Progresista leaders, unofficially and see how he reacted.[129] Until Palmerston had some idea of the Progresista reaction to his proposal he could not consider official overtures embodying the idea to the eastern powers; in any case he did not wish to make any such proposal until he was either forced or ready to do so. He thought of the re-introduction of the Salic Law as both a long-term affair and as a last resort; the difficulties it involved were formidable. Only Clarendon and Russell[130] knew that he was toying with the idea; if Palmerston were to take it further he would need to ensure that none of his colleagues opposed it, even if their support was not enthusiastic. Palmerston was well aware that cabinet support was unlikely for a policy that would necessitate such active participation in Spanish politics. In Spain, too, the plan would require skilful handling: even if the Progresistas agreed to support it, it would still be necessary to restore them to power and, once there, to hold them to their promises. Palmerston knew as well as anyone that there were few certainties in Spanish politics. Moreover, even successful execution of the plan would afford Palmerston no short-term satisfaction: there would be no immediate setback for Guizot, no spectacular triumph for himself. Until it became clear that the eastern powers were resolute in their refusal to take the British view of Utrecht, Palmerston concentrated his efforts on eliciting from them a statement that would enable him to claim that the four powers agreed in regarding the Duchess of Montpensier and her descendants as excluded from the succession to the Spanish throne.

On 31 December Palmerston informed Westmorland that he

[129] 'I have written to ask Olozaga what his opinion is of re-establishing the Salic Law as the speediest and most effectual means of excluding a French Prince from the throne of Spain.' Clarendon to Palmerston, 23 Dec. 1846. B.P. GC/CL/466.

[130] Russell was not very enthusiastic about the plan. 'If indeed the French will consent to waive the Infanta's claims, I shall be very glad to see the succession run in the line of Isabella, Francisco, Enrique, Carlos or Isabella, Carlos, Francisco, Enrique as the Spaniards might prefer. But our Quadruple Alliance binds us, as I think, to support the two daughters of Ferdinand the first in the succession. Any arrangement which altered that succession would only be made with the assent of the four parties to that treaty. We stand at present clear of violating any treaty, Utrecht or Vienna, and we must keep that honourable position.' Memorandum of Lord John Russell, 29 Nov. 1846. B.P. GC/RU/127.

had abandoned his attempt to induce the northern Courts to join Great Britain in a protocol on the Spanish succession. Brunnow, the Russian ambassador in London, had drafted a protocol,[131] but the two Imperial governments had refused to sign it.[132] On 1 January 1847 Palmerston instructed Ponsonby that the British government was prepared to address to the Austrian government a note in which it would ask for the opinions of the Imperial government on the Treaty of Utrecht and the Montpensier succession. If the Austrian reply was satisfactory, the two notes could be published. Palmerston hoped that this new proposal would achieve two things. In his conversations with Ponsonby Metternich had objected more to the form of a protocol than to the opinions expressed in it; an exchange of notes would avoid this difficulty. Palmerston was also beginning to suspect Metternich of an attempt to deceive him by leading him on as far and as long as possible without ever committing Austria to the British view of Utrecht. Ponsonby was to inform Metternich that the British government would only accept an answer that was 'plain, simple and decisive'; if preliminary discussions convinced Ponsonby that the Austrian answer was likely to be hedged round with 'reserves and qualifications', he was to drop the matter.[133]

Ponsonby believed that he could secure from Metternich the reply Palmerston wanted; he assured Stockmar that he stood 'well with Metternich' and that a sincere desire to be on 'the most intimate terms of friendship' with England prevailed at Vienna.[134] In an official note of 15 January 1847 Ponsonby stated to Metternich that:

Her Majesty's Government believe the Austrian Government maintain that the treaties and Laws and renunciations [of Utrecht] do preclude the Duke of Montpensier and his descendants from succeeding to the throne of Spain, but Her Majesty's Government are nevertheless very desirous to obtain from the Austrian cabinet a distinct answer that such is their opinion.[135]

[131] There is a copy of Brunnow's draft, dated Dec. 1846, in F.O. 65/329.
[132] Palmerston to Westmorland, 31 Dec. 1846. F.O. 64/262.
[133] Palmerston to Ponsonby, 1 Jan. 1847. F.O. 7/334.
[134] Ponsonby to Stockmar, 4 Jan. 1847. R.A. H/49/34.
[135] Ponsonby to Metternich, 15 Jan. 1847. F.O. 7/336.

Metternich's reply, delayed until 23 January, justified Palmerston's apprehensions. He avoided the 'distinct answer' requested by the British government, and contented himself with stating that the Austrian government based its attitude on the Treaty of Utrecht and the Pragmatic Act.[136] He did this, he informed Ponsonby, because the ground he stood on was 'stronger than the grounds adopted by Her Majesty's Government'. Ponsonby considered the Austrian reply satisfactory.[137] Westmorland hoped that Palmerston would accept it even though it was not quite what he wanted. Together with Bloomfield they thought it could provide the basis of a *détente* between England and the eastern powers, which could be transformed into an anti-French alliance.[138] Palmerston, however, whose suspicions that Metternich was playing a double game with England and France had received confirmation, rebuked Ponsonby for accepting so unsatisfactory a reply.[139]

During January 1847 the anxiety of Guizot and Flahaut about relations between England and Austria and their negotiations on the Spanish succession revived. The French were perturbed in early January when Metternich sent Hummelauer, an official of the Austrian Foreign Office, to London to discuss matters of general interest with Palmerston,[140] despite Hummelauer's categorical denial that he was empowered to negotiate on Spain.[141] Their fears increased when Metternich suggested to Flahaut on 22 January that the only solution to the Anglo-French difference over the Spanish succession lay in the re-establishment of the Salic Law,[142] when news of Palmerston's new overture of 1 January was leaked to Flahaut, and when Aberdeen warned the French government to be vigilant at Vienna.[143] Guizot was shocked by Metternich's suggestion that the Salic Law should be restored in Spain; if it were associated

---

[136] Metternich to Ponsonby, 23 Jan. 1847. F.O. 7/336.
[137] Ponsonby to Palmerston, 23 Jan. 1847. F.O. 7/336.
[138] Westmorland to Bloomfield, 1 Feb. 1847. Westmorland Papers, B.M.M. 516; Bloomfield to Westmorland, 4 Feb. 1847. Ibid.
[139] Palmerston to Ponsonby, 8 Feb. 1847. F.O. 7/334.
[140] Guizot to Flahaut, 1 Feb. 1847. G.P. 42/AP/9.
[141] Flahaut to Guizot, 6 Jan. 1847. G.P. 42/AP/68; Sainte Aulaire to Guizot, 22 Jan. 1847. A.A.E.C.P. Angleterre 667.
[142] Flahaut to Guizot, 22 Jan. 1847. G.P. 42/AP/68.
[143] Sainte Aulaire to Guizot, 29 Jan. 1847. G.P. 42/AP/66.

with any attempt to restore Montemolin to the succession it would, he assured Metternich, plunge Spain once more into civil war and anarchy. In this event Austria would suffer as much as France:

La France a besoin que l'Espagne soit pacifiée et monarchique et conservatrice...L'Autriche surtout a besoin que la France continue à soutenir la politique de conservation. Elle a besoin du concours, de l'action morale de la France en Italie, en Suisse. Ressusciter à notre porte, en Espagne, l'état révolutionnaire, c'est ôter à la France non seulement tout moyen, mais peut-être toute envie de persévérer ailleurs dans cette politique. Si le désordre renaît en Espagne, il peut naître en Italie.[144]

The Austrian response to Guizot's warning was immediate and favourable. Metternich assured Flahaut that his answer to Ponsonby's note of 15 January was written with the intention of maintaining Austria's neutral position between England and France.[145]

In February 1847 the Russian and Austrian governments made determined efforts to extricate themselves from the negotiation on the Spanish succession. After Ponsonby's note of 15 January Metternich realised that equivocation was no longer possible. Moreover, there was no longer any need for an ambiguous policy; the debates in the British Parliament and the French Chambers on Cracow were over and it was clear that there would be no reconciliation between England and France in the near future. Metternich believed that the position he had adopted had enabled him to overcome short-term difficulties without prejudice to his future relations with either England or France. The British government, though it had failed to secure the full or immediate support of Austria, could comfort itself with the reflection that Austria's position differed as much from that of France as it did from that of Great Britain, and that

[144] Guizot to Flahaut, 1 Feb. 1847. G.P. 42/AP/9.
[145] Flahaut to Guizot, 6 Feb. 1847. A.A.E.C.P. Autriche 343. On 15 Feb. Flahaut informed Guizot that Metternich 'sait que l'influence Anglaise, c'est Espartero, les progressistes, la révolution et l'anarchie, substitués à l'ordre, au principe monarchique et conservateur'. Flahaut to Guizot, 15 Feb. 1847. G.P. 42/AP/68. On 25 Feb. Metternich wrote to Apponyi instructing him to assure Guizot that he would not depart from the position he had adopted in 1833. See Metternich, *Mémoires*, vii, 383–8.

future co-operation with the northern Courts would be possible if Britain agreed to support the re-introduction of the Salic Law.[146] The French were relieved that Austria had not upheld the British view of Utrecht, and would be anxious for continued Austrian support in view of continuing bad relations with England. Metternich believed that this would considerably ease the difficulties of taking direct action in Switzerland and Italy should it become necessary.[147] The immediate task was therefore to end the negotiations with Palmerston. On 11 February Canitz regretted that the two Imperial Courts seemed anxious to end negotiations 'without that concert or communication with England which he had expected'.[148] On 23 February Bloomfield informed Palmerston that Nesselrode was 'shifting his ground on the Montpensier Marriage question'; on 3 March he concluded regretfully that Nesselrode was 'most anxious. . . that the subject will be allowed to drop'. Both he and Ponsonby failed in their valiant efforts to revive discussion on the Spanish succession at St Petersburg and Vienna. 'I am sorry to have to repeat my impression', wrote Bloomfield on 17 March, 'that this Court desires above all to remain in statu quo on the Spanish question, and that I fear there is a secret understanding with the Court of Austria on the subject'.[149] At St Petersburg it was reported that Metternich was 'disinclined to move hand or foot'.[150] By the beginning of April Palmerston had reached the conclusion that he could expect only unsatisfactory answers from Metternich to his questions on the Spanish succession. 'The fact is', wrote Palmerston to Bloomfield on 3 April,

Metternich has broken his word to us about the Montpensier Marriage question and has thrown us over for France. His note of January was a Jesuitical equivocation worthy of Loyola or of a Delphic Oracle, but it was paying us a very bad compliment to suppose us dull enough to be satisfied with it. But Guizot has caught Metternich, having baited his hook with promises to take the

[146] Ponsonby to Palmerston, 18 Feb. 1847. F.O. 7/336.
[147] Metternich, *Mémoires*, vii, 322–5, 331–2.
[148] Westmorland to Palmerston, 11 Feb. 1847. F.O. 64/272.
[149] Bloomfield to Palmerston, 23 Feb. 1847. B.P. GC/BL/167; Bloomfield to Palmerston, 3 Mar. 1847. B.P. GC/BL/168; Bloomfield to Palmerston, 17 Mar. 1847. B.P. GC/BL/169.
[150] Bloomfield to Westmorland, 17 Mar. 1847. Westmorland Papers, B.M.M. 516.

absolutist line about Switzerland, Italy and Germany; and I give up entirely any expectation of seeing Austria take part against France in any political question for some time to come. Sooner or later Guizot will throw over Austria, and then Metternich will be very angry and we shall laugh at him.[151]

To Ponsonby Palmerston contented himself with pointing out that 'it is not love but fear which impels' Metternich towards France.[152]

French diplomats in eastern Europe were jubilant at Palmerston's failure to secure the support of the eastern powers for his interpretation of Utrecht. Flahaut considered it another triumph for Guizot's diplomacy, and urged him to establish an immediate and intimate understanding with Metternich.[153] This Guizot attempted to do in March 1847 when the Chevalier Klindworth went to Vienna as his special emissary for secret discussions with Metternich. Guizot himself was pleased that Metternich had refused to support the British view of Utrecht, but he realised that it was not Austria's attitude towards Spanish affairs but Palmerston's refusal to consider a reconciliation with France that formed the real basis of his new intimacy with Metternich. A temporary danger had been averted, but Guizot knew that his diplomacy was entering a new phase in which he would encounter difficulties he had always hoped to avoid. Palmerston, on the other hand, felt that his diplomacy had received only a temporary setback. As far as he was concerned, the battle over the Spanish succession was by no means over.

[151] Palmerston to Bloomfield, 3 Apr. 1847. B.P. GC/BL/223.
[152] Palmerston to Ponsonby, 6 Apr. 1847. B.P. GC/PO/544.
[153] Flahaut to Desages, 5 Mar. 1847. G.P. 42/AP/68.

CHAPTER VII

Currents of Thought

Guizot attributed Palmerston's refusal to act in concert with France over Cracow to personal antipathy towards himself, and to the opportunism which, he believed, had led Palmerston to abandon Cracow in the hope of gaining the support of the eastern powers over the Spanish succession. He did not think that Palmerston's decision reflected the considered views of the British cabinet, nor the tenor of public opinion, that good relations between England and France were impossible while the Duchess of Montpensier remained heiress presumptive to the Spanish throne.[1] In November and December Jarnac had reported that none of Palmerston's cabinet colleagues shared to the same extent his obsession with the Spanish succession.[2] Moreover, Guizot had reason to believe that there was increasing dissatisfaction outside the cabinet with Palmerston's policy: Aberdeen expressed his contempt for it both privately to Jarnac[3] and in his directives to Reeve and Delane of *The Times*;[4] Jarnac reported that Disraeli and Stanley, the two Protectionist leaders, were preparing to attack Palmerston's extreme stand on the Spanish succession, an issue which in their view did not affect the vital interests of Great Britain, at the opening of the new session of Parliament.[5] In Guizot's view one of the main tasks of French diplomacy at the end of 1846 should be to afford the goodwill and desire for a *rapprochement* that existed on both sides of the Channel an opportunity to manifest themselves.[6] He

[1] Guizot to Flahaut, 3 Dec. 1846. G.P. 42/AP/9.
[2] Jarnac to Desages, 22 Dec. 1846. G.P. 42/AP/69.
[3] Jarnac to Desages, 5 Dec. 1846. G.P. 42/AP/69.
[4] Aberdeen to Delane, 22 Nov. 1846. Printing House Square MSS., Delane Correspondence, vol. 2.
[5] Lyndhurst to Brougham, n.d., enclosure Jarnac to Desages, 5 Dec. 1846. G.P. 42/AP/69.
[6] On 22 Dec. Sainte Aulaire informed Guizot that 'our friends in the cabinet hope your speech in the Chamber will not be aggressive and will include general statements of goodwill'. Sainte Aulaire to Guizot, 22 Dec. 1846. G.P. 42/AP/66.

was convinced that a widespread and widely publicised spirit of compromise would force Palmerston to take a more moderate attitude to France and to abandon his efforts to remove the Duchess of Montpensier from the Spanish succession.[7] Although Guizot did not expect that Anglo-French relations could be restored to the level of confidence and cordiality they had reached when he and Aberdeen had presided over them, he hoped that they could be redeemed from the nadir to which they had sunk since September 1846.

In December 1846 Guizot looked to the forthcoming debates on the Spanish marriages in the new sessions of the French Chambers and the British Parliament to reveal the goodwill from which he expected so much. He believed that the negotiations of July and August should be treated as a series of regrettable misunderstandings; it was essential that the debates should be friendly in tone.[8] This desire to use the debates as the basis for an improvement in Anglo-French relations, constantly reiterated in Guizot's correspondence with Jarnac and Sainte Aulaire throughout December 1846, was undoubtedly sincere, but it was not his sole consideration. The debates would be primarily a discussion of the negotiations of July and August. Guizot knew that he would have to defend his conduct, produce the evidence on which he based his defence, and repel the charges levelled against him by Palmerston and Thiers. The way to avoid a re-opening of old wounds, he believed, was to keep discussion on the negotiations of July and August as short as possible.[9] This wish was not entirely high-minded; the briefer the debate on the *procédés*, the less likely were the weaknesses of Guizot's defences to be exposed.

Early in January 1847 Guizot began to take measures to ensure that the debates in the French Chambers went as he wanted and caused him the minimum of embarrassment. The new session of the Chambers was due to open on 11 January, a week before the English Parliament. Guizot believed that this would give him the advantage of creating the first impressions.[10]

[7] Guizot to Jarnac, 21 Dec. 1846. G.P. 42/AP/7.
[8] Guizot to Jarnac, 31 Dec. 1846. G.P. 42/AP/7.
[9] Ibid.
[10] Ibid.

Normanby, who had urged Palmerston to publish the British documents on the Spanish marriages before the French issued their version, was clearly annoyed that Guizot would have the opportunity of defending his conduct without the evidence that condemned him being available to Thiers and the opposition.[11] Even before the Chambers met or any documents were presented to them, the *Revue des Deux-Mondes* published extracts from the correspondence of the British and French governments in July and August, selected and supplied by Guizot.[12] Through Jarnac he had made careful preparations to ensure that the French documents and his first speech in the Chambers received immediate coverage and sympathetic comment in the English press.[13]

In his speech from the throne on 11 January 1847 Louis Philippe claimed that the Montpensier marriage had led to an improvement in relations with Spain, but he omitted to mention the deterioration it had effected in Anglo-French relations.[14] Normanby wrote with evident annoyance that Guizot was trying to set the scene for conciliation.[15] His despondency, however, was short-lived. On 13 January Guizot presented to the Chambers the French documents on the negotiations of July and August[16] which seemed to Normanby to offer the British government a brilliant opportunity to expose Guizot for the

---

[11] Normanby to Palmerston, 4 Jan. 1847. Normanby Papers, Box P, bundle 13.

[12] *Revue des Deux-Mondes*, Jan. 1847. The article was written by the journalist and commentator on foreign affairs, D'Haussonville. 'Every advantage is now daily taken', wrote Normanby, 'to print in the different periodicals here articles insinuating facts and spreading erroneous impressions as to the procédés.' Normanby to Palmerston, 4 Jan. 1847. Normanby Papers, Box P, bundle 13. The *Journal des Débats* on 7 Jan. 1847 reprinted the documents published in the *Revue des Deux-Mondes*, and stated that they showed Guizot's arguments to be conclusive.

[13] On 21 Dec. 1846 Guizot informed Jarnac that he would send him a complete translation of the French documents for him to give to *The Times* to publish on the same day as the documents were published in France. On 31 Dec. Guizot instructed Jarnac not to give Palmerston a copy of the French documents until after they had been published in *The Times*, otherwise, he wrote, all the advantages of early communication to *The Times* would be lost. Guizot to Jarnac, 21 and 31 Dec. 1846. G.P. 42/AP/7.

[14] *Discours du Roi—Séance Royal du 11 Janvier 1847*. There is a copy of the printed version of this speech in F.O. 27/778.

[15] Normanby to Palmerston, 15 Jan. 1847. B.P. GC/NO/39.

[16] *Documents communiqués aux Chambres par le ministre des affaires étrangères: Mariages Espagnols*.

'low, cunning Frenchman' that he was.[17] The French documents were not only a very inadequate account of the negotiations which culminated in the double marriages; they also deliberately falsified two of the key documents, Aberdeen's note of 22 June 1846 to Sotomayor and Palmerston's despatch of 19 July 1846 to Bulwer. These were the documents on which Guizot rested his assertions that Palmerston had departed from Aberdeen's policy and that he had championed Prince Leopold's candidature. The former was summarised to suggest that Aberdeen had never departed from the line that Queen Isabella must marry a Bourbon, and the latter was condensed so as to suggest that Palmerston had recommended the Coburg candidate. Guizot was clearly staking everything on first impressions; when the British documents were published his falsifications would be evident. The risk of exposure was one Guizot felt he had to take since the documents in his versions were essential to his defence. Moreover, he believed that in France the discussions of the *procédés* would have ended by the time the British documents were published.[18] Public reception of the French documents in both France and England was as favourable as Guizot could have hoped for.[19] Both the *Journal des Débats* and *The Times* published them in full.[20] *The Times*, while exonerating Palmerston from blame for the unfortunate conclusion of the affair, refrained from harsh condemnation of Guizot, and concluded the article with an attack on the style of Palmerston's despatches.[21] Normanby, however, made an immediate protest to Guizot about the misrepresentation of the two British documents. After an acrimonious correspondence, Guizot agreed to publish the texts in full, but he delayed doing

[17] Guizot, wrote Normanby, had indulged in 'a systematic perversion of fact'. Normanby to Palmerston, 15 Jan. 1847. B.P. GC/NO/39. Greville, who was in Paris in Jan. 1847, was surprised that Guizot should think it worthwhile 'to practise a piece of deceit which could be exposed in 48 hours'. Greville to Clarendon, 13 Jan. 1847. Clar. Dep. C521.
[18] Guizot to Jarnac, 10 Jan. 1847. G.P. 42/AP/7.
[19] Hervey to Reeve, 18 Jan. 1847. Hervey Papers, 941/61/1. Prince Albert wrote: 'The extracts Guizot has laid before the Chambers are mostly garbled and most unfairly put together; they have produced in France and even here an impression in his favour.' Memorandum by Prince Albert, 19 Jan. 1847. R.A. J/47/24.
[20] *Journal des Débats*, 13 Jan. 1847; *The Times*, 14 Jan. 1847.
[21] *The Times*, 14 Jan. 1847.

so until he had defended his conduct in the Chambers.[22] The risk paid off.

Guizot opened the debate in the Chamber of Deputies on 13 January. His long speech dwelt mainly on the consistency of his Spanish policy and the legitimacy of unilateral action in view of Palmerston's departure from the policy of Aberdeen. In reply, Thiers dismissed Guizot's alleged fears as groundless and condemned the conclusion of the marriages as an act with disastrous consequences for the *entente* and for the liberal cause in Europe.[23] Guizot's speech was warmly received by the Deputies; Normanby admitted that the applause was greater than he had expected.[24] From London, Sainte Aulaire reported that the publication of the French documents, coupled with Guizot's speech, had produced a 'très grand effet sur le public anglais, et déjà quelques personnes y voient la chute de Lord Palmerston'.[25] The Duke of Broglie opened the debate on the Spanish marriages in the House of Peers on 18 January. His speech was well received in both France and England; one of the foremost Anglophile politicians of the July Monarchy, Broglie succeeded in defending French policy in Spain without being offensive to England.[26] On 21 January Guizot spoke to the Peers; his discussion of the *procédés* was perfunctory, the greater part of his speech being devoted to proving himself a sincere friend of England and to expressing the hope that it would not be long before good relations were restored.[27] For the first few days,

[22] Normanby to Guizot, 13 Jan. 1847. F.O. 27/778. Greville, who saw a copy of this note, informed Clarendon that he thought it was very strong, and would make it impossible for Normanby 'to go on with him [Guizot] in any tolerably satisfactory way'. Greville to Clarendon, 13 Jan. 1847. Clar. Dep. C521; Guizot to Normanby, 13 Jan. 1847. F.O. 27/778; Normanby to Palmerston, 18 Jan. 1847. F.O. 27/778.

[23] Guizot's speech was printed in full in the *Journal des Débats*, 14 Jan. 1847, and Thiers' in *Le Constitutionnel*, 14 Jan. 1847.

[24] Normanby to Palmerston, 13 Jan. 1847. F.O. 27/778.

[25] Sainte Aulaire to Guizot, 15 Jan. 1847. G.P. 42/AP/66.

[26] Hervey to Reeve, 18 Jan. 1847. Hervey Papers, 941/61/1.

[27] *Journal des Débats*, 22 Jan. 1847. Greville wrote, 'Guizot's speech was very adroit, in as much as it shirks all the difficulties of the question and does not attempt to grapple with the strong points of ours. He knows that whatever he says here will do for his own people, and for us he is moderate and conciliatory in his language. He never mentioned Aberdeen's dispatch to Sotomayor, butters Aberdeen and throws the blame on Palmerston.' Greville to Clarendon, 21 Jan. 1847. Clar. Dep. C520.

therefore, the debates appeared to be going as Guizot wanted.

In England, the debate on the Spanish marriages opened on 19 January. Prince Albert noted that 'the debate is to be conducted on the part of the members of the government with the greatest of forbearance towards France'.[28] Sainte Aulaire was elated by the tone adopted by the principal participants.[29] Stanley expressed his belief that it was 'essential that this country should be on terms, not of amity merely, but of cordial co-operation and union' with France; he did not consider the Montpensier marriage detrimental to the interests of England, although he did regard the method of its conclusion as discourteous to the British government.[30] Lansdowne, speaking on behalf of the government, claimed that in the Spanish policy of the Whig government:

> There had been no departure...from a wish to maintain that cordial understanding between the French Government and that of Great Britain, which he admitted to be so much for the benefit of Europe and the rest of the world, and which he for one would never relinquish without great regret. With regard to that understanding he would say no more on the present occasion than suggest to the Noble Lords that the less there was of angry debate on the subject, the more likely and the more speedily would the good understanding between the two countries be resumed...[31]

In the Commons Russell spoke more critically of Guizot's policy in Spain and towards England, contending that it was the duty of the British government to resist any attempt by France 'to govern the destinies of Spain'. He regretted that the French government attached so little value to good relations with England, but indulged in no bitter recriminations or detailed exposure of Guizot's bad faith; nor did he rule out good relations with France even while the Duchess of Montpensier remained heiress presumptive to the Spanish throne.[32] The debate was remarkable not only for its friendly tone towards France but also for the silence of both Aberdeen and Palmerston. Aberdeen

---
[28] Memorandum by Prince Albert, 19 Jan. 1847. R.A. J/47/24.
[29] Sainte Aulaire to Guizot, 25 Jan. 1847. G.P. 42/AP/66.
[30] *Hansard*, 3rd series, lxxxix, 22–5: House of Lords, 19 Jan. 1847.
[31] Ibid., 41.
[32] Ibid., 144–7: House of Commons, 19 Jan. 1847.

abstained from participation on the grounds that he wished neither to defend Palmerston nor to criticise Guizot.[33] Palmerston's silence is less explicable. He may have intended to speak after publication of the British Blue Book; he may have wished to avoid discussing the question while he was negotiating with the eastern powers on the Spanish succession. Neither the parliamentary debate nor the publication of the Blue Book on 24 January aroused much public interest in England. Lord George Bentinck, the Protectionist leader, was right in his assertion that the British public 'was more interested in the Spanish carrying trade than in the Spanish Marriages'.[34] Hervey and Normanby were disgusted by the 'low tone' adopted towards France in the British Parliament; Normanby thought it would persuade the eastern powers that there was no point in joining England in a protest against the succession rights of the Duchess of Montpensier, and make it more difficult for Thiers to launch any further attacks on Guizot in the Chambers.[35] At the end of January 1847 a determined effort on both sides of the Channel to end the debates seemed probable. On 29 January Aberdeen called for the cessation of discussion and correspondence on the Spanish marriages;[36] his appeal was taken up by *The Times*,[37] and on 3 February Normanby reported that in Paris further discussion in the Chambers was said to be unlikely.[38] On 5 February, however, the debate was unexpectedly revived in the Chamber of Deputies. Guizot was questioned by members of the opposition on certain discrepancies between his account of the negotiations and that in the British Blue Book. This was what Guizot had hoped to avoid, and he obviously found it difficult to answer their questions. In reply he

[33] Sainte Aulaire to Guizot, 18 Jan. 1847. G.P. 42/AP/66. Greville, who was generally well disposed to Aberdeen, thought that he would not speak because he had too much to answer for, 'especially with the memorandum of February. What answer did he make to this very insulting menace? and what was the necessity for making such a communication to him, whom they assert was already acting with them? What event had occurred, or what was doing at that time to make the step necessary? How did he receive it?' Greville to Clarendon, 21 Jan. 1847. Clar. Dep. C520.
[34] *Hansard*, 3rd series, lxxxix, 107: House of Commons, 19 Jan. 1847.
[35] Normanby to Palmerston, 22 Jan. 1847. B.P. GC/NO/42.
[36] *Hansard*, 3rd series, lxxxix, 602: House of Lords, 29 Jan. 1847.
[37] *The Times*, 1 Feb. 1847.
[38] Normanby to Palmerston, 3 Feb. 1847. F.O. 27/778.

alleged that Normanby's despatch of 25 September to Palmerston contained an inaccurate account of his interview with Guizot on that day.[39] In that interview Guizot had announced to Normanby that the two marriages would take place on the same day. Normanby had thereupon reminded Guizot that on 1 September he had said that the two marriages would not take place at the same time. Guizot 'denied at first having used such words', but when Normanby

> reminded him that I had the next day read to him what I had written to Your Lordship as having passed between us and received his assent as to its accuracy...he then admitted that he had said something to that effect but only that the Queen's marriage should take place first; "and so", he added, "it will, she will be married first".'[40]

Normanby's report of 25 September had clearly suggested that on 1 September Guizot had deliberately deceived the British government; in fact, however, Guizot had given the original assurance in good faith and in an attempt to underplay the significance of the Montpensier marriage. It was only later, under pressure from Queen Christina and Bresson, that he had agreed to the marriages taking place on the same day. Normanby's reminder of 25 September of his assurances of 1 September had clearly embarrassed Guizot, and he had attempted to evade its implications. On 5 February, therefore, Guizot's only obvious way of explaining the discrepancies was to deny the accuracy of Normanby's report; the temptation to do this was increased by his belief that the questions had been put by the opposition at Normanby's instigation.

Since the arrangement of the Spanish marriages, relations between Guizot and Normanby had deteriorated rapidly. Their dislike was mutual; Normanby considered Guizot a pedant,[41] and Guizot thought Normanby lacking in respect and discretion.[42] Thiers and the opposition soon exploited their antipathy by courting Normanby. By frequent attendance at the British embassy, the opposition undoubtedly hoped to gain

[39] Normanby to Palmerston, 6 Feb. 1847. F.O. 27/778.
[40] Normanby to Palmerston, 25 Sept. 1846. *Accounts and Papers, 1847*, lxix, 283–4.
[41] Normanby to Palmerston, 4 Jan. 1847. Normanby Papers, Box P, bundle 13.
[42] Guizot to Sainte Aulaire, 20 Feb. 1847. G.P. 42/AP/9.

information which would enable them to damage Guizot and to create the impression that they were the friends of England and the defenders of the *entente*. Molé was as assiduous in his attendance at Normanby's *salon* as Thiers.[43] Guizot was convinced that Normanby was intriguing to engineer his fall from power; he and Princess Lieven made no secret of this, and statements to this effect appeared in the *Journal des Débats* and *La Presse*.[44] Guizot realised that these rumours were not without their value: they enabled him to discredit Normanby and the opposition by suggesting that their criticisms had no other motive than to displace him. The hint of foreign intrigue would rally Guizot's colleagues and the Deputies behind him. Guizot was doing to Normanby what Palmerston had already done to Jarnac.[45]

Normanby reacted precipitately to Guizot's accusation in the Chamber of Deputies by demanding an official and public apology, and withdrawing an invitation which Guizot had already received to a reception at the British embassy.[46] Thiers and Molé were informed of his resentment and anger, and within days the quarrel between Guizot and Normanby was being discussed in the French press. 'L'affaire Normanby' replaced Guizot's conduct in July and August and Cracow as the major topic of discussion. Guizot refused to apologise because this would be to admit that he had lied to the Chamber.

[43] Greville thought that the frequent appearance of the leaders of the French opposition at the British embassy 'has a very bad air, and even if the coming discussions should leave a possibility of a rapprochement, such clear communication with Guizot's bitterest enemies, will render the relations of the [French] Foreign Office and the Embassy very difficult and uneasy. I find it is now the common report and belief that the Embassy is in constant communication with Thiers and others and the fact is, that it is true.' Greville to Clarendon, 15 Jan. 1847. Clar. Dep. C520.
[44] Normanby faithfully reported all these rumours to Palmerston. See for example Normanby to Palmerston, 16 Feb. 1847. F.O. 27/778. Palmerston minuted on this despatch: 'H.M. Govt feel confident that in this matter as in all others he has acted with perfect propriety.'
[45] In a letter to Russell of 9 Jan. Normanby wrote that Guizot was saying that Normanby was intriguing to bring about his fall. 'He certainly wishes to remain in power and he cunningly enough conceives that nothing would so much mend his chance of doing so as if he could persuade the French that there was an effort on the part of a foreigner to get rid of so national a minister as he.' Normanby to Russell, 9 Jan. 1847. Russell Papers, P.R.O. 30/22/6A.
[46] Guizot to Sainte Aulaire, 20 Feb. 1847. G.P. 42/AP/9.

CURRENTS OF THOUGHT

Normanby retaliated by suspending all contact with the French government, a move that received the full support of Palmerston.[47] The quarrel between the two men threatened to become a major diplomatic incident. Palmerston warned Sainte Aulaire that if Normanby did not receive satisfaction he would return to London and no successor would be appointed; the Paris embassy would be reduced to a legation.[48] Without authority from Guizot, Sainte Aulaire asserted that if Normanby returned to London, he would return to Paris.[49]

Normanby had played into Guizot's hand, delivering insult for insult, by his withdrawal of the invitation to the embassy reception and by ensuring that it received publicity in the opposition press. Guizot's cabinet colleagues stood by him: all refused to attend the reception.[50] Normanby had forfeited his position as the injured party by his breach of etiquette, and Guizot was able to play on the fact that the French government had been insulted; he stated that he would only give an apology if Normanby gave him one.[51] Although Russell sympathised with Normanby, he was anxious for a reconciliation with Guizot in order to avoid the cessation of diplomatic relations on the ambassadorial level, which he felt would meet with strong criticism in England.[52] At the beginning of March a compromise was reached. Guizot and Normanby agreed to meet and shake hands at the Austrian embassy, and contact between the French government and the British embassy was resumed.[53] Normanby did not conceal the fact that he had agreed to a reconciliation under pressure from London, and he informed Palmerston that he proposed to keep future contacts with Guizot to a minimum.[54]

[47] Palmerston to Normanby, 26 Feb. 1847. B.P. GC/NO/436.
[48] Palmerston told Sainte Aulaire, 'That if the result of this affair should be that you [Normanby] should be forced to leave Paris...no other ambassador would be sent and the diplomatic relations between the two countries would be brought down to the nature of those which now exist between France & Russia; there to remain until Guizot might chuse to drive away our chargé d'affaires also.' Palmerston to Normanby, 19 Feb. 1847. Normanby Papers, Box P, bundle 19.
[49] Guizot rebuked Sainte Aulaire for having made this threat. Guizot to Sainte Aulaire, 25 Feb. 1847. G.P. 42/AP/8.
[50] Guizot to Flahaut, 24 Feb. 1847. G.P. 42/AP/9.
[51] Ibid.
[52] Russell to Palmerston, 22 Feb. 1847. B.P. GC/RU/138.
[53] Guizot to Sainte Aulaire, 1 Mar. 1847. G.P. 42/AP/8.
[54] Normanby to Palmerston, 8 Mar. 1847. B.P. GC/NO/44.

Appearances were restored, but the antipathy between Normanby and Guizot remained as strong as before.[55] Their quarrel assumed exaggerated proportions largely because it arose not only out of personal distrust but out of the struggle of the parties within France, and because it was exploited by the French press. It was also symptomatic of the state of irritation, mistrust and rancour that characterised relations between the two governments. Despite Guizot's hopes to the contrary, the friendly tone of the debates on the Spanish marriages in both England and France in January had done nothing to improve the relations between them.

By the end of February 1847 it was evident that no immediate improvement in Anglo-French relations was likely. In Palmerston's view the Montpensier marriage had revealed the true spirit of French foreign policy; in September 1846 he declared to Clarendon that French aggression in Spain made it his duty 'in future to pursue an English policy and to act with reference to English interests', sacrificing nothing for a 'pretended entente cordiale'.[56] While the 'fatal marriage question remains unsolved', Normanby was instructed to inform Molé, good relations with France were 'hardly possible'.[57] *The Times* and *La Presse*, reflecting the views of Aberdeen and Guizot, asserted that England and France were estranged only by Palmerston's 'recollection of his defeat'.[58] This suggestion was the calumny of his enemies, Palmerston informed Sainte Aulaire; the real 'question between England and France was not one of persons, or of procédés, but of substantial things'.[59] The only remedy was for 'a law to be passed in Spain settling this question in the only way in which it can be settled, for the mere renunciation of the Infanta unless made law by the Cortes would of course not be sufficiently conclusive': this was Palmerston's verdict to James Rothschild, a member of the French

[55] In Sept. 1847 Guizot informed Broglie that Normanby remained 'vif et hostile' towards him, but that their relations were 'poli mais froid et de courte conversation'. Guizot to Broglie, 16 Sept. 1847. G.P. 42/AP/214.
[56] Palmerston to Clarendon, 30 Sept. 1846. Clar. Dep. C561.
[57] Palmerston to Normanby, 4 Feb. 1847. Normanby Papers, Box P, bundle 20.
[58] *The Times*, 9 Dec. 1846; *La Presse*, 7 Dec. 1846; Aberdeen to Delane, 22 Nov. 1846. Printing House Square MSS., Delane Correspondence, vol. 2.
[59] Palmerston to Normanby, 7 Dec. 1846. Normanby Papers, Box P, bundle 20.

banking house and a friend of Guizot, who visited London in December 1846.[60]

Palmerston did not expect the French government to pay the price he demanded for a *rapprochement*. He was convinced that Guizot only wanted to restore good relations to ease his domestic difficulties. Sincerity, in his experience, was not a characteristic of French foreign policy. The French, Palmerston informed Russell, 'talk of renewing the entente as if it was a military position which could be evacuated or occupied by word of command instead of its being a temper of mind dependent not upon will, but upon the conduct of men in dealing with things'.[61] In his view the French would always do what they thought would most damage and thwart England.[62] This would remain the guiding principle of every French government, because all French politicians shared a general hatred of England. More important than the hostility of the politicians was the attitude of Louis Philippe and the officials of the French Foreign Office, whom Palmerston believed to 'have far more power in France than they have here' and to 'direct very much the course of events'.[63] In response to Normanby's frequent comments on the friendly disposition of Louis Philippe, Palmerston wrote:

Depend upon it whatever he may say or swear to the contrary Louis Philippe hates England as a power from the very bottom of his heart as the natural obstacle to the aggrandizement of France and he will always do everything he can or which he dares to do, to weaken us, to hamper us, and to thwart us, and if ever he could put his heel on our neck it would be shod with iron.[64]

Like Louis Philippe, the officials of the French Foreign Office 'hate and detest England, and thirst for vengeance upon us for all the humiliations we have made France undergo'.[65] Palmerston's opinion was that for the French the only purpose of good

[60] Palmerston to Normanby, 18 Dec. 1846. Normanby Papers, Box P, bundle 19.
[61] Palmerston to Russell, 21 Aug. 1847. B.P. GC/RU/1025.
[62] 'The French will always be found everywhere doing that which they think the reverse of what England wishes, or whatever they fancy most adverse to English policy and interests.' Palmerston to Southern, 13 Dec. 1846. B.P. GC/SO/273.
[63] Palmerston to Easthope, 25 Nov. 1846. B.P. GC/EA/55.
[64] Palmerston to Normanby, 14 Mar. 1847. B.P. GC/NO/438.
[65] Palmerston to Easthope, 25 Nov. 1846. B.P. GC/EA/55.

relations with England was 'to keep us quiet or even induce us to play their game'. Any illusions the British might have about French foreign policy only afforded them an advantage which their government would exploit, for the French themselves 'have no illusions; they act upon system, and not from any erroneous notions of what we are about—if they deceive themselves in anything, it is only as to the extent to which they are able to carry their schemes into execution'.[66] Palmerston viewed the Montpensier marriage as part of a long-term plan of aggrandisement, illustrative of the basic character of French foreign policy. Their inordinate ambition and fundamental hostility towards England made it impossible for the two countries to work together.

Palmerston's belief that a *rapprochement* between England and France was impossible while the Spanish situation remained unchanged was shared by almost all his diplomats and by many of his colleagues. Some of the latter, like Lansdowne, Grey and Wood, remained in principle well disposed towards France, and believed that time and goodwill on both sides would heal the breach. In the autumn of 1847 Lansdowne regretfully told Broglie that he could not envisage any improvement in Anglo-French relations until the Queen of Spain had a child; he was, however, anxious to prevent the further deterioration of relations between the two countries.[67] Others, like Russell and Clarendon, regretted the estrangement but could see no alternative. Russell did not 'see much hope' of any change 'so long as the affairs of Spain remain in their present state and Guizot at the head of affairs'.[68] In April 1847 Clarendon replied to a letter from Reeve which was strongly critical of Palmerston's policy towards France:

I do not expect that the divergent interests of England and France will ever run in the same line. The fact is we are too honest for co-operation with France, when we interfere in the affairs of other countries it is with the bona fide wish of benefiting them. When France interferes it is with the mala fide wish of benefiting herself at their expense...[69]

[66] Palmerston to Bulwer, 11 June 1847. B.P. GC/BU/548.
[67] Broglie to Guizot, 13 Oct. 1847. A.A.E.C.P. Angleterre 668.
[68] Russell to Palmerston, 22 Aug. 1847. B.P. GC/RU/157.
[69] Clarendon to Reeve, 1 Apr. 1847. Clar. Dep. C534.

The Queen and Prince Albert were of much the same mind as Russell and Clarendon. In his final despatch to Guizot before relinquishing his post as ambassador in London, Sainte Aulaire reported that, although the Queen retained some affection for the Orleans family, she and the Prince were still bitter about the treatment they had received over the Spanish marriages.[70] The frequent attempts of King Leopold of the Belgians to effect a reconciliation between Queen Victoria and Louis Philippe were unavailing. Prince Albert sent one of his letters to Peel with the dismissive comment: 'My uncle's love for peace and for the French Royal Family seems quite [to] obscure his sight...'[71]

For Palmerston's cabinet colleagues the parting of friends was a sad fact to which they had to adjust; for most British diplomats the breach with France resulted in a state of affairs which they did not hesitate to exploit. They were thorough disciples of Palmerston. Wellesley, the acting chargé d'affaires at Constantinople in the spring of 1847, informed Palmerston that he believed 'all Frenchmen to be without exception, a mass of intrigue'.[72] To Ponsonby the object of the French, 'I speak of all of them, is national aggrandizement'.[73] Bulwer wrote to Clarendon that the Montpensier marriage had inaugurated 'a new epoch' in Anglo-French relations, calling for 'a new policy': the attention of Englishmen must be drawn to foreign affairs, as nothing was 'more likely to affect our commercial greatness...than the unchecked system of aggrandizement in the Mediterranean, which has marked the policy of France, of late years especially...'[74] Hervey's opinion was similar: 'if we are to have the policy of Louis XIV over again', he wrote to Reeve, 'it is impossible that we should long continue friends'. He was convinced that Palmerston's policy towards France was right: 'it is the duty of all those who are really interested in the prosperity of England to endeavour to nip all such [French] projects in the bud'.[75] Criticism of Palmerston's policy seemed

[70] Sainte Aulaire to Guizot, 29 June 1847. G.P. 42/AP/66.
[71] Prince Albert to Peel, 17 Feb. 1847. Peel Papers, B.M. Add. MS. 40441.
[72] Wellesley to Palmerston, 19 Apr. 1847. Cowley Papers, F.O. 519/144.
[73] Ponsonby to Palmerston, 30 Dec. 1847. B.P. GC/PO/550.
[74] Bulwer to Clarendon, 22 Oct. 1846. Clar. Dep. C525.
[75] Hervey to Reeve, 5 Feb. 1847. Hervey Papers, 941/61/1.

to him unpatriotic.⁷⁶ Guizot himself was under no illusions as to the attitude of British diplomats towards France: 'le travail des agents anglais contre nous et notre influence est très actif', he informed Broglie in the autumn of 1847. He knew too that there was no likelihood of their activities meeting with disapproval in London.⁷⁷

Palmerston's hatred of France and his conviction that the French government was determined to extend her interests and influence wherever possible and at the expense of England, meant that he regarded opposition to French aggrandisement and the vigorous defence of English interests as the necessary and unquestionable bases of English foreign policy. To Normanby he wrote: 'We must labour to bring things right, convinced that our friends at Paris will be equally industrious in keeping them wrong.'⁷⁸ This policy raised no problems of principle, only of practice: to what lengths should it be taken? should it be a policy of reserve and caution, implemented only when British interests were attacked, or should it be what Clarendon called a policy of 'counter-irritation',⁷⁹ taking the offensive by attacking French influence wherever it was superior to that of Great Britain? Palmerston pursued the second alternative. He believed that only vigorous and active opposition would contain France and remind her that her schemes would not go unnoticed nor her ambitions unchecked. In his view a passive policy would lead eventually to war; if the French were free to follow their own course their ambition would be limitless and their policy more intrepid. To Palmerston it seemed certain that the diplomacy of resistance would make armed resistance less likely in the future. Moreover, both his restless character and his belief in the benefits conferred by British influence made him unsuited to conduct a quiet and inactive foreign policy. In Spain, in Portugal, in Greece, in any country where he saw French influence in the ascendant or appearing to challenge that of England, Palmerston attacked it by whatever means were at his disposal. For

[76] Hervey to Reeve, 26 Feb. 1847. Hervey Papers, 941/61/1.
[77] Guizot to Broglie, 10 Nov. 1847. G.P. 42/AP/214.
[78] Palmerston to Normanby, 30 Mar. 1847. B.P. GC/NO/441.
[79] Clarendon to Reeve, 1 Apr. 1847. Clar. Dep. C534.

him there were no absolute standards of diplomatic conduct; local conditions had always to be taken into account, and exploited if necessary. Local conditions, however, must be seen in the perspective of great power rivalry. Parties and politicians belonged to two distinct categories, those who were 'independent' and 'liberal' in their outlook and therefore naturally pro-British, and those who were 'corrupt' and 'reactionary' and in the pay of France. Active opposition to France therefore implied active opposition to her agents. In Spain, for example, Palmerston believed that the aim of British policy should be to oust the Moderados. He explained this view to Clarendon, who in turn informed Reeve:

We should support the Progresistas, because not withstanding all their blunders and imprudence and the little use they make of experience they are Spaniards and not Frenchmen like the Moderados. They are the only men who can avert the Montpensier succession and undo the work of Louis Philippe because they wish to see their country independent and have a firm belief in its possibility.[80]

Palmerston was not alone in his conviction that it was the duty of the British government to oppose French influence everywhere. Russell was in general sympathy with Palmerston's aims; he believed that 'we should be more on an equality with the French' in the Mediterranean, and was prepared to extend Anglo-French rivalry to Tunis and Morocco, where he thought British diplomats should be upgraded so 'that they may equal the French in rank'.[81] Despite financial stringency, Auckland made every possible effort to put more men and money at the disposal of the Mediterranean fleet,[82] and throughout 1847 Clarendon loyally supported Palmerston's policies. Where his colleagues differed from Palmerston was over means, not aims. While Russell agreed that the return to power of the Progresistas in Spain would be in English interests, he was not prepared to countenance Bulwer's active involvement in Spanish politics to

[80] Clarendon to Reeve, 18 Sept. 1847. Clar. Dep. C534.
[81] Russell to Palmerston, 10 Dec. 1846. B.P. GC/RU/128.
[82] See Palmerston to Auckland, 9 Oct. 1847. B.P. GC/AU/67; and Auckland to Napier, 26 Jan. 1847. Napier Papers, B.M. Add. MS. 40022.

achieve this end.[83] Palmerston believed that to refuse to overstep the bounds of convention in these matters was to play into the hands of the French, as they were prepared to use whatever means would serve their ends. Guizot liked to believe that it was Palmerston who was unscrupulous and British agents who intrigued with foreign parties and politicians. In fact his strictures on the devious conduct of the British were sheer hypocrisy:[84] he was himself quite content to give a free hand to agents who claimed that they could make and break governments.[85]

Palmerston realised that, if they were known, the extent to which hatred of France determined his foreign policy, the lengths to which he was prepared to go, and the means he was willing to use to subvert French intrigues, would meet with the strong disapproval of the Queen and some of his cabinet colleagues. He therefore attempted to conceal much of what he and British diplomats were doing, and presented his policy as more moderate than it actually was. In November 1846 he advised Easthope to see that the language of the *Morning Chronicle* was not too violent. Although Palmerston admitted that strong language would have a salutary effect on the French, 'the only thing to be regarded is that many of our friends in this country are still duped as to the real sentiments and character of our august ally and that it would not be useful to seem too strongly against their prejudices'.[86] After discussing Anglo-French relations with Palmerston at Windsor in January 1847, Peel informed Aberdeen that:

Palmerston is very cool and temperate in speaking of the Spanish Marriages. He says that France has deceived England, that an unworthy and unfair advantage has been taken. But the thing is done and although confidence is destroyed he has no wish that the feelings of the two countries towards each other should be further exasperated.[87]

---

[83] Russell to Palmerston, 20 Oct. 1847. B.P. GC/RU/164.
[84] See for example Guizot to Sainte Aulaire, 10 Dec. 1846. G.P. 42/AP/8.
[85] In Apr. 1847 Guizot wrote to Glucksburg, French chargé d'affaires at Madrid, 'Je ne puis vous donner des directions précises et spéciales. Vous savez le fond de notre politique. Vous avez latitude quant aux moyens.' Guizot to Glucksburg, 10 Apr. 1847. G.P. 42/AP/7.
[86] Palmerston to Easthope, 25 Nov. 1846. B.P. GC/EA/55.
[87] Peel to Aberdeen, 6 Jan. 1847. Aberdeen Papers, B.M. Add. MS. 43295.

CURRENTS OF THOUGHT

In 1847 Palmerston successfully ensured that considerable ignorance prevailed both within the cabinet and in British political circles as to the real nature of his policies.

Although he made it clear that he was not likely to push the rivalry with France to the point of war, Palmerston was anxious that Great Britain's defences should be improved. He believed that the poor state of the national defences weakened Britain's negotiating power and encouraged the French to take risks. To improve our defences, wrote Palmerston to Napier, 'is the best way to prevent it being necessary to employ them'.[88] This view was shared by many.[89] In 1845 Peel had used the same argument to Parliament to justify proposed increases in defence expenditure. Palmerston was convinced that the only way to prevent France from subjugating Spain completely was by a demonstration of Britain's strength and willingness to resist her. Moreover, the hatred of the English which prevailed in France meant that a sudden surprise attack on England was always a possibility. 'England and France', wrote Palmerston in a memorandum of April 1847 on national defence,

come into contact and often into something like conflict politically and commercially in almost every part of the globe. The insolence or the indiscretion of a subordinate officer, the rival jealousy of grasping merchants, a hundred possible incidents may at any moment give rise to questions which, inflaming national feelings on one side of the Channel or the other, may place the most peace loving Governments to say the least of it, in great embarrassments and which might furnish fair ground of quarrel to a government in France desirous of finding occasion for a rupture.[90]

Were France to make a surprise attack, Palmerston believed that Great Britain would be in grave danger.

I am not afraid of our losing our naval superiority if we can keep the French out of the United Kingdom for a twelvemonth after the

[88] Palmerston to Napier, 23 Jan. 1848. Napier Papers, B.M. Add. MS. 40022.

[89] 'Unless the world can be made to believe that we possess some physical as well as moral power they will pay less and less attention to our opinions and wishes every day, and Louis Philippe will go on till he has fairly got hold of the Spanish throne, just as Louis XIV did.' Hervey to Clarendon, 27 Mar. 1847. Clar. Dep. C529.

[90] Memorandum by Lord Palmerston on Defence, 10 Apr. 1847. Russell Papers, P.R.O. 30/22/6C.

beginning of a war, by that time we should be unassailable. But our danger would be during the first fortnight, three weeks or month, and before we had got our ships in ordinary equipped and manned, and before we had our regular army augmented and our militia ballotted.[91]

While Great Britain's defences remained in their present state, Palmerston warned Russell, 'we should be obliged to go to an extreme point of humiliation or to put the whole country into confusion, either by hurried measures for defence, or by the disturbance of an actual invasion'.[92] He therefore considered that the government would 'be guilty of treason to the country and the Crown if we allowed...the United Kingdom...to be as defenceless as at present'.[93] Improvements were urgently needed. The only thing to do, wrote Normanby, was to create and maintain 'salutary alarm...as to the disgraceful state of our national defences'.[94] This Palmerston did.[95] He was indefatigable in his advocacy of increased naval expenditure[96] and of the reorganisation of the militia.[97] His proposals met with opposition, not from Russell or Wellington, but from Wood, the Chancellor of the Exchequer, who objected on financial grounds.[98] In January 1848 the government laid before Parliament proposals for increased defence expenditure. Although less ambitious than Palmerston wanted, the measures

[91] Palmerston to Normanby, 19 Oct. 1847. Normanby Papers, Box P, bundle 19.
[92] Palmerston to Russell, 11 Jan. 1848. Russell Papers, P.R.O. 30/22/7A.
[93] Palmerston to Clarendon, 23 Sept. 1847. B.P. GC/CL/1361.
[94] Normanby to Palmerston, 16 Oct. 1847. Normanby Papers, Box P, bundle 13.
[95] 'We are all of us', wrote Palmerston to Clarendon, 'sleeping on a barrel of gunpowder and fancying it a feather bed; and some fine day some hot headed Frenchman will apply the match and blow us up. It is mere childish fatuity to be discussing Poor Laws, and Free Trade and Education and Health of Towns and other such like things when we are liable to be swept away as an independent nation whenever France chuses to make the effort. If the country is worth improving it is worth defending and there is no defence for a country but men armed, organised and trained.' Palmerston to Clarendon, 14 Apr. 1847. Clar. Dep. C561.
[96] Palmerston to Auckland, 9 Oct. 1847. B.P. GC/AU/67.
[97] Memorandum on the Defenceless State of the Country, Dec. 1846. B.P. ND/A/2.
[98] Wood to Russell, 21 Mar. 1847. Russell Papers, P.R.O. 30/22/6B. Wood also thought 'it will be better to postpone this matter [defence] till after the general election. I entertain a strong opinion that this will be very unpopular amongst the class of persons from whom we generally derive our support at elections.'

were shelved after the February revolution in France and a cool reception by the House of Commons.[99] Discussions about the national defences in the cabinet throughout 1847 and in Parliament in February 1848 revived discussions as to whether an improvement or a deterioration in relations with France was to be expected. To Palmerston this was immaterial to the fact that Great Britain was 'defenceless', but his expectation was that relations would either remain unchanged or would deteriorate. Unlike Normanby, who believed that 'little Thiers...will support any Govt which should be constructed on the basis of re-establishing the English Alliance',[100] Palmerston thought that Thiers in office would, if anything, be worse for Great Britain than Guizot:

As long as Louis Philippe lives and Guizot remains his chief clerk, the French will only endeavour to cheat us and trick us in every way and to every extent to which we may allow them to go; but Louis Philippe is old and not immortal and Guizot may sink himself and be replaced by Thiers, and if new men were to come into power in France they would not be content with cheating or treachery but might (and Thiers certainly would) be inclined if they thought us defenceless to try what a little quick bullying would do.[101]

[99] C. J. Bartlett, *Great Britain and Sea Power, 1815–1853* (Oxford, 1963), 251. See pp. 183–95 for an excellent discussion of the debate within the cabinet in 1847 on the national defences.
[100] Normanby to Palmerston, 27 Nov. 1846. Normanby Papers, Box P, bundle 12.
[101] Palmerston to Auckland, 9 Oct. 1847. B.P. GC/AU/67. Palmerston was remarkably consistent in his attitude to Thiers. In Sept. 1840 he informed Minto that Thiers was, in his opinion, 'a little rogue and no dependence can be placed upon his pretended love for the English Alliance. But we ought to cease to care who governs France, for govern her who may, we shall always find her hostile at heart...' Palmerston to Minto, 3 Sept. 1840. B.P. GC/MI/580. In 1845 Palmerston refused Thiers' offer of co-operation between the English and French oppositions against the policies of Aberdeen and Guizot. Palmerston was well aware that Thiers was more anxious to get Guizot out and himself back in office than he was to establish good relations with England. Normanby, who seems to have fallen for Thiers' charm, was quite taken in by his protestations of friendship. Halévy undoubtedly exaggerated Normanby's attitude to, and relationship with, the French opposition when he wrote: 'He [Normanby] lost no time in adopting the typical attitude of the Palmerstonian diplomat and attempted to do in Paris what his fellows were doing in Madrid, Lisbon and Athens, to make the Liberal Opposition an Anglophile party inspired and led by himself.' E. Halévy, *Victorian Years, 1841–1895* (London, 1951), 220. Halévy sees the letters that passed between Thiers and Panizzi, an Italian refugee in London, which the latter passed on to Palmerston, as part of a plot by Thiers 'in collusion with Palmerston' to oust Guizot. Ibid., 221. The full

The sad fact, wrote Hervey to Reeve, was that no French government would be 'more ready' than the present one 'to relinquish the Spanish project in which France is now embarked'.[102] Palmerston remarked that no ministerial change in France could succeed in 'impregnating the Queen of Spain',[103] and 'whoever may succeed [Guizot] will be equally the instrument of Louis Philippe's policy'.[104] As long as the Queen of Spain was childless and the Orleans dynasty remained on the French throne, Palmerston saw no chance of the restoration of good relations with France. Although not as pessimistically expressed as Palmerston's, Clarendon's outlook amounted to the same. To Brougham he said that Louis Philippe regarded an intimate alliance with England 'as a marketable commodity, to be exchanged at any time for a dynastic or pecuniary advantage. I do not see how any united action between the two countries will in future be possible.'[105] The effect of the Montpensier marriage had thus been to revolutionise the attitude of most

text of these letters may be found in L. Fagan, *The Life of Anthony Panizzi* (London, 1880). The letters are mainly concerned with Guizot's conduct over the Spanish marriages and with the publication of the British Blue Book on this subject in Jan. 1847. They hardly support Halévy's somewhat wild assertion. Palmerston was obviously willing to see Thiers damage Guizot in the Chambers as much as possible, and supplying him with an advance copy of the British Blue Book on the Spanish marriages would help him to do this. On the other hand, it must be remembered that Palmerston did not make nearly such elaborate preparations to see that the French opposition was furnished with information as Guizot did for the English opposition. Palmerston's attitude to Thiers and his private correspondence, to which Halévy did not have access, show that he in fact preferred Guizot in power to Thiers. He believed that Thiers was more warlike than Guizot. Palmerston, who regularly read the French press, could not have failed to recognise the aggressive tone of *Le Constitutionnel* throughout 1847 towards Austria. Although he differed from both Metternich and Guizot in his attitude to Italy, Palmerston was anxious that Italian problems should be settled peaceably and without intervention. Thiers, on the other hand, advocated French intervention in Italy to forestall Austrian intervention. See *Le Constitutionnel*, 15 Dec. 1847. To Easthope, Palmerston wrote: 'Of course Thiers, being more than anybody French, would cling even more than Guizot to the hold which they all think the Montpensier Marriage would give them over Spain, and he would gladly have the national advantage of the King, and reap the private advantage of ousting Guizot on account of the manner of doing it. But we care not which is Minister; the King will always be the real one...' Palmerston to Easthope, 27 Nov. 1846. B.P. GC/EA/54.

[102] Hervey to Reeve, 23 Apr. 1847. Hervey Papers, 941/61/1.
[103] Palmerston to Russell, 21 Aug. 1847. B.P. GC/RU/1025.
[104] Palmerston to Easthope, 28 Nov. 1846. B.P. GC/EA/55.
[105] Clarendon to Brougham, 22 Nov. 1846. Clar. Dep. C525.

Whigs to foreign policy: they abandoned their enthusiasm for the *entente*, since 1830 the keystone of their policy. In March 1847 Clarendon confessed to Lord Holland, the son of the man with whom in 1840 he had opposed Palmerston's separation from France, that formerly the *entente cordiale* had been his 'beau idéal of unbounded power applicable to universal good', but 'like many an other illusion this one has passed away'.[106]

In a leader in *The Times* in the spring of 1847 Reeve claimed that a diplomatic revolution had taken place. The two groupings which since 1830 had dominated Europe—the 'liberal alliance' and the Holy Alliance—had been replaced by two new combinations—an Austro-French *entente* and an Anglo-Prussian *entente*.[107] Prussian hostility towards France, her willingness to support the British view of Utrecht, and the granting of a limited constitution in February 1847 had, he argued, detached her from her Imperial allies and drawn her closer to Great Britain. Guizot was undoubtedly concerned about the growing intimacy between London and Berlin; he instructed Dalmatie to warn the Prussians of the dangerous consequences of a *rapprochement* with England,[108] and it was one of the questions which Klindworth discussed with Metternich in March 1847.[109] Palmerston, on the other hand, although favourably disposed towards Prussia for her attitude over the Spanish succession,[110] did not regard her as likely to detach herself from Russia

[106] Clarendon to Holland, 9 Mar. 1847. Clar. Dep. C561.

[107] *The Times*, 7 Mar. 1847. Palmerston appears to have made no comment on this leader. Aberdeen, however, read it with 'some apprehension'. It seems to me, he wrote to Delane, 'to indicate a new system of foreign policy, greatly at variance with that which we have hitherto pursued, and which you have supported. Of course we must be friendly to all constitutions, whether good or bad, or whether in Prussia or anywhere else. This is the condition of our existence. But I should have thought that good will and support might have been extended to the Prussian constitution without putting an end altogether to the French Alliance, which is done by your article pretty nearly in express terms.' Aberdeen to Delane, 8 Mar. 1847. Printing House Square MSS., Delane Correspondence, vol. 2.

[108] Guizot to Dalmatie, 4 Mar. 1847. G.P. 42/AP/8.

[109] Conversation between Klindworth and Metternich, 30 Mar. 1847. G.P. 42/AP/68.

[110] 'Pray thank Baron Arnim from me for the kind and friendly part which he has taken in these late and important matters; and assure him that we all feel strongly how important it is to England to maintain a cordial and intimate union with Prussia.' Palmerston to Normanby, 7 Jan. 1847. Normanby Papers, Box P, bundle 19.

and Austria in order to act in concert with England. According to Westmorland, the King and the Prussian government lacked the courage to break with Austria and Russia.[111] Metternich assured Klindworth that Frederick William IV was only flirting with England under the influence of the Anglophile Bunsen and Arnim; his Protestantism and his heart, said Metternich, might push him towards England, but in the last resort his head would pull him back to Austria and Russia.[112]

In fact, after failing to secure their support over the Spanish succession, Palmerston made no attempt to establish a close connection between England and Prussia, or an anti-French coalition with the eastern powers. He was anxious that Prussia should be well disposed towards England, but realised that except in Greece she could offer Great Britain little effective assistance. At Madrid she was not even represented. Palmerston believed that Metternich had 'gone over to France'; in any case in 1847 an immense gulf separated Austria and England on most of the major problems confronting the great powers. The Minto mission to Italy in the autumn of 1847 demonstrated the gap between England and Austria on an issue which touched Austrian interests more closely than any other.[113] Palmerston recognised that England and the eastern powers were separated in 1847 by a basic difference of attitude and priorities: the eastern powers were concerned primarily with problems in their own dominions and in neighbouring states such as Switzerland; England was more concerned to resist French expansionism in western Europe and the Mediterranean. In Palmerston's view, only when the eastern powers recognised the dangers France posed to the peace of Europe and were willing to join Great Britain in resistance to her policies would any real co-operation be possible.[114]

Metternich's expectation that the estrangement between

[111] Westmorland to Bloomfield, 1 Feb. 1847. Westmorland Papers, B.M.M. 516.
[112] Metternich concluded the conversation with Klindworth by stating that the King of Prussia 'ne se séparera pas de moi, il me traite comme son père'. Conversation between Klindworth and Metternich, 30 Mar. 1847. G.P. 42/AP/68.
[113] For the Minto mission and the Italian background to it, see A. J. P. Taylor, *The Italian Problem in European Diplomacy, 1847–49* (Manchester, 1934), ch. i; and *Gran Bretagna e Italia nei Documenti della Missione Minto*, ed. F. Curato (Rome, 1970).
[114] Palmerston to Ponsonby, 6 Apr. 1847. B.P. GC/PO/544.

England and France would force both to continue to make concessions in return for promises of Austrian support was vain. Palmerston did not quickly forget Metternich's deception over the Spanish succession,[115] nor did he fear that France would join the eastern powers in order to form a continental coalition against England. 'France', Palmerston informed Clarendon,

> must go with us in Italian affairs. Metternich thinks he has her in his pocket because he has had promises from Louis Philippe and Guizot, but public opinion in France must be stronger than the King and his minister and as they broke their word to us last year about Spain, so will they be compelled to break their word this year to Metternich about Italy.[116]

By the beginning of March 1847 Guizot had resigned himself to the fact that no immediate improvement in Anglo-French relations was possible. To a certain extent this surprised him as he could see no real barrier to a *rapprochement*. He had made it quite clear in his speeches of January on the Spanish marriages that France had no intention of violating the independence of Spain, that he had acted out of fear and not ambition, and that he was anxious for the restoration of good relations between England and France. He had expected the English Francophiles to take these statements at their face value. He was therefore genuinely disappointed when they did not. Guizot found an explanation for the failure of his friendly overtures in the perversity of Palmerston, who in his view had no appreciation of the true interests of Great Britain. In Guizot's mind the right policy for England was the maintenance of good relations on equal terms with France, each country pursuing its own interests, making concessions to one another where their interests conflicted and co-operating where their interests and aims coincided. For England to pursue this wise and peaceful policy was 'si nécessaire aux intérêts de nos deux pays', Guizot informed Lord Howden, the British diplomat.[117] Guizot

[115] '. . .if we brought [Guizot] back to our ground about Switzerland', wrote Palmerston to Normanby in Nov. 1847, 'and made him desert Metternich on that question, it would be a partial retribution to Metternich for having jilted us about the Spanish Marriages.' Palmerston to Normanby, 16 Nov. 1847. Normanby Papers, Box P, bundle 19.
[116] Palmerston to Clarendon, 23 Sept. 1847. B.P. GC/CL/1361.
[117] Guizot to Howden, 24 Feb. 1847. G.P. 42/AP/7.

believed that Palmerston's policy was the exact opposite of what it ought to be. It was a sad fact which France must accept, Guizot informed Flahaut in late February 1847, that Palmerston:

est entré dans la politique méfiante et isolée. Plus que cela; dans la politique jalouse et rivale. Je doute qu'il vise sérieusement à la guerre et je suis sûr que son pays ne la veut pas. Mais il provoquera, il engagera partout l'hostilité secrète, la lutte d'influence.[118]

Like Guizot, Desages could see no motive in Palmerston's policy other than to satisfy 'son esprit de vengeance contre nous'.[119] Although Guizot had no illusions about Palmerston's attitude towards himself and France, and realised that he would have to adapt his policy to meet the challenge this posed, he never believed that the estrangement of England and France over the Montpensier marriage was more than a temporary misunderstanding. He was convinced that sooner or later Palmerston would inevitably be exposed as a warmonger and as the only obstacle to a restoration of good relations with France. Guizot never thought that the Whig cabinet as a whole would lose its 'engouement pour l'entente'. He believed that as soon as Palmerston's colleagues became aware of the dangers inherent in his policy, they would rid themselves of him. But before this could happen the Russell government might itself fall; English politics were so unstable that anything could happen. He informed Broglie on the eve of his assumption of the post of ambassador to London that one day, and perhaps in the near future, there would be:

en Angleterre quelque revirement des partis et des hommes qui remettra les idées justes et les intérêts vrais à la place de toutes ces susceptibilités, jalousies, vanités et chimères nationales et individuelles. C'est à attendre ce moment et à prévenir, en l'attendant, tout accident grave que nous travaillons vous et moi.[120]

The fact that Guizot believed that there was no real issue that separated England and France and that it was the ignorance of Palmerston's colleagues as to the true nature of his policy which kept him in power meant that the difficulties which

[118] Guizot to Flahaut, 24 Feb. 1847. G.P. 42/AP/9.
[119] Desages to Bourqueney, 17 Nov. 1846. Bourqueney Papers, A.E. France 1900.
[120] Guizot to Broglie, 8 July 1847. G.P. 42/AP/214.

CURRENTS OF THOUGHT 209

confronted French foreign policy in 1847 could be seen as not of Guizot's own making, but entirely attributable to Palmerston's hatred of France. By the spring of 1847, therefore, Guizot's most fervent hope, the answer to all his problems, was that Palmerston would be dismissed or that the Whig government would fall; until this happened, he wrote to Bresson, 'nous avons un rude défile à traverser'.[121] Unlike Palmerston and his diplomats, who hated all things French, Guizot and his diplomats regarded themselves as only anti-Palmerston and not anti-English. As Guizot saw it, the task of French policy was not just to oppose Palmerston's policy, but also to expose it for the folly it was.

Guizot regretted that Palmerston's enmity towards France and the complexity of the European situation in 1847 made it impossible for him to pursue a policy which looked straightforward and consistent. He regretted this partly because he attached great value to the consistency of his policy; it was this, he believed, that gave it its strength and was its chief recommendation in France.[122] He knew too that his opponents in France would find it easier to misrepresent and attack a complex policy. As Flahaut told Metternich: 'La politique compliquée est difficile pour les Ministres qui ont à s'expliquer devant les Chambres et l'opinion publique.'[123] Guizot believed that while Palmerston remained in office and while the situation in central Europe was tense, France would have to reckon with the bitter enmity of England in the Mediterranean.[124] In central Europe France would have to stand between 'les conspirations radicales fomentées de Londres et les routines absolutistes de Vienne'.[125] Guizot realised that there was no easy solution to these problems. What he hoped to do was to treat these two major areas of conflict separately. He was determined not to sacrifice French interests, but to safeguard them by a policy of careful balance.[126]

It would be difficult, wrote Desages to Glucksburg, to find in

[121] Guizot to Bresson, 5 Dec. 1846. G.P. 42/AP/8.
[122] Guizot to Flahaut, 24 Feb. 1847. G.P. 42/AP/68.
[123] Flahaut to Guizot, 31 Jan. 1847. G.P. 42/AP/68.
[124] See Guizot to Bourqueney, 6 July 1847. Bourqueney Papers, A.E. France 1901.
[125] Guizot to Broglie, 30 July 1847. G.P. 42/AP/214.
[126] Guizot to Flahaut, 2 Mar. 1847. G.P. 42/AP/9.

England twenty people who were not convinced that France was bent on the complete subjection of Spain: 'c'est assurément fâcheux et regrettable; mais cela ne nous empêchera pas de conduire notre fiacre'.[127] Guizot and Louis Philippe were determined to uphold French interests and influence in Spain. In the struggle with Palmerston, wrote Guizot, 'après Paris, Madrid est le point capital'.[128] The result of the Montpensier marriage and Palmerston's opposition to it was that Guizot regarded Spain as the touchstone of French prestige; any French setback in Spain would be a triumph for Palmerston. He was as determined to maintain the Moderado régime and the succession rights of the Duchess of Montpensier as Palmerston was to replace the former and deny the latter;[129] Guizot was therefore prepared to run even greater risks in Spain after the marriage than before it. He hoped that a defensive policy would be sufficient, but he was prepared to sanction almost anything that would keep the Moderados in power and well disposed towards France, since he believed that only these conditions could ensure the continuation of French influence over Spain and the maintenance of the succession rights of the Infanta.[130]

In so far as Spanish issues were of European concern, Guizot hoped for the support of Austria,[131] although at Madrid France would have to defeat Palmerston's intrigues alone. To counteract the advocates of revolution, said Guizot, the advocates of order must submerge their differences and stand together.[132] In March 1847 Guizot sent the Chevalier Klindworth on a secret mission to Vienna. His task was to inform Metternich of Guizot's views on the major problems confronting the great powers, and to assure Metternich that Guizot was a champion of order and anxious to work with Austria. In fact Guizot was trying to conceal the expediency that dictated his approach to Metternich

[127] Desages to Glucksburg, 14 Aug. 1847. G.P. 42/AP/53.
[128] Guizot to Bresson, 5 Dec. 1846. G.P. 42/AP/8.
[129] Guizot to Bresson, 15 Dec. 1846. G.P. 42/AP/8.
[130] See above, pp. 214–17.
[131] 'Quelle politique vaut le mieux pour la cause de l'ordre et de la monarchie en Espagne, celle de Lord Palmerston ou la nôtre? Posez ainsi la question au Prince de Metternich, car elle est toute là. Je ne puis douter de sa réponse.' Guizot to Flahaut, 2 Mar. 1847. G.P. 42/AP/9.
[132] Conversation between Klindworth and Metternich, 29 Mar. 1847. G.P. 42/AP/68.

behind a parade of supposedly common principles. In some ways Guizot's outlook on the issues facing the great powers in Italy, Switzerland and Germany was nearer Metternich's than Palmerston's—like Metternich and unlike Palmerston, he was fundamentally out of sympathy with the aspirations of the German and Italian nationalists, and he bitterly disliked the Swiss radicals[133]—but whereas Guizot feared change he did not despair of it completely. He thought that government must eventually adapt itself to and reflect the society it ruled. Metternich, on the other hand, was prepared neither to admit the truth of this proposition nor to permit its practice or anything resembling it in the Habsburg dominions or her client states. Guizot's actual policy towards Italy, Switzerland and Germany was likely to be less conservative than he led Metternich to think it would be. Even though he was a determined opponent of revolution Guizot realised that he could not completely identify France with the counter-revolutionary eastern powers. 'Le succès du parti modéré', he wrote to Broglie, 'est partout notre succès.'[134] The different outlooks of Metternich and Guizot were not all that separated Austria and France. In Italy and Switzerland they were traditional rivals; if France were now to range herself behind Austria in these countries, Guizot thought that this would be as inimical to French interests as it would be offensive to French liberals. The understanding between Guizot and Metternich[135] was designed, as far as Guizot was concerned, to protect France against the rancour of Palmerston rather than to establish a basis for joint action on common problems. Flahaut told Russell that his 'office at Vienna...was simply to oppose England'.[136] Guizot's rejection of Metternich's approaches in June 1847 for joint action on Swiss affairs showed how reluctant he was to range

[133] See P. Thureau-Dangin, 'La France et l'Europe à la veille de la révolution de 1848', *Revue d'Histoire Diplomatique*, 1892, 110–31.
[134] Guizot to Broglie, 30 July 1847. G.P. 42/AP/214.
[135] For the relations between Guizot and Metternich in 1847, see Thureau-Dangin, op. cit., and Prince Clemens Metternich, *Mémoires et Documents*, ed. Prince Richard Metternich, vii, 388–405. The conversations between Metternich and Klindworth in Mar. 1847, the accounts of which run to over a hundred pages, can be found in G.P. 42/AP/68.
[136] Greville to Delane, 13 Nov. 1847. Printing House Square MSS., Delane Correspondence, vol. 2.

France behind Austria even when their outlooks were the same.[137]

Although Guizot was anxious for Austrian support against Palmerston, he also wanted British support in restraining the forces both of revolution and of reaction in central Europe. He believed that Palmerston was a partisan of the revolutionaries in Italy and Switzerland because chaos on France's eastern borders and sharp conflict with Austria would absorb French attention and prevent her from making a vigorous defence of her interests in Spain and the Mediterranean.[138] In the final resort, he was convinced that Palmerston would have to abandon the cause of revolution and co-operate with France in central Europe, partly because of pressure from his cabinet colleagues and public opinion, partly to avoid isolation and exclusion from the affairs of Europe.[139] Like Palmerston, Guizot believed that on certain issues and problems each was necessary to the other. Palmerston thought he could force Guizot to abandon Metternich. Guizot thought he could force Palmerston to abandon his revolutionary sympathies.

In the spring of 1847, therefore, Guizot's hopes for the future depended on his ability to perform an elaborate balancing act between England and Austria. Although this would be difficult, at least the cabinet was united and the majority of the French nation would, he felt sure, understand and support his policy: 'nous avons pour nous le sentiment public aussi bien que l'appui du Roi et de la majorité'. Public opinion would, he assured Flahaut, 'approuve et soutient sans crainte ce qui l'alarmerait beaucoup sous un autre drapeau'. Palmerston and Thiers would persist in their tactics of intimidation, but Guizot was convinced that he would triumph: 'on ne nous forcera point la main'; we shall cling, Guizot wrote, to 'l'esprit d'ordre du gouvernement régulier et de conservation'.[140]

[137] Guizot to Flahaut, 25 June 1847. A.A.E.C.P. Autriche 434.
[138] Guizot to Bourqueney, 6 July 1847. Bourqueney Papers, A.E. France 1901.
[139] Guizot to Broglie, 30 July 1847. G.P. 42/AP/214.
[140] Guizot to Flahaut, 24 Feb. 1847. G.P. 42/AP/9.

CHAPTER VIII

Iberian Problems,
October 1846–February 1847

In 1847 the struggle over the Spanish succession was the most bitter and unrestrained conflict in which England and France were involved; it was certainly the most divisive issue between them and easily the most productive of tension. Palmerston was convinced that Louis Philippe and Guizot were bent on the complete subjugation of Spain to France, and he saw the Montpensier marriage as a step towards this goal. He was quite sure that, given the chance, Louis Philippe would attempt to 'establish the Montpensiers in the Escurial'. 'You are quite right', Palmerston informed Normanby, 'in thinking that we must keep our eyes sharply fixed on the proceedings of the French about Spain; as they have broken the ice they will probably be less scrupulous about a future plunge.'[1] If the French were to succeed in placing Spain under their tutelage, Palmerston feared disastrous consequences for both Spain and England. Spanish constitutionalism would be dealt a fatal blow: Spain would be governed from Paris by means of Bourbon tyranny and corrupt politicians; material progress and prosperity would disappear with the constitutional institutions which alone could guarantee them. If the Spaniards resisted—and Palmerston felt sure that a large number of them would—England would inevitably be drawn into 'a new war for the independence of Spain'. Palmerston further feared that if Paris controlled the politics of Madrid, Portuguese independence and constitutionalism would also be in jeopardy. In his view the insatiable appetite for power manifested by the French would not be satisfied by dominion over Spain. Unless France were resisted, England would before long be fighting a war for the

[1] Palmerston to Normanby, 19 Mar. 1847. B.P. GC/NO/439.

independence of the small states of western Europe. Palmerston's genuine, albeit exaggerated, fears for Spanish independence and peace in western Europe were never understood by Guizot; to him Palmerston's Spanish policy seemed merely vindictive.

The restoration of a close relationship between France and Spain was, in Guizot's view, one of the corner-stones of his foreign policy, and certainly its greatest achievement. He saw a return to the historic traditions of French policy as the most effective way of weaning the French nation away from their more recent revolutionary traditions. In his opinion his Spanish policy and its success were contributions to stability in France and peace in western Europe. More than this, he believed that the exercise of French influence over Spain was both legitimate for France and in the best interests of Spain. France, as a great power, needed outlets for her energy and opportunities to manifest her equality with the other great powers, all of whom exercised influence over one or other of their less powerful neighbours. Stability in Spain depended, in Guizot's view, on French support for the alliance between the Crown and the Moderados, the only political combination likely to endure and ensure material prosperity by reason of the compromise it represented between old and new forces in Spanish society. Guizot feared that Palmerston's policy would plunge Spain into anarchy and revolution merely to satisfy his injured pride and to humiliate France. On his side, Palmerston was as insensible to the aims and fears underlying Guizot's policy as Guizot was to his. Their misunderstanding was total, and it was therefore in an atmosphere of intense suspicion that each developed and pursued his Spanish policies. This in its turn gave their struggle its own momentum: each was prepared to take desperate steps to alter a situation which appeared desperate. Moreover, the conflict was exacerbated by the presence at Madrid of British and French diplomats who detested one another. Bresson's return to Paris in the spring of 1847 did nothing to reduce the tension at Madrid as his temporary successor, the young Duke of Glucksburg, hated Bulwer with even greater intensity than Bresson had done.

In December 1846 Guizot warned Sainte Aulaire that in 1847 the struggle over the Spanish succession would be fought on three fronts: 'il y a un triple travail en train', he wrote.² In the immediate aftermath of the Montpensier marriage both Guizot and Palmerston had concentrated their efforts on gaining the support of the northern powers, but by December 1846 they had both evolved new policies for the situations that confronted them in Spain and Portugal. We must, wrote Guizot, defeat Palmerston's diplomacy in Europe, frustrate his intrigues at the Court of Queen Isabella, and prevent him from exploiting the situation in Portugal to the detriment of the established order in Spain.³

At Madrid there was a new Court. In theory Queen Isabella had been in full possession of her sovereign powers since 1839, but they had in practice been exercised first by Espartero, and after his fall by Queen Christina. Immediately after her marriage, however, at the age of sixteen, the Queen began to transact official business; Queen Christina was in eclipse. Christina's decline was in part the natural result of her daughter's assumption of royal authority. The swiftness with which she was superseded, however, reflected Queen Isabella's resentment at being forced by her mother into a marriage with a man she disliked. Within two or three months Spanish Court politics turned full circle from domination by Christina to hatred of her. Bulwer and Palmerston hoped to exploit the new situation at Court, and in time to wean Isabella away from the Moderados. If Queen Isabella will accept 'a Liberal Govt—we may foil the French cabinet yet', wrote Palmerston.⁴ They also hoped that the family of Don Francisco de Paula would, out of hatred of Christina, self-interest,⁵ and as a consequence of their association with the Progresistas, persuade the Queen to accept a ministry committed to denying the Duchess of Montpensier her succession rights. Once again the emphasis of British policy was on reconciliation between the anti-French forces in Spain and the Court.⁶

² Guizot to Sainte Aulaire, 10 Dec. 1846. G.P. 42/AP/8.
³ Guizot to Bresson, 15 Dec. 1846. G.P. 42/AP/8.
⁴ Palmerston to Normanby, 19 Mar. 1847. B.P. GC/NO/439.
⁵ If the Infanta were removed from the line of succession Don Francisco de Paula and his sons would follow the Queen immediately in the order of succession.
⁶ 'The battle must now', wrote Palmerston, 'be fought at the elections, in the Cortes, in the newspapers and at last in the Court and at the Palace. But we must carry our objects by sap and not by storm. Your endeavours to unite parties for Spanish and national purposes against French influence are just what we wish.' Palmerston to Bulwer, 15 Nov. 1846. B.P. GC/BU/525.

Palmerston was aware that this would be a matter of time and careful preparations. 'We must be patient', he informed Bulwer.[7]

Guizot, on the other hand, was determined that Palmerston should not exploit the divisions and enmities within the Spanish royal family. Queen Isabella must be made to realise that the stability of her throne depended on the maintenance of a Moderado ministry, and the family of Don Francisco de Paula must be made to pledge their support for the existing order of succession. The first of these tasks he left to Bresson:

L'essentiel pour nous, le capital, c'est donc d'empêcher la formation d'un Ministère progressiste et de retenir dans le camp modéré, sous le drapeau modéré, par crainte ou par amour, la Reine et le Roi. Toute notre politique doit être là.[8]

Louis Philippe applied himself to the second task. He informed Don Francisco de Paula that if Palmerston succeeded in changing the order of succession it would inevitably be at the expense of the rights of his family and in favour of the Carlists.[9] Don Enrique, who had in September presented a formal protest to the Cortes against the succession rights of the Infanta, was summoned from Brussels to Paris to be informed that he could return to Madrid only if he withdrew his protest.[10] Towards the end of 1846, therefore, both the British and the French were adopting new tactics in response to changed circumstances at

[7] Ibid.
[8] Guizot to Bresson, 15 Dec. 1846. G.P. 42/AP/8.
[9] Louis Philippe to Guizot, 13 Nov. 1846. G.P. 42/AP/286.
[10] The summons was sent by Louis Philippe to Rumigny, the French ambassador at Brussels. Guizot to Rumigny, 17 Oct. 1846. G.P. 42/AP/9. Towards the end of October Don Enrique agreed to come to Paris and to withdraw his protest in return for Louis Philippe arranging for him to return to Spain. Rumigny to Guizot, 30 Oct. 1846, Guizot to Rumigny, 3 Nov. 1846. G.P. 42/AP/9. On 20 Nov. Louis Philippe informed Guizot that Don Enrique's disposition was excellent and that it was safe for him to return to Spain. Louis Philippe to Guizot, 20 Nov. 1846. G.P. 42/AP/286. On 26 Nov. 1846 Palmerston informed Bulwer that he had received a message from Don Enrique. 'The message was that I might rely upon it that he is not changed and never will change. That he is a Spaniard and a liberal and an anti-Gallican. That he is going back to Madrid; that when there his object will be to get rid of the present government and to get a liberal government in its place and then to drive out French influence and Frenchified Spaniards; and that he will place himself in communication with you on these matters.' B.P. GC/BU/527.

the Spanish Court. The struggle would really begin, wrote Bresson to Guizot, when the Isturiz ministry lost its unity or came into conflict with the Queen.[11]

Late in 1846 the struggle between England and France over Spain was extended to Portugal, completing what Guizot called 'le triple travail'. This was by no means a surprising development: both the British and the French shared the belief of the Spanish and Portuguese themselves that the fortunes of the two Iberian kingdoms were closely linked. 'The liberal party here', wrote Bulwer to Palmerston, 'look upon their cause as intimately connected with the success of the liberal party in the neighbouring Kingdom';[12] and the Moderado press claimed that 'the conservative Governments of France, Spain and Portugal could defy the world'.[13] The post-civil war political structures in both kingdoms were roughly comparable; Queen Dona Maria of Portugal had been as reluctant as Queen Christina to play a strictly constitutional rôle, and like her she had been active in party struggles rather than remaining above them. She detested the Portuguese liberals (the Septembrists) much as Christina detested the Progresistas. The Portuguese conservatives (the Cabralists) used similar corrupt practices to the Moderados to maintain themselves in power. Identity of outlook was not all that united the two governing and the two opposition parties: the Moderados and the Cabralists thought that they had a mutual interest in assisting one another to suppress their rivals, and the Progresistas and the Septembrists thought it was in their interests to afford one another refuge and to concert their opposition.

By the end of 1846 there was a state of near civil war in Portugal. The Septembrists resented the partisanship of the Court, which they attributed to the evil influence of Dona Maria's German adviser, Dietz, and their permanent exclusion from power. Their vocal opposition to the absolutist tendencies of the Court and the corrupt electoral practices of the Cabralists led the latter to adopt increasingly oppressive measures. Some opposition members were arrested, and the opposition press was

[11] Bresson to Guizot, 21 Dec. 1846. G.P. 42/AP/65.
[12] Bulwer to Palmerston, 30 Oct. 1846. B.P. GC/BU/291.
[13] Bulwer to Clarendon, 22 Oct. 1846. Clar. Dep. C525.

muzzled. In the late summer of 1846 the Septembrists, fearing for their survival, withdrew from the Cortes, establishing themselves in a state of semi-insurrection in the town of Oporto, their main stronghold. They refused to return to Lisbon or to reestablish royal authority at Oporto until the Queen dismissed the Cabralist ministry and revoked a number of unconstitutional and repressive laws.

Britain and France adopted diametrically opposite attitudes to the Portuguese situation. Palmerston hoped that Queen Dona Maria would be peacefully reconciled with the Septembrists, and would in future stand above party politics and act according to the constitution.[14] He saw a settlement on these lines as desirable for Portugal and the means of affording an object lesson to Spain. 'It would certainly be a great point for the pacification of the whole peninsula if we could settle affairs in Portugal by a compromise. . .', wrote Bulwer.[15] Like Palmerston, he believed that a liberal government at Lisbon would dishearten the Moderados and encourage Queen Isabella and the Progresistas to seek a reconciliation. Guizot was as anxious to maintain the Cabralists in power as Palmerston was to oust them; he believed that monarchy and order in Spain, and thus French influence and Moderado supremacy, needed the support of similar institutions in Portugal. If the Septembrists returned to power at Lisbon, Guizot feared that Portugal would become the base for Progresista and English intrigues against the Spanish government.[16] Indeed, he was convinced that the sole object of Palmerston's Portuguese policy was to create this situation.[17] Thus, by the beginning of 1847 both Palmerston and Guizot were attempting to pursue integrated Iberian policies rather than separate Spanish and Portuguese policies. This was easier for Guizot than it was for Palmerston. For Guizot Portugal was only of secondary importance; he did not wish to establish French ascendancy at Lisbon—the British naval presence in the Tagus rendered this impossible—but only to maintain the political *status quo* at Lisbon, not so much for its

[14] Palmerston to the Queen, 25 Nov. 1846. R.A. B/10/60.
[15] Bulwer to Palmerston, 20 Dec. 1846. B.P. GC/BU/306.
[16] Guizot to Sainte Aulaire, 10 Dec. 1846. G.P. 42/AP/8.
[17] Guizot to Bresson, 26 Dec. 1846. A.A.E.C.P. Espagne 828.

own sake as in the interests of Spain. If left alone, Guizot believed that the Moderados and the Cabralists could look after their own and each other's interests. At the outset of the Portuguese crisis, therefore, Guizot confined himself to expressing the friendly disposition of the French government to Dona Maria and to urging the Spanish government not to take precipitate action in support of the Cabralists, which would give the British an excuse to intervene on behalf of the Septembrists.[18] Guizot hoped that the Portuguese army under Marshal Saldanha would be able to force the Septembrists into submission.[19]

For Palmerston an integrated Iberian policy was more difficult to achieve; British policy lacked the singleness of purpose that characterised French policy. Palmerston wanted above all to overthrow French influence at Madrid and change the Spanish law of succession, but he was also committed by treaty to defend the throne of Queen Dona Maria. Although these aims and commitments were not necessarily incompatible, there was always the possibility of conflict between them. If the Queen of Portugal and the Septembrists, or either of them, refused to accept a compromise settlement and civil war broke out, the British government would be forced to intervene on the side of the Queen. This would inevitably weaken and dishearten the liberal cause in Portugal, and thus in the Peninsula as a whole; '...any moral support given to the present Govt at Lisbon will be unfortunately connected with a support given to a party against ourselves here', wrote Bulwer to Admiral Parker in October 1846.[20] The only way to avoid this, Palmerston thought, was to induce both sides in Portugal to accept a compromise,[21] and from late 1846 onwards it was to this end that his efforts were directed.[22] By January 1847 the situations in Spain and Portugal were so confused that the British and the French were able to think that they could both achieve their ends. 'If we only have the courage required', wrote

[18] Guizot to Varenne, 29 Jan. 1847. A.A.E.C.P. Portugal 177; Guizot to Bresson, 26 Dec. 1846. A.A.E.C.P. Espagne 828.
[19] Guizot to Varenne, 23 Dec. 1846. A.A.E.C.P. Portugal 177.
[20] Bulwer to Parker, 21 Oct. 1846. Bulwer Papers, S/33.
[21] Palmerston to Southern, 13 Dec. 1846. B.P. GC/SO/273.
[22] Palmerston to Bulwer, 31 Dec. 1846. F.O. 72/695.

Hervey to Bulwer in January 1847, 'we shall gain a great victory.'[23] Bresson voiced similar sentiments to Guizot.[24]

By January 1847 the new situation at the Spanish Court was beginning to affect Spanish politics. The Isturiz ministry had depended on Christina's support to bring it into power and to retain it there.[25] As soon as it became clear that Christina's power was in decline and that the ministry did not enjoy the favour of Isabella, it began to disintegrate from within. Isabella could not dismiss Isturiz, however, until she had found someone able and willing to replace him. Her search for a new ministry inaugurated a series of hectic intrigues in which both Bulwer and Bresson were active participants. Bulwer aimed to convince the Queen, the King and Don Enrique that an anti-French coalition of liberal Moderados and Progresistas was the only combination that would govern in the interests of Spain. Palmerston thought it premature to hope for the formation of a ministry committed to denying the Duchess of Montpensier her succession rights, but he did not oppose Bulwer's attempts to overthrow the Isturiz ministry. It was, he wrote, the ministry which had made the marriages, and therefore 'no change can be much for the worse'.[26] After the failure of his attempts to prevent a change of ministry by reconciling Christina and Isabella, Bresson concentrated on preventing the replacement of Isturiz by Bulwer's favourite candidate, Pacheco, the leader of the liberal Moderados and one of the few Moderados to have opposed the Montpensier marriage.[27] In this he succeeded. On 28 January 1847 Sotomayor, formerly Spanish ambassador in London, formed a new government. From the beginning it was considered to be a weak caretaker government. The new ministry depended, not on royal favour, but on the absence of royal disapproval. This was an inadequate basis for a strong government, and by mid-February both Bulwer and Bresson were considering new combinations which might succeed it.[28]

[23] Hervey to Bulwer, 16 Jan. 1847. Bulwer Papers, S/26.
[24] Bresson to Guizot, 3 Jan. 1847. G.P. 42/AP/65.
[25] Bulwer to Palmerston, 9 Jan. 1847. F.O. 72/719.
[26] Palmerston to Bulwer, 21 Jan. 1847. B.P. GC/BU/533.
[27] Bresson to Guizot, 19 Jan. 1847. A.A.E.C.P. Espagne 830.
[28] Bulwer to Palmerston, 14 Feb. 1847. F.O. 72/719; Bresson to Guizot, 14 Feb. 1847. G.P. 42/AP/65.

Bulwer was convinced that the intrigues of January and the formation of the Sotomayor ministry proved his frequently reiterated argument that Great Britain ought to try to organise a coalition of liberal Moderados and Progresistas instead of relying on the Progresistas alone, whom he regarded as 'impractical'.[29] He therefore set himself two tasks: to form such a coalition, and then to persuade the Queen to call it to power.[30] In the context of Spanish politics, Bulwer was advocating a middle course; he believed that an exclusively Progresista government would be too radical a change for Queen Isabella to accept, and that it would be unreliable on the succession issue. Although Palmerston accepted Bulwer's arguments and endorsed his policies, it was clear that he had a higher regard for the Progresistas than Bulwer, and unlike Bulwer he tended to see a coalition not as the ultimate goal but merely as the prelude to the formation of a completely Progresista government.[31] To Bresson the intrigues of January suggested that in default of a strong Spanish ministry the caprices of a sixteen-year-old girl would jeopardise French influence at Madrid and the existing order of succession. In his view Spain needed a minister able to command respect or inspire fear at Court, and to control the factions within the Moderado party.[32] There was only one such man: General Narvaez. The French therefore also set themselves two tasks: to prevent further ministerial changes,

---

[29] 'The more I see of these people', wrote Bulwer to Clarendon, 'the more I am convinced that the policy I set out with namely that of having no party is the right one...I think Lord Palmerston will find every day more that what I said to him when he first came into office about Don Enrique and Don Enrique's friends was but too correct.' Bulwer to Clarendon, 2 Mar. 1847. Clar. Dep. C525. To Palmerston Bulwer wrote, 'Two great parties the Moderados and the Progresistas who alone take a part in public affairs are so divided and subdivided by personal jealousies and ambitions that neither of them offers a strong or compact body which could either follow out a particular policy or impose one upon the Court.' Bulwer to Palmerston, 14 Feb. 1847. F.O. 72/719.
[30] Bulwer to Clarendon, 15 Feb. 1847. Clar. Dep. C525.
[31] See for example Palmerston to Russell, 15 Mar. 1847, enclosure Russell to the Queen, 16 Mar. 1847. R.A. J/57/12 and 13. '...the loss', wrote Palmerston, 'of [English] influence [over Spain] has been owing not to the English Government having taken up the Progresistas but to its having abandoned them; it has been the natural and inevitable result of what I must ever think the short sighted and fatal policy of the late Government in regard to Spanish affairs.'
[32] Bresson to Guizot, 3 Feb. 1847. G.P. 42/AP/65.

but if this proved impossible to prepare the way for the return of Narvaez.[33]

In view of the fact that the overriding issue in Spanish politics was that of the succession, the private lives of the Spanish royal family, particularly those of the Queen and the King, were of great concern to the British and French governments. In December 1846 Bresson informed Guizot that the rumours of the Queen's pregnancy were unfounded.[34] In late January Bulwer reported that the Queen had taken a young army officer as a lover,[35] and in February he wrote that Don Enrique and his two sisters intended to marry into the Spanish nobility.[36] All these developments had important implications for the succession question. Both the British and the French hoped that Queen Isabella would produce an heir as quickly as possible, thus removing the Duchess of Montpensier from her position as heiress presumptive. The Queen's failure to conceive, and thus resolve the succession problem naturally and speedily, increased tension between England and France.[37] The British government began to fear that the Duchess of Montpensier might after all succeed to the Spanish throne, and the French had to acknowledge that her succession rights, which since September 1846 they had treated as a matter of prestige and principle, might become a matter of real and pressing importance.

The power wielded by the Crown in Spain meant that the Queen's private life inevitably affected Spanish politics. In 1847 the Queen's amours became a real problem for both England and France. The British considered it important to ensure that Isabella risked neither her life nor her reputation by a career of dissipation,[38] and that her peccadilloes were conducted with due

---

[33] Desages to Glucksburg, 13 Mar. 1847. G.P. 42/AP/53.
[34] Bresson to Guizot, 12 Dec. 1846. G.P. 42/AP/65.
[35] Bulwer to Palmerston, 19 Jan. 1847. B.P. GC/BU/309.
[36] Bulwer to Palmerston, 7 Feb. 1847. F.O. 72/719.
[37] Several reasons for the Queen's barrenness were advanced. Some attributed it to the King's impotence. Rose to Palmerston, 9 Feb. 1847. R.A. J/49/108. Others claimed on the authority of secret and reliable Palace sources that the Queen was incapable of bearing a child: see Normanby to Palmerston, 28 June 1847. B.P. GC/NO/60. Others alleged that all would be well if both the Queen and the King underwent slight operations: see Decazes to Guizot, 24 May 1847. A.A.E.C.P. Espagne 831.
[38] Bulwer to Palmerston, 20 Mar. 1847. B.P. GC/BU/327.

regard for decency: she must at all costs continue to live under the same roof as the King and be seen with him in public.[39] Moreover, neither the British nor the French overlooked the potential influence of the Queen's lovers on her political outlook and decisions. Bulwer argued that if they were of the right political persuasion they could be exploited to serve British interests on the succession question. This was what the French feared: if Isabella took a Progresista lover he might persuade her to accept a Progresista ministry, and Palmerston's plans would be half-way to fruition.[40] The greatest French fear, however, was that the Queen and her lovers would act irresponsibly and bring the Crown into total disrepute, causing the politicians to look for some alternative to Isabella. Whatever the alternative —a republic or the Duchess of Montpensier—France would face a grave situation. For the sake of political stability in Spain the French were therefore anxious to prevent the Queen's conduct from becoming a matter of public scandal. They were not, as some suggested,[41] trying to guard against her conceiving a child by someone other than the King. To prevent this would have been impossible without controlling or restricting the Queen's movements.

Don Francisco's unmarried children presented a greater problem to the British government than to the French: any marriage with a member of the Spanish nobility would be morganatic, and the issue would have no succession rights. The British government would consequently have to alter its plans for revising the order of succession or rely on the Cortes passing yet another succession law to give the issue of such marriages succession rights.[42] Palmerston was exasperated by Don Enrique's unreliability, and Bulwer informed Clarendon that 'matters will come to the point where Montemolin or

[39] By Jan. 1847 this was already a difficult task. On 19 Jan. 1847 Bulwer reported that as far as the King was concerned the question of a new ministry was getting one 'ugly enough to please him'. Bulwer to Palmerston, 19 Jan. 1847. B.P. GC/BU/309. On 5 Apr. Bulwer reported that he was trying to bring the relations between the Queen and the King 'into at least a state of decency, since they are at present a scandal to the public'. Bulwer to Palmerston, 5 Apr. 1847. F.O. 72/721.
[40] Glucksburg to Guizot, 19 Mar. 1847. G.P. 42/AP/67.
[41] Palmerston to Normanby, 20 Apr. 1847. Normanby Papers, Box P, bundle 19.
[42] Bulwer to Palmerston, 5 Feb. 1847. B.P. GC/BU/314.

Montpensier will carry the day'.[43] By February 1847, therefore, Bulwer and Bresson were trying to cope with the day to day intrigues at Madrid,[44] while Palmerston and Guizot considered the fundamental problems raised by the political and personal turmoil within the Spanish royal family.

In late February and March 1847 a series of sudden and dramatic events in Spain, and new developments in Portugal, deflected the attention of both Palmerston and Guizot from these basic issues. The fall of the Isturiz ministry and to a lesser extent the eclipse of Christina had brought about a marked decline in Bresson's influence over Spanish politics. He had relied on Mon and Isturiz even more than on Christina,[45] and it was their fall which deprived him of effective means of influence. He found this dispiriting. The acute instability which led to his suicide in late 1847 was already showing itself, and his dejection was increased by the reluctance of Louis Philippe and Guizot to promote him to an embassy at one of the great Courts.[46] By the end of February Bresson could bear Madrid no longer, and Guizot reluctantly granted him leave of absence. No successor was appointed since Guizot hoped to persuade him to return; the young Duke of Glucksburg, the first secretary of the French embassy at Madrid, was appointed minister plenipotentiary in his absence.[47] By the British government Bresson's sudden departure from Madrid was interpreted as presaging a new French offensive in Spain.[48] Suspicion increased when Christina also left for Paris in March 1847.[49] In fact, however, the combination which had made the marriages and dominated Spanish politics for a few months afterwards was disintegrating. In 1841 Christina had been forced into exile, but in 1847, after

[43] Bulwer to Clarendon, 15 Feb. 1847. Clar. Dep. C525.
[44] Bulwer to Hervey, 13 Feb. 1847. Bulwer Papers, S/26; Bresson to Guizot, 14 Feb. 1847. G.P. 42/AP/65.
[45] Desages advised Glucksburg in Mar. 1847 to remain faithful to Mon as he had been Bresson's most useful contact and ally. Desages to Glucksburg, 13 Mar. 1847. G.P. 42/AP/53.
[46] Bresson had sounded Minto as to how good were his chances of being received by the British government as French ambassador in London. Palmerston instructed Normanby to state that it would be impossible. Palmerston to Normanby, 30 Mar. 1847. B.P. GC/NO/441.
[47] Guizot to Glucksburg, 20 Mar. 1847. A.A.E.C.P. Espagne 830.
[48] Normanby to Russell, 12 Mar. 1847. Russell Papers, P.R.O. 30/22/6B.
[49] Palmerston to Normanby, 14 Mar. 1847. B.P. GC/NO/438.

her prestige and her power had waned, she chose voluntary exile. The departure of Christina and Bresson finally liberated Isabella from the influences she was already discarding. By 9 March 1847 it seemed to Bulwer that the time had come for a change of ministry.[50] Serrano, the Queen's new lover and a prominent army officer of supposedly Progresista leanings, agreed with Bulwer that the Sotomayor ministry could not last.[51] March 1847, like January, witnessed a series of hectic and complex intrigues in which Bulwer and Glucksburg played major parts.[52] Bulwer hoped to persuade Isabella to appoint a liberal ministry which would be a fusion of Progresistas and liberal Moderados. If the anti-French Moderados led by Pacheco could be detached from the 'ultras' such as Isturiz and Mon, he believed that he could induce the Progresistas either to join them immediately or to abstain from opposing them, thus preparing the ground for a subsequent coalition. He believed that the Queen would accept such a ministry, partly out of hatred of the Moderados who had made her marriage, partly to spite her mother, and partly because of Serrano's influence.[53] French tactics, Guizot wrote to Glucksburg, were dictated by Palmerston's attempts to divide the Moderado party and make Serrano the chief influence over the Queen; the French must therefore unite with the Moderado party and make the King the main influence over the Queen.[54] Bulwer's tactics triumphed. The circumstances were too difficult for the French plan to have much chance of success: the Moderados were too divided among themselves for Glucksburg to rally them in time to save the Sotomayor ministry,[55] and relations between the Queen and the King were too strained for the latter to avert a change which the Queen eagerly sought.[56] On 28 March Pacheco formed a

[50] Bulwer to Palmerston, 9 Mar. 1847. F.O. 72/720.
[51] Bulwer to Palmerston, 11 Mar. 1847. F.O. 72/720.
[52] Bulwer and Glucksburg each claimed that he was trying to make his activity as unobtrusive as possible. Bulwer to Palmerston, 11 Mar. 1847. F.O. 72/720; Glucksburg to Guizot, 19 Mar. 1847. G.P. 42/AP/67.
[53] Guizot to Glucksburg, 22 Mar. 1847. G.P. 42/AP/7.
[54] Ibid.   [55] Glucksburg to Guizot, 28 Mar. 1847. G.P. 42/AP/67.
[56] The King wanted to prevent the formation of a Pacheco ministry because it was urged on the Queen by Serrano. As soon as he heard of the formation of the new ministry, the King wrote to Glucksburg, 'Dieu nous protège et nous tire de ce faux pas.' The King of Spain to Glucksburg, 28 Mar. 1847. G.P. 42/AP/67.

liberal Moderado government which Bulwer hoped and Glucksburg feared would be pro-British and anti-French.[57] The French government was undoubtedly worried by developments in Spain. In Paris the feeling in favour of engineering the return to power of Narvaez became stronger.[58] In London, on the other hand, Palmerston was jubilant at the news of the formation of the Pacheco ministry: 'we may now look forward to a reign of the Liberals in Spain, long enough at least to do some good things', he wrote to Normanby.[59] As well as being a good augury for the future of Spain, the formation of the Pacheco ministry also afforded immediate relief to Palmerston and Bulwer, who felt that the new government would be 'disposed to follow a policy in Portugal more in accordance with our own than their predecessors'.[60]

At the end of October 1846 the British government reluctantly abandoned its attitude of neutrality towards the dispute between Queen Dona Maria of Portugal and the Septembrists in favour of a more active mediatory rôle. This change of policy was a response to two factors. Southern, the British chargé d'affaires at Lisbon, had warned Palmerston that, with the situation in Portugal rapidly deteriorating, only external pressure on both parties to negotiate a settlement could prevent their dispute from degenerating into prolonged and inconclusive armed conflict.[61] Secondly, Palmerston feared that if Great Britain did not assert her influence in Portugal, Spain, prompted and guided by France, would intervene on behalf of Dona Maria, thus securing the triumph of absolutism throughout the Peninsula. Late in October Normanby warned Palmerston 'that there is danger of imminent action in this question from hence through Spain unless either forestalled or prevented by us'.[62] British diplomats in the Iberian peninsula were con-

---

[57] Glucksburg to Guizot, 28 Mar. 1847. G.P. 42/AP/67; Bulwer to Palmerston, 28 Mar. 1847. F.O. 72/720.
[58] Guizot admitted that Narvaez had many faults, but he had the right qualities for a desperate situation. Guizot to Glucksburg, 3 Apr. 1847. G.P. 42/AP/7.
[59] Palmerston to Normanby, 2 Apr. 1847. Normanby Papers, Box P, bundle 19.
[60] Ibid.; Bulwer to Palmerston, 3 Apr. 1847. F.O. 72/721.
[61] Southern to Palmerston, 14 Oct. 1846. F.O. 63/619.
[62] King Leopold of the Belgians informed Normanby after discussions with Louis Philippe and Guizot on Portugal that if England did not take immediate action it would make it 'difficult for the other powers [France and Spain] to recognise

vinced that both France and Spain were urging Dona Maria to crush the rebels, and assuring her that she might depend on Spanish military assistance if her own troops were unable to achieve this.[63] Southern believed that the appointment of Marshal Saldanha as Prime Minister of Portugal in October 1846 was part of a 'plan...in which I believe Spanish intervention and an intimate union for the future between the governments of Lisbon and Madrid figure as principal features'.[64]

Palmerston hoped that the more active policy he was forced to pursue would not only avert the danger of a long civil war in Portugal and the 'ejection of England from all influence whatever in the Peninsula',[65] but would also be a means of undermining Moderado ascendancy and French influence at Madrid. A peaceful reconciliation between the Queen of Portugal and the Septembrists and the re-establishment of constitutional government at Lisbon would be an object lesson for Queen Isabella and a source of strength and inspiration for the Progresistas. Palmerston was also well aware that, if England did not play an active mediatory rôle and if the Portuguese situation deteriorated so far as to endanger the monarchy, Britain's treaties of alliance with Portugal would compel her to defend the throne against its opponents. If she were forced to assist the anti-liberal and pro-French forces in Portugal, England would become the instrument of her own undoing in the Peninsula. Palmerston therefore aimed to persuade the Queen and the Septembrists to negotiate a settlement as soon as possible. 'Our policy', wrote Bulwer to Admiral Parker, the commander of the British fleet in the Tagus, 'is to establish a middle course between two extremes; a revolution sweeping away the throne and a royal triumph which will act against the liberal cause in the Peninsula'.[66] At the outset the British

England's predominant influence and Spain might feel herself in danger and thus intervene'. Normanby to Palmerston, 28 Oct. 1846. Normanby Papers, Box P, bundle 12.

[63] Bulwer to Parker, 28 Oct. 1846. Bulwer Papers, S/33; Southern to Palmerston, 30 Oct. 1846. F.O. 63/619.
[64] Southern to Palmerston, 22 Oct. 1846. F.O. 63/619.
[65] Stanley to Bulwer, 3 Nov. 1846. Bulwer Papers, S/40.
[66] Bulwer to Parker, 28 Oct. 1846. Bulwer Papers, S/33.

government had to decide how far it was prepared to go to achieve this aim. Palmerston thought that the most the British government could do was to try to establish the internal and external conditions necessary for a negotiated settlement, and to suggest to the disputants the principles on which such a settlement should be based.[67] In November 1846 Palmerston began to apply himself to these tasks.

Palmerston's assessment of the measures necessary for the opening of negotiations between the two sides in Portugal was based on his opinion as to who was responsible for the outbreak of the dispute and who was to blame for the impasse that had been reached. His opinions reflected closely those of Southern and of Colonel Wylde, an equerry to Prince Albert who was sent on an unofficial mission to Portugal at the end of October 1846.[68] Wylde and Southern both believed that the despotic tendencies of the Court and the corrupt and unconstitutional practices of the Cabralists had driven the Septembrists to adopt unconstitutional means of opposition.[69] Soon after his arrival in Portugal, Wylde informed Prince Albert that the 'people were acted upon by the idea that the Queen wished with the assistance of France and Spain to become absolute',[70] and he sent Palmerston a devastating indictment of the political outlook of the Portuguese Court. 'It is to be borne in mind', he wrote, that the Queen of Portugal is a 'mindless, truthless, heartless' woman, thoroughly French in her predilections and 'wholly under the influence of the King' whose 'predominant passion is hatred of constitutional government in all its forms'. To Wylde it seemed clear that the struggle was 'the defence of a nation against the aggressions on it of a sovereign who has violated her solemn engagements to it'.[71] Palmerston did not for one moment doubt the truth of Southern's and Wylde's reports. They confirmed his impression that the struggle in Portugal was part of the wider contest in the Peninsula between absolutism

[67] Palmerston to Southern, 26 Nov. 1846. F.O. 63/614.
[68] Wylde had fought with the British volunteer forces in the Spanish civil war in the 1830s, and was well acquainted with both Spanish and Portuguese politicians.
[69] Southern to Palmerston, 22 Oct. 1846. F.O. 63/619.
[70] Wylde to Prince Albert, 8 Nov. 1846. R.A. J/56/1.
[71] Wylde's Memorandum on Portugal, [?] Nov. 1846. B.P. GC/WY/15.

backed by France and constitutionalism supported by England.[72] Palmerston's low opinion of Dona Maria and her government and his sympathy for the Septembrists brought him into conflict with Queen Victoria and Prince Albert, who were both first cousins of the King of Portugal and keenly interested in Portuguese affairs.[73] Southern had fallen foul of Dona Maria because he had shown some independence of judgment in refusing to approve her arbitrary policies. In their correspondence with the English Court, the King and Queen of Portugal had suggested that Southern was a Septembrist partisan,[74] consequently Queen Victoria dismissed his reports as deriving from 'an ultra progresista and a most violent party man'.[75] Although not entirely uncritical of their Portuguese cousins, the Queen and the Prince had no sympathy whatever for 'the revolutionary movements of the democratic party'.[76] They believed that, in order to create an atmosphere conducive to negotiation, the British government should make it clear to the rebels that they were determined to support the Portuguese throne and the authority of Dona Maria. Moreover, they believed that strictures on the Queen and her government not only caused offence at Lisbon but also encouraged the rebels to hold out for terms which it was impossible for Dona Maria to accept.[77] The conflict over Portuguese affairs which arose between the Court and Palmerston in the autumn of 1846 was never resolved to the satisfaction of either side. The result was that the Queen lost all remaining confidence in Palmerston, who in turn became increasingly resentful of royal interference in the affairs of his department. Fundamentally the dispute was over aims: whereas Palmerston wished his Portuguese policy to serve his wider objectives in the whole Peninsula, the Queen and the Prince thought only of the stability and prestige of the

[72] Palmerston to Normanby, 17 Nov. 1846. Normanby Papers, Box P, bundle 19.
[73] A large part of the correspondence between the Queen and Palmerston on Portuguese affairs in 1846 and 1847 has been published in Brian Connell, *Regina v. Palmerston* (London, 1962), ch. ii, and in R. A. Leitao, *Documentos dos Arquivos de Windsor* (Coimbra, 1955).
[74] See for example the Queen of Portugal to Queen Victoria, 30 Nov. 1846. Leitao, op. cit., 21-2.
[75] The Queen to Palmerston, 19 Oct. 1846. R.A. B/10/28.
[76] Ibid.
[77] The Queen to Palmerston, 28 Oct. 1846; Connell, op. cit., 48.

Portuguese monarchy. In October and November 1846, however, neither the Queen nor Palmerston showed any disposition to push their difference over Portugal to extremes; each stressed their common ground, and Palmerston seemed to concede the Queen's point about Southern's partisanship by his agreement to the Wylde mission and to the necessity of appointing a new British minister at Lisbon who would possess the confidence of both Courts.[78] Palmerston undoubtedly hoped that a new minister at Lisbon would send reports similar to Southern's, and thus convince the Queen that it was she who was being misled. The critical reports on the Portuguese Court that Wylde sent in November 1846 were of great value to Palmerston, as the Queen and Prince Albert trusted him and believed him to be impartial.

Despite the wishes of the Queen, Palmerston's instructions to Southern in late November as to finding a way out of the current difficulties had a strong anti-Court bias. Palmerston began by pointing out that, although the British government was prepared to do anything that could reasonably be expected of a friendly and allied power, the Portuguese could not expect the government or its agents either to negotiate or to guarantee any settlement; the Portuguese must do this themselves.[79] He confined British assistance to suggesting the means of creating in Portugal a political climate that would make possible the speedy and amicable termination of the dispute. The Queen of Portugal, wrote Palmerston, must make concessions to regain the confidence of the Septembrists;

She should give to the nation the most distinct and binding pledges that it is Her Majesty's intention to govern according to constitutional forms and in a constitutional spirit, and the best assurance and proof which Her Majesty could give of such an intention would be the appointment of an administration consisting of men who while on the one hand they should deserve to be trusted by the Crown, should on the other possess the confidence of the nation.

[78] It was Russell who suggested sending Sir Hamilton Seymour, British minister at Brussels, to Lisbon. Russell thought that 'as he knows King Leopold' he 'would be well-received'. Russell thought it 'a great misfortune' to have a minister at Lisbon 'that neither here nor at Lisbon has the confidence of the Court'. Russell to Palmerston, 11 Oct. 1846. B.P. GC/RU/120.
[79] Palmerston to Wylde, 25 Nov. 1846. B.P. GC/WY/28.

The formation of such a government, thought Palmerston, should be accompanied 'by a general amnesty for all political offences connected with the late outbreak'.[80] Palmerston believed that the Septembrists would accept a compromise settlement, primarily because they were not strong enough to hold out for total victory, but also because he judged their leaders to be sensible and moderate men driven to desperate measures by the repressive policy of the Court.[81] The real problem, therefore, was to convert the Portuguese Court to the course which he advocated. Palmerston hoped that a marked change in the outlook of the King and Queen of Portugal would result from the removal of Dietz from the Portuguese Court[82] and the presence of Wylde, supported as he was by Queen Victoria, Prince Albert and King Leopold of the Belgians. He could not, however, rely exclusively on the triumph of reason at the Portuguese Court; he believed that Dona Maria was more likely to adopt his plan of pacification through lack of an alternative than as a voluntary gesture of conciliation. He therefore made clear to her that she could not expect foreign military assistance for any attempt to crush the rebels. An indispensable element in Palmerston's new Portuguese policy was 'to keep the French and the Spaniards in check'.[83] In December 1846 Bulwer was instructed to inform the Spanish government that Great Britain would not allow the Spaniards either to supply arms to the Portuguese government or to intervene on its behalf;[84] and

[80] Palmerston to Southern, 26 Nov. 1846. F.O. 63/614.
[81] Palmerston to Russell, 23 Nov. 1846. B.P. GC/RU/1008.
[82] Ibid.
[83] Palmerston to Doyle, 30 Oct. 1846. B.P. GC/DO/95.
[84] Palmerston to Bulwer, 19 Dec. 1846. Bulwer Papers, S/30. Russell suggested that Palmerston should 'write to Madrid that we rely upon the written promise of the Spanish ministers not to send troops into Portugal'. Russell to Palmerston, 24 Nov. 1846. B.P. GC/RU/126. On 23 Nov. 1846 Palmerston sent the following question to the law officers of the Crown: 'Is there anything in our treaties with Portugal, of any date, which bears upon the question of Portugal asking assistance from Spain, for interference in her internal affairs?' The law officers replied: 'No stipulation can be found in any treaty between Portugal and Gt. Britain, binding Portugal by anticipation not to apply for such assistance. But the comprehensive terms in which the alliance and guarantee between Portugal and Great Britain are described in some of the ancient treaties between the two powers might perhaps be considered as sufficient to entitle Gt. Britain...to remonstrate with Portugal, if not to interpose between Portugal and Spain, in the event of such a transaction.' Memorandum on Portugal, 23 Nov. 1846. B.P. FO/9/28.

Normanby was instructed to reply to an overture from Guizot on Portugal to the effect that the British government 'would not inquire whether the French government minded or not that which we feel ourselves called upon...to do' in Portugal.[85] Palmerston was convinced that the prospect of a long and inconclusive struggle in Portugal combined with British pressure in favour of negotiations and the exclusion of any possibility of help from Spain would force the two sides to seek a settlement, the outcome of which would be the restoration of constitutional government in Portugal and a triumph for British policy in the Peninsula.[86]

It soon became clear that Palmerston's optimism was unfounded. An inherent weakness in his policy was the unrealistic suggestion that Dona Maria should appoint a ministry of moderate men able and willing to pursue a policy of conciliation. As Wylde pointed out, there was 'no juste milieu party' in Portugal in 1846;[87] politics were polarised around the Cabralists and the Septembrists. No group of men enjoyed the trust of both parties and the confidence of the Crown. Palmerston's proposal that the formation of a government of independent men should precede a settlement thus depended on a situation which could only be achieved long after the dispute was ended. A coalition was also out of the question; it would require some degree of reconciliation between the Queen and the Septembrists, and could thus only follow a settlement. The second weakness in Palmerston's proposal was the lack of a British guarantee for the settlement. Basic to the dispute was the inability of the disputants to trust one another; the Queen believed that the Septembrists wished to deprive her of all her power and authority, and the Septembrists were convinced that the Queen and the Cabralists wished to destroy them as a political party. By autumn 1846 these fears were held with great intensity, and would not easily be removed. Another difficulty was that Palmerston's emphasis was on an early settlement to the dispute; 'our object', he informed Wylde in December 1846, 'must be to get the Queen and the King through the present crisis, and let

---

[85] Palmerston to Normanby, 17 Nov. 1846. Normanby Papers, Box P, bundle 19.
[86] Palmerston to Wylde, 13 Dec. 1846. B.P. GC/WY/29.
[87] Wylde's Memorandum on Portugal, [?] Nov. 1846. B.P. GC/WY/15.

the future take care of itself'.[88] The Portuguese, not unnaturally, had a long-term perspective; the two sides wished to end the dispute in such a way as to safeguard their future: the Queen hoped to reaffirm royal authority by crushing the rebels, and the Septembrists hoped to strengthen themselves by chastening the Crown and weakening the Cabralists.

The manifest deficiencies of Palmerston's proposals contributed to their poor reception in December 1846 and January 1847. The disputants rejected not only the specific measures which the British government proposed as a possible basis for negotiation, but also the spirit of compromise which underlay them. The Queen of Portugal and her Prime Minister, Saldanha, concentrated on pointing out the impediments to the British plan of pacification, but were also offended by the tone and tenor of Palmerston's advice. What Dona Maria wanted was unconditional support for her course, and she had looked to England to provide it. She was bitterly disappointed when it was not forthcoming. Since neither was prepared to compromise, Dona Maria and Saldanha could see only three courses of action open to them: firstly, to attempt to crush the rebels with the troops who had remained loyal to the throne; secondly, to try to change the policy of the British government; and thirdly, to continue to explore the possibility of Spanish intervention against the Septembrists.[89] The uncertainty of Portuguese military and financial affairs, the instability of Spanish politics and of diplomatic relations in the Peninsula, obliged the Portuguese government to keep all three possibilities in mind rather than to concentrate exclusively on one of them.

For the Septembrists the major shortcoming of the British plan of pacification was the lack of a guarantee. They had judged the Queen and the Cabralists not by their words but by their deeds, and were resolved to continue to do so.[90] Besides their justifiable misgivings as to the wisdom of committing themselves to a negotiated and unguaranteed compromise, the Septembrists, like the Queen, were convinced that they were on

[88] Palmerston to Wylde, 13 Dec. 1846. B.P. GC/WY/29.
[89] Southern to Palmerston, 18 Jan. 1847. F.O. 63/643; Bulwer to Palmerston, 30 Jan. 1847. F.O. 72/719.
[90] Southern to Palmerston, 28 Nov. 1846. F.O. 63/620.

'the high road to success'.[91] Their belief that permanent and exclusive power would shortly be theirs made them ill disposed to accept anything less than a total victory.[92] In December 1846 and January 1847, therefore, the reports of Southern and Wylde on the prospects of a speedy settlement were gloomy. In January Wylde was authorised by Palmerston to convey to the Junta at Oporto the terms which the British government had succeeded in extracting from the reluctant Portuguese government.[93] These differed slightly from the original proposals in that the Queen had agreed to form a new government and to call the Cortes after, rather than before, the insurgents had laid down their arms.[94] The attempt by the Portuguese government to enlist a promise of British aid in suppressing the rebels if they refused to accept the terms failed. Palmerston and Russell remained adamantly opposed to such a commitment[95] despite pressure from Queen Victoria in support of the Portuguese government.[96] The inadequacy of the terms offered, Russell's insistence that it be made absolutely clear to the Septembrists 'that the terms must be terms granted by the Queen of Portugal and...must depend upon her royal word for their fulfilment',[97] combined with the military optimism at Oporto,[98] made the rejection of the proposals almost inevitable. By the beginning of 1847 Palmerston's plan for the pacification of Portugal was nowhere nearer accomplishment than it had been when first mooted, and the situation in Portugal showed signs of rapid deterioration. In November and December both Southern and Wylde reported rumours that the Septembrists had joined forces with the Miguelites,[99] the supporters of the Portuguese pre-

[91] Wylde to Prince Albert, 16 Nov. 1846. R.A. J/56/3.
[92] Wylde also believed that the Junta at Oporto 'stood in great awe of [the military] force of their own creation'. He estimated that there were 8,000 men under arms in Oporto. Wylde to Prince Albert, 8 Nov. 1846. R.A. J/56/1.
[93] Palmerston to Wylde, 26 Jan. 1847. B.P. GC/WY/30.
[94] Ibid.
[95] Russell to Palmerston, 28 Jan. 1847. B.P. GC/RU/132.
[96] Queen Victoria to Russell, 7 Jan. 1847. Q.V.L., 1st series, ii, 137–8; Prince Albert to Palmerston, 28 Jan. 1847. R.A. J/56/35.
[97] Russell to Palmerston, 28 Jan. 1847. B.P. GC/RU/132.
[98] Wylde to Prince Albert, 30 Jan. 1847. R.A. J/56/43.
[99] Wylde to Prince Albert, 3 Dec. 1846. R.A. J/56/11; Southern to Palmerston, 28 Nov. 1846. F.O. 63/620.

tender, Dom Miguel; and by January it was evident that the rumours were true.[100] For the Septembrists combination with the Miguelites was in one way natural and desirable. Both parties were hostile to Dona Maria, and the Miguelites had men, military experience and money at their command. In other respects, however, it compromised their position; it became more difficult for them to claim that they sought merely the redress of legitimate grievances. Association with the Miguelites made them seem bent upon the deposition of Dona Maria and hostile to the established order of succession.[101] The Portuguese government and its supporters quickly began to exploit the Miguelite character of the opposition, and from January 1847 Palmerston was under increasing pressure from Queen Victoria, the Portuguese, Spanish and French governments to abandon his policy of conciliation in favour of support for Dona Maria, either on the basis or in the spirit of the Quadruple Alliance of 1834.

Dona Maria and Saldanha believed that the Septembrists had played into their hands by joining forces with the Miguelites. They hoped that the Miguelite character which the revolt had assumed would enable them to abandon their desultory efforts to meet Palmerston's demand that a basis for compromise be established by providing what they had hitherto lacked—a good reason for not doing so. They also welcomed it because it offered them a better case than before for demanding foreign assistance in crushing the rebels. The Queen of Portugal claimed that the coalition of the Septembrists and the Miguelites threatened her throne and her dynasty, and that England was

[100] Southern to Palmerston, 5 Jan. 1847. F.O. 63/643.

[101] '...a change in the policy and language of both the Miguelites and the Junta towards each other and in their publications has certainly taken place, such as leaving out the name of the Queen, alluding to the throne as if vacant, and ceasing to oppose each other in the field, also naming General Povas, a notorious Miguelite, to the command of the province of Beira.' Wylde to Prince Albert, 30 Jan. 1847. R.A. J/56/43. Varenne, the French minister at Lisbon, informed Guizot that although the Miguelites and the Septembrists had combined their forces, the Septembrists did not want a Miguelite government if they succeeded in defeating the government troops. They intended to place Dona Maria's eldest son on the throne with the Princess Isabella, the Queen's aunt, as Regent. Isabella was, wrote Varenne, very clerical in her outlook, and her appointment would be regarded with satisfaction by the Miguelites. Varenne to Guizot, 19 Jan. 1847. A.A.E.C.P. Portugal 177.

therefore bound by treaties to come to the aid of Portugal.[102] Moreover, the Portuguese government also claimed that the Miguelite character of the revolt was 'a terrible precedent for Spain and the Spanish government cannot allow such a thing to go on in its neighbourhood without paying the greatest attention to it'.[103] The implication was clear, as Count Thomar, the Portuguese minister at Madrid, reminded the Spanish government: to forestall a Carlist insurrection in Spain the Spanish government must assist the Portuguese government to suppress the Miguelites.[104] Thus in January 1847 the Queen of Portugal and Saldanha abandoned their remaining hopes of crushing the rebels with their own forces, and concentrated on trying to change British policy from conciliation to coercion, and on securing Spanish military assistance. The Portuguese wanted a declaration by England and Spain against the Junta, the blockade of Oporto by English ships, and the entry into Portugal of Spanish troops. On 22 January 1847 Saldanha expressed to Wylde his conviction that the Portuguese question had 'now become a European one' and that 'the moment has now arrived for intervention'.[105] In order to secure both British and Spanish assistance, the Portuguese government invoked the Quadruple Alliance of 1834 in which Great Britain and Spain had co-operated to expel Dom Miguel from Portugal.[106] In February 1847 the Portuguese government formally requested assistance under the provisions of this treaty.[107]

The French and Spanish governments gave unequivocal support to the demands of the Portuguese government for foreign intervention. Like the Portuguese government, they had been unable actively to oppose Palmerston's efforts to bring about a negotiated compromise, although both governments had attempted to subvert them by encouraging Dona Maria not

[102] Southern to Palmerston, 18 Jan. 1847. F.O. 63/643.
[103] Saldanha to Wylde, 22 Jan. 1847. R.A. J/56/44.
[104] Bresson to Guizot, 3 Feb. 1847. A.A.E.C.P. Espagne 830.
[105] Saldanha to Wylde, 22 Jan. 1847. R.A. J/56/44.
[106] For the Quadruple Treaty of 1834, see Webster, *Palmerston*, i, ch. v.
[107] Thomar to Sotomayor, 5 Feb. 1847, copy F.O. 72/719. The requests for assistance to the British and French governments were made through the Portuguese ministers in London and Paris. Palmerston to Russell, 10 Feb. 1847. Russell Papers, P.R.O. 30/22/6B; Guizot to Sainte Aulaire, 16 Feb. 1847. A.A.E.C.P. Angleterre 667.

to be deflected from her aim of crushing the rebels.[108] The Spanish government had also supplied arms to the Portuguese government.[109] The union of the Septembrists and the Miguelites enabled the French and Spanish governments to be much more active and open in their support of Dona Maria, both in response to Portugal's request for assistance under the Quadruple Alliance, and on the pretext that the Miguelite rising provided a direct threat to Spain by the example it set to the Carlists.[110] On 16 February, therefore, Guizot made it clear that the French government was willing to accede to Portugal's request for assistance under the Quadruple Alliance of 1834, and to begin consultations with a view to intervention with the other three signatories to that treaty.[111] Guizot had several reasons for his willingness to reactivate the Quadruple Alliance. In the first place, it would enable him to support Dona Maria and the Cabralists, and thus the *status quo* throughout the Peninsula, without openly avowing it: the official basis of his policy was anti-Miguelite rather than pro-absolutist. Secondly, like the Portuguese government he saw it as a means of forcing Palmerston to change his policy from one of conciliating the rebels to intervention on behalf of the Queen. Thirdly, it was his one hope of preventing Palmerston from excluding France from any intervention. Guizot was particularly anxious to avoid the exclusion of France from intervention in Portugal, since this would be interpreted in France as a deliberate rebuff; if, however, England and France were to co-operate in Portugal on the basis of the Quadruple Alliance of 1834, with its evocations of the 'liberal alliance' of the 1830s, Guizot would be able to deny Thiers' assertion that the government had abandoned the cause of liberalism. Above all, Guizot hoped that co-operation on the basis of the Quadruple Alliance would prevent Palmerston from making a separate arrangement with Spain in an attempt to weaken her connection with France, thus forcing Spain to play a rôle in Portugal that was not in her best interests.[112]

[108] Guizot to Varenne, 29 Dec. 1846. A.A.E.C.P. Portugal 177; Southern to Palmerston, 18 Jan. 1847. F.O. 63/643.
[109] Palmerston to Bulwer, 4 Jan. 1847. F.O. 72/717.
[110] Guizot to Sainte Aulaire, 16 Feb. 1847. A.A.E.C.P. Angleterre 667.
[111] Ibid.
[112] On 25 Jan. 1847 Varenne informed Guizot that even if Great Britain were

During January and February the Spanish government was even more active than the French in support of Dona Maria. Not content with sending arms to help her cause, Spain intimated her willingness to use the troops she was amassing on the frontier to intervene in Portugal in support of the government, and warned the British government that Spain could not indefinitely hold aloof from the conflict in Portugal.[113] The Sotomayor government was genuinely convinced that only the immediate suppression of the Miguelites at Oporto would dissuade the Carlists from following their example. Moreover, as Thomar and Bresson pointed out to them, Palmerston's hope of a return to constitutionalism in Portugal was directed as much against the Moderados as against the Cabralists.[114] In January 1847 both Bulwer and Southern expressed concern about the intimacy between Bresson, Thomar and the Spanish government on Portuguese affairs;[115] both believed that the Portuguese government's request for assistance under the Quadruple Alliance was inspired by them.[116] In order to prevent the Spanish government from taking precipitate and unilateral action over Portugal, Bulwer wrote on 4 February 1847 without instructions from London to Sotomayor to ask whether he was 'willing to consider the state of affairs of Portugal, either as a question resulting from the Quadruple Alliance to which England is a party, or as a special one particularly concerning the Governments of England and Spain'.[117] On the following day Sotomayor assured Bulwer that Spain would take no action over Portugal without consulting Great Britain.[118] Bulwer believed that his independent action had averted the imme-

prepared to intervene immediately in Portugal, her naval intervention alone would be insufficient to restore order; troops would be needed to suppress opposition to royal authority in the centres of population, and particularly at Oporto. He therefore assumed that if intervention took place it would be a combined operation with British naval and Spanish land forces. Varenne to Guizot, 25 Jan. 1847. A.A.E.C.P. Portugal 177.

[113] Bulwer to Palmerston, 30 Jan., 5 Feb. 1847. F.O. 72/719.
[114] Bresson to Guizot, 3 Feb. 1847. A.A.E.C.P. Espagne 830.
[115] Southern to Palmerston, 18 Jan. 1847. F.O. 63/643; Bulwer to Palmerston, 19 Jan. 1847. F.O. 72/719.
[116] Southern to Palmerston, 31 Jan. 1847. F.O. 63/643.
[117] Bulwer to Sotomayor, 4 Feb. 1847. Copy, F.O. 72/719.
[118] Bulwer to Palmerston, 5 Feb. 1847. F.O. 72/719.

diate danger of Spanish intervention in Portugal and had afforded Palmerston an opportunity not only of detaching Spain from France but also of excluding France from any intervention in Portugal. The Spanish government, however, assumed intervention in the near future to have been the implicit basis of the agreement with Bulwer.[119] Palmerston, on the other hand, was by no means committed to intervention, and if he decided against it Bulwer would obviously find difficulty in holding the Spanish government to its promise. Everything therefore depended on the attitude adopted in London both to the new situation in Portugal and to the request of the Portuguese government, backed by France and Spain, for assistance under the Quadruple Treaty.

Queen Victoria and Prince Albert were convinced that the collaboration between the Septembrists and the Miguelites had completely altered the situation in Portugal. They made determined efforts to secure from Palmerston and Russell a promise that if the Miguelite insurrection 'became seriously dangerous we would be ready to give the assistance we are bound to do by the Quadruple Treaty. A promise to do what treaties already oblige us to do, can in the Queen's opinion create no difficulty for us.'[120] Palmerston realised that the Queen was seeking to alter his policy. His reply skilfully evaded the differences between them over Portugal by concentrating on the practical difficulties in the way of the Queen's suggestion.[121] To Russell Palmerston was more frank: the Queen's proposal, he wrote,

would be a very unusual measure for the British Government to take and would be much more after the fashion of Austria and Russia than of England. It would be, to a certain degree, to erect ourselves as judges between the parties, but to bind ourselves to pronounce judgement according to the dictation of one alone.[122]

Palmerston did not consider that the appearance of the Miguelites at Oporto made conciliation no longer possible and commitment to intervention necessary. In his view the Miguelite

[119] Bresson to Guizot, 7 Feb. 1847. A.A.E.C.P. Espagne 830.
[120] The Queen to Russell, 2 Feb. 1847. R.A. C/7/34. See also the Queen to Palmerston, 2 Feb. 1847. R.A. J/56/37.
[121] Palmerston to the Queen, 3 Feb. 1847. R.A. J/56/39.
[122] Palmerston to Russell, 10 Feb. 1847. Russell Papers, P.R.O. 30/22/6B.

threat was not serious; in so far as it existed it had been 'secretly encouraged by those who thought it might afford a pretext for foreign intervention'.[123] On 11 February Palmerston informed Bulwer that the British government saw no reason to change its policy towards Portugal. 'Military interference in Portugal' was neither necessary nor justifiable. Great Britain's ancient treaties with Portugal bound her only to protect Portugal against foreign aggression, and:

the Quadruple Treaty as far as Portugal is concerned is worked out; and was worked out within a few weeks after it was signed and ratified. It had a specified object, the expulsion of the two Infants from the territory of Portugal. But it was not a standing engagement to give military aid to the Sovereigns of Portugal whenever a set of ragged guerilras might throw up their tattered caps and call out long live Dom Miguel. There can be no difference in this respect between a Miguelite insurrection and any other insurrection in Portugal.[124]

In an official despatch of the same day Bulwer was instructed to warn the Spanish government that Portugal could not request assistance from Spain alone under the Quadruple Treaty, and that Spain could not intervene in Portugal without the consent of England.[125] Stanley, the Under Secretary at the Foreign Office, recognised that Palmerston's instructions would disappoint Bulwer, who had restrained the Spanish from immediate intervention in the anticipation of future joint intervention; he frankly admitted to Bulwer that 'you will have some trouble' after the Spanish government heard Palmerston's views.[126]

Before Palmerston's instructions of 11 February reached Madrid, Russell called a cabinet meeting to consider Portuguese affairs. This was partly in response to royal pressure for a reappraisal of British policy towards Portugal, and partly because Russell himself had begun to doubt the wisdom of Palmerston's course. Before the meeting Russell asked Lansdowne for his opinion on Portuguese affairs. Lansdowne's view

[123] Palmerston to Bulwer, 4 Feb. 1847. Bulwer Papers, S/30.
[124] Palmerston to Bulwer, 11 Feb. 1847. B.P. GC/BU/536.
[125] Palmerston to Bulwer, 11 Feb. 1847. F.O. 72/717.
[126] Stanley to Bulwer, 11 Feb. 1847. Bulwer Papers, S/40.

as to the legal standing of the 1834 treaty coincided with Palmerston's, but his recommendations as to the future course of English policy were nearer those of the Court than those of the Foreign Secretary. He thought the impression that England favoured the insurgents should be corrected, and stated in addition that: 'it would be no unfair construction to consider [the Quadruple treaty] as applying to the case of [Dom Miguel] re-entering Portugal or any attempt made to place him on the throne by force'.[127] The cabinet arrived at an opinion which combined Palmerston's and Lansdowne's views: that England 'cannot interfere between the Queen of Portugal and the Junta', but that 'if Dom Miguel should appear in Portugal the spirit of the Quadruple Treaty would authorize interference' and that Great Britain ought to initiate consultations with Spain to provide for this eventuality.[128] After the cabinet meeting Russell reconsidered the issue and moved closer to a commitment to intervention than Palmerston thought desirable or the cabinet had authorised. In his view Great Britain must consider not only the situation in Portugal and the legal implications of the 1834 treaty, but the situation in the whole of the Peninsula. He felt that Palmerston's policy of conciliation required more time than was available, and a greater degree of passivity from France and Spain than they were disposed to observe.[129] Russell favoured the course advocated by Bulwer, 'an understanding with Spain' respecting Portugal 'with a view to intervention'.[130] Palmerston disagreed with Russell and argued that intervention in support of absolutism would create more problems than it would solve. England should only commit herself to intervention, in his view, if she also made clear her refusal to underwrite the absolutist system of Dona Maria. This could be done only if England intervened as mediator or umpire:

As mediator we should simply have to convey from one belligerent to the other any proposal which either might be disposed to make...If we are to assume the character of umpire we must see that justice is done by both parties; and while we exact submission from the

[127] Lansdowne to Russell, 12 Feb. 1847. Russell Papers, P.R.O. 30/22/6B.
[128] Russell to the Queen, 13 Feb. 1847. R.A. J/56/30.
[129] Memorandum by Russell, 13 Feb. 1847. Russell Papers, P.R.O. 30/22/6B.
[130] Russell to Palmerston, 13 Feb. 1847. B.P. GC/RU/135.

Junta, we must require from the Queen all those acts and arrangements on her part which may appear to us to be due to her subjects and essential for her own well understood interests; such as the departure of Dietz, the appointment of a respectable administration, freedom of elections, an early meeting of the Cortes, general amnesty for all political offences...[131]

Palmerston sought to make any policy, whether conciliation or intervention, serve the cause of constitutionalism in the Peninsula. Russell quickly accepted Palmerston's contention that it was necessary to impose safeguards for Portuguese constitutionalism upon any intervention. On 14 February Russell prepared a new memorandum for the cabinet which combined a recommendation to begin consultations with Spain and to commit Great Britain to intervention if Dom Miguel should appear in Portugal with Palmerston's reservation that England could only act as mediator or umpire.[132] The cabinet met again on 16 February, and agreed to adopt the memorandum as the basis of British policy.[133] Palmerston immediately sent new instructions to Bulwer and Sir Hamilton Seymour, the new British envoy at Lisbon, transmitting the cabinet decision; he stressed that the commitment to intervention was contingent, that if it took place it would represent a change of means but not of ends.[134]

On 17 February 1847 Sainte Aulaire intimated to Palmerston the willingness of the French government to begin consultations about intervention in Portugal on the basis of the Quadruple Treaty. Palmerston replied that he regarded that treaty as worked out; if intervention were to take place, it would require careful consideration and new engagements. Palmerston's response to Sainte Aulaire's question whether France would be invited to participate if intervention were decided upon was

[131] Palmerston to Russell, 13 Feb. 1847. B.P. GC/RU/1009.
[132] Memorandum by Russell for the cabinet, 14 Feb. 1847. R.A. J/56/55.
[133] Russell to the Queen, 16 Feb. 1847. R.A. J/56/64.
[134] Palmerston to Bulwer, 16 Feb. 1847. F.O. 72/717; Palmerston to Seymour, 16 Feb. 1847. F.O. 63/640. On 17 Feb. Palmerston wrote to Wylde, 'Do not let the Court deceive themselves into a belief that we shall allow a Miguelite insurrection to draw us into an interference between the Queen and the Junta. We shall take good care to avoid that. We will not expose ourselves to the imputation of having been instrumental in the suppression of constitutional government in Portugal.' Palmerston to Wylde, 17 Feb. 1847. B.P. GC/WY/31.

uncertain: 'ce serait une question à examiner.' Of one thing, however, Palmerston was certain: 'les principes du Gouvernement Anglais ne lui permettent pas d'intervenir dans les affaires intérieures d'un pays au profit du despotisme'.[135] Sainte Aulaire concluded that British policy was inspired by sympathy for the Portuguese revolutionaries, and that its ultimate goal was the restoration to power of the Progresistas in Spain.[136] Palmerston was far more explicit to Normanby than to Sainte Aulaire about the rôle France should play in any intervention in Portugal. There seems to be (he wrote) no particular part that could be assigned to France in an intervention in Portugal; England and Spain could perfectly well manage it themselves, and moreover there was 'some disinclination in the cabinet to let France in unnecessarily into an affair which concerns Portugal alone, or to have anything whatever to do jointly with her where it is possible to avoid it'.[137]

The French government was well aware that Palmerston was attempting to exclude them from any part in an intervention in Portugal. Dietrichstein, the Austrian representative in London, told Sainte Aulaire that he had heard it from Palmerston himself,[138] and from Lisbon Varenne reported that Southern was very hostile to any plan of intervention that included France.[139] At the beginning of March 1847 Desages warned Glucksburg to be on his guard against British manœuvres to separate Spain from France on Portuguese affairs.[140] On 25 March the French government received news that Palmerston had proposed to the governments of Spain and Portugal that they should send their representatives in London full powers to negotiate a convention to regulate the co-operation of English naval and Spanish land forces should intervention in Portugal become necessary.[141] On Desages' instructions, Glucksburg warned Sotomayor of the great dangers for Spain if she were to negotiate 'sans nous avec l'Angleterre',[142] and secured from him an undertaking that the

[135] Sainte Aulaire to Guizot, 18 Feb. 1847. A.A.E.C.P. Angleterre 667.
[136] Sainte Aulaire to Guizot, 18 Feb. 1847. G.P. 42/AP/66.
[137] Palmerston to Normanby, 17 Feb. 1847. Normanby Papers, Box P, bundle 19.
[138] Sainte Aulaire to Guizot, 24 Feb. 1847. G.P. 42/AP/66.
[139] Varenne to Guizot, 26 Feb. 1847. A.A.E.C.P. Portugal 177.
[140] Desages to Glucksburg, 3 Mar. 1847. G.P. 42/AP/53.
[141] Desages to Glucksburg, 25 Mar. 1847. G.P. 42/AP/53.   [142] Ibid.

Spanish government would not act without France on the affairs of Portugal.[143] The isolation of France in the Peninsula, Glucksburg informed Guizot, had been averted.[144] The day after these conversations the Sotomayor government fell, and in their first interview the new Prime Minister, Pacheco, informed Glucksburg that, although the Spanish government sincerely wished to co-operate with France over Portugal, its interests there were too important for it to refuse to work with Great Britain if France were not invited to participate.[145] In early April Louis Philippe expressed to Guizot his deep anxiety about the turn of events in the Peninsula; only vigilance and firmness on the part of France, he wrote, could prevent Palmerston from destroying the achievements of five years of French diplomacy.[146]

In late February and March, the British government had achieved some success in its attempts to draw Spain to Britain's side over Portugal. Sotomayor had frequently assured Bulwer that the Spanish government would take no action without first consulting the British government,[147] and he acceded to Palmerston's request that the Spanish government should send full powers to Tacon, the Spanish minister in London, to negotiate a convention with Palmerston and the Portuguese envoy, Moncorvo, should the need arise.[148] Sotomayor was, however, as Bulwer noticed, hardly 'delighted' by the British offer;[149] indeed, unknown to Bulwer, immediately after agreeing to Palmerston's request, Sotomayor promised the French not to act on Portugal without them. Before he had to find a way out of these contradictory commitments, Sotomayor fell. The British government's only hope of holding Spain to her

[143] 'Votre Excellence m'a assuré...qu'en aucun cas elle n'accepterait soit à Madrid, soit à Lisbonne, soit à Londres aucune négociation et aucune convention sur des bases qui ne fussent pas une conservation formelle du traité de la quadruple alliance ou qui, soit directemment, soit indirectemment pussent impliquer l'exclusion de la France.' Glucksburg to Sotomayor, 27 Mar. 1847. A.A.E.C.P. Espagne 830.
[144] Glucksburg to Guizot, 28 Mar. 1847. A.A.E.C.P. Espagne 830; Glucksburg to Guizot, 29 Mar. 1847. G.P. 42/AP/67.
[145] Glucksburg to Guizot, 1 Apr. 1847. A.A.E.C.P. Espagne 830.
[146] Louis Philippe to Guizot, 1 Apr. 1847. G.P. 42/AP/286.
[147] Bulwer to Palmerston, 23 Feb. 1847. F.O. 72/719.
[148] Palmerston to Bulwer, 20 Feb. 1847. B.P. GC/BU/538; Bulwer to Palmerston, 2 Mar. 1847. F.O. 72/720.
[149] Bulwer to Palmerston, 2 Mar. 1847. B.P. GC/BU/320.

promise of bilateral action, in face of contrary French pressure, would have been to offer almost immediate intervention.[150] In fact, however, on 27 March Russell decided that 'there is at present no case for interference either by the letter or by the spirit of the Quadruple Treaty'. The British government, he concluded, could only agree to intervene to suppress the Miguelites if Dona Maria first made an effort to detach the Septembrists from the Miguelites by offering them 'a complete amnesty, a promise to abide by the constitution and convoke the Cortes within six months [and] nominate moderate ministers', and the Junta were to reject these concessions.[151] Immediate intervention, which the Portuguese government was pressing for and Spain was eager to offer, was again rejected by the British government in favour of conciliation. The response of the Pacheco government to the British insistence that the Portuguese government should make a further attempt to reach a compromise was very different from the response that could have been anticipated from the Sotomayor government. Pacheco informed Bulwer that, in his government's view, the Portuguese throne was threatened only by the Miguelites, not by the Septembrists; Spain's best course was therefore to send a representative to Lisbon to unite with the British diplomats in urging on Dona Maria conciliatory measures that would detach the Septembrists from the Miguelites.[152] The formation of a new government in Spain, Bulwer concluded, had averted an international crisis over Portugal, and he looked forward to close co-operation between England and Spain on Portuguese affairs.[153]

[150] On 26 Mar. Bulwer informed Palmerston that he thought that he could 'prevent the intervention of a Spanish force' in Portugal 'for a while', but that if the situation in Portugal remained the same and Great Britain opposed to intervention he thought Sotomayor would 'ultimately' sanction unilateral intervention. Bulwer to Palmerston, 26 Mar. 1847. F.O. 72/720.
[151] Memorandum by Russell, 27 Mar. 1847. Russell Papers, P.R.O. 30/22/6B.
[152] Bulwer to Palmerston, 30 Mar. 1847. F.O. 72/720.
[153] Bulwer to Palmerston, 3 Apr. 1847. F.O. 72/721.

CHAPTER IX

Iberian Problems,
March 1847–February 1848

On 30 March 1847 Palmerston informed Bulwer of the new British proposals for a negotiated settlement of the Portuguese dispute. The terms of settlement differed little from those offered to the Junta in late January: the Septembrists were required to lay down their arms and submit to the Queen's authority, and Dona Maria was to make the concessions necessary to re-establish constitutional government in Portugal. If, however, the Junta rejected this final chance of compromise, they would be coerced into submission. This new attempt at conciliation, unlike its predecessor, was in the nature of an ultimatum. Since the alternative was total defeat and humiliation, Palmerston believed that the Junta would accept the new proposals. 'I cannot believe', he informed Bulwer, 'that they would hesitate two hours upon the matter.'[1] In Palmerston's view a definite threat of intervention made actual intervention less likely. The fact was, however, that the British government had to prepare to follow the logic of its own policy: if the mediation proposals were rejected at Oporto, intervention would become inevitable. Palmerston and Russell had thus to reconsider the major questions which intervention raised. On what grounds was it to be justified, and which powers were to take part in it?

Palmerston and Russell held unswervingly to the opinion that the Quadruple Alliance was inapplicable to the situation in Portugal in 1847.[2] With characteristic bluntness Palmerston

[1] Palmerston to Bulwer, 30 Mar. 1847. B.P. GC/BU/541. Palmerston thought that if the Junta refused the terms offered to them 'there will be such a defection from their ranks by the submission of all moderate men, that the civil war will necessarily end from the weakness of the Junta'. Palmerston to Queen Victoria, 30 Mar. 1847. Connell, *Regina v. Palmerston*, 54–5.

[2] Palmerston to Seymour, 5 Apr. 1847. F.O. 63/640. Bulwer told Pacheco on

informed Bulwer that the only reason why the British government was prepared to intervene was to prevent Portugal from 'going to the Dogs'.³ If England allowed the dispute to continue, Portugal would be devastated by civil war, Spain would intervene, and Portugal would end as a satellite of France and Spain. Intervention, if it proved necessary, would be defended as the only way to avert the ruin of Portugal and preserve the balance of power in the Peninsula.⁴

Having once again declared the Quadruple Treaty inapplicable, the British government was free to determine what other powers, if any, were to join in the intervention. Spanish participation was never in any doubt. The British government had already offered joint intervention to the Spanish government in the hope of dissuading it from unilateral intervention; moreover, Spanish land forces would be needed in any intervention to complement British naval forces in restoring Dona Maria's authority. The crucial question in late March remained as before: would France be invited to participate in intervention in Portugal? The French had little expectation that they would. On 30 March Sainte Aulaire informed Guizot that Palmerston was bent on the total exclusion of France from Portuguese affairs, and that in his opinion France was helpless to prevent it since the British government had rejected the Quadruple Treaty as the basis for intervention. This left France no treaty right on which to claim to participate, and Moncorvo, the Portuguese minister, and Isturiz, the new Spanish minister in London, although well disposed towards France, could not be expected to hold out for the inclusion of France in a matter of

---

7 Apr. that intervention on the basis of the Quadruple Treaty 'would be establishing a perpetual right for all the parties to the Quadruple Alliance to interfere for ever and in any circumstances in a kingdom which it is our interest and fixed determination to keep independent'. Bulwer to Palmerston, 7 Apr. 1847. F.O. 72/721.

³ Palmerston to Bulwer, 30 Mar. 1847. B.P. GC/BU/541.
⁴ See Palmerston's Memorandum on Portuguese Affairs, July 1847, B.P. MM/PO/50, where Palmerston states that in March 1847 'we found

1. That the Portuguese Government would not come to terms with the Junta.
2. That the Spanish Government would interfere in spite of us if the throne of Maria should be in imminent danger.
3. That Maria's throne was in imminent danger.
4. That the whole country was going to ruin by reason of the Civil War.'

such vital importance to their governments.[5] On 1 April, in a stormy interview with Sainte Aulaire, Palmerston accused the French government of instructing Varenne to offer Dona Maria unilateral French assistance should she require it, and warned him of the grave threat to peace in western Europe if France encroached upon a well-established British sphere of influence.[6] Angered by Palmerston's accusation, Guizot and Louis Philippe insisted that a formal denial that France had offered assistance to Portugal be made and placed on record.[7] On 2 April Guizot drafted a despatch to Sainte Aulaire, again contesting the British assertion that the Quadruple Treaty was inapplicable to the Portuguese situation, and petulantly suggesting that British participation in any intervention not based on the Quadruple Alliance was as unnecessary as French, since the matter could safely be left to the Spanish and Portuguese governments.[8] Guizot did not expect this despatch to be taken seriously in London; it was merely an expression of his anger at being excluded from intervention. Before it was sent, he received news that on 2 April Palmerston had informed Sainte Aulaire that if British mediation were to fail, he proposed to invite the representatives of Spain, Portugal and France to a conference to decide upon the best mode of intervention.[9] Guizot was surprised and relieved, although puzzled by the British change of mind.[10] Although there was still a strong disinclination in Britain to work with France, both Palmerston and Russell had been aware from the outset that, even though her inclusion might bring no positive advantages, the exclusion of France had

[5] Sainte Aulaire to Guizot, 30 Mar. 1847. G.P. 42/AP/66.
[6] Sainte Aulaire to Guizot, 1 Apr. 1847. G.P. 42/AP/66. See also Seymour to Palmerston, 20 Mar. 1847. F.O. 63/645.
[7] Louis Philippe to Guizot, 3 Apr. 1847. G.P. 42/AP/286. Guizot instructed Jarnac on the same day to make a formal denial of the offer. Guizot to Jarnac, 3 Apr. 1847. G.P. 42/AP/7. There is no evidence other than Seymour's assertion of any offer having been made by the French government to the Portuguese government. It seems unlikely that any such offer was ever made as Guizot knew that Palmerston would regard it as a direct challenge. King Leopold perhaps best summed up the question when he wrote to Queen Victoria on 23 Apr.: 'The French were tempted to assist Portugal but they always did subordonner the thing au bon plaisir de l'Angleterre.' R.A. Y/73/39.
[8] Guizot to Sainte Aulaire, 2 Apr. 1847. A.A.E.C.P. Angleterre 667.
[9] Sainte Aulaire to Guizot, 2 Apr. 1847. G.P. 42/AP/66.
[10] Guizot to Sainte Aulaire, 3 Apr. 1847. A.A.E.C.P. Angleterre 667.

inherent dangers. Frustrated, France might work behind the scenes at Madrid to undermine Anglo-Spanish co-operation; if this happened after Spanish troops had crossed the Portuguese frontier, it could be a real hazard. Above all, they feared that France might retaliate for her exclusion from intervention in Portugal by excluding England from intervention in Spain should a similar crisis occur there.[11] It was with reluctance that Palmerston admitted the necessity of co-operating with France, and he made it clear that the invitation to join in any intervention reflected no change in his attitude to France. He was, in any case, confident that the Junta would accept the terms of mediation, thus making the offer of co-operation one in principle only.

On 5 April Palmerston sent the new mediation proposals to Lisbon. Seymour was empowered to offer the services of Colonel Wylde as the official mediator between Lisbon and Oporto. Immediately the Junta submitted to her authority, Dona Maria was required to grant a full and general amnesty for all political offences committed since October 1846, to recall all those exiled for political offences, to revoke all the decrees issued since October 1846 which infringed established laws, and to appoint a new administration composed of neither Cabralists nor Septembrists. As soon as the elections had been held—and these were to take place without delay—she was to convoke the Cortes. If the Junta refused the proposed terms, they would be compelled to submit by Great Britain, France and Spain, but Dona Maria must clearly understand, wrote Palmerston, that 'if intervention does become necessary she will be expected to carry out all the above stipulations except the granting of the amnesty...'[12] Although he was committed to joint intervention

[11] On 20 Feb. Palmerston informed Bulwer: 'if we exclude France she may be more likely to take a separate line about Spain if any disturbances should break out there, and perhaps with a view to such contingencies it may be prudent to take her with us to Portugal'. Palmerston to Bulwer, 20 Feb. 1847. B.P. GC/BU/538. On 22 Mar. Russell informed Palmerston: 'Upon considering the whole matter I think France should be invited to join us as a principal. If she is not, she may form some separate alliance with Spain respecting Don Carlos which would be very objectionable. To be sure when admitted Guizot may play all sorts of tricks. We must be on our guard against them; that is all. On the whole we shall be safer as allies than as separate parties.' B.P. GC/RU/140.
[12] Palmerston to Seymour, 5 Apr. 1847. F.O. 63/640.

if mediation failed, Palmerston made no effort to consult the French and Spanish governments on the terms offered, nor did he ask them to urge Dona Maria to accept them. He expected France and Spain to stand aside and wait until he invited them to further consultations.[13] This, Guizot observed, reflected his intense suspicion of France and Spain, and his desire to claim all the credit should mediation succeed, but not all the responsibility should intervention become necessary. In private Guizot condemned Palmerston's high-handedness,[14] but he recognised that France was helpless to stand out for better terms for Dona Maria; Palmerston would not support them, and would undoubtedly attempt to discredit Guizot by a public declaration that England could not join France in supporting absolutism in Portugal. The French and Spanish governments would have either to intervene on terms dictated by Britain, or to refuse to intervene.[15] Thus, although Palmerston's threat of intervention had in large measure arisen from suspicion and doubt as to the Portuguese policies of France and Spain, he exploited their anxiety to intervene and Guizot's fear of being accused of absolutist sympathy to dictate terms of intervention without reference to them, and of which they did not fully approve. Palmerston believed that he had made the best of a bad situation. All that remained was for both sides in Portugal to accept the mediation proposals.

The Pacheco government in Spain was prepared to follow a policy towards Portugal more in accordance with that of Great Britain than its predecessor. This gave rise to bitter criticism in Spain, the high Moderados claiming that Pacheco had abandoned the cause of monarchy and order in the Peninsula.[16] After little more than a week in office, Pacheco felt it necessary to make his Portuguese policy look more independent; he informed Bulwer that, while he remained in favour of a compromise settlement, the time had come to deal firmly with the Junta to stop them flouting the authority of the Queen.[17] Bulwer had expected these developments: he knew Pacheco

[13] Palmerston to Normanby, 6 Apr. 1847. Normanby Papers, Box P, bundle 19.
[14] Guizot to Jarnac, 19 Apr. 1847. G.P. 42/AP/7.
[15] Guizot to Sainte Aulaire, 15 Apr. 1847. A.A.E.C.P. Angleterre 667.
[16] Bulwer to Palmerston, 6 Apr. 1847. B.P. GC/BU/332.
[17] Bulwer to Palmerston, 7 Apr. 1847. F.O. 72/721.

to be under considerable pressure from the high Moderados to intervene immediately in Portugal, and that Glucksburg, who did not hear from Guizot until 8 April that Palmerston had decided to include France in any intervention, was urging him not to co-operate with Great Britain on any basis other than the Quadruple Treaty.[18] Bulwer considered that the best way of securing Pacheco's support for Palmerston's new policy was not to inform him of it, but by judicious prompting to lead Pacheco to suggest it himself. Despite opposition from Glucksburg, Pacheco fulfilled Bulwer's hopes by agreeing on 11 April that the Spanish government would join with Great Britain to urge the Portuguese government to accept a peaceful settlement; for this purpose Ayllon, the new Spanish ambassador at Lisbon, was to begin consultations with Seymour. If a peaceful solution failed, Spain would act in perfect accord with Great Britain in any further measures.[19] The only difference between the agreement concluded between Pacheco and Bulwer on 11 April and the proposals which Palmerston had communicated informally to Bulwer on 30 March was that the former envisaged some degree of Spanish participation in the proposed mediation whereas the latter did not. Bulwer urged Palmerston and Seymour to make a small concession to Spanish *amour-propre* by accepting this. It was of no importance to England, whereas its effect in Spain, argued Bulwer, would be incalculable: it would strengthen Pacheco against his critics, and create the impression that England was prepared to treat Spain with respect and confidence in a way that France was not.[20]

The new disposition of the Spanish government towards Portuguese affairs had little effect at Lisbon. Palmerston and Bulwer hoped that Dona Maria would accept with alacrity the new English plan of conciliation once she realised that she could no longer hope for unilateral Spanish assistance, but Seymour reported on 14 April that the reaction of the Portuguese Court to the British proposals of 5 April was 'not very satisfactory'.[21]

[18] Glucksburg to Guizot, 8 Apr. 1847. G.P. 42/AP/67.
[19] Bulwer to Palmerston, 12 Apr. 1847. B.P. GC/BU/334; Bulwer to Palmerston, 13 Apr. 1847. F.O. 72/721.
[20] Bulwer to Palmerston, 13 Apr. 1847. F.O. 72/721; Bulwer to Seymour, 12 Apr. 1847. Bulwer Papers, S/43.
[21] Seymour to Palmerston, 14 Apr. 1847. F.O. 63/646.

This was surprising in view of the recent deterioration of the Queen's position *vis-à-vis* the rebels. At the beginning of April a detachment of rebel troops under the command of Sa da Bandeira had left Oporto to march on Lisbon; the commander of the Lisbon garrison had warned Dona Maria that if the rebel troops reached the capital he could not guarantee her safety because he feared that at least half his troops would defect to the rebels. Seymour hoped that this new danger would force Dona Maria to accept Palmerston's plan in its entirety. On 14 April, however, he informed Palmerston that the Court was against a complete amnesty and he expected the government to ask 'that a very limited number of persons should be excluded from the immediate benefit of an amnesty'.[22] Before deciding whether to accept mediation, Dona Maria consulted Ayllon and Varenne. It was apparent to Varenne that she was unwilling to accept the British proposals and wished the French and Spanish governments to suggest an alternative. Ayllon recommended acceptance, whereas Varenne stated that he had no instructions which would allow him to comment on the British proposals.[23] The defection of Spain to the side of compromise prevented Varenne from employing his usual tactic of relying on the Spaniards to oppose British policy by advocating an extreme stand against the rebels. Silence was therefore his only way of expressing the sympathy of his government for Dona Maria's plight.[24] In default of French and Spanish support against mediation, on 15 April Dona Maria accepted the British plan on condition that twelve Septembrist leaders were excepted from the amnesty. This condition was sharply rejected by Seymour.[25] In late April Dona Maria succumbed to pressure from Seymour and accepted the British plan of mediation in its entirety. Saldanha, who opposed this course, was dismissed and a new government was formed.

By the beginning of May mediation was under way. As a preliminary to offering terms to the Junta, Colonel Wylde had visited the headquarters of Sa da Bandeira on 30 April to pro-

[22] Ibid. See also Wylde to Prince Albert, 15 Apr. 1847. R.A. J/57/64.
[23] Varenne to Guizot, 15 Apr. 1847. A.A.E.C.P. Portugal 177.
[24] Varenne, wrote Seymour, has become an 'indifferent spectator' of the events in Portugal and expresses no opinion whatever. Seymour to Palmerston, 24 Apr. 1847. F.O. 63/647.
[25] Seymour to Palmerston, 16 Apr. 1847. F.O. 63/647.

pose an armistice until the Junta should either accept or reject mediation. Bandeira agreed,[26] but Wylde's departure for Oporto was delayed by a dispute as to whether Ayllon should accompany him. The Portuguese government objected to the inclusion of a Spanish diplomat in the negotiations, presumably because they feared it would increase the chances of acceptance by the Junta.[27] A compromise, which allowed Wylde to proceed to Oporto with the Spanish chargé d'affaires, satisfied neither the Portuguese nor the Spaniards. Pacheco and Ayllon both felt neglected and insulted; the former complained to Bulwer 'that by acting with us instead of listening to the advice of the French he has been excluded from all credit' for a peaceful settlement. The fact is, wrote Bulwer, that Spain will only follow our lead 'if we do so in a manner suited to please her vanity'.[28] Varenne refused to follow a British lead; he informed Seymour that he had no instructions to authorise Wylde to state to the Junta that in offering mediation the British government had the full support of the French government.[29] His sole action was to give a reception at the French legation on 1 May, Louis Philippe's birthday; la fête du Roi was announced, wrote Varenne, as 'une solennité pour les hommes d'ordre de tous les pays';[30] it was attended exclusively by Cabralist politicians. On 11 May the Junta refused mediation. Seymour took immediate steps to gain time for the British government to organise measures of coercion. To prevent Lisbon from falling into the hands of the rebel army,[31] on 15 May Seymour suggested to Ayllon and Varenne that they should demand from Sa da Bandeira an extension of the armistice; he was to be informed that any attack on Lisbon would be regarded as an act of

[26] Seymour to Palmerston, 2 May 1847. F.O. 63/648.
[27] Seymour to Palmerston, 5 May 1847. F.O. 63/648.
[28] Bulwer to Seymour, 6 May 1847. F.O. 72/722. See also Bulwer to Clarendon, 6 May 1847. Clar. Dep. C525.
[29] Varenne to Guizot, 30 Apr. 1847. A.A.E.C.P. Portugal 177.
[30] Varenne to Guizot, 2 May 1847. A.A.E.C.P. Portugal 177. 'As long as there was an appearance of Her Majesty's Government standing aloof', wrote Seymour, 'there was certainly...an inclination on the part of the French to draw nearer to this government. The timely assistance offered by Her Majesty's Government appears now to have produced a corresponding desire on the part of France to assume an inactive—for I will not say an unfriendly attitude.' Seymour to Palmerston, 12 May 1847. F.O. 63/648.
[31] Seymour to Palmerston, 14 May 1847. F.O. 63/648.

hostility against Great Britain, France and Spain. Ayllon agreed; Varenne at first refused on the familiar grounds that he had no instructions, but agreed to the suggestion on the following day.[32] His change of mind was the result of the fact that on 16 May the commander of the French ships in the Tagus informed Varenne that he had been placed under his instructions.[33]

On 15 May Jarnac informed Guizot that, according to telegraphic information received by *The Globe*, the Junta had refused mediation; he, Isturiz and Moncorvo were therefore waiting to be called to the Foreign Office to concert the means of intervention.[34] Guizot instructed Jarnac on 17 May to press Palmerston to act without delay.[35] Palmerston was well aware of what needed to be done; on 15 May he informed Bulwer that he was making arrangements for intervention, with France and Spain 'playing second fiddle to us'.[36] On 20 May the cabinet authorised Palmerston to 'take immediate steps to enforce the mediation on the Junta of Oporto'.[37]

On 21 May 1847 Palmerston invited Moncorvo, Isturiz and Jarnac to the Foreign Office to join in drawing up a protocol which would regulate the intervention of England, France and Spain in Portugal. The terms of the intervention, which were identical to those of the mediation proposal of 5 April, were agreed without discussion; on this point Palmerston had already committed France and Spain, whether they liked it or not. Jarnac and Isturiz insisted, however, that the grounds for intervention must be a request for assistance from the Portuguese government 'to those of her allies who had been parties to the Treaty of the 22nd of April, 1834'.[38] When Jarnac made it clear that this was the *sine qua non* of French participation, Palmerston waived his first objections and amended his draft protocol accordingly. Jarnac regarded this as a great triumph,

---

[32] Seymour to Palmerston, 17 May 1847. F.O. 63/649.
[33] Varenne to Guizot, 16 May 1847. A.A.E.C.P. Portugal 178.
[34] Jarnac to Guizot, 15 May 1847. A.A.E.C.P. Angleterre 667.
[35] Guizot to Jarnac, 17 May 1847. A.A.E.C.P. Angleterre 667.
[36] Palmerston to Bulwer, 15 May 1847. Bulwer Papers, S/1.
[37] Russell to the Queen, 21 May 1847. R.A. J/58/27.
[38] Protocol of a Conference relating to the Affairs of Portugal, 21 May 1847. *Accounts and Papers, 1847*, xxv, 5–6.

demonstrating that the French interpretation of the bearing of the Quadruple Alliance had been correct from the outset; in France, moreover, he claimed that intervention based on that treaty would be considered 'comme un gage nouveau de la fidelité de son gouvernement aux grands principes qui dirigent sa politique extérieure'.[39]

The subjection of the Junta to the Queen's authority was to be accomplished by British and French naval assistance and the entry into Portugal of Spanish troops. Palmerston recognised that Spanish military intervention was indispensable if the dispute were to be ended swiftly and decisively, but in order to save Portugal from long-term 'political dependence on Spain'[40] he insisted that Spanish troops should withdraw from Portugal either as soon as the Septembrists submitted or not later than 'two months after the time when they shall enter'.[41] Jarnac made no objection to this stipulation since the French government feared that the prolonged absence of a considerable number of Spanish troops in Portugal would afford an opportunity to the Progresistas to foment disorder within Spain.[42]

The decision to intervene in Portugal pleased the French more than the British. Forth-Rouen, the French chargé d'affaires at Lisbon, wrote to Guizot that the British government was doing France's work for her in the Peninsula, in that intervention to compel the submission of the Junta would make it impossible to intervene a second time to compel Dona Maria to fulfil the terms of the protocol of 21 May. Dona Maria would thus be at liberty to defy Palmerston, and Forth-Rouen predicted that she would.[43] Moreover, as Glucksburg pointed out, Palmerston had already alienated Dona Maria and the Cabralists, and intervention would alienate the Septembrists as well; the French could therefore exploit the enmity of both parties in Portugal towards Great Britain.[44] Guizot and Desages deferred for a while any assessment of the consequences of the

[39] Jarnac to Guizot, 21 May 1847. A.A.E.C.P. Angleterre 668.
[40] Palmerston's Memorandum on Portuguese Affairs, July 1847. B.P. MM/PO/50.
[41] *Accounts and Papers, 1847*, xxv, 5–6. See also Palmerston to Bulwer, 22 May 1847. Bulwer Papers, S/1.
[42] Desages to Glucksburg, 25 May 1847. G.P. 42/AP/53.
[43] Forth-Rouen to Guizot, 29 May 1847. A.A.E.C.P. Portugal 178.
[44] Glucksburg to Guizot, 25 June 1847. G.P. 42/AP/76.

intervention in Portugal on France's Peninsular policy, and concentrated on exploiting the advantages offered by apparent Anglo-French co-operation. They knew that Palmerston resented having to work with France but assumed that he would not say so publicly.[45] The four-power decision to intervene in Portugal could therefore be represented as a triumph for the goodwill which the French government had continued to show towards England despite the rupture over the Spanish marriages;[46] in the Chamber of Deputies Guizot went so far as to hint that he would not be surprised to see the *entente* revived.[47]

Palmerston was undoubtedly disappointed at the failure of his plans for a peaceful settlement in Portugal and fully alive to the dangers of his new course. He anticipated considerable parliamentary disapproval of intervention, and he realised that to overcome the resistance of the Junta would be easier than to hold Dona Maria to her promise to re-establish constitutional government.[48] As always, he tried to make the best of a bad situation, consoling himself with the reflection that whatever perils had still to be encountered, the worst dangers had been avoided. This sanguine outlook was not shared by Seymour and Bulwer. Seymour clearly did not relish the prospect of having to work closely with Varenne, an awkward colleague under any circumstances.[49] Bulwer was dismayed by the intervention itself and even more by French participation. He regarded this as a definite setback for British policy in the Peninsula. On 26 May he informed Palmerston:

[45] In early June Jarnac reported that it was generally believed in London that the British government had been forced to intervene in Portugal by the fear that France and Spain would if she did not. This, according to Jarnac, was what Palmerston told Peel. Jarnac to Guizot, 5 June 1847. A.A.E.C.P. Angleterre 668; Jarnac to Guizot, 8 June 1847. G.P. 163/MI/52. The French were irritated when the British Blue Book on Portugal was published as it contained Seymour's despatches on the imminence of French intervention in Portugal. See *Accounts and Papers, 1847*, xxv, 253, 269. Jarnac admitted that it would be difficult to lodge a formal protest as the papers were presented in such a way as to suggest that the British government did not believe that the French had offered assistance to Dona Maria. Jarnac to Guizot, 11 June 1847. A.A.E.C.P. Angleterre 668.
[46] *Journal des Débats*, 25 May 1847.
[47] Guizot's speech in the Chamber of Deputies, 14 June 1847. There is a printed copy in G.P. 42/AP/53.
[48] Palmerston to Bulwer, 22 May 1847. Bulwer Papers, S/1.
[49] Seymour to Palmerston, 28 May 1847. F.O. 63/649.

When I brought England and Spain together into this business it was because I felt sure that Spain alone was sure to act according to the views of Great Britain; I apprehend, however, that if France, England and Spain act together, it is by no means impossible that France and Spain may at any time unite in favour of a course of which we do not approve.[50]

The Moderado press was demanding that intervention should aim at 'crushing the liberal party in Portugal', and claimed that 'Spain in conjunction with France' could achieve this.[51] Bulwer's fears concerned Spain as much as Portugal: 'remember', he wrote to Seymour, 'you are not managing a Portuguese affair but an European affair'. A Cabralist triumph in Portugal would, he believed, make the ultra-Moderados much more intrepid; the return to power of Narvaez, the forced abdication of Isabella, and the proclamation as Queen of the Duchess of Montpensier were all possible consequences of their increased confidence. The Progresistas were already disheartened, and interpreted British intervention in Portugal on behalf of the Queen as tantamount to the abandonment of the cause of liberalism in the Peninsula. In Bulwer's opinion, England's last chance of retaining a shred of influence in Portugal lay in conciliating the Septembrists once intervention was over: 'if possible they should be brought back to power to aid the English party in Spain'.[52]

Palmerston and Seymour hoped to avoid the dangers Bulwer predicted, provided the Junta were quick to admit defeat and Dona Maria prompt to implement the terms of the intervention. The confidence of the Junta and the recalcitrance of Dona Maria largely destroyed these hopes. The new Portuguese government led by Bayard began well by announcing its decision to withdraw Thomar from Madrid because of his close association with the Cabralists. Both Ayllon and Varenne approved of this.[53] On 4 June, however, Seymour came into conflict with Bayard over the proclamation restoring constitutional government to be issued by the Queen. Seymour

[50] Bulwer to Palmerston, 26 May 1847. F.O. 72/722.
[51] Bulwer to Palmerston, 27 May 1847. B.P. GC/BU/349.
[52] Bulwer to Seymour, 29 May 1847. Bulwer Papers, S/43.
[53] Seymour to Palmerston, 1 June 1847. F.O. 63/650.

considered the draft proclamation totally inadequate since it stated merely that once the civil war was over the Septembrists would enjoy the protection of the law. He persuaded Ayllon and Varenne to join him in a demand that a new proclamation be drawn up.[54] Redrafting was delayed because the Bayard government insisted on exceptions being made to the amnesty; Seymour pointed out that this would contravene the protocol of London, and advised Dona Maria to change her government.[55] Ayllon and Varenne, however, did not support this advice.[56] On 8 June the Bayard government agreed to grant a general amnesty, preferring, wrote Seymour, their places to their principles.[57]

The coercion of the rebels seemed to be progressing faster than royal compliance with the terms of intervention. On 13 June Seymour and Admiral Parker decided to strengthen the blockade of Oporto, Spanish troops continued their advance, and Parker left Lisbon for St Ubes with a squadron of steamers to demand the submission of Sa da Bandeira.[58] These measures soon achieved success: Sa da Bandeira submitted within a few days, and early in July royal authority was re-established at Oporto.[59] By the end of July the British ships from the home and Mediterranean fleets, sent to augment the Tagus squadron, had left Portuguese waters, and the Spanish troops returned to Spain.[60] Dona Maria's throne was no longer in imminent peril.

The success of intervention destroyed the fragile unity which Seymour had established at Lisbon between himself, Ayllon and Varenne. On 18 June Varenne authorised the release of some Septembrists captured by a French frigate without consulting his English and Spanish colleagues.[61] Seymour recognised that Varenne was intent on exploiting the antipathy of both parties in Portugal towards Great Britain by refusing to support the British demand that all Cabralists should be removed from

[54] Seymour to Palmerston, 4 June 1847. F.O. 63/650.
[55] Seymour to Palmerston, 5 June 1847. F.O. 63/650.
[56] Seymour to Bulwer, 7 June 1847. Bulwer Papers, S/43.
[57] Seymour to Palmerston, 8 June 1847. F.O. 63/650.
[58] Seymour to Palmerston, 14 June 1847. F.O. 63/650.
[59] Seymour to Palmerston, 17 June 1847. F.O. 63/651; Seymour to Palmerston, 4 July 1847. F.O. 63/652.
[60] Bulwer to Palmerston, 25 July 1847. Bulwer Papers, S/11.
[61] Wylde to Prince Albert, 18 June 1847. R.A. J/59/12.

official positions while at the same time conciliating the Septembrists.[62] In late June 1847 Varenne received instructions to abandon joint action with Seymour, and maintain an attitude of complete reserve.[63] In the French view intervention had served its purpose: the Junta had been coerced. On 17 June Louis Philippe informed Guizot that France should have nothing more to do with intervention in Portugal; he expected that great embarrassments would follow the armistice, and thought that it would not be in French interests to become involved in them.[64] At the same time as new instructions were sent to Varenne, Glucksburg informed Pacheco that the French government hoped that Ayllon would not be authorised to support British schemes for restoring the Portuguese 'revolutionaries' to power. In July and August 1847 Pacheco seemed more disposed to follow the advice of Glucksburg than that of Bulwer on Portuguese affairs. Although Pacheco had shown a greater willingness than Sotomayor to work with Great Britain in Portugal, the basic aim of Spanish policy had always remained the same: the restoration of order in Portugal. Pacheco was as alive as Sotomayor to the potential danger to Spain of a Septembrist government in Portugal. A coalition between Pacheco and the Progresistas, on which Bulwer had pinned his hopes, never materialised; although Pacheco's government was never identified with the extreme right of his party, he nevertheless remained a Moderado. Like the French government, he was therefore unwilling to do anything that might destroy Cabralist ascendancy in Portugal. Thus Palmerston's belief that he had forced the French and Spanish governments into assisting to re-establish constitutional government in Portugal by agreeing to coerce the Junta was unjustified; as soon as the civil war was over, all efforts by the French and Spanish governments to make Dona Maria comply with the terms of the protocol of 21 May ceased. They left this task to Seymour and Palmerston, secure in the knowledge that they would be unable to accomplish it.[65]

[62] Seymour to Palmerston, 18 June 1847. F.O. 63/651.
[63] Guizot to Varenne, 26 June 1847. A.A.E.C.P. Portugal 179.
[64] Louis Philippe to Guizot, 17 June 1847. G.P. 42/AP/286.
[65] Glucksburg to Guizot, 18 June 1847. A.A.E.C.P. Espagne 831.

The fourth stipulation of the terms of intervention was that Dona Maria should entrust the task of reconciling the two parties in Portugal to a non-partisan and moderate ministry. This condition was crucial; unless it could be accomplished, certain of the other conditions, such as free elections, would be impossible. Palmerston was determined that Dona Maria should observe scrupulously the terms under which she had received foreign assistance.[66] Dona Maria was equally determined not to; her aim after the intervention remained as before, the destruction of the Septembrist party. She feared that if a new government, which faithfully honoured the stipulations of the protocol of 21 May, were formed, she would shortly be faced with a Septembrist majority in the Cortes. The intervention had dispersed and dispirited the Septembrist leaders; Dona Maria realised that this, combined with the destruction of their military power, put her in a stronger position than ever before to exclude them from power and to weaken them as a party. She therefore defied the British government, well aware that they would not intervene a second time to compel her to fulfil the terms of the protocol. Apart from the *Morning Chronicle* and the *Globe*, the English press had condemned the intervention, and the government had only just avoided parliamentary censure for its Portuguese policy. At one stage in the parliamentary debate on Portugal, Russell had warned the Queen that the government might well fall.[67] Further measures of coercion in Portugal were therefore unlikely; Dona Maria could defy the British government with impunity. The acerbity of Palmerston's comments on Dona Maria and her régime only reflected his complete inability to influence the one or change the other.[68] During July and August the connection between the Bayard government and the Cabralists, and its hostile measures against the Septembrists, became daily more overt.[69] Even Queen Victoria felt it necessary in August 1847 to express to Dona Maria her regret that the conditions of the London protocol remained unful-

[66] Palmerston to Seymour, 22 June 1847. F.O. 63/641; Palmerston to the Queen, 26 June 1847. R.A. J/59/14.
[67] Russell to the Queen, 13 June 1847. R.A. J/58/72.
[68] See for example Palmerston to the Queen, 6 Aug. 1847. R.A. J/59/49.
[69] Seymour to Palmerston, 4 July 1847. F.O. 63/652; Seymour to Bulwer, 16 Aug. 1847. Bulwer Papers, S/43.

filled.⁷⁰ There could be no doubt that intervention had achieved the very result Palmerston had sought from the outset to avoid; it had strengthened a party and a political system of which he did not approve and which would in no way serve British aims in Spain. Bulwer proved correct in his gloomy prediction of early June that intervention could only be a setback for Palmerston's Iberian policy. For the French it was a triumph, although they contributed little to Palmerston's reverse: the determined resistance of Dona Maria was the rock on which British policy foundered. It was sufficient for France—concerned as she was to maintain the *status quo* in Portugal—to encourage Dona Maria to resist compromise and to allow the Spanish government to push itself forward with the threat of intervention. After the intervention, the questions facing the French were how actively and how openly should they support the Cabralists. Glucksburg thought that the reluctance of the British government to intervene again in Portugal would enable France to pursue a much bolder Portuguese policy.⁷¹ Guizot, however, was unwilling to acquire the responsibilities and complications which a more active policy in Portugal would inevitably entail. For him French ascendancy at Madrid was, as it had always been, 'l'intérêt véritable, clair [et] direct' in the Peninsula.⁷² In the early autumn of 1847 it was the crisis in Spain to which Guizot was devoting his attention. Dona Maria was now in a position to look after herself.

In an interview with Lord Normanby on 5 April 1847, after the news of the formation of the Pacheco government had reached Paris, Queen Christina expressed the hope that 'things might now go on quietly in Spain', but she added that 'nothing ever seemed permanent there'.⁷³ No one knew better than Christina how difficult it was to form a ministry in Spain which had any real prospect of stability, and which could devote some of its energies to the practical problems of government rather than just to fending off intrigues. The Pacheco government was in a particularly difficult position. In dismissing Sotomayor and

⁷⁰ Queen Victoria to the Queen of Portugal, 6 Aug. 1847. R.A. J/59/50.
⁷¹ Glucksburg to Guizot, 25 June 1847. G.P. 42/AP/67.
⁷² Guizot's speech in the Chamber of Deputies, 14 June 1847. (printed copy) G.P. 42/AP/53.
⁷³ Normanby to Palmerston, 5 Apr. 1847. B.P. GC/NO/50.

inviting Pacheco to form a government, Isabella had followed the advice of her lover, Serrano; the fortunes of the new government were thus closely linked to the fickle affections of a sixteen-year-old girl. The high Moderados, whom Serrano had excluded from office, were determined to displace him and the ministry he had made either by reconciling the Queen to the King or by finding her a new lover whose political views accorded with their own.[74] Meanwhile they were ideally placed to embarrass Pacheco by denying him their support in the Cortes. He was therefore forced to look for a majority from the ranks of the liberal Moderados and the Progresistas. The support of the latter was uncertain despite Bulwer's efforts to persuade them that their interests would best be served by keeping Pacheco in power until they were ready and able to replace him.[75] Pacheco's position was very difficult: he had little firm support and many determined opponents.

As far as the British and French governments were concerned, the Pacheco government occupied something of an intermediate position: the French regarded it as a step in the wrong direction and the British as a step in the right direction. Neither believed that it could endure for long or provide a permanent solution to the problem of Spanish politics. The French regarded the new government with profound suspicion: Pacheco had been one of the few Moderados to oppose the Montpensier marriage, Salamanca, the Finance Minister, was a known Francophobe, and Serrano, the patron of the ministry, was suspected of Progresista leanings.[76] Moreover, Bulwer's approval was enough to condemn the ministry in French eyes.[77]

[74] In a series of articles in early April the *Heraldo*, the paper of the high Moderados, claimed that if necessary the Moderados could regain and retain power despite the hostility of the Court. Bulwer to Palmerston, 12 Apr. 1847. F.O. 72/721.

[75] Bulwer to Palmerston, 5 May 1847. F.O. 72/722. The Progresistas disapproved of Pacheco's Portuguese policy almost as strongly as they had condemned Sotomayor's, and they were particularly hostile to Salamanca, and were determined to oppose any measures which he brought before the Cortes. Bulwer to Palmerston, 3 May 1847. F.O. 72/722.

[76] Guizot to Sainte Aulaire, 3 Apr. 1847. A.A.E.C.P. Angleterre 667. As far as Salamanca was concerned, Desages informed Glucksburg on 17 Apr.: 'Il faut user Salamanca; il faut préparer sa chute, mais de telle sorte qu'elle soit inévitable et complète.' G.P. 42/AP/53.

[77] Glucksburg to Guizot, 28 Mar. 1847. G.P. 42/AP/67.

Pacheco knew that he could expect no support from Paris. What was not clear, however, was the tactics the French would employ to oppose the ministry. There were two courses open to them: they could initiate a series of new intrigues aimed at bringing down the government as soon as possible, or they could wait until they had re-established their influence at Court and restored some unity to the Moderado party.[78] In part the tactics of the French would depend upon what Pacheco did. If it became apparent that Pacheco was prepared to meet Palmerston's wishes on the succession question, or to follow Bulwer's advice about a fusion with the Progresistas, or to attempt to weaken the high Moderados by dissolving the Cortes and calling new elections, then the French were prepared to work for the immediate downfall of the government. Guizot hoped to avoid this: it would be a desperate measure to meet a desperate situation, and could only be a short-term solution. A new government formed under these circumstances would inevitably be an unstable and ephemeral combination.[79] In Guizot's view, France should follow the second course and play a waiting game. It had obvious advantages: firstly, the Pacheco government would be overthrown by purely Spanish forces acting apparently on their own initiative; secondly, if the Queen were reconciled to both the King and the Moderados, and if the Moderados were united, the succeeding government would be both strong and stable, and this would put an end to Palmerston's schemes for altering the succession. Glucksburg's task, as defined by Guizot, was to work unobtrusively but effectively for the reunion of the Moderados, for the re-establishment of their ascendancy at Court, and for the reconciliation of the Queen with the King. The choice of means was left to Glucksburg.[80]

The British government welcomed the formation of the Pacheco ministry, not only because it averted a crisis over Portugal but also because it augured well for Spain.[81] Palmerston, however, wanted more than a ministry of moderate and independent-minded men, free from French domination; in his

[78] Guizot to Glucksburg, 10 Apr. 1847. G.P. 42/AP/7; Glucksburg to Guizot, 18 Apr. 1847. G.P. 42/AP/67.
[79] Guizot to Glucksburg, 13 Apr. 1847. G.P. 42/AP/7.
[80] Guizot to Glucksburg, 10 Apr. 1847. G.P. 42/AP/7.
[81] Palmerston to Normanby, 16 Apr. 1847. Normanby Papers, Box P, bundle 19.

view the exclusion of the Duchess of Montpensier and her descendants from the succession to the Spanish throne was essential, and he wanted a government committed to this. Soon after Pacheco took office, Bulwer informed Palmerston that he could expect no co-operation from the new government on the succession question. Pacheco, though more liberal than his predecessors, remained a Moderado, and in the autumn of 1846 all the new ministers had supported the high Moderados in rejecting the Progresista interpretation of the Treaty of Utrecht and the succession law of 1845. Moreover, even had it wanted to, the government could not accede to Palmerston's wishes on the succession question, since this would inevitably reunite the Moderado factions in the Cortes and bring about its own fall.[82] In the long term, therefore, the Pacheco government was almost as unsatisfactory an agent as its predecessor in achieving the ultimate objective of Palmerston's Spanish policy. Palmerston knew this: 'our success in Spain', he wrote to Normanby, 'is as yet incomplete'.[83]

On the tactics to be employed to achieve the British aims in Spain Palmerston and Bulwer were agreed that while the high Moderados remained the alternative government Pacheco must be supported. In the longer term, they believed that they must ensure that, when the Pacheco government fell, its successor was still more anti-French and was willing to act in accordance with British views on the succession.[84] To Palmerston this could only mean a Progresista government. As he frequently informed Bulwer, Spain needed 'a Progresista ministry, a purification of the army and if necessary a new Cortes'.[85] Bulwer disagreed with Palmerston: he had a much lower opinion of the Progresista leaders and a more realistic assessment of the strength of their party. Palmerston believed that the weakness of the Progresistas derived from governmental control of elections and the exile of its leaders, notably Espartero; if new and free elections were held and Espartero returned, he assumed that the party would immediately revive. In fact the Progresista party was in process of distintegrating; the divisions which were to lead to its break-

[82] Bulwer to Palmerston, 6 May 1847. B.P. GC/BU/341.
[83] Palmerston to Normanby, 3 May 1847. B.P. GC/NO/445.
[84] Palmerston to Bulwer, 15 May 1847. Bulwer Papers, S/1.
[85] Palmerston to Bulwer, 4 June 1847. B.P. GC/BU/547.

up in 1848 were already apparent.[86] Bulwer was aware that the Progresistas, in addition to being distrusted by the Court and a large part of the army, were incapable of forming a government had they been invited to do so. He believed that he should work towards the formation of a coalition of liberal Moderados and conservative Progresistas, and should persuade the Queen that such a coalition government would protect her and govern in the interests of Spain.[87] This fundamental difference of opinion between Palmerston and Bulwer was never eliminated: Palmerston continued to hope for a Progresista ministry whilst Bulwer tended to work for a coalition, although he never completely ruled out the possibility of bringing the Progresistas to power. This difference was regarded by Palmerston as one of circumstances; the position, which changed 'from week to week', dictated what could be achieved at any particular moment, and Palmerston accordingly left Bulwer 'to deal with each new contingency as it arises without any instructions from hence'.[88] The French by contrast were much more sure about the government they wanted to succeed Pacheco.

In April and May 1847 Bulwer and Glucksburg applied themselves to the task of creating new alignments which they hoped would determine the future course of Spanish politics. Neither achieved much success. The existence of the Pacheco government made it difficult for Glucksburg to reunite the Moderado factions; the high Moderados regarded the liberal Moderados as renegades, and the latter were reluctant to move too close to their old associates for fear of alienating those Progresistas who supported them in the Cortes. Equally, Pacheco would not fall in with Bulwer's schemes and collaborate closely with the Progresistas in case he should thereby sacrifice the support of members of his own Moderado faction. His policy of delicate balance between the factions in the Cortes made it

[86] See J. Quero Molares, 'Spain in 1848', in *The Opening of an Era: 1848*, ed. F. Fejtö (New York, 1966), 143–60. On 6 June Decazes informed Guizot that the Moderado party 'était assez fort pour lutter contre ses adversaires sur lesquels il a l'avantage de l'homogénéité qui n'existe pas dans l'autre parti, si on peut donner ce nom à un assemblage occasionnel de tant de fractions hétérogènes.' A.A.E.C.P. Espagne 831.
[87] Bulwer to Palmerston, 20 May 1847. F.O. 72/722.
[88] Palmerston to Bulwer, 4 June 1847. B.P. GC/BU/547.

almost impossible for Bulwer and Glucksburg to create new combinations which had any prospect of permanence.[89] This was not the only difficulty encountered by Bulwer and Glucksburg: Bulwer complained constantly that the Progresistas were impractical and unwilling to accept compromises to achieve power; Glucksburg found the high Moderados unwilling to entertain the possibility of sharing power even temporarily with the liberal Moderados. Both men believed that purity of principle could only be overcome by the offer of place, and that the only way to bring the various factions to their senses was to hold out to them the prospect of office. But office depended on the attitude of the Court. Both Bulwer and Glucksburg therefore attempted to secure Court favour for their preferred political combination, but this proved an even more difficult task than realigning the parties.

'The confusion at Court', Bulwer informed Clarendon in May 1847, 'is terrible.'[90] The Queen was commonly said to be 'a pluralist in lovers', although Serrano remained the favourite. She lived apart from the King, who was suspected of Carlist sympathies and involvement in a military conspiracy. Don Francisco de Paula, who had exercised considerable influence over the Queen in the first few months of her marriage, had taken the side of the King, and was said to be involved in an intrigue to replace Pacheco by a government that would insist on a reconciliation between the Queen and the King. 'There never was', wrote Palmerston after reading Bulwer's account of the problems at the Spanish Court, 'a more embarrassing situation of things invented in a novel or a melodrama.'[91] To a certain point royal favourites and the intrigues of various members of the royal family were accepted as an endemic feature of Spanish politics. The danger, however, was that Isabella would behave so outrageously as to bring her person and her crown into total disrepute and that the Court intrigues would become so numerous and so open that the politicians would come to regard the Court as utterly irresponsible. Queen Christina had neither had impeccable morals nor eschewed

[89] Decazes to Guizot, 4 May 1847. A.A.E.C.P. Espagne 831.
[90] Bulwer to Clarendon, 6 May 1847. Clar. Dep. C525.
[91] Palmerston to Bulwer, 4 June 1847. B.P. GC/BU/547.

intrigue, but she had possessed a keen sense of political reality. This was the redeeming quality which Isabella seemed to lack, and Spanish politicians as well as Bulwer and Glucksburg feared that she was pursuing a reckless course. The situation at Court was further complicated by the Queen's failure to conceive a child and her announcement in the summer of 1847 that she wanted a divorce.[92] Her extra-marital activities made it clear that her barrenness could not be attributed solely to the King's impotence, and it was commonly said that she was incapable of bearing a child.[93] It was in this context that the British and French governments had to reconsider the problem of the succession in the summer of 1847, and both Bulwer and Glucksburg stressed that it was a matter of great urgency. The deposition of Isabella was not impossible, and she herself talked of abdication if she could not secure a divorce.[94] As early as April 1847 Glucksburg wrote to Guizot that 'pour tout le monde, la question politique est complètement dominée par la question du Palais'.[95] On 23 May Bulwer too informed Palmerston that the deplorable situation at the Court had led 'people to think about the succession and parties are already forming on one side or the other'.[96]

For the French government the problem of the succession in

[92] Buschenthal, a Spanish agent, informed Palmerston on 8 May 1847: 'In my humble opinion a separation, divorce or whatever it may be called must soon take place as the antipathy which existed before the marriage took place has degenerated into hatred and is growing in gigantic dimensions.' Copy, R.A. J/48/34.

[93] On 28 June 1847 Normanby informed Palmerston that Louis Philippe had managed to purchase from Isabella's doctor a report on the state of her health which concluded: 'she is not in a state to have children principally from an internal tumour of a scrofulous character which is not dangerous but which would be difficult to cure'. B.P. GC/NO/60. On 16 July Palmerston wrote to Bulwer: 'Let me know whether if we were to send to Madrid some man experienced in female complaints, in the interior department, you could get him consulted by and employed by the Queen. This would be a grand recovery if it could be accomplished.' Bulwer Papers, S/15.

[94] Bulwer to Palmerston, 27 May 1847. F.O. 72/722; Decazes to Guizot, 4 May 1847. A.A.E.C.P. Espagne 831. 'It is probable in my opinion, that unless great events call out what is good and great in the Queen's character, her reign will end some day or other by an abdication, forced on her or adopted by her voluntarily.' Bulwer to Palmerston, 26 May 1847. B.P. GC/BU/347. On 25 May Bulwer reported to Palmerston that the Queen had told Serrano that she would like to abdicate and live with him in Italy. F.O. 72/722.

[95] Glucksburg to Guizot, 11 Apr. 1847. A.A.E.C.P. Espagne 830.

[96] Bulwer to Palmerston, 23 May 1847. B.P. GC/BU/344.

1847 was an unexpected and unwelcome development of its double marriages policy of 1846. Guizot's attitude to the succession question was determined by his belief that Palmerston was exploiting it, as he had attempted to exploit the marriage question, to humiliate France and to substitute dominant English influence for dominant French influence at Madrid. In French eyes Palmerston's policy lacked perspective: as Guizot remarked, the possibility that one day a daughter-in-law or a cousin of the King of the French might occupy the Spanish throne no more threatened the peace of Europe than the fact that close relatives of the Queen of England already reigned in Belgium and Portugal.[97] In the autumn of 1846 Guizot hoped that the succession question would solve itself. By the summer of 1847, however, Isabella had failed to produce an heir, her disreputable conduct was endangering her throne, and Palmerston was still bent on the exclusion of the Duchess of Montpensier from the line of succession. What, in these circumstances, Glucksburg demanded of Guizot, was the policy of France?[98] Guizot and Louis Philippe both believed that they had no alternative but to follow the logic of their own policy. In August 1846 they had accepted the risk that the Infanta might one day succeed to the throne; in the autumn they had resisted Palmerston's attempt to humiliate France and reduce her influence at Madrid by changing the order of succession. To alter their policy, by allowing the Duchess to renounce her rights voluntarily or the Cortes to remove her from the succession, would inevitably involve serious loss of prestige and influence. Our policy, wrote Guizot to Glucksburg, is dictated by that of our adversary: Palmerston wishes to deny the Duchess her natural rights, we must therefore support them.[99] It was not, however, only Palmerston and the Progresistas who constituted a threat to the Duchess of Montpensier's succession rights. In June and July 1847 Queen Isabella talked of abdication unless she could

[97] Guizot to Rayneval, 4 Dec. 1846. G.P. 42/AP/9.
[98] Glucksburg to Guizot, 18 Apr. 1847. G.P. 42/AP/67.
[99] Guizot to Glucksburg, 25 Apr. 1847. G.P. 42/AP/7. In March Guizot advised Glucksburg: 'Ne perdez jamais de vue que la politique adverse a une idée fixe, un but immuable; "Amener un ministère progressiste qui fasse élire des Cortes Progressistes qui changent l'ordre de succession."' Guizot to Glucksburg, 22 Mar. 1847. G.P. 42/AP/7.

obtain a divorce, and the high Moderados said that if Isabella continued to behave irresponsibly she would force Spain to look for another sovereign, one who displayed greater respect for the dignity of the Crown and more responsibility in the exercise of royal authority. In their minds the candidate was obvious: the Duchess of Montpensier.[100] To Guizot such talk was alarming. The abdication of Isabella, whether voluntary or forced, would precipitate both a Spanish and an international crisis which would leave France in a false position, torn between her desires to support the rights of the Duchess and to avoid conflict with England which might lead to war. Isabella must therefore be disabused of any notion that she could abdicate, and the high Moderados of the idea that they could replace the Queen by her sister: 'Nous garderons ici le duc et la duchesse de Montpensier. Le jour où leurs droits s'ouvriraient naturellement, nécessairement nous verrons. D'ici là, nous ne serons point à la merci des fantaisies folles ou d'intrigues coupables', wrote Guizot to Broglie at the end of July 1847,[101] and Glucksburg's instructions were to put an end to discussion of the succession question. If necessary Narvaez must be brought back to power to restore order at Court and in the Moderado party.[102] The aim of the French was therefore to maintain the existing order of succession and to avert a succession crisis.

Palmerston, however, was convinced that the aim of the French was to engineer a crisis in Spain and then to place the Duchess of Montpensier on the throne. Normanby's reports from Paris and events in Spain seemed to him to afford proof of this. On 2 June 1847 Normanby wrote:

the King . . . dreams of living to see Montpensier on the throne of Spain, and though Guizot does not go his length of wishing for the abdication of the Queen he feels that his only chance of maintaining himself in power here is some great and speedy success in Spain.[103]

There can be no doubt, wrote Palmerston to Bulwer on 19 June, that the French are working for 'a change of Government in Spain and the re-establishment of Narvaez in power, to be

[100] Glucksburg to Guizot, 29 July 1847. G.P. 42/AP/67.
[101] Guizot to Broglie, 30 July 1847. G.P. 42/AP/214.
[102] Guizot to Glucksburg, 31 July 1847. G.P. 42/AP/7.
[103] Normanby to Palmerston, 2 June 1847. B.P. GC/NO/57.

followed by a declaration of the Cortes in favour of the Montpensier succession and probably such proceedings...as might induce the Queen to abdicate'.[104] Guizot's standing in France, wrote Palmerston three days later, was so shaken that he would try to recover prestige by a bold stroke in Spain.[105] Palmerston considered it his duty to resist in every way possible Guizot's bid to save himself and satisfy the ambition of Louis Philippe by 'leading or driving [Isabella] into some scrape'.[106] It also convinced him that the basis of his Spanish policy since the autumn of 1846, the exclusion of the Duchess of Montpensier from the line of succession as 'the landmark which we ought to steer for',[107] was the right one; only when the succession question was settled would Spain be free from French interference. The belief that a succession crisis was imminent made the British government realise that despite their determination to prevent the Montpensiers from mounting the throne of Spain they had no alternative candidate ready and willing to take the field against them. It was of pressing importance to the anti-French party in Spain, wrote Bulwer on 6 May 1847, to know which candidate the British government favoured and the extent to which they would support him: 'The assurance that England will support the Spanish Government against that of France if the French undertake by arms to sustain the Duchess's pretensions...is of course the most important and is even now asked for when the subject is alluded to.'[108] Palmerston could not commit the British government on the latter question; that decision would be taken by the cabinet when the time came. The decision would, wrote Palmerston, be greatly influenced by the situation in Spain: if there was widespread resistance to the succession of the Duchess of Montpensier, the British government would probably assist the anti-French party, and the best way to ensure nation-wide opposition was by the choice of a popular candidate. In 1846 Palmerston thought he had found a suitable prince in Don Enrique, but by the summer of 1847 he

[104] Palmerston to Bulwer, 19 June 1847. B.P. GC/BU/550.
[105] Palmerston to Bulwer, 22 June 1847. F.O. 72/717.
[106] Palmerston to Bulwer, 25 June 1847. F.O. 72/717.
[107] Palmerston first used this phrase in Apr. 1847. Palmerston to Bulwer, 19 Apr. 1847. B.P. GC/BU/543.
[108] Bulwer to Palmerston, 6 May 1847. B.P. GC/BU/341.

was forced to admit that Enrique was neither reliable nor responsible; he had quarrelled with his Progresista friends, and in June 1847 he married a Spanish noblewoman. 'Under no circumstances', wrote Bulwer in May 1847, 'is it likely that Don Henry would have sufficient influence to mount the throne of Spain, while the law excludes at all events his succession from [*sic*] it.'[109] Palmerston and Bulwer had therefore to look beyond the established order of succession for a suitable candidate. In the autumn of 1846 Palmerston had been prepared to consider the Carlist Count of Montemolin, primarily because he hoped thereby to secure the support of the eastern powers. Palmerston met Montemolin in November 1846 and was favourably impressed, believing him to have renounced his father's absolutist principles and to be prepared to accept and defend a constitutional régime. During 1847 Palmerston came to the conclusion that Montemolin stood a better chance of success than Don Enrique as an alternative to the Duchess of Montpensier. Don Enrique could be the candidate only of the Progresista party and England whereas, if the Progresistas could be persuaded to accept him, Montemolin would have the support of two parties in Spain as well as bringing the eastern powers over to the side of England in Europe. As early as April 1847, before Enrique had finally ruined his chances, Palmerston instructed Bulwer to inform the Progresistas that they 'should consider the possibility of their being called upon one day to choose between Montemolin and Montpensier'; he added, 'I cannot doubt that they would in such case stand by Montemolin the Spaniard.'[110] Bulwer agreed that 'Montemolin is perhaps the simplest and most likely course...for defeating in a solid and legitimate manner the French succession', but he anticipated difficulty in convincing the Progresistas that he would be their strongest candidate.[111] After discussing the question with some Progresista leaders in May, Bulwer reported that if Montemolin became the British candidate, 'then a great number of the Liberals and Moderados would be driven to the side of the Duchess of Montpensier'. Olozaga, a Progresista leader with

[109] Bulwer to Palmerston, 19 May 1847. F.O. 72/722.
[110] Palmerston to Bulwer, 22 Apr. 1847. B.P. GC/BU/544.
[111] Bulwer to Palmerston, 6 May 1847. B.P. GC/BU/341.

whom Bulwer discussed the succession question, suggested the Prince of Portugal as an alternative to Montemolin, claiming that many who would otherwise support the Duchess of Montpensier would back him, since his candidature held out the prospect of a united Iberian kingdom which many Spaniards wanted.[112] Bulwer's first enthusiasm for this alternative waned on reflection: 'I see many difficulties in its way', he wrote on 26 May.[113] Palmerston and Russell also gave serious consideration to a Braganza candidate; like Bulwer they were initially attracted to the idea but later ruled it out on the grounds that it would not be in Britain's best interests if Portugal were incorporated into a united Iberian kingdom.[114] By June 1847 the British government was forced to recognise that Montemolin was the only alternative to the Duchess of Montpensier: he was the only Spanish prince in the field, and in a struggle in which the rallying cry would be the defence of Spanish independence against French aggression, only a Spanish prince would do. If the occasion should arise, wrote Palmerston on 30 June, for the Spanish people to resist the domination of France and the Montpensier succession, then Montemolin 'is at present the only candidate who would be likely to combine in his own person the conditions necessary for holding out a fair prospect of success in such a contest'.[115] This conclusion was not a happy one for Palmerston. The awkward fact that Montemolin was a Carlist was offset by the advantage that it would secure him the support of the eastern powers, and his supposed conversion to constitutionalism enabled Palmerston to claim that support for Montemolin was compatible with his Spanish policy since 1833, the aim of which had been the creation of a truly constitutional and independent Spain. The difficulty inherent in his candidature was, as Bulwer frequently pointed out, the impossibility of persuading 'the Progresistas or the liberal portion of the Moderados to take up the son of Don Carlos'.[116] The ineluctable fact was that the anti-French forces in Spain would not support the only anti-French Spanish prince; and the chances of an

[112] Bulwer to Palmerston, 23 May 1847. B.P. GC/BU/344.
[113] Bulwer to Palmerston, 26 May 1847. B.P. GC/BU/347.
[114] See below, pp. 277–8.
[115] Palmerston to Bulwer, 30 June 1847. F.O. 72/717.
[116] Bulwer to Palmerston, 26 May 1847. B.P. GC/BU/347.

immediate declaration in his favour should Isabella die or abdicate were thus very slight. Palmerston would consequently be hard pressed to persuade his cabinet colleagues to afford British assistance to Montemolin. The Progresistas must be informed, Palmerston wrote to Bulwer, that while they have no candidate they cannot expect the British government to pledge them their support.[117] Faced with the dilemma posed by their determination to prevent the Montpensier succession coupled with no sure means of accomplishing it, Palmerston and Bulwer took the most obvious and effective way of avoiding the problem, at least in the short term, by making every possible effort to save and strengthen Isabella. 'In all matters', wrote Palmerston to Bulwer on 15 June,

the first thing is to consider what are the facts which one has to deal with and not what are the different state of events which one might possibly prefer. The basis then on which our policy must be founded is the existence and possibly long life of the Queen. The question is how can we assist and make the best of her?[118]

To Palmerston the answer was clear:

The course which I think would be the best...would be to get a Progresista Government appointed, to dissolve the Cortes, and have a new one elected under Progresista auspices, and that either then or now the Queen should take the necessary steps for obtaining a divorce...[119]

Russell and Normanby agreed with Palmerston that Isabella should 'throw herself boldly upon the support of the Cortes and her people';[120] and Prince Albert also thought that the only way out was to cut 'the Gordian knot'.[121] Towards the end of June,

[117] Palmerston to Bulwer, 30 June 1847. F.O. 72/717.
[118] Palmerston to Bulwer, 15 June 1847. Bulwer Papers, S/1.
[119] Palmerston to Bulwer, 19 June 1847. B.P. GC/BU/550.
[120] Normanby to Palmerston, 21 June 1847. Normanby Papers, Box P, bundle 13; Russell to Palmerston, 8 June 1847. Enclosure, B.P. RC/H/18.
[121] On 8 June 1847 Prince Albert wrote to Palmerston: 'The immoral "Marriage Scheme" is producing all the evil fruits which follow iniquity and may yet embroil Europe in a war. It is clear from Mr. Bulwer's statements that the plots are thickening and nobody sees a way out of them. I think, if salvation is still to be hoped for, it must be got by cutting the Gordian Knot. Let the Queen be advised to assemble the Cortes, to appear there herself to declare that she is a most unhappy woman... that she appeals as a woman to the sympathy of her Cortes and as a Queen throws

therefore, the aim of the British government was to save Isabella by means of a divorce and a Progresista government. The French government was equally determined to save Isabella from ruin, but it was convinced that only a reconciliation with the King and the appointment of a new high Moderado government could avert crisis in Spain.[122]

By late May 1847 the French began to fear that a crisis in Spain was imminent. The relations between the Queen and the King had degenerated to a point where the Progresista press openly urged the Queen to petition the Pope for a divorce. The *Clamor Publico* also revived the discussion of the succession question, reiterating the arguments it had used in the autumn of 1846 against the succession rights of the Duchess of Montpensier.[123] The French felt that they could not wait for the fall of the Pacheco government to end public debate about a divorce and the succession, which they believed Bulwer and Palmerston were encouraging as part of their plan to persuade the Queen to turn to the Progresistas as the only party likely to agree to a divorce. Immediate action seemed necessary, especially as Decazes reported that the articles in the Progresista press were being well received in Madrid.[124] In late May the Moderado press accused Bulwer of initiating the public discussion of a divorce, for which they claimed there was no support in Spain beyond a few 'revolutionary Progresistas'.[125] On 27 May Desages instructed Rossi, the French ambassador at Rome, to warn the Pope that the idea of a divorce had originated with the English, and to suggest that the best way to answer any request for an annulment of the Queen's marriage would be 'par un non sans appel'.[126] On 13 June Glucksburg demanded of Pacheco that the Spanish government should suppress attacks in the press on the succession rights of the

herself upon her people, to get her marriage ties severed and herself married to a person whom she can respect and who could become the founder of a future line of Kings.' R.A. J/48/43.
[122] Guizot to Glucksburg, 1 July 1847. G.P. 42/AP/7.
[123] Glucksburg to Guizot, 24 May 1847. A.A.E.C.P. Espagne 831.
[124] Decazes to Guizot, 24 May 1847. A.A.E.C.P. Espagne 831.
[125] See *La Presse*, 28 May 1847.
[126] Desages to Rossi, 27 May 1847. G.P. 42/AP/9; Desages to Glucksburg, 22 May 1847. G.P. 42/AP/53.

Duchess of Montpensier on the grounds that they infringed the constitution and the laws of the kingdom. Pacheco agreed, and on 14 June the *Royal Gazette* published an ordinance banning further discussion of the succession.[127] Although the prompt response of the Moderados and the Pacheco government pleased Guizot, he knew that the basic dangers remained: the Queen continued to live apart from the King, she was still under the influence of Serrano, and her desire for a divorce might at any moment induce her to take the desperate step of inviting the Progresistas to form a government.[128] On 20 June 1847 Glucksburg reported that Serrano was prepared to head a Progresista ministry,[129] and a few days later that Bulwer was urging the Queen and Serrano to dismiss Pacheco and form a government prepared to act decisively on the question of a divorce and the succession.[130] Glucksburg saw only one possible answer to such a situation: General Narvaez.[131]

On 2 June Normanby informed Palmerston that 'it is obvious that delay in any proceedings on the part of the Queen now weakens her own case and gives opportunity for reopening those counter intrigues which are no doubt going on both here and at Madrid...'[132] On 4 June Klindworth suggested to Hervey that the British government should devote all its energies to exploiting the favourable disposition of the Spanish Court towards the Progresistas as the party likely to promote a divorce, and to forestall French counter-intrigues.[133] Russell, Palmerston, Prince Albert and Normanby all agreed with Klindworth's assessment of the Spanish situation, and with their assent Palmerston instructed Bulwer on 11 June to inform Isabella that her only chance of securing a divorce lay in a Progresista

[127] Glucksburg to Guizot, 14 June 1847. A.A.E.C.P. Espagne 831. See also Bulwer to Palmerston, 14 June 1847. F.O. 72/723.
[128] Desages to Glucksburg, 26 June 1847. G.P. 42/AP/53.
[129] Glucksburg to Guizot, 20 June 1847. A.A.E.C.P. Espagne 831.
[130] Glucksburg derived this information from his perusal of Bulwer's private correspondence, copies of which were sold to him by Bulwer's Spanish secretary who, wrote Glucksburg, had great financial embarrassment. Glucksburg to Guizot, 27 June 1847. G.P. 42/AP/67. On 1 July Guizot advised Glucksburg that it was too dangerous to buy copies of Bulwer's correspondence; oral accounts, he wrote, were sufficient and they leave no trace. Guizot to Glucksburg, 1 July 1847. G.P. 42/AP/7.
[131] Glucksburg to Guizot, 27 June 1847. G.P. 42/AP/67.
[132] Normanby to Palmerston, 2 June 1847. B.P. GC/NO/57.
[133] Hervey to Palmerston, 4 June 1847. Extract, R.A. J/48/38.

government and a new Cortes.¹³⁴ Bulwer, however, doubted whether such a course was either possible or desirable; the Progresistas were not ready for office, and he did 'not think things have come to that point at which it is necessary...to take a course from which one cannot draw back'.¹³⁵ Palmerston thought Bulwer insufficiently alive to the danger of French designs in Spain: the fact is, he wrote on 19 June, that 'if we cannot be allowed to go on quietly in Spain, we must accept the war which Guizot thus declares and fight it out to extremity... Was there any point', he asked, 'keeping any longer in the motley administration which is more Moderado than Progresista?' and he again advocated 'a bold and determined push for a real Progresista government'.¹³⁶ Bulwer again counselled caution: the most that could be hoped for, he intimated, was a new government headed by Serrano which would keep 'the Queen and the Liberal party well disposed towards each other'. If he were to urge the Queen to appoint a Progresista government, Bulwer feared that the French and the Moderados would use the occasion to force Narvaez on her.¹³⁷ With reluctance Palmerston deferred to Bulwer's judgment, although this was tantamount to an admission that England was impotent to prevent a French *coup* in Spain. This, combined with the unwillingness of the anti-French factions in Spain to support Montemolin, the only anti-French Spanish prince, seemed to Palmerston to augur ill for the future. The British government could only hope that Bulwer's skill and the good sense of liberal Spaniards would bring Spain through the crisis confronting her.¹³⁸

Russell was as disturbed as Palmerston by the imminence of crisis in Spain: we must 'be prepared with some plan of conduct for any sudden but not unforeseen emergency', he wrote to Palmerston. The British government must decide what it would do if Isabella were to die, abdicate or be deposed. In Russell's opinion, 'Should the Cortes and the nation (in spite of the articles in the Spanish Constitution) generally acknowledge the

¹³⁴ Palmerston to Bulwer, 11 June 1847. B.P. GC/BU/548.
¹³⁵ Bulwer to Palmerston, 14 June 1847. B.P. GC/BU/358.
¹³⁶ Palmerston to Bulwer, 19 June 1847. B.P. GC/BU/550.
¹³⁷ Bulwer to Palmerston, 22 June 1847. F.O. 72/723.
¹³⁸ Palmerston to Bulwer, 30 June 1847. B.P. GC/BU/551.

Infanta Fernanda Luisa, I confess I do not think the danger to the balance of power is such to justify us in opposing the presumed will of the Spanish nation.' If, however, the Spaniards resisted the 'virtual annexation of Spain to France' and the French government were tempted 'to assist a son of France', Russell thought that: 'We might fairly ask Louis Philippe to do what Louis XIV consented to do, namely to leave Montpensier the French claimant to fight his own battles, we doing more than Marlborough would have consented to do, namely stand neutral in the contest.' Russell believed that the government should 'take means next session of putting this country in a state of defence'; meanwhile they could only try to prevent a crisis in Spain.[139] Unlike Palmerston, Russell did not believe that the British government could rely solely on Bulwer to do this. It was the French who were bent on provoking a crisis in Spain and only they could avert it. He therefore decided to appeal directly to the French government. On 17 July, without informing Palmerston, he asked Broglie, the new French ambassador in London, to help preserve 'peace and the friendship of our two governments'. I hope, wrote Russell to Broglie:

...you will do all you can to preserve Spain from foreign interference. I fear the worst consequences from any measure which should create an apprehension in England that France was not content with the present position in Spain. Time may make things better. Precipitate action may make them much worse.[140]

Broglie's non-committal reply, that nobody 'ne sont plus intéressés que nous au maintien de l'ordre de chose actuel en Espagne' and that neither England nor Spain had anything to fear from France,[141] disappointed Russell. Moreover, throughout July the reports received from Bulwer and Normanby contained repeated assertions that the French were preparing new plots and intrigues at Madrid.[142] Russell therefore concluded

[139] Russell to Palmerston, 11 July 1847. B.P. GC/RU/153.
[140] Russell to Broglie, 17 July 1847. Enclosure, Broglie to Guizot, 19 July 1847. G.P. 42/AP/214.
[141] Broglie to Russell, 17 July 1847. Russell Papers, P.R.O. 30/22/6D.
[142] Bulwer to Palmerston, 20 July 1847. B.P. GC/BU/369; Bulwer to Palmerston, 26 July 1847. Bulwer Papers, S/14; Normanby to Russell, 29 July 1847. Russell Papers, P.R.O. 30/22/6D.

that although the British government could do no more at the moment than 'to sustain Queen Isabella', it ought for the future to 'hold out to the Liberals of Spain the prospect of the Union of the two Crowns, in the person of the Prince of Portugal'. Russell did not think that the British government could give the Prince of Portugal and his Spanish supporters any active assistance; in his view all the British could do for the anti-French forces in Spain was to ensure that they were not taken by surprise and that they had a candidate who could command widespread support.[143] Palmerston agreed, but he doubted whether the Prince of Portugal would be a popular candidate, and he was convinced that 'we should be paying too dearly for the exclusion of the Montpensiers from the throne of Spain if we bought that exclusion by the annexation of Portugal to Spain'.[144] If Isabella were to die or abdicate, concluded Palmerston, the situation 'would be most embarrassing'. Thus by August 1847 both Russell and Palmerston had reluctantly decided that their chances of changing the order of the Spanish succession or of resisting the succession of the Duchess of Montpensier were very slight indeed. They virtually admitted the necessity of accepting what in the autumn of 1846 they had vowed never to accept: 'the total subjection of Spain to France'. Once again they had to rely on Isabella's readiness to recognise where her real interests lay and Bulwer's ability to foresee and forestall French intrigues.

Guizot was as surprised as Broglie by Russell's overture of 17 July, and believed his reply to have been the right one; any more explicit assurance would limit Glucksburg's freedom of action at Madrid, and no amount of French denials would allay the exaggerated suspicions of London as to French designs on Spain. Moreover, Guizot saw no reason why the French government should have to quieten fears which Palmerston had aroused. In his opinion France could only continue as before, and strive to restore order in Spain;[145] he advised Glucksburg on 31 July: 'Tenez toujours à ces trois points fixes 1. Ecarter

---

[143] Russell to Palmerston, 31 July 1847. B.P. GC/RU/152.
[144] Palmerston to Normanby, 2 Aug. 1847. B.P. GC/NO/451; Palmerston to Russell, 9 Aug. 1847. Russell Papers, P.R.O. 30/22/6E.
[145] Guizot to Broglie, 30 July 1847. G.P. 42/AP/214.

les Progressistes. 2. Réconcilier le Roi et la Reine. 3. Maintenir les droits de l'Infante. Toute notre politique est là. Nous ne voulons rien de plus, rien de moins.'[146] The only practical result of Russell's approach to Broglie was to make the French more confident of success. Why, reasoned Guizot, would Russell have made such a move if he thought there was any chance of the Progresistas returning to power? Combined with Glucksburg's reports that total confusion reigned in Progresista circles, this convinced Guizot that determination and patience were all that was required of France: it would not be long before the Moderados were restored to office and order imposed on the Court.[147] In fact, however, Glucksburg found it as difficult in August 1847 as it had been before to reunite the Moderado factions, and he repeatedly informed Guizot that only Narvaez could accomplish it.[148] On 14 August Pacheco informed Glucksburg that Court intrigues and the Queen's irresponsibility had so undermined his government that it was impossible to carry on, and that he had advised Isabella to send for Narvaez, who was the only man who could form a strong government.[149] On 21 August Narvaez arrived in Madrid: 'la situation est à nous une seconde fois', wrote Glucksburg to Guizot.[150]

The British were alarmed by the return of Narvaez: to Normanby he appeared as the chosen instrument of French aggression; Bulwer predicted that he would attempt to establish a violent despotism; and Palmerston once again thought that Isabella could only save herself by appointing 'a Liberal Government and a new Cortes'.[151] Instead of transmitting Palmerston's advice, Bulwer attempted to keep Narvaez out of office by urging Isabella to refuse to appoint any government that insisted on a reconciliation with the King. This tactic succeeded, and when Pacheco resigned on 27 August he was replaced not by Narvaez, as Glucksburg had confidently

[146] Guizot to Glucksburg, 31 July 1847. G.P. 42/AP/7.
[147] Desages to Glucksburg, 7 Aug. 1847. G.P. 42/AP/53.
[148] Glucksburg to Guizot, 12 Aug. 1847. G.P. 42/AP/67.
[149] Glucksburg to Guizot, 14 Aug. 1847. G.P. 42/AP/67.
[150] Glucksburg to Guizot, 21 Aug. 1847. G.P. 42/AP/67.
[151] Bulwer to Palmerston, 24 Aug. 1847. F.O. 72/724; Palmerston to Bulwer, 26 Aug. 1847. F.O. 72/718.

expected, but by the comparatively unknown liberal-Moderado, Goyena.[152]

Like its predecessor, the Goyena government had been brought to power by Serrano, who saw his own disgrace as inevitable if Narvaez returned to power and the Queen and the King were reconciled. From the outset Bulwer admitted that the new government had only a tenuous hold on office, and that Goyena and Serrano were no match for Narvaez, who had behind him the French, the army and the majority of the Moderado party. If he remained in Madrid, Bulwer was sure that Narvaez would make another bid for power. As Bulwer wrote to Palmerston, the difficulty was that Britain could not do without Serrano but could do nothing with him; in these circumstances he felt that the British government could only try to 'keep afloat and hope some favourable wind may yet take us into port'.[153] Guizot advised Glucksburg to urge Narvaez to rally all the Moderado factions behind him, thus leaving Goyena without support in the Cortes and the Queen no alternative but to invite Narvaez once again to form a government.[154] Isabella's position, as Bulwer recognised, was impossible: she could not continue without a party without soon having 'all the parties against her...If she takes up the Moderado party...she will no longer be able to count on the Progresistas. If she takes up the Progresistas it will be a struggle of life and death with the Moderados.'[155] By the end of September it was clear that Isabella had no such choice: Narvaez, Glucksburg and the Moderados had succeeded in bringing the Goyena government to its knees, and Serrano admitted that Isabella would risk her throne if she attempted to form a Progresista ministry in defiance of the Moderado majority in the Cortes and the Moderado garrison at Madrid. There is 'no chance at all' of the Progresistas being asked to form a government, wrote Bulwer to Palmerston on 3 October, 'and it is best that you should know it'.[156] On the following day Glucksburg informed Guizot that the struggle was over: Narvaez had

[155] Bulwer to Palmerston, 25 Sept. 1847. Bulwer Papers, S/13.
[156] Bulwer to Palmerston, 3 Oct. 1847. B.P. GC/BU/403.
[152] Bulwer to Palmerston, 2 Sept. 1847. F.O. 72/725.
[153] Bulwer to Palmerston, 13 Sept. 1847. Bulwer Papers, S/13.
[154] Guizot to Glucksburg, 11 Sept. 1847. G.P. 42/AP/7.

formed a ministry. Bulwer had to admit defeat; all we can do now, he wrote to Palmerston, is 'to remain quiet...until new jealousies and divisions afford one a fair field for conflict'.[157]

Bulwer was slow to recognise that the return to power of Narvaez ended a distinct phase in Spanish politics. Eighteen months earlier, in March 1846, Christina and the Moderado politicians, resentful of Narvaez's ascendancy, had combined to oust him. Christina realised that she could only exclude Narvaez from office as long as she retained the confidence of the Moderado leaders; she therefore treated them with the respect which their position as equal ally of the Crown against the military dictator demanded. Isabella, however, treated with contempt the men who had arranged her marriage and refused her a divorce, not realising that if pushed too far they might turn against her. The exclusion of the ultra-Moderados from office in March 1847, and their conviction that Isabella, following the advice of Serrano and Bulwer, would appoint a Progresista government, destroyed the alliance between the Crown and the Moderado politicians. The latter therefore combined with the military dictator to chasten the Crown and protect the ascendancy of their party. Thus in October 1847 Isabella became the victim of a situation which her own reckless conduct had done much to create. Retribution for her political ineptitude was swift: Serrano was sent to a provincial garrison, a reconciliation with the King was forced on Isabella, and Narvaez sent for Christina to maintain order within the royal family and at Court.[158] The Moderado politicians accepted Narvaez as the necessity he was: the ultra-Moderados regarded him as the only guarantor of order; the liberal Moderados believed in his liberal pretensions and hoped, under his stable rule, to inaugurate a programme of reform.

The return of Narvaez led the British government to expect that at any moment their worst fears would be realised. What was now being enacted 'on the theatre of Madrid under the direction of the great stage manager at the Tuileries', wrote

[157] Bulwer to Palmerston, 4 Oct. 1847. B.P. GC/BU/406.
[158] Bulwer to Palmerston, 8 Oct. 1847. F.O. 72/726; Bulwer to Palmerston, 9 Oct. 1847. Bulwer Papers, S/13; Normanby to Palmerston, 13 Oct. 1847. B.P. GC/NO/80; Glucksburg to Guizot, 13 Oct. 1847. G.P. 42/AP/67.

Palmerston to Queen Victoria, was the 'last performed act of the tragedy of "Isabella or the fatal marriage"'.[159] He was convinced that 'the errand on which Louis Philippe sent Narvaez was to get rid of [Isabella] and bring in her sister and Montpensier in her room'.[160] Bulwer believed that Narvaez's

> principal plan is to secure the succession of the Duchess of Montpensier, ruling in the meantime in the Queen's name if he can, or if he cannot removing her out of the way. I believe moreover his object and instructions are to win over if he can to this plan the Progresistas, or at all events to break up and dissolve their party by employing and conciliating them.[161]

Bulwer expected at any moment the return of the Duchess of Montpensier to Madrid, and he admitted that if:

> Her Royal Highness does come and conducts herself with prudence and tact it will be almost impossible to prevent her taking that station in the country which must sooner or later lead to her mounting the throne.[162]

To the British government the situation in Spain in October 1847 looked more critical than at any time since the worst days of the Carlist War. Palmerston was convinced that Isabella's only hope of salvation lay in the adoption of the course he had so frequently advocated: she ought 'boldly to throw herself for support on the Progresistas'. He authorised Bulwer, if he thought it necessary, to inform the Progresistas that England would provide 'a good general at Gibraltar and some muskets and our moral support to prevent French interference'.[163] Bulwer thought that Great Britain ought to decide whether to concentrate on organising 'a counter-intrigue' or fomenting 'a revolution'. The former would require patience, the latter money. The Progresistas assured Bulwer that they 'had the means of attempting this revolution, probably with success'; if Palmerston could supply the large sum of money required, Bulwer believed that 'in the end it would be a great economy'.[164]

[159] Palmerston to the Queen, 25 Oct. 1847. R.A. J/49/25.
[160] Palmerston to Bulwer, 5 Oct. 1847. B.P. GC/BU/562.
[161] Bulwer to Palmerston, 16 Oct. 1847. B.P. GC/BU/415.
[162] Bulwer to Palmerston, 17 Oct. 1847. F.O. 72/726.
[163] Palmerston to Bulwer, 5 Oct. 1847. B.P. GC/BU/562.
[164] Bulwer to Palmerston, 12 Oct. 1847. B.P. GC/BU/409-11.

Revolution was ruled out in October 1847 for the same reasons as it had been in September 1846; Palmerston regretted that there was insufficient money in the Secret Service fund to finance it,[165] and Russell and the Queen thought that 'an insurrection would be calamitous for its authors, for Spain and for us'.[166] At the end of October Palmerston concluded that Great Britain could only 'try to ride a beaten horse with patience and perseverance and hope that in the course of events some chance may turn up in our favour'.[167] A week later Palmerston decided that perseverance was more important than patience. 'I should', he wrote, 'be better pleased to see a change effected without waiting for the intervention of the Montpensiers. The knot does not require such a vindex.'[168]

Whilst Palmerston and Bulwer were trying to turn out Narvaez and the Moderados, Guizot was trying to restrain them. On the day the Narvaez government was formed Glucksburg told Guizot that the presence of the Montpensiers at Madrid was necessary to ensure the total exclusion of English influence.[169] Guizot did not agree; Christina could deal with the Palace and Narvaez with the politicians; this should suffice to ensure that 'la monarchie Espagnole se sauvera'.[170] On 17 October Guizot informed Broglie that the return of Narvaez and Christina had taught Palmerston, Bulwer and the Progresistas a lesson he hoped they would not forget, and had put Spanish politics back on the right course; France, he hoped, would no longer need to be so preoccupied with Spanish problems.[171] Also on 17 October Narvaez informed Glucksburg that Isabella had made quite clear her resentment at his own return to power and Christina's return to Madrid, and that she was

---

[165] In any case Palmerston did not have as much faith as Bulwer in the power of money. 'Louis Philippe has everything his own way for the moment and has bought everybody right and left; but one may buy a man today and not have him the bit the more a few days later.' Palmerston to Bulwer, 18 Oct. 1847. B.P. GC/BU/563.
[166] The Queen to Russell, 18 Oct. 1847. R.A. C/7/84; Russell to Palmerston, 20 Oct. 1847. B.P. GC/RU/164.
[167] Palmerston to Bulwer, 28 Oct. 1847. B.P. GC/BU/565.
[168] Palmerston to Bulwer, 4 Nov. 1847. Bulwer Papers, S/15.
[169] Glucksburg to Guizot, 4 Oct. 1847. G.P. 42/AP/67.
[170] Guizot to Glucksburg, 10 Oct. 1847. G.P. 42/AP/7.
[171] Guizot to Broglie, 17 Oct. 1847. G.P. 42/AP/214.

looking for an opportunity to dismiss Narvaez and send her mother into exile. Narvaez went on to state that he believed the time was ripe for the return of the Duchess of Montpensier: her presence in Spain, far from encouraging revolution, would calm the turbulent elements. Glucksburg agreed with Narvaez: the Duchess of Montpensier, he wrote, was the heiress presumptive, and if the Cortes called her back she must come.[172] On 20 October Glucksburg made a similar, but even more emphatic, appeal to Guizot: the Duchess of Montpensier must raise her flag before everyone took the side either of Montemolin or the revolution.

Pour venir à nous les masses n'attendront qu'une chose, la conscience de notre détermination et de notre résolution. Il faut un fait pour la leur donner et ce fait ne peut-être que le retour en Espagne de notre Infante. Il ne sera pas une menace...il sera la confession et la proclamation d'un droit, d'une situation légale à côté du trône, rien de plus.[173]

Guizot was unmoved by Glucksburg's appeals. He knew that Narvaez wanted the Duchess of Montpensier at Madrid as a counterpoise to the Queen and to make Isabella more docile for fear of being deposed in favour of her sister. He also knew that Narvaez and Christina were inveterate opponents, and that the former hoped to strengthen his position by dividing the royal family. It suited him better to create rivalry between the Queen and her sister than to face a situation in which Christina emerged once again as the real power behind the throne. Guizot felt that Narvaez needed a lesson in constitutional theory, and he instructed Glucksburg to remind him that 'la monarchie, c'est les inconvénients comme les avantages de la royauté, c'est les défauts comme les qualités de la personne royale. Et la monarchie constitutionnelle, c'est la liberté, pour tout le monde et par conséquent la lutte et le péril continuel.'[174]

---

[172] Glucksburg to Guizot, 17 Oct. 1847. G.P. 42/AP/67.
[173] Glucksburg to Guizot, 20 Oct. 1847. G.P. 42/AP/67.
[174] Guizot to Glucksburg, 21 Oct. 1847. G.P. 42/AP/7. On 30 Oct. Guizot instructed Glucksburg to inform Narvaez that only if the Duchess of Montpensier did not come to Spain would he gain the confidence of Isabella, as then she 'ne pourra plus penser qu'il veut servir, à tout prix, les intérêts de l'Infante sa sœur'. Guizot to Glucksburg, 30 Oct. 1847. G.P. 42/AP/7.

As for Glucksburg, Guizot diagnosed his disease as that endemic among British and French diplomats at Madrid: the desire for a spectacular triumph. Glucksburg admitted that there was no greater partisan of the Duke and Duchess of Montpensier than he,[175] and he believed that their return to Spain need cause no apprehension in France provided Narvaez and the Moderados remained firmly entrenched in power and Bulwer could be got rid of by Narvaez demanding his recall.[176] What happened thereafter would be the responsibility of the Spaniards, not of the French. After consultations with Louis Philippe and the Queen, and with the Duke of Montpensier, but not the cabinet, Guizot wrote to Glucksburg on 30 and 31 October that a visit to Spain by the Duke and Duchess of Montpensier was too dangerous under present circumstances: it would be regarded as

un calcul d'ambition impatiente et illégitime...Il faut que le duc et la duchesse de Montpensier n'arrivent pas à Madrid comme une menace à la Reine, comme un instrument hostile qui va se placer dans les mains des partis. Si cela était, le duc de Montpensier perdrait toute sa valeur d'avenir, car il se classerait, dès à présent, parmi les faiseurs d'intrigues et les préparateurs de révolutions.

If the Montpensiers were ever to be called upon to rule Spain, Guizot believed that it must not seem to derive from their own initiative. A visit to Spain at this moment would implicate them in Spanish politics and benefit their enemies rather than themselves. When, wrote Guizot,

un voyage de Monsieur le duc et de Madame la duchesse de Montpensier ne soit plus un grave événement politique et presque une perspective de crise, alors ce voyage deviendra possible en devenant simple...Le premier intérêt du duc et de la duchesse de Montpensier, et par conséquent de l'Espagne et de la France, c'est de ne donner à personne aucun motif de croire et aucun prétexte de dire qu'on veut exploiter un péril momentané pour attendre précipitamment un but illégitime.[177]

Glucksburg was to reassure Narvaez that it was unnecessary for the Montpensiers to visit Madrid: the situation was improving

[175] Glucksburg to Guizot, 27 Oct. 1847. G.P. 42/AP/67.
[176] Glucksburg to Guizot, 20 Oct. 1847. G.P. 42/AP/67.
[177] Guizot to Glucksburg, 30 Oct. 1847. G.P. 42/AP/7.

daily, he was becoming stronger and his enemies weaker. The real dangers had been averted.[178]

Glucksburg was greatly disappointed by Guizot's letters of 30 and 31 October. On 7 November he returned to the attack: you are quite wrong, he assured Guizot, to suppose that the crisis is over; it was the Queen who was liable to provoke the crisis, not the Moderados, who could not carry on without some hope or security for the future. Narvaez was very disheartened, according to Glucksburg, and contemplated resignation.[179] Guizot remained adamant. On 14 November he declared that the Infanta must conduct herself as Louis Philippe did before 1830.

J'espère qu'il n'y aura point de 1830 en Espagne, et que les droits de l'Infante, s'ils doivent jamais s'ouvrir, ne s'ouvriront que naturellement. Mais en tout cas, une nécessité absolue, évidente, incontestable, prouvée par des événements et non pas affirmée d'avance, peut seule imprimer et légitimer le mouvement.[180]

Glucksburg's letter of 7 November convinced Guizot of the necessity of a public declaration that France was determined to support the rights of the Duchess of Montpensier as heiress presumptive to the Spanish throne. His letter of 14 November sent to Madrid by a special emissary, the young Duke of Talleyrand, was designed to reassure the Moderados that the French government, by refusing to allow the Montpensiers to visit Madrid, was not contemplating the abandonment of the rights they had defended since August 1846. A declaration to this effect would be made in the Chamber of Deputies when an appropriate opportunity presented itself.[181] At the same time as he publicly reassured the Moderados of his support, Guizot also took steps to ensure that they did not take advantage of it by provoking a showdown with Isabella. Christina was warned to keep a close watch over the Queen; and Louis Philippe and the cabinet agreed that Piscatory, the French minister at Athens, should be sent as ambassador to Madrid. Piscatory, a known

---

[178] Guizot to Glucksburg, 31 Oct. 1847. G.P. 42/AP/7.
[179] Glucksburg to Guizot, 7 Nov. 1847. G.P. 42/AP/67.
[180] Guizot to Glucksburg, 14 Nov. 1847. G.P. 42/AP/7.
[181] Glucksburg gave an account of his conversation with Talleyrand in his letter to Guizot of 21 Nov. 1847. G.P. 42/AP/67.

Anglophobe, was a more experienced diplomat than Glucksburg, and Guizot believed that he was the only French diplomat who could handle Narvaez and the Moderados.[182] At the end of 1847, therefore, the French government was trying to prevent an irreparable breach between Isabella and the Moderados, which would result in her deposition. At the same time, however, Guizot made it clear that if such a situation were to develop despite French efforts to the contrary, France would support the right of the Duchess of Montpensier. The extent of French support was left vague: for Guizot, as for Palmerston, the question of military assistance was not one which could be decided in advance.

During November Bulwer was encouraging Isabella to break with Narvaez and the Moderados in the belief that there was 'a better chance for a national government if this falls to the ground than there has been before'. The only practical result of his attempts to create a national party and to provoke a breach between Isabella and Narvaez was to strain his relations with the new government to breaking point. The attacks on Bulwer in the Moderado press became more frequent and more violent until in late November Narvaez instructed Isturiz to ask Palmerston to recall him, a task which Isturiz refused to undertake.[183] With the politicians and the Queen ignoring his advice, Bulwer could foresee only imminent disaster: he remained convinced that the aim of Narvaez was no other than the deposition of Isabella. The fact that the Queen was a prisoner in her own palace, and the bitter attacks on her in the Moderado press, suggested to Bulwer that her reign, perhaps even her life, would soon be over.[184] Russell was again seriously perturbed by Bulwer's reports: 'I entirely believe in the probability of Narvaez and his gang having the intention of deposing and perhaps murdering the Queen', he informed Palmerston. He did not, however, believe that Louis Philippe was party to such schemes or that he would support them. He saw the French as

[182] For the background of this appointment, see Douglas Johnson, *Guizot*, 249-50, and Glucksburg to Guizot, 19 Dec. 1847. G.P. 42/AP/67. Lord Cowley thought Piscatory's nomination to Madrid was 'a fresh slap in the face to our government'. Cowley Papers, F.O. 519/144.
[183] Palmerston to Bulwer, 24 Nov. 1847. B.P. GC/BU/568.
[184] Bulwer to Palmerston, 16 Nov. 1847. F.O. 72/727.

the only possible restraining influence on the Moderados, and believed that they knew it was in their own interests to 'retard the Montpensier succession'.[185] Would they do so? Russell tried another confidential approach: on 4 December he wrote to Broglie that he thought it his duty to inform him of the reports which the British government had received 'concerning the Queen of Spain'. 'These rumours', Russell concluded,

> may not be at all or wholly true. If, however, the desperate politicians who now hold power in Spain should endeavour to fix their positions by ridding themselves of a Queen who has several times shown an inclination to dismiss them, this might be their gain but the hazard and the loss of character would attach to those who were their manifest protectors and friends. Excuse this warning, which I hope is needless.[186]

Broglie returned Russell's letter, saying that if he were to continue to work for good relations between England and France he had no alternative but to forget that he had ever received it.[187] Russell realised that he had overstepped the bounds of propriety and agreed that the letter should be withdrawn.[188] This last exchange on Spanish affairs between the British and French governments before the fall of the July Monarchy in February 1848 revealed the total misunderstanding that existed on both sides about the attitude and intentions of the other. It was only Russell's intense fears which resulted in any contact at all; Palmerston was convinced that the French would allow nothing to stand in the way of their ambition, and that there was no point in reasoning with them. All that could be done was to make every effort to thwart them. Guizot thought similarly that discussion of Spanish affairs with the British government would be useless; it was foolish to suppose that any accounts the French were to give of their Spanish policy would 'désarmer l'injustice et la calomnie'.[189]

In January 1848 the British government was relieved and surprised to find Isabella still on the throne of Spain. Bulwer

---

[185] Russell to Palmerston, 26 Nov. 1847. B.P. GC/RU/167.
[186] Russell to Broglie, 4 Dec. 1847. G.P. 42/AP/214.
[187] Broglie to Russell, 4 Dec. 1847. G.P. 42/AP/214.
[188] Russell to Broglie, 5 Dec. 1847. G.P. 42/AP/214.
[189] Guizot to Broglie, 1 Nov. 1847. G.P. 42/AP/214.

became more optimistic and concluded that 'as long as things can be kept in their present position...that is as long as the Moderado party is in possession of power and there is a probability of keeping the Queen under the Queen Mother's authority' there would be no attempt to depose the Queen and place the Duchess of Montpensier on the throne.[190] In early February 1848 Normanby returned to the subject of what Great Britain could do if the Duchess of Montpensier did ascend the throne of Spain. It is certain, he wrote, that the Progresistas would support her and not Montemolin; she would in fact be the national candidate. He therefore concluded that:

> we seem to have nothing else to do but quietly (should the case occur) to make up our minds to accept what we have been accustomed to consider the worst which will after all be much less bad than might have been anticipated. The throne of July has latterly been shorn of so much of its lustre that the reflected brilliancy of a second Orleans dynasty need not quite extinguish our lights.[191]

Normanby's conclusion differed from that Russell and Palmerston had reached in the autumn of 1847 only in the fact that he accepted the succession of the Duchess of Montpensier to the Spanish throne without panic or despair, and without regarding it as a major setback for British policy. Within three weeks the July Monarchy had been replaced by a republic, and the possibility of a close dynastic union between France and Spain was, for the time being at least, a thing of the past.

Palmerston believed that the fall of the Orleans Monarchy had increased the chances of removing the Duchess of Montpensier from the succession. He doubted the ability of Narvaez and the Moderados long to survive the eclipse of those who had placed them in power, and expected 'to hear that the Progresistas will have again reared their heads'. A new government would be able to do as it pleased about the succession, with the French too preoccupied with their own affairs 'to trouble themselves much about Spain'.

Now would be the time for [the Spaniards] to make a settlement of the Crown, so as to bar out the Duchess of Montpensier and her

---

[190] Bulwer to Palmerston, 30 Jan. 1848. F.O. 72/740.
[191] Normanby to Palmerston, 6 Feb. 1848. B.P. GC/NO/111.

290   IBERIAN PROBLEMS

issue. It is true that the Montpensiers do not at the present moment stand in the same relation to France in which they stood a fortnight ago, but still he is a French prince and all his feelings and partialities will still and ever be French. Besides it seems to me scarcely possible that the present order, or rather disorder, of things in France can be lasting. I have no expectation that France will permanently settle down into a Republic. Sooner or later there will be a reaction in favour of monarchy...and in that case I think the Comte de Paris is as good a horse to back for winning the Plate as any other in the field.[192]

A new government in Spain, preceded by the prevention of the exiled Montpensiers from settling in Spain, was, believed Palmerston, all that was necessary finally to resolve the succession question.[193] His conviction that Britain ought still to press for the exclusion of the Duchess of Montpensier was strengthened when Bulwer informed him that it was commonly stated among Moderado politicians at Madrid that the Spanish government would offer asylum to the Orleans family and assist them to organise a counter-revolution in the south of France.[194] Bulwer thought that these circumstances would justify a proposal to the new French government that Britain and France should make joint representations to the Spanish government on the succession question.[195] Palmerston did not think this necessary; the sole requisite was a liberal government in Spain. The need for a change in the law of succession was the ultimate motive behind his despatch of 16 March 1848, which strongly criticised the Narvaez government and urged the Queen of Spain to enlarge 'the basis upon which the administration is founded' and to call to her councils 'some of those men who possess the confidence of the Liberal party'.[196] Bulwer was instructed to make the

[192] Palmerston to Bulwer, 4 Mar. 1848. B.P. GC/BU/572. On 10 Mar. Palmerston wrote to Bulwer, 'Lamartine's circular must show to the Spaniards that the Montpensier succession is no longer a French object; nevertheless the prevention of it must still remain an English object.' Bulwer Papers, S/15. Russell, however, did not agree. He informed Palmerston that he thought it was 'imprudent and unwise to keep up a chronic quarrel in Spain on account of the bad faith of an old and deposed sovereign and his baffled and exiled Minister'. Russell to Palmerston, 27 Mar. 1848. B.P. GC/RU/194.
[193] Palmerston to Normanby, 11 Mar. 1848. Normanby Papers, Box P, bundle 14.
[194] Bulwer to Palmerston, 16 Mar. 1848. F.O. 72/739.
[195] Bulwer to Palmerston, 16 Mar. 1848. Bulwer Papers, S/20.
[196] Palmerston to Bulwer, 16 Mar. 1848. F.O. 72/739.

contents of the despatch known to Queen Christina should an opportunity occur. Palmerston also informed Isturiz that a 'close and friendly connection' between England and Spain, more than ever necessary after France became a republic, was not possible 'as long as there remained open between us the wide gulf of separation occasioned by the Montpensier marriage'.[197] In April and May 1848 all Palmerston's hopes of a triumph over the Orleans family were destroyed. In early April the Montpensiers arrived in Madrid, and shortly afterwards Narvaez suspended the Cortes indefinitely. Palmerston recognised that without a Cortes there could be no law to change the succession.[198] Bulwer, in an effort to bring some Progresistas into the government, on 12 April handed the Spanish government a copy of Palmerston's despatch of 16 March, because he had

reason to believe not only that the present Spanish Government will make no concessions on the subject of the Montpensiers but that they actually meditate stirring up a counter revolution in the south of France in favour of the Prince de Joinville, that member of the Orleans family most inimical to England.[199]

Narvaez strongly resented Palmerston's remarks on his government and informed Bulwer that he 'had no more right to speak of the course of conduct which the Spanish government was pursuing in Spain than the Spanish minister in London had to speak of the conduct which the English government was pursuing in England'.[200] A bitter correspondence between Bulwer and the Spanish government ensued, in which each side published letters in the press before communicating them to the other side. On 12 May the Spanish government ordered Bulwer to leave Spain within forty-eight hours. Palmerston had 'no doubt that the intrigues of the Orleans Family and ministers have had their full share in bringing about this result'. They feared that if England and Spain were reconciled, the Montpensiers would be

sacrificed as offerings on the altar of reconciliation. It was therefore

[197] Palmerston to Bulwer, 24 Mar. 1848. B.P. GC/BU/575.
[198] Palmerston to Bulwer, 9 Apr. 1848. B.P. GC/BU/577.
[199] Bulwer to Palmerston, 12 Apr. 1848. Bulwer Papers, S/20.
[200] Bulwer to Palmerston, 20 Apr. 1848. F.O. 72/741.

their political interest to get up a breach between the English and Spanish governments, and if that breach could be made in any way subservient to a mortification to Bulwer and to me by some affront to be given to the English government personal feelings would be gratified while family interests were served.[201]

The expulsion of Bulwer and the lack of a French ambassador at Madrid meant that Spanish politics ceased to be dominated by Anglo-French rivalry, and with the consolidation of the republic in France the Spanish succession ceased to be a divisive issue between England and France. When in 1868 the Spanish throne became vacant as a result of the deposition of Isabella, both Don Enrique and Montpensier offered themselves as candidates, and their rivalry culminated in a duel in which Enrique was killed. By 1868, however, Palmerston was dead, and England remained a passive spectator in a great power struggle over the Spanish succession which did alter the balance of power in Europe.

[201] Palmerston to Normanby, 30 May 1848. Normanby Papers, Box P, bundle 20.

CHAPTER X

The *Sonderbund* Crisis, 1847–8

Although in the autumn of 1847 Guizot discounted the possibility of a *détente* between England and France on Spanish problems, he was nevertheless particularly anxious to promote a close understanding between the two powers on Swiss affairs. He saw no reason why he should not have the best of both worlds: in his opinion bitter rivalry at Madrid was no barrier to cooperation at Berne. For Guizot the primary aim of an Anglo-French accord over Switzerland was not to improve the relations between the two countries, although if this occurred it would be welcomed, but to confound his critics. He hoped that, by acting with England in a concert of five powers, he would avoid the domestic opprobrium and international dangers which would be inevitable if France were to act with the eastern powers alone.

During the spring and summer of 1847 Guizot had tried to shroud his relations with Metternich in mystery. He never boasted of his *entente* with Austria as he had of his good understanding with Aberdeen; in the Chambers he described Austro-French relations as good rather than as intimate and cordial. The most important exchanges of view between Guizot and Metternich by-passed the official channels of French diplomacy: in the spring of 1847 Guizot sent the Chevalier Klindworth, a secret agent, to Vienna for confidential talks with Metternich,[1] and thereafter he communicated confidentially with Metternich either by private letter[2] or through Count Apponyi, the Austrian ambassador at Paris. Guizot had good reasons for such secrecy. An important group in the cabinet—it is now impossible to say exactly how many—led by Duchâtel, the Minister of the Interior, regarded with disapproval a close connection between France and Austria. In their view Metternich

[1] See above, pp. 210–11.
[2] Some, but not all, of Guizot's letters to Metternich are printed in Metternich, *Mémoires et Documents*, ed. Prince Richard Metternich (Paris, 1880–4), vii, 388–405.

was the epitome of sterile reaction; they also believed that France and Austria were traditional rivals in Italy and Switzerland; moreover, they were convinced that an Austro-French accord following so soon on the suppression of Cracow would be unpopular in France.[3] Outside the government, opposition to close relations with Austria was even stronger. The Republicans, who regarded Guizot as capable of anything, sweepingly condemned his foreign policy as a betrayal of the true interests of France in particular and of mankind in general, struggling as it was to free itself from the fetters of reaction. Thiers and the dynastic opposition focused their attack on the government's foreign policy on the accusation that Guizot had not only sacrificed good relations with England by his Spanish policy, but also delivered himself into the hands of Metternich, and was thus forced to abandon the policy of protecting liberal and constitutional movements in central Europe. Thiers' accusation that Guizot and Louis Philippe had forsaken the principles of 1830 for dynastic aggrandisement was undoubtedly popular; it was even sufficiently powerful to conceal the bankrupt opportunism that had led Thiers to make it.

Guizot was well aware of the need for circumspection in his relations with Metternich. His desire neither to offend his colleagues nor to play into the hands of the opposition was certainly a real and important restraint on close and open Austro-French collaboration, but it was not the only one: Guizot had reservations of his own. He realised that he and Metternich had common enemies rather than common aspirations. Both were opposed to violent and far-reaching change and thus, by inference, to revolutionaries, but beyond this their identity of outlook ceased. Metternich believed that all movements which aimed at changing the *status quo* must be suppressed, any form of discontent with the established order was in his view potentially revolutionary. Guizot, by contrast, distinguished between the forces of progress and the forces of disruption, and was prepared to concede that a slow programme of conciliatory reform was under certain circumstances the best

---

[3] For the relations between Guizot and Duchâtel and their differences on foreign policy, see Douglas Johnson, *Guizot*, 249–50, and Rémusat, *Mémoires de ma Vie*, ed. Charles H. Pouthas (Paris, 1958–62), iv, 126–7.

antidote to revolution. There could thus only be a basis for co-operation between France and Austria when both statesmen were agreed that violent radicals were actively fomenting revolution or trying to bring about changes directly detrimental to both countries.[4] Moreover, even when there were grounds for joint action Guizot was unwilling to co-operate with Austria unless it was made abundantly clear that Austria was following a French lead. He feared that any appearance of French subservience to Austria would result in a loss of French prestige, particularly in Italy where the liberal groups looked to France for protection against Austria.[5] In his relations with Metternich Guizot therefore tried to strike a balance between his desire to retain Metternich's support and so guard against an Austrian agreement with Palmerston on the Spanish succession, and his desire to avoid any definite commitment to Austria which might result in loss of popularity in France and of standing abroad. For the most part, Guizot attempted to delude Metternich into accepting professions of goodwill as adequate substitutes for joint action. This policy had a fair chance of success while the situations in the central European states remained subjects for discussion rather than for action. When they became critical, Metternich wanted more than fair words from Guizot.

In the autumn of 1846 Metternich made several overtures to Guizot for joint Austro-French action to restrain the Swiss radicals.[6] He was anxious that the two powers should take a firm stand on Swiss affairs for several reasons. Metternich profoundly distrusted the radical groups who since the 1830s had been gaining ground in Switzerland, and whose basic aim

[4] Both Guizot and Metternich had profound misgivings as to the effect of German unification on their respective states. Guizot hoped that opposition to a Prussian-led movement for the unification would be a fruitful source of Austro-French co-operation. Metternich, however, refused to admit to the French that there were any differences between Austria and Prussia on German affairs in 1847. See P. Thureau-Dangin, 'La France et l'Europe à la veille de la révolution de 1848', *Revue d'Histoire Diplomatique*, 1892, 110–31.

[5] For Guizot's Italian policy in 1847, see A. J. P. Taylor, *The Italian Question in European Diplomacy, 1847–1849* (Manchester, 1944), and S. Mastellone, 'Pellegrino Rossi ambasciatore a Roma', *Rivista Storica Italiana*, 1949, 68–81.

[6] For Guizot's Swiss policy in 1846 and early 1847, see my 'Guizot and the Sonderbund crisis, 1846–1848', *English Historical Review*, July 1971, lxxxvi, 497–526.

was the reform of the Federal Pact of 1815. In addition to making Switzerland the first neutral country, the peacemakers at Vienna had given the Swiss a constitution heavily weighted in favour of cantonal sovereignty, in the belief that a weak central government was the best way of ensuring that the Swiss scrupulously observed their neutral status.[7] This constitution rested on the ascendancy over the cantonal governments of aristocratic cliques which were conservative and, in the Catholic cantons, clerical in outlook. These narrow oligarchies soon came under attack, and the July revolution of 1830 in France was followed by democratic revolutions in twelve cantons. Rivalry between the radical and conservative cantons centred around the issue of Federal reform: the radicals wished to strengthen the Federal Diet and the Federal Executive, arguing that neither unity nor progress was possible while the Federal Pact of 1815 remained unchanged, whereas the conservatives saw their only hope of survival in the maintenance of the constitutional *status quo*. During the 1840s the question of Federal reform became linked with another issue, that of the position and influence of the Jesuits in Swiss society. The Society of Jesus, together with other Catholic religious orders, was regarded by the radicals with deep hostility because of their unconcealed support for the conservative clericals. When in 1841 the radicals gained control of the cantonal government of Aargau they therefore regarded the closure of the monastic establishments in that canton as a necessary measure of self-defence. The conservative clerical cantons appealed to the Diet to intervene to protect religious liberty; its failure to comply led them to take measures for self-defence by summoning a meeting in 1843 outside the auspices of the Diet, an act expressly forbidden by the 1815 constitution. In 1844 the radicals also infringed the constitution by an armed attack on the canton of Lucerne in an attempt to overthrow its pro-Jesuit government. In 1845 the radical cantons proposed in the Diet that the Jesuits should be expelled from the whole of Switzerland; although this proposal was rejected, it led to a rapid deterioration of the situation in Switzerland. The conservative govern-

---

[7] For an account of Swiss constitutional development between 1815 and 1848, see William E. Rappard, *La Constitution Fédérale de la Suisse* (Neuchâtel, 1948), part 1.

THE *SONDERBUND* CRISIS, 1847-8

ments of three cantons which had voted against the proposal were replaced by radicals; in December 1845 seven Catholic conservative cantons concluded a defensive alliance, the *Sonderbund*, in order to protect the Jesuits and preserve the constitutional *status quo*. This was followed almost immediately by radical victories in more cantons, which ensured the radicals a majority in the next Diet. The *Sonderbund* cantons, anticipating that the radicals would not fail to make use of their majority and knowing that in 1847 the Federal Executive was due to rotate to the cantonal government of Berne led by Ulrich Ochsenbein, a former leader of the radical volunteers who had attacked Lucerne, placed their only hope of survival in some form of interference by the great powers. Their first step was to turn to Austria for support.

The *Sonderbund* cantons found in Metternich a willing champion of their cause. He viewed with alarm the prospect of a centralised and democratic Switzerland. 'A Swiss Republic constituted on the principle of supreme central authority' could not, he believed, long remain independent or neutral;[8] a democratic Switzerland could not fail to be a beacon of hope for radicals and malcontents everywhere. Do not forget to remind Guizot, said Metternich to Flahaut in November 1847, that the tranquillity of Italy depends upon the defeat of the Swiss radicals by France and Austria.[9] Metternich was anxious to assist the *Sonderbund* in whatever way he could. He hoped that a stern warning to the radicals that they could not be permitted to harass and attack the conservatives with impunity nor to change the Federal Pact without the consent of the signatories to the General Act of the Congress of Vienna would suffice to restrain them. If not, Metternich was prepared to intervene in Switzerland to defend the *Sonderbund* and the constitutional *status quo*. He realised, however, that warnings would not be efficacious nor intervention possible without the support of France, hence his overtures to Guizot.

By the autumn of 1846 Guizot had abandoned his earlier view that the Swiss situation was far from critical, needing no more

---

[8] Ponsonby to Palmerston, 4 Dec. 1847. F.O. 7/337.
[9] Flahaut to Guizot, 10 Nov. 1847. G.P. 42/AP/68.

than friendly advice from the great powers.[10] He now agreed with Metternich's diagnosis of Swiss affairs, regarding the radicals as an unstable and dangerous force in Swiss society, and their aim of a more centralised state as potentially detrimental to the interests of France. He wanted a democratic state on France's borders no more than Metternich did on Austria's. In theory, therefore, the Swiss question afforded an ideal opportunity for Austro-French co-operation, with Metternich and Guizot in agreement on both the causes of the crisis and the measures necessary to prevent its further deterioration. For Guizot, however, what he ought to do and what he could do were quite different things. Although combined Austro-French pressure was the surest way to restrain the Swiss radicals, Guizot knew that it was also the surest way of dividing his cabinet and making his government unpopular in France. He therefore felt constrained to reject Metternich's suggestion of joint Austro-French action. He did not, however, wish to remain totally inactive, since this would both offend Metternich whose support he was anxious to retain, and allow the Swiss radicals to press ahead unchecked. Guizot therefore proposed in October 1846 a *démarche* of all the powers 'to regulate in common the affairs of Switzerland'.[11] If England were to agree to co-operate with the other four powers to restrain the Swiss radicals, Guizot believed that he would have successfully disarmed his critics. Guizot was denied this neat solution to his difficulties by Palmerston's rejection of the proposal on the grounds that the Swiss situation was not sufficiently critical to require great-power supervision, and that the Swiss were quite capable of solving their own problems.[12] Guizot was thus forced to make the choice he had tried to avoid, between inaction and Austro-French co-operation. British diplomats in Paris were delighted to see Guizot in such an embarrassing position, and Normanby hoped that the opposition would do its utmost to discredit Guizot on the Swiss question.[13] In January 1847, however, Guizot thought that he had found a way out of his Swiss

[10] Guizot to Flahaut, 24 Oct. 1846. A.A.E.C.P. Autriche 433.
[11] Ibid.
[12] Palmerston to Normanby, 6 Nov. 1846. B.P. GC/NO/430.
[13] Normanby to Palmerston, 22 Dec. 1846. Normanby Papers, Box P, bundle 19.

dilemma which, though far from ideal, was better than nothing. He hoped that a policy of covert and limited co-operation with Austria would enable him to take a firm stand against the Swiss radicals, satisfy Metternich, and guard against the attacks of his critics at home. Bois-le-Comte, the new French minister to the Helvetic Confederation, was instructed to join with his Austrian colleague, Kaiserfeld, in giving friendly advice to the *Sonderbund* and stern warnings to the radicals.[14] This cooperation was to be as unobtrusive as possible: Guizot instructed Bois-le-Comte: 'évitez de fournir au public français aucun fait, aucun acte dont on puisse s'emparer et se faire une arme contre notre marche en Suisse'.[15] Whilst authorising Austro-French collaboration in Switzerland, Guizot made it clear to Metternich that there were definite limits beyond which France would not go: armed intervention to defend the *Sonderbund* was, in Guizot's opinion, only to be contemplated in the most extreme circumstances; and Guizot warned Metternich that France could never stand aside and allow Austria to intervene alone.[16] Guizot was reasonably confident that discreet Austro-French co-operation would secure the desired results in Switzerland: if it failed, however, Guizot was prepared to abandon this policy in favour of concerted action by the five powers.[17] He knew that Metternich would prefer Austro-French co-operation to five-power action, but assumed that he would accept the latter if France were to insist on it as the basis of action on Swiss affairs. Guizot was also confident of securing British participation in five-power action. He believed that his October proposal had been rejected only because the Whigs were inadequately acquainted with recent developments in Switzerland; any further advances by the Swiss radicals would, he felt sure, alert Russell and Palmerston to the gravity of the situation. Once they realised that action was necessary, Guizot expected that the British government would agree to work with France, firstly because no great power representations would

[14] Guizot to Bois-le-Comte, 26 Feb. 1847. A.A.E.C.P. Suisse 554.   [15] Ibid.
[16] Guizot to Flahaut, 24 Feb. 1847. G.P. 42/AP/68.
[17] Jarnac informed Aberdeen in July 1847 that France would not take any new steps to bring the Swiss situation under control 'until we have done our best to go with England and failed'. Jarnac to Aberdeen, 8 July 1847. Aberdeen Papers, B.M. Add. MS. 43296.

influence the Swiss unless the French government was party to them, and secondly because Metternich could only be restrained in co-operation with France. 'Guizot hopes', wrote Hervey to Clarendon in January 1847, 'that if Metternich sent troops to the Swiss frontier it would compel us to come to an understanding with him', and Hervey admitted that 'it will be a difficult case to deal with if it arises'.[18]

By June 1847 it was clear that Austro-French pressure had had no effect on the Swiss radicals; their confidence in their cause remained undimmed, and the radical cantons announced their firm intention to raise the questions of the Jesuits and of Federal reform when the Diet met at Lucerne in July.[19] At Vienna, according to Ponsonby, Switzerland was 'the great subject of anxiety and alarm',[20] and at Paris the opposition press espoused the cause of the Swiss radicals[21] and congratulated Ochsenbein on his curt replies to the repeated remonstrances of Bois-le-Comte.[22] The Swiss radicals had refused to yield to Austro-French pressure for two reasons. Firstly, Ochsenbein believed that the co-operation of the two powers had definite limits, and that further radical moves against the *Sonderbund* would incline Metternich towards intervention, and thus separate him from Guizot. If this happened, Ochsenbein was sure that the radicals would be able to move steadily ahead, with Austria and France condemned to inaction by their differences. Secondly, Austro-French diplomacy in Switzerland between January and June 1847 lacked any constructive suggestions for the settlement of either the Jesuit or the constitutional problem; they proposed no compromise, but merely encouraged the *Sonderbund* cantons to resist all change in the religious and constitutional *status quo*. To the radicals this seemed no more than minority rule under great power auspices.

Metternich was the first to recognise the failure of Austro-French collaboration in Switzerland. On 15 June he informed

[18] Hervey to Clarendon, 29 Jan. 1847. Clar. Dep. C529.
[19] Hervey to Palmerston, 9 June 1847. F.O. 27/780.
[20] Ponsonby to Palmerston, 15 June 1847. F.O. 7/336.
[21] P. Thureau-Dangin, *Histoire de la Monarchie de Juillet* (Paris, 1880–94), vii, 181–2.
[22] *Le Constitutionnel*, 9 June 1847; Hervey to Palmerston, 11 June 1847. F.O. 27/780.

Ponsonby that 'a civil war is most imminent' and that Austria 'must resist the establishment of one universal democratic republic by arms, if all peaceable means for the maintenance of the existing constitution shall fail'.[23] Unknown to Ponsonby, however, Metternich had on 7 June proposed to Guizot that the four continental powers should warn the Swiss that they could not be expected to stand aside if cantonal sovereignty were violated or attempts made to alter the Federal Pact. Metternich regretted the exclusion of Great Britain, but doubted her willingness to join in the proposal; France too might be prevented by domestic restraints from joining in such a *démarche*.[24] To Normanby, the Chevalier Klindworth confided that Metternich's proposal 'was the beginning of a complete separation between France and Austria', since Metternich was determined 'to enter Switzerland with a hundred thousand men' should civil war break out.[25] Klindworth was clearly exaggerating: Metternich knew that he could not intervene in Switzerland without the concurrence of France. His aim was to elicit from Guizot a counter-proposal which could provide the basis for a firmer Austro-French stand than hitherto against the Swiss radicals. Whereas Palmerston, who heard unofficially of Metternich's proposal in late June 1847, treated it with studied indifference,[26] Guizot reacted sharply by rejecting the suggestion on the grounds that it would inevitably lead to armed intervention in Switzerland. He warned Metternich that if the eastern powers were to send troops into Switzerland, the resultant indignation in France would be so great that it would be almost impossible for the French government to avoid

[23] Ponsonby to Palmerston, 15 June 1847. F.O. 7/336.
[24] Metternich to Apponyi, 7 June 1847. Metternich, *Mémoires*, vii, 451–4. Although Metternich did not inform Ponsonby of his proposal to Guizot of 7 June he did say that although Louis Philippe was with Austria 'in opinion' on Swiss affairs, 'it was most probable that the King would be afraid of the cry, which would be raised in France, and would not act in conformity with his own opinions'. Ponsonby to Palmerston, 15 June 1847. F.O. 7/336. Normanby informed Klindworth that if Austria did intervene in Switzerland, then it would result in the separation of England and Austria, which could only be of benefit to France, and that if Austrian intervention occurred 'before our elections it would be the one foreign topic on our hustings and Louis Philippe would escape quite scot free'. Normanby to Palmerston, 25 June 1847. Normanby Papers, Box P, bundle 19.
[25] Normanby to Palmerston, 25 June 1847. Normanby Papers, Box P, bundle 19.
[26] Palmerston to Normanby, 8 July 1847. B.P. GC/NO/448.

counter-intervention.[27] Although he rejected Metternich's proposal, Guizot hoped to turn it to good account; he planned to use it as an opportunity to renew his proposal for a common stand by the five great powers on Swiss affairs.

On 30 June 1847 he instructed Jarnac to sound out Palmerston's views on the possibility of a five-power declaration requesting both the *Sonderbund* and the radicals to maintain strictly the principle of cantonal sovereignty.[28] Guizot hoped that his proposal would be well received in London since Palmerston was aware of the Austrian proposal with its implied threat of armed intervention in Switzerland and its exclusion of England from whatever action was taken. Broglie, who had recently arrived in London, was surprised by Palmerston's indifference to the threatened isolation of England when he presented Guizot's proposal, and was even more astonished by Palmerston's suggestion that Austria and France, as the two great Catholic powers, should co-operate to end the Swiss dispute by urging the Pope to withdraw the Jesuits from Switzerland. He pressed Palmerston to accept the French proposal, arguing that the Swiss radicals would only respond to a unanimous declaration of the powers, and that armed intervention in Switzerland could only be avoided if England and France co-operated to prevent Metternich from embarking on an extreme course. Palmerston refused Broglie's request for an immediate five-power declaration, although he did not rule out future co-operation between France and England on Swiss affairs.[29] In view of the unpopularity of the recent intervention in Portugal, Broglie considered it unlikely that Palmerston would commit himself on Swiss affairs until after the July general election.[30] In an attempt to induce Palmerston to make an immediate decision, Guizot, at Louis Philippe's suggestion, extended his proposal by suggesting a five-power conference to be held in London under Palmerston's auspices as the best method of settling Swiss problems.[31] Contrary to Guizot's

[27] Guizot to Flahaut, 25 June 1847. A.A.E.C.P. Autriche 434.
[28] Guizot to Jarnac, 30 June 1847. A.A.E.C.P. Angleterre 668.
[29] Broglie to Guizot, 5 July 1847. A.A.E.C.P. Angleterre 668.
[30] Broglie to Guizot, 5 July 1847. G.P. 42/AP/214.
[31] Guizot to Broglie, 5 July 1847. G.P. 42/AP/214. Normanby was surprised when Guizot suggested a conference in London on Swiss affairs. 'In the first place

expectations, Palmerston did not jump at a proposal consciously designed to flatter his vanity. The French were at a loss to understand Palmerston's caution which Guizot and Broglie ascribed, after reflection, to the fear of domestic unpopularity. By doing so they failed to perceive the gulf between their view of Swiss affairs and Palmerston's. The latter was well aware that Guizot hoped that English support over Switzerland would enable him to extricate himself from domestic difficulties and to save the *Sonderbund*. Palmerston was determined not to play Guizot's game: he wished neither to spare Guizot from embarrassment nor to save the *Sonderbund*. He did not fear a combination of the continental powers on Swiss affairs since he did not believe that Guizot would defy French public opinion by supporting the *Sonderbund* in conjunction with Metternich.[32] Moreover, Palmerston genuinely believed that the withdrawal of the Jesuits from Switzerland was an essential preliminary to a settlement of the Swiss dispute; if the Pope would not recall them, the radicals must be given an opportunity to expel them.[33] He would not, therefore, give British support to any proposal aimed at preserving the religious *status quo* in Switzerland. This was not the only difference between England and France. Palmerston believed that Guizot's proposal of 30 June was open to the same objections as Guizot had raised against Metternich's overture of 7 June: that it carried with it a threat of armed intervention. He wrote on 8 July:

A conference must contemplate some result and some action to bring that result about. We should begin by advising. Nothing better if the advice is good and properly given. But say the advice is neglected and things are done which we advise people not to do. What are we, the 5 powers, then to do? Shall we wish each other goodbye and say we have thrown pearls to swine and so much the worse for those who

because he would feel justly that Europe would consider it as taking the Swiss question out of her hands to put it in yours [Palmerston's]. [Secondly because] the duc de Broglie's sympathies...are in favour of Swiss independence. He [Guizot] would not like to expose to him [Broglie] some of the expectations he had held out to Metternich in the winter when he wanted his assistance on the Spanish question, being aware that the Duke is a man whom he could neither induce to trick nor venture to disavow.' Normanby to Palmerston, 7 July 1847. B.P. GC/NO/65.

[32] Palmerston to Abercrombie, 19 Jan. 1847, quoted in D. M. Greer, *L'Angleterre, la France et la Révolution de 1848* (Paris, 1925), 135.
[33] Palmerston to Normanby, 16 July 1847. F.O. 27/775.

have not known their own interests? This would be laughable and better not meet than so to part. But then should we proceed to compel the Swiss to act upon our advice? That would be military interference and the very thing which we really and the others professedly wish to avoid.

Guizot's proposal seemed to Palmerston both premature and drastic; 'my own opinion', Palmerston informed Normanby, 'is that the knot might be untied instead of being cut'.[34] Palmerston believed that if a crisis developed in Switzerland it would be more the result of the shortcomings of Austrian and French diplomacy than of the folly of the Swiss radicals, as he was convinced that constructive and conciliatory diplomacy by Switzerland's great power neighbours could soon end the dispute.[35] Guizot therefore waited in vain for British acceptance of his proposal. Although Metternich accepted it promptly and promised Russian and Prussian support, Guizot regarded a four-power declaration as impossible.[36] His hope that the powers would deliver a stern warning to the Swiss before the Diet met was destroyed. On 19 July the Diet met in Lucerne. To mark their disapproval of its domination by the radicals, the eastern powers instructed their representatives neither to take up residence in Lucerne nor to attend the opening sessions; Metternich urged Guizot to issue similar instructions to Bois-le-Comte.[37] Guizot felt unable to comply unless the British government did the same, as it would associate France too closely with the eastern powers. Bois-le-Comte and Peel, the British chargé d'affaires, therefore travelled together to Lucerne where they attended the opening of the Diet. Guizot's second attempt to defend the *Sonderbund* by five-power action had failed. He recognised that he had lost a battle, but still hoped to win the campaign.[38]

[34] Palmerston to Normanby, 8 July 1847. B.P. GC/NO/448.
[35] '...the French and the Austrians might induce the Pope to recall the Jesuits from the 7 cantons. The French might persuade the Protestant and Liberal cantons to put an end to their free corps, Austria might induce the 7 cantons to dissolve their unconstitutional Sonderbund; and when all that was done, there would be nothing more left for the cantons to quarrel about...' Ibid.
[36] Guizot to Broglie, 12 July 1847. G.P. 42/AP/214.
[37] Flahaut to Guizot, 2 June 1847. A.A.E.C.P. Autriche 434; Metternich to Kaiserfeld, 1 July 1847. Metternich, *Mémoires*, vii, 463.
[38] Guizot to Broglie, 25 July 1847. G.P. 42/AP/214.

The Swiss radicals were swift to take advantage of their majority in the Diet and of the dissensions between the great powers. By the beginning of August 1847 they had in principle secured everything they wanted; resolutions were passed which condemned the *Sonderbund* as an illegal union, called upon each canton to expel the Jesuits, and set up a committee, composed mostly of radicals, to consider reform of the Federal Pact. The radicals claimed that these resolutions were binding on all the cantons; there could be no doubt of their determination to enforce them, if necessary by force of arms. The protests of the *Sonderbund* cantons against these resolutions went unheeded, and by the time the Diet adjourned in mid-August both sides knew that a negotiated settlement of their differences was unlikely. In late August and September the radicals and the *Sonderbund* both began open preparations for civil war.

Palmerston was both surprised and alarmed by these developments. In his opinion Austria and France, by their refusal to urge the *Sonderbund* cantons to dissolve their illegal union and the Pope to recall the Jesuits, were as much responsible for this crisis situation as the Swiss themselves.[39] Palmerston felt that what the Swiss lacked was the advice of a 'wise friend, free from selfish interest', and he took it upon himself to give it. On 18 September he wrote to Lord Minto, the Lord Privy Seal, who was in Switzerland before beginning his special mission to the Italian states,[40] that he should urge the Swiss that they should 'amicably and moderately settle their differences'.[41] Minto did not receive these instructions until he reached Turin, but the reports he sent Palmerston of his visits to Berne and Lucerne and of his unofficial discussions with Ochsenbein tended to confirm Palmerston's fear that civil war was imminent. Unless the Pope could be induced to recall the Jesuits, Minto concluded, 'civil war is I fear inevitable'.[42] Minto believed Bois-le-Comte and Kaiserfeld to be uncritical partisans of the *Sonderbund*, and that neither was likely 'to smooth the way to

[39] Palmerston to Normanby, 16 Aug. 1847. Normanby Papers, Box P, bundle 13.
[40] For the Minto mission to Italy and its background, see *Gran Bretagna e Italia Nei Documenti della Missione Minto*, ed. Federico Curato (Rome, 1970), 2 vols.
[41] Palmerston to Minto, 18 Sept. 1847. Ibid., i, 68–73.
[42] Minto to Palmerston, 19 Sept. 1847. B.P. GC/MI/459.

accommodation'.[43] Palmerston's apprehensions were increased by a report from Normanby of the existence of a secret Austro-French understanding to intervene on behalf of the *Sonderbund* in the event of civil war.[44] In reply to Russell's question as to the course England should pursue if France and Austria were to intervene in Switzerland, Palmerston replied that as sovereign states the cantons were perfectly 'entitled to seek assistance for their own defence wheresoever they can get it'.[45] By late October 1847 Palmerston admitted that all he could do was to appeal to the Pope to 'prevent much bloodshed and evil by a timely' withdrawal of the Jesuits,[46] but, as Normanby pointed out, without Austrian and French support such an appeal would be vain.[47] By early November Palmerston expected almost daily to hear of the outbreak of hostilities in Switzerland and of the intervention of Austria and France on behalf of the *Sonderbund*.

Guizot did not share Palmerston's surprise about the imminent crisis in Switzerland, nor was he as despondent about the future. He believed that when the Swiss situation became sufficiently critical Palmerston would consent to do what he had twice refused: join France in a five-power concert. Guizot believed this not only because he wanted to, but also because of Broglie's belief that an Anglo-French accord on Swiss affairs was likely if Palmerston thought that it was the only alternative to allowing Switzerland to degenerate into anarchy and civil war.[48] Guizot was not alone in thinking along these lines. In July Normanby had urged Palmerston to bear in mind the fact that, if Austrian intervention were imminent, British cooperation with France, however distasteful, 'would be a step in the protection of Swiss independence'.[49] In Guizot's view, therefore, the Swiss situation had to get worse before it could get better. By late October reports received from Bois-le-Comte convinced Guizot that Swiss affairs had deteriorated far

---

[43] Minto to Palmerston, 22 Sept. 1847. B.P. GC/MI/460.
[44] Normanby to Palmerston, 19 Oct. 1847. B.P. GC/NO/26; Normanby to Palmerston, 23 Oct. 1847. F.O. 27/756.
[45] Palmerston to Russell, 10 Oct. 1847. Russell Papers, P.R.O. 30/22/6F.
[46] Palmerston to Minto, 29 Oct. 1847. B.P. GC/MI/583.
[47] Normanby to Palmerston, 5 Nov. 1847. B.P. GC/NO/86.
[48] Broglie to Guizot, 5 July 1847. G.P. 42/AP/214.
[49] Normanby to Palmerston, 7 July 1847. B.P. GC/NO/65.

enough; once again the time had come for him to take the initiative. On 4 November the French cabinet met to discuss Swiss affairs. Normanby believed that the outcome would be another attempt to gain the support of the British government, and he reminded Palmerston of the importance of ensuring that Great Britain did not lose her position as 'the only power which has not shewn ill-will towards the Federal Government'.[50]

Immediately after the cabinet meeting on 4 November Guizot wrote to Broglie and Flahaut instructing them to deliver to Palmerston and Metternich a new French plan for the settlement of the Swiss dispute. It was time, wrote Guizot, to restore the unity and moral authority of the great powers in Switzerland, and for them to assume their responsibilities as signatories to the 1815 treaty. He therefore proposed that the five powers should adopt the rôle of mediators. They should demand first, either by one collective note or five identic notes, the immediate cessation of hostilities on the basis suggested by the *Sonderbund* cantons, that the question of the Jesuits be submitted to papal arbitration. If mediation was accepted, the second stage would be the establishment of a conference to which both sides could send delegates to discuss with the powers the means of ending the crisis and the question of Federal reform. If either party or both refused mediation, the powers should inform the Swiss that they regarded the Confederation at an end and Switzerland deprived of her neutral rights.[51] Guizot did not attempt to conceal the partisan nature of his proposals, the adoption of which would undoubtedly ensure the complete triumph of the *Sonderbund* over the radicals—Palmerston described it as 'a proposal to the majority that they should submit to the terms offered by the minority'.[52] Firstly, mediation would save the *Sonderbund* from military defeat; although Guizot was not aware of the full extent of the military inferiority of the conservatives,[53] he certainly knew them to be the weaker side. Secondly, the submission of the Jesuit question to papal arbitration would ensure the preservation of the religious *status quo* in Switzerland,

[50] Normanby to Palmerston, 5 Nov. 1847. B.P. GC/NO/86.
[51] Guizot to Broglie, 4 Nov. 1847. A.A.E.C.P. Angleterre 669; Guizot to Flahaut, 4 Nov. 1847. A.A.E.C.P. Autriche 214.
[52] Palmerston to Normanby, 9 Nov. 1847. Normanby Papers, Box P, bundle 19.
[53] Guizot, *Mémoires*, viii, 465–7.

since the Pope was hardly likely to decide against his co-religionists. Thirdly, the submission of the question of Federal reform to a conference dominated by the four continental powers, all known to oppose the radical stand on this issue, would result in the preservation of the constitutional *status quo*.

Guizot felt sure that Metternich would accept his proposals, that Russia and Prussia would follow suit, and that their adoption by the powers would leave the Swiss radicals no alternative to the acceptance of mediation. The implied threat of intervention if mediation was refused was not a real one; Guizot inserted it as the best way to persuade the radicals to accept what they might otherwise reject. As before, it was Palmerston's acquiescence which Guizot wanted most and which he thought would be most difficult to secure. Guizot knew Palmerston to be more sympathetic to the radicals than to the *Sonderbund*, and recognised his reluctance to commit Great Britain to interference in the internal affairs of another country so soon after the intervention in Portugal. He believed, however, that Palmerston would accept the French proposals if the alternative were clearly seen to be the total exclusion of England from Swiss affairs, and her isolation in Europe. Broglie had instructions to stress the danger of the isolation of England when he presented Guizot's proposals to Palmerston, and to inform him that England's refusal to join with the other powers would mean that 'la déclaration se ferait à quatre'.[54] Broglie was faithful to his instructions: he warned Palmerston that the circumstances gave France 'une belle occasion de prendre notre revanche de votre traité de 15 juillet 1840, et de nous mettre ici quatre contre un'.[55] Palmerston ignored this as French hyperbole, and dismissed Guizot's proposals as no more than the means to establish a basis for French and Austrian intervention in Switzerland and to afford them an opportunity to 'faire croisade contre les Radicaux'.[56] Broglie thus failed to get the immediate and unconditional support for the French proposals

---

[54] Guizot to Broglie, 4 Nov. 1847. G.P. 42/AP/214.
[55] Broglie to Guizot, 6 Nov. 1847. A.A.E.C.P. Angleterre 669.
[56] Ibid. See also Palmerston to Normanby, 7 Nov. 1847. Normanby Papers, Box P, bundle 19.

that Guizot wanted. In Palmerston's opinion, England could do one of two things:

> We shall either agree to join in a combined offer of mediation between the contending parties with a view to effect a settlement of the points practically at issue; namely the Jesuits and the Sonderbund and the Free Corps but leaving alone the revision of the compact until that question may assume such a shape as to call for or justify our interposition; or else we shall propose to unite with the other powers in an application to the Pope to withdraw the Jesuits and in an appeal to the contending parties to pause till the result of that application shall be known.[57]

Palmerston did not, however, inform Broglie in the course of their interview on 6 November that he was prepared to consider proposals on these lines. He saw no reason why he should reassure Guizot by revealing a willingness, under certain circumstances, to work with France. Palmerston was confident that France would not act with the eastern powers; this was corroborated by Louis Philippe's admission to Normanby on 7 November that it would be 'very awkward for his position here to act with Austria alone on [Swiss] affairs'.[58]

Palmerston's refusal to join with the other powers in a note to the Swiss which, in his opinion, bore 'a strong resemblance to the manifesto of the three powers upon the incorporation of Cracow'[59] left Guizot in a difficult position. Time was running out; to be effective mediation must be offered and accepted without delay. Guizot had to choose between immediate action with the eastern powers which might divide his cabinet and would certainly be unpopular in France, and further negotiations with Palmerston in an attempt to reach a *modus operandi* which might fail or be overtaken by events, and would certainly entail making concessions to the radicals. It was a straightforward choice between upholding his principles in Switzerland or his position at home; Guizot chose the latter. This was in line with Broglie's advice after Guizot's proposal had been coldly received by Palmerston and after Broglie had discussed it with

[57] Palmerston to Normanby, 7 Nov. 1847. Normanby Papers, Box P, bundle 19.
[58] Normanby to Palmerston, 8 Nov. 1847. F.O. 27/783.
[59] Palmerston to Prince Albert, 9 Nov. 1847. R.A. J/102/15.

Bunsen, the Prussian minister in London.[60] Unless the proposals had the concurrence of England, wrote Broglie on 10 November, the Swiss radicals would only respond to force; unless France was prepared to draw back, she would thus be dragged into intervention with Austria, which would result in a public outcry in France and the accusation that the government had thrown in its lot with 'les souverains de Cracovie'. Broglie suggested the removal from Guizot's proposal of the threat of intervention; the most Palmerston was likely to accept was 'la menace de retirer la garantie de neutralité, ce qui rend à chacun sa liberté naturelle'.[61] After consulting the King and the cabinet, Guizot agreed to the modification suggested by Broglie in order to secure the adherence of London. He was in fact satisfied with this solution; he regarded the sacrifice of the threat of intervention as a small concession. The important fact was that the proposals were still heavily weighted in favour of the *Sonderbund*.[62] Before the modified French proposals could be presented to Palmerston, Broglie was informed by Bunsen, at Palmerston's instigation, that the British were preparing a counter-project of mediation. Broglie was unperturbed; he thought that Palmerston was merely trying to ensure that he cut a good figure when the papers on Switzerland were published as a Blue Book.[63] He remained confident that the revised French plan would be the basis for negotiation in his next interview with Palmerston on Swiss affairs, fixed for 16 November. He was therefore disconcerted when Palmerston brusquely dismissed the modified French note and presented a counter-project of mediation, based on a memorandum of Lord John Russell's of 11 November and already approved by the cabinet as the basis for negotiation.[64]

---

[60] Bunsen told Broglie: '1. There was a sin of omission: nothing said to prove that the proposal of the Pope's mediation was honest. He seemed ashamed. He said what ought to be done? I answered, what the Grison Catholics have done; tell the Pope they are ready to give up the Jesuits if he will command or advise it. 2. A sin of commission; at the end there was the armed intervention announced which he before had disclaimed.' Bunsen to Palmerston, 9 Nov. 1847. B.P. GC/BU/591.

[61] Memorandum by Broglie, 10 Nov. 1847. G.P. 42/AP/214.

[62] Guizot to Broglie, 11 Nov. 1847. G.P. 42/AP/214.

[63] Broglie to Guizot, 12 Nov. 1847. A.A.E.C.P. Angleterre 669.

[64] 'In Switzerland', wrote Russell, 'our objects should be those which have been pointed out. 1. The removal of the Jesuits. 2. The dissolution of the Sonderbund. 3. The maintenance of the independence of the Cantons, as prescribed by the

Palmerston's plan of mediation was threefold: it insisted firstly on the complete withdrawal of the Jesuits from Switzerland, and secondly on the immediate dissolution of the *Sonderbund* which both Russell and Palmerston considered an illegal union. Finally, and only after these points had been accepted by both sides, were all warlike measures to cease. If either side rejected mediation, the proposals would lapse without further consequences. There was no threat of intervention, no forfeiture of neutral status if either side were to reject mediation, and reform of the Federal Pact was treated as outside the terms of reference which the powers should adopt for settlement of the dispute.[65] Where Guizot's proposals amounted to a total victory for the *Sonderbund* cantons, Palmerston's were designed to secure a radical triumph. Palmerston even hoped that the radicals would take advantage of the delay which was inevitable while the powers considered the proposals to take Freybourg and Lucerne and expel the Jesuits from those cantons. If they did so, he confided to Normanby, they 'will have lessened the difficulties of making a peaceful arrangement'.[66] Palmerston was delighted that his counter-project put Guizot in an extremely difficult position: 'Guizot will have to choose', he wrote to Minto on 17 November, 'between us and the three powers.'[67]

Although Broglie was extremely irritated by what he considered Palmerston's underhand manner of preparing his proposal and his offensive way of presenting it, he told Palmerston that it was his 'personal and private opinion' that France would

Federal Compact. 4. The restoration of peace. In walking upon this line we must be clear in our explanations to France. We cannot join in hostilities in Switzerland.' Russell's Memorandum on Swiss Affairs, 11 Nov. 1847. R.A. I/102/31. On the same day as the cabinet met to discuss Swiss affairs Palmerston informed Minto that 'we are willing to join the other powers in an endeavour to put an end to the civil war by an offer of mediation but not willing to meddle with a revision of the Federal Compact'. Palmerston to Minto, 11 Nov. 1847. B.P. GC/MI/584. Palmerston asked Stratford Canning, who had helped draw up the Federal Compact in 1815, for his views on the situation in Switzerland in 1847. Canning did not submit his memorandum to Palmerston until 12 Nov., the day after the cabinet had discussed Swiss affairs. For Canning's memorandum, see Ann G. Imlah, *Britain and Switzerland, 1845–1860* (London, 1966), Appendix I.

[65] Palmerston to Normanby, 16 Nov. 1847. F.O. 27/777; Broglie to Guizot, 16 Nov. 1847. A.A.E.C.P. Angleterre 669.
[66] Palmerston to Normanby, 16 Nov. 1847. Normanby Papers, Box P, bundle 19.
[67] Palmerston to Minto, 17 Nov. 1847. B.P. GC/MI/585.

accept it,[68] and he urged Guizot to do so. He believed that Palmerston would consider modifications to his plan, and his frank opinion to Guizot was that a revised version of Palmerston's plan of mediation was preferable to four-power action on the basis of the French proposals, with the associated threat of intervention. Moreover, as he pointed out, mediation of any kind would at least save the *Sonderbund* from military defeat. Guizot recognised the force of Broglie's arguments, and on 18 November he informed Normanby that, although he could not commit himself without consulting the King and the cabinet, 'he did not see any difficulties of importance which would prevent him from acceding to [Palmerston's] proposal'.[69] After a cabinet meeting Guizot instructed Broglie to accept the British proposals provided Palmerston would accept two modifications. Guizot insisted firstly that the Jesuit question be submitted to papal arbitration; he felt that Palmerston's proposal for their total exclusion smacked of religious intolerance since it allowed the Catholic cantons no freedom of choice in matters relating to their own religion. Secondly, Guizot thought it unreasonable to expect the powers, especially Austria and France, to impose upon themselves a self-denying ordinance as far as intervention was concerned. Circumstances might arise, he wrote, when intervention was unavoidable. Moreover, he felt that the specific denial by the powers of the right of intervention would encourage the radicals to reject mediation. Broglie was also instructed to insist that Palmerston's draft proposals be amended and despatched to the other three Courts without delay.[70]

Guizot knew that Metternich would disapprove of the British mediation proposals. Their adoption would mean giving up the stronger French note which Metternich had already accepted; they were also too favourable to the radicals; and their acceptance by France was an indication of Guizot's anxiety not to separate France from England or to act alone with the eastern powers. Nevertheless, Guizot did not think that Metternich would reject the British plan of mediation, because

[68] Ibid.
[69] Normanby to Palmerston, 18 Nov. 1847. B.P. GC/NO/89.
[70] Guizot to Broglie, 18 Nov. 1847. G.P. 42/AP/214.

the effect of rejection would be to separate Austria from France, to condemn his country to inaction in Swiss affairs, and thus ultimately to ensure a radical victory. On 20 November Palmerston joined Guizot in urging Metternich to accept the British proposals; Ponsonby was instructed to inform Metternich that between the British and French mediation plans there were 'really only differences of form', and that Palmerston's formula was adopted in preference to Guizot's because the British government was trying to avoid 'having to encounter the difficulties with regard to public feeling in this country which might be insurmountable'.[71]

When Broglie presented Guizot's required amendments to the British proposals on 20 November he met no apparent opposition from Palmerston. Palmerston was prepared to allow the Jesuit question to be referred to papal arbitration as a face-saving device provided Austria and France would both urge the Pope to recall them; he was also willing to concede to the powers the rights 'which they at present possess' if mediation were to fail.[72] As soon as Palmerston's acceptance of the emendations was known, Guizot began to make determined efforts to persuade the eastern powers to accept the British proposals. He pointed out that his revisions had greatly strengthened the original proposals, and that the urgency of the situation would make it impossible now to draw up new proposals, secure the agreement of the five powers, and present them to the Swiss before the outbreak of hostilities.[73] What Guizot was in fact arguing was that something was better than nothing. Only the Prussian minister, Arnim, responded favourably to Guizot's pleading. Normanby attributed his acceptance of the British proposals to the fact that Palmerston had clearly thwarted Guizot's attempt to take the lead in the great power negotiations over Switzerland.[74] Apponyi and Kisselef did not at first hold out much hope that their governments would accept the British mediation proposals,[75] but at the moment when

[71] Palmerston to Ponsonby, 20 Nov. 1847. F.O. 7/335. See also Palmerston to Ponsonby, 20 Nov. 1847. B.P. GC/PO/804.
[72] Broglie to Guizot, 20 Nov. 1847. G.P. 42/AP/214.
[73] Guizot to Broglie, 24 Nov. 1847. G.P. 42/AP/214.
[74] Normanby to Palmerston, 24 Nov. 1847. Normanby Papers, Box P, bundle 19.
[75] Guizot to Broglie, 24 Nov. 1847. G.P. 42/AP/214. Nesselrode told Bloomfield

Guizot most despaired of Austrian and Russian support, Apponyi and Kisselef agreed to recommend to their Courts the adoption of the English note.[76]

By the last week of November it was clear that Guizot's fears that great power negotiations were not proceeding fast enough to avoid being overtaken by events were well grounded. On 22 November the radical forces attacked Lucerne, the largest Jesuit stronghold. Guizot immediately suspected Palmerston of double-dealing, of encouraging the radicals to attack Lucerne and delaying the mediation until they had done so.[77] Broglie was instructed to inform Palmerston that if England did not immediately sign the identic note and despatch it to Switzerland, the French would revive their own mediation proposals and act *à quatre*.[78] Palmerston apparently regarded this as an idle threat. To Broglie's surprise and consternation, Palmerston's final draft of the mediation was word for word identical with the first draft. Palmerston claimed that he had understood their discussion on the 20th to have been a clarification only of the original draft, not a revision. He accepted the modifications, however, after Broglie pointed out that the four continental powers regarded them as an essential part of the proposals.[79] Palmerston did this primarily because he knew that the radicals were advancing on Freybourg and Lucerne, and he expected the Jesuits to have been expelled before the Pope recalled them officially.[80] By 28 November only the Russian government had still not accepted the British mediation proposals.[81] Stratford Canning, who was to deliver the British identic note to the Swiss, was in Paris awaiting orders to proceed to Berne. Bois-le-Comte was already in receipt of the French note and only needed instructions to deliver it. Although Guizot regretted that

that he hoped the other powers would place 'the question of Switzerland under the direction of Prince Metternich who was a master hand...in such matters, and whose experience rendered his opinions of the greatest value'. Bloomfield to Palmerston, 24 Nov. 1847. F.O. 63/323.

[76] Guizot to Broglie, 26 Nov. 1847. G.P. 42/AP/214.
[77] Ibid.
[78] Ibid.
[79] Broglie to Guizot, 26 Nov. 1847. G.P. 42/AP/214. See also Palmerston to Broglie, 26 Nov. 1847. F.O. 27/791.
[80] Palmerston to the Queen, 26 Nov. 1847. R.A. I/102/66.
[81] Guizot to Broglie, 29 Nov. 1847. G.P. 42/AP/214.

unity among the powers had not been established earlier, he was well pleased with the outcome of the negotiations; he felt that it was a signal triumph for French diplomacy. No previous government under the July Monarchy, he reminded Broglie, had succeeded in guiding the Concert of Europe. 'Nous sommes évidemment à ce point critique', he wrote, 'où la bonne politique Française peut devenir, de gré ou de force, conviction ou nécessité, la politique Européenne.'[82] Just as Guizot expected the concert of the powers to act decisively, it collapsed since on 28 November Lucerne fell to the radicals. Palmerston's reaction to this news was that it left nothing for the great powers to do, while Metternich thought it called for firm and decisive action. Palmerston ordered Stratford Canning to remain in Paris, and Metternich instructed Kaiserfeld not to deliver the identic note. Guizot decided to act alone. His Swiss policy was in shreds; and future developments might call for stronger action, perhaps with Austria alone. Guizot believed that the best way to prepare his party and French public opinion for such a step was to demonstrate that France had tried to work with all the powers on the basis of moderate proposals. On 1 December therefore Bois-le-Comte was instructed to deliver the French note. Guizot did not expect the Swiss radicals to heed it;[83] he merely wished it widely reported in France. He knew that any policy which attempted to deny the Swiss radicals the fruits of their military victory would meet with strong opposition in France: Guizot was resigned to the fact that 'la lutte sera très rude dans les Chambres'. To Broglie he confessed that 'au fond, et pour ces choses, cela est inévitable'.[84]

Early in December British and French policy towards Switzerland began to diverge significantly. Hervey, acting chargé d'affaires at Paris in Normanby's absence, reported that Guizot was extremely hostile to the radicals and was meditating measures to safeguard the rights and independence of the defeated *Sonderbund* cantons.[85] Metternich told Ponsonby that

[82] Ibid.
[83] For Ochsenbein's reply to the French note, see *La Presse*, 10 Dec. 1847.
[84] Guizot to Broglie, 3 Dec. 1847. G.P. 42/AP/214.
[85] Hervey to Palmerston, 6 Dec. 1847. F.O. 27/743. On 5 Dec. Hervey informed Reeve, 'I have no confidence in the wisdom of Metternich, Canitz or Guizot... They are meditating some fresh step.' Hervey Papers, 941/61/1.

Austria was determined to maintain the principle of cantonal sovereignty, and that even if the other powers refused to cooperate with him, he could not abandon his principles and the public law of Europe.[86] Palmerston feared that the Swiss radicals would be vindictive in their hour of triumph, and that the continental powers would seize upon any excess of vengeance as a pretext for intervention. Throughout December Palmerston therefore devoted his efforts to urging moderation on both the Swiss radicals and the great powers. Stratford Canning was instructed to proceed to Switzerland and to lose no opportunity 'of endeavouring to keep them [the radicals] to moderate measures'.[87] He might assure the radicals of English sympathy as long as they pursued a sensible and generous policy towards the defeated cantons, but 'above all do not let them suppose, if you find them inclined to do so, that England will go to war with France and Austria and Prussia in order to back the Swiss up...'[88] To the four continental powers Palmerston made it clear that he did not regard the refusal of the Swiss 'to yield to foreign influence in regard to the settlement of their internal disputes' as grounds for armed interference.[89] 'So long as Switzerland abstains from any act at variance with its neutral character', Normanby was instructed to inform Guizot, 'the inviolability of her territory should be respected.'[90] Palmerston did not stop at reminding the powers that they had no right to intervene in Switzerland; he warned Metternich that French intervention in Switzerland would have a disastrous effect on Austria's position in Italy: 'if there is one maxim of policy which Metternich ought to hold by more than another', Palmerston wrote to Ponsonby, 'it is to keep the French out of Switzerland'.[91] Normanby, Hervey and Russell hoped that Louis Philippe, the French cabinet and French public opinion would restrain Guizot, and thus ensure inaction on the part of the

[86] Ponsonby to Palmerston, 4 Dec. 1847. F.O. 7/337.
[87] Palmerston to Russell, 1 Dec. 1847. Russell Papers, P.R.O. 30/22/6H.
[88] Palmerston to Stratford Canning, 1 and 2 Dec. 1847. Canning Papers, P.R.O. F.O. 352/30.
[89] Palmerston to Westmorland, 6 Dec. 1847. Copy, Canning Papers, P.R.O. F.O. 352/30.
[90] Palmerston to Normanby, 27 Dec. 1847. F.O. 27/777.
[91] Palmerston to Ponsonby, 21 Dec. 1847. B.P. GC/PO/805.

continental powers.⁹² *The Times*, relying on information which Reeve received from Hervey, confidently asserted on 14 December that Austria and France would not intervene in Switzerland: 'We do not believe that this is a line of policy which the French nation, the Chambers or even his own colleagues, will allow the French minister to pursue.'

Guizot was determined that the Swiss radicals should not go unchecked. They had already defeated and dissolved the *Sonderbund* and expelled the Jesuits; if nothing were done to prevent them from implementing their plans for the reform of the Federal Pact, Austria and France would find themselves confronted with a unitary republic on their borders, which would be, as Metternich predicted, 'un foyer de trouble et de révolution'.⁹³ The reports from Berlin and Vienna strengthened Guizot's resolve to act against the radicals. He was especially pleased by the attitude of Prussia: Frederick William IV sent General Radowitz to Vienna to discuss Swiss affairs with Metternich, with authority to proceed to Paris for further discussions if Metternich thought this desirable. The coolness which had marked Franco-Prussian relations since the autumn of 1846 was fast disappearing; in the eyes of the Prussian King, Louis Philippe, the citizen king, had become 'le bouclier des monarques européens'.⁹⁴ On 7 December Guizot put forward a new plan for the great power management of Swiss affairs: he proposed that a conference be convened by the five powers at Neuchâtel as soon as possible. Its first act should be to demand the immediate evacuation of the *Sonderbund* cantons by Diet troops, and the restoration of full political liberty to the defeated cantons. It should next demand an assurance from the Diet that no change in the Federal Pact would be effected without the unanimous consent of all the cantons.⁹⁵ Guizot hoped for Palmerston's acceptance of his latest proposal, but he made it clear that this time he was determined to proceed without England if Palmerston rejected his proposals. Palmerston not

⁹² Hervey to Reeve, 12 Dec. 1847. Hervey Papers, 941/61/1. Normanby to Palmerston, 12 Dec. 1847. Normanby Papers, Box P, bundle 19. Russell to Prince Albert, 7 Dec. 1847. R.A. I/103/34.
⁹³ Flahaut to Guizot, 29 Dec. 1847. G.P. 42/AP/68.
⁹⁴ P. Renouvin, *Histoire des Relations Internationales* (Paris, 1954), v, 192.
⁹⁵ Guizot to Broglie, 7 Dec. 1847. G.P. 42/AP/214.

only dismissed the idea of a conference, but also sent Normanby a strongly worded condemnation of any further deliberations on Swiss affairs for communication to Guizot. He also informed Doyle of the *Morning Chronicle* that he disapproved of the idea of a conference on Switzerland,[96] and *The Times* followed the lead of the *Morning Chronicle* in criticising the French proposals.[97] Hervey hoped that the hostile reaction of the British government and the British press to the idea of a conference would result in Swiss affairs being 'allowed to blow over without any act of violence on the part of the four powers'.[98] Guizot, however, was not prepared to endure another humiliating defeat at the hands of Palmerston. On the morning of 13 December he informed Broglie of his determination to proceed with the conference despite English opposition.[99] Later the same day Duchâtel and other members of the cabinet called on Guizot to warn him that they believed that if the government were to act without England and with the eastern powers on the Swiss conference proposal there would be a tremendous outcry in France and the government's popularity would be greatly reduced. Guizot was unimpressed by this argument; he pointed out that France would be leading the continental powers, not following in Metternich's wake. He did, however, agree to consider modifications to the conference proposal in order to secure English support.[100] Broglie knew that no amount of modification would secure Palmerston's participation in a conference, and he regarded the unity of the French cabinet as infinitely more important than the chatisement of the Swiss radicals; he therefore urged Guizot to yield to Duchâtel and his supporters. He proposed an honourable retreat as the only way out: the four powers should, he suggested, send to the Swiss Diet an identic note which should clearly uphold the principles of cantonal sovereignty and of unanimity over revisions to the constitution, and should reserve to the powers all their right of action for the future. Broglie thought that once the retreat from the Swiss question had been accomplished, France should

---

[96] Palmerston to Doyle, 9 Dec. 1847. B.P. GC/DO/96.
[97] *The Times*, 14 Dec. 1847.
[98] Hervey to Reeve, 24 Dec. 1847. Hervey Papers, 941/61/1.
[99] Guizot to Broglie, 13 Dec. 1847. G.P. 42/AP/214.   [100] Ibid.

establish a close concert with the other three powers; this would effect the exclusion of England from the affairs of Europe, and so hasten the fall of the Whig government.[101] In the face of continued cabinet opposition, Guizot was forced to adopt the course suggested by Broglie. According to Normanby, Radowitz and Colleredo, an Austrian representative, both sent by Metternich to discuss Swiss affairs in Paris, were surprised to meet with a cold reception from Guizot.[102] He informed them that the idea of a conference was being reconsidered, and that negotiations could not begin until they had fresh instructions from Metternich. Guizot made sure that they received the right instructions. On 25 December he instructed Flahaut to inform Metternich that a conference of the powers, conducted in the public eye and issuing stern warnings to the Swiss, would soon find itself forced either to abandon its attempt to restrain the Swiss radicals in face of their refusal to accept its suggestions, or to enforce their views by armed intervention. The former would be humiliating, the latter contrary to the interests of peace. Guizot therefore recommended that the idea of a conference be dropped. If Metternich was not convinced by Guizot's argument, Flahaut was further to inform him that domestic reasons had forced the French government to abandon

[101] Broglie to Guizot, 16 Dec. 1847. G.P. 42/AP/214. In July 1847 Broglie accepted the post of French ambassador in London because he believed that he could bring about a marked improvement in Anglo-French relations. He was convinced that if he gained the confidence of Russell and the Whig Francophiles, they would restrain the excesses of Palmerston's Francophobia. By December 1847 Broglie had lost faith in the Whigs. The failure of Lansdowne to exercise the degree of vigilance over Palmerston necessary to ensure some improvement in the relations of the two western powers greatly disappointed him. Broglie was even more disappointed in Russell. Like Guizot, he believed that Russell was constantly deceived by Palmerston, and he hoped that the exposure of Palmerston's conduct would lead Russell to take a firm line with him. In October 1847 Guizot and Broglie thought they had an opportunity to expose Palmerston's handling of the River Plate negotiations and perhaps bring about his fall, but Russell's timidity and Palmerston's back-tracking denied them the opportunity. (See D. Johnson, *Guizot*, 278, and J. F. Cady, *Foreign Intervention in the Rio de la Plata, 1835–50* (Philadelphia, 1929), 233–4. As Johnson points out, Cady wrongly dates Guizot's memorandum on the River Plate.) The effect of Russell's failure to support Broglie's side in his disputes with Palmerston was to convince Broglie that there could be no improvement in Anglo-French relations while the Whigs remained in office. Thus by December 1847 Broglie was anxious to see the Whigs fall as quickly as possible.

[102] Normanby to Palmerston, 27 Dec. 1847. B.P. GC/NO/91.

its conference proposals.[103] Metternich knew that he could not proceed against the Swiss radicals without the full support of France, and was therefore forced to follow the French in an honourable retreat. Characteristically, Metternich hoped that something could be salvaged from the situation; whereas he told Flahaut that his willingness to abandon the conference and agree to the declaration proposed by the French arose from his wish 'to be personally agreeable to M. Guizot',[104] in reality he hoped to secure French neutrality in case Austria found it necessary to intervene in Italy. In the last resort—and Metternich knew that this was the point he had reached—French support for Austrian policy in Italy was more important than Austro-French co-operation over Switzerland.[105] On 5 January Guizot, Colloredo and Radowitz drafted for presentation to the Swiss Diet a note demanding that cantonal sovereignty be respected and the 1815 Federal Pact maintained.[106] The Swiss radicals received this note later in January with complete indifference. They knew that only Austria and France acting in complete harmony and with determination could rob them of their victory, and the collective note was, as Nesselrode observed, merely 'une déclaration à l'eau de rose'.[107]

Despite his last-minute retreat, Guizot had, as Palmerston had anticipated, some difficulty in explaining 'this mess'.[108] In a debate on foreign policy on 31 January the opposition made a bitter attack on Guizot's Swiss policy, using the collective note of the four continental powers to illustrate their contention that the government had aligned itself with the reactionary powers. According to Hervey, even Guizot's friends and supporters were at a loss to understand his Swiss policy.[109] Normanby urged Palmerston to publish a Blue Book on the Swiss negotiations without delay; Guizot, he wrote, dreads 'the counter-effect in the Chambers of the knowledge of your opinion...[on] the

---

[103] Guizot to Flahaut, 20 Dec. 1847. G.P. 42/AP/9.
[104] Flahaut to Guizot, 28 Dec. 1847. G.P. 42/AP/68.
[105] For Metternich's Italian policy in Dec. 1847, see Renouvin, op. cit., 190–1.
[106] D. M. Greer, *L'Angleterre, la France et la Révolution de 1848*, 161. Guizot to Flahaut, 5 Jan. 1848. G.P. 42/AP/9.
[107] Nesselrode, *Lettres et Papiers* (Paris, n.d.), ix, 54.
[108] Palmerston to Minto, 31 Dec. 1847. B.P. GC/MI/590.
[109] Hervey to Reeve, 7 Jan. 1848. Hervey Papers, 941/61/1.

independence of Switzerland and therefore he gave strict orders that your dispatch [of 28 December] should be concealed from everyone here'.[110] Palmerston did not think this necessary: 'the opposition will make some fun of it and it would not surprise me if Guizot was to go out at last'.[111] In little over a month Guizot did go out. Palmerston was, however, surprised to see Louis Philippe go with him.

[110] Normanby to Palmerston, 6 Jan. 1848. B.P. GC/NO/95.
[111] Palmerston to Normanby, 9 Jan. 1848. Normanby Papers, Box P, bundle 19.

CHAPTER XI

England and the Fall of the Orleans Monarchy

Throughout 1847 Normanby and Hervey frequently predicted that Guizot would soon fall from power. In the early part of the year they argued that his dynastic policy in Spain and the rupture with England would be the direct cause of his dismissal. They believed that a number of factors, either individually or in various combinations, could bring him down. Louis Philippe, who was known to regret the collapse of the *entente cordiale*, might replace Guizot with a minister able and willing to restore good relations with England; the government might disintegrate from within if Duchâtel and other ministers resigned in protest against Guizot's foreign policy; popular indignation at a policy of dynastic aggrandisement, combined with opposition charges of gross ineptitude in the conduct of foreign policy, might destroy Guizot's majority in the Chambers. In these speculations Normanby and Hervey were not entirely free from wishful thinking; their dislike of Guizot predisposed them to believe that antipathy to him was more widespread than it really was and that his government was as weak as his critics claimed. They undoubtedly saw his fall as a vindication of their own conduct and of the British government's foreign policy. It would, however, be wrong to suggest that the two senior British diplomats in Paris allowed their judgments to be completely obscured by their hostility towards Guizot. The belief that Louis Philippe dispensed with his ministers when it suited his purpose was commonly held, and the difficulty which governments had in maintaining a majority in the Chamber of Deputies was generally recognised to be one of the major problems of French politics. Moreover, the expectation that the mistakes of his foreign policy would lead to Guizot's fall was not confined to Normanby, Hervey and the French opposition; in France it was shared by the Duke of Joinville, the son of Louis Philippe, and by many Deputies on the government side.[1] In England it was commonplace amongst those who took an informed interest in French politics. Peel, for example, in August 1847 claimed that Guizot's defiance of England was a 'fatal error' which would permanently and irreparably weaken his government.[2] The fact that Guizot was still in office in the summer of 1847 did not alter Normanby's conviction that he would fall as a direct consequence of his mismanagement of foreign affairs. In July he assured Palmerston that the developments of the past six months had confirmed rather than undermined this opinion:

Considerations of foreign policy exercise a very different degree of influence upon public opinion in this country than in England. Much dissatisfaction has been felt at the abandonment, for purely dynastic objects, of a useful alliance to which those most interested in the permanence of the present system were attached, certainly not by sentiment but from a feeling of security. Still more indignation has been expressed that the Government should have sought new strength in the sympathies of those absolute powers who are at the moment endeavouring by threats of force to repress peaceable movements in favour of liberal reforms in different parts of Europe.[3]

In this despatch Normanby was elaborating a theme first developed by Thiers and the opposition press, that the collapse of the *entente* was in itself bad, but its consequences were even worse; France had become a conservative power, and Guizot was betraying in Europe the principles on which the Orleans monarchy was based.

By the autumn of 1847 Normanby had thus shifted the emphasis of his argument that Guizot's foreign policy would cause his fall: he now claimed that the alignment of France with the reactionary powers was making the government even more unpopular than the breach with England had done. This coincided with other changes in his assessment of the state of French politics. He became gradually less concerned with the

[1] Normanby to Palmerston, 15 Mar. 1847. Normanby Papers, Box P, bundle 13; Hervey to Reeve, 28 May 1847. Hervey Papers, 941/61/1.
[2] Peel to Aberdeen, 19 Aug. 1847. Aberdeen Papers, B.M. Add. MS. 43297.
[3] Normanby to Palmerston, 30 July 1847. F.O. 27/781.

effect of a change of government in France on Anglo-French relations and more concerned with the domestic implications of a crisis in French politics. He also began to argue that it was not Guizot's foreign policy alone that accounted for the widespread popular dissatisfaction with the government, but its policy as a whole and its increasingly tarnished image. Normanby contended that Guizot's refusal to consider proposals for widening the narrow franchise during the present session of the Chambers was damaging his reputation, not only in the country but also amongst the more liberal of the government's adherents in the Chambers.[4] At the same time Hervey informed Reeve that he had heard from a reliable source that conservatism in both domestic and foreign affairs was rapidly undermining the unity of the cabinet, since Duchâtel believed some concessions to the liberal forces in France to be necessary if the government were to survive.[5] According to Normanby the charges that 'ministerial corruption and the abuse of patronage' had enabled the government to win the last election had produced a profound impression on the public mind.[6] Normanby's reports in the autumn of 1847 not only suggested that opposition to Guizot was becoming more widespread but also contained a new note of urgency. He thought that as long as Louis Philippe kept Guizot in office, dissatisfaction with the institutions of the monarchy and with the monarch himself was bound to increase:

...there exists in the present political state of France no attachment to any individual, no respect for any institution...the system [is] maintained by its identification with the material interests of the middle classes. 'Enrichissez-vous' has long been said to be the paternal admonition addressed from the Throne to the people.[7]

In the short term, however, Normanby saw the increasing unpopularity of Louis Philippe as a more serious and potentially more dangerous development. By keeping Guizot in office, Normanby thought that the King was giving substance to the charge that he was sacrificing the real interests of France to

[4] Normanby to Palmerston, 19 July 1847. Normanby Papers, Box P, bundle 13.
[5] Hervey to Reeve, 12 July 1847. Hervey Papers, 941/61/1.
[6] Normanby to Palmerston, 30 July 1847. F.O. 27/781.
[7] Normanby to Palmerston, 23 July 1847. Normanby Papers, Box P, bundle 13.

advance his ambitions for his fifth son in Spain.[8] By December 1847 Normanby feared that together Louis Philippe and Guizot were seriously endangering the monarchy itself. Palmerston was impressed by Normanby's reports on the state of French politics, describing them as 'able, luminous and comprehensive', and he circulated them among his cabinet colleagues.[9] Thus, by the end of 1847 it was commonly believed in British government circles that a ministerial crisis at least was imminent in France. Palmerston was convinced of it; in December 1847 he informed Minto that he thought 'Guizot very rickety'.[10] Others feared that the régime itself was in peril; if Louis Philippe 'does not look sharp, while he is grasping the Crown of Spain he will find his own tottering on his head', wrote Greville to Clarendon.[11]

In January 1848 the feeling in Paris, according to Normanby, was 'that the government are at once both weak and violent and both these qualities seem to react upon each other and to go on increasing every day'.[12] Guizot's total dependence on the King, the divisions within the cabinet, and the widening gulf between the government and its supporters within the Chamber, wrote Normanby, formed 'the principle topics of the day'.[13] The disclosures in early January that Guizot's private secretary, Génie, had been engaged in the 'corrupt traffic in places' were condemned in all sections of the French press, and Normanby thought that 'Guizot's character must suffer in consequence'; he also repeated a rumour that Duchâtel planned to use this as 'the occasion he has been seeking for a quarrel' with Guizot.[14] Later in January the French government's handling of the Swiss crisis was the subject of bitter criticism. The arrival in Paris of Radowitz and Colleredo, and the four-power declaration to the Swiss Diet were regarded as an open proclamation of the alignment of France with the conservative powers. According to Molé there was 'a sufficient number of conservatives determined

---

[8] In July 1847 Normanby heard that Guizot's friends had persuaded Louis Philippe 'that the Montpensier succession would be in danger with any other minister, especially Molé'. Normanby to Palmerston, 28 July 1847. B.P. GC/NO/70.
[9] Minute by Palmerston on Normanby to Palmerston, 30 July 1847. F.O. 27/781.
[10] Palmerston to Minto, 18 Dec. 1847. B.P. GC/MI/589.
[11] Greville to Clarendon, 30 Dec. 1847. Clar. Dep. C521.
[12] Normanby to Palmerston, 20 Jan. 1848. B.P. GC/NO/99.
[13] Normanby to Palmerston, 7 Jan. 1848. B.P. GC/NO/96. [14] Ibid.

to get rid of Guizot to make his fate certain before long' and 'they had been much confirmed in their determination by these last papers on the Swiss question'.[15] Normanby's reports of January 1848 intensified the feeling in England that a crisis was imminent in France. Palmerston and Clarendon were particularly anxious about the state of French politics. Guizot, wrote the former, 'seems playing like a reckless and desperate gambler for all or nothing; one should say he was more likely to get nothing than all. One would be glad to see him out but one does not want his ejectment to be brought about by a revolution'.[16] Clarendon informed Reeve that he thought *The Times* ought to begin 'to differentiate between the French government and the French people; praise the latter for their honest attachment to the principles of July and condemn the former for their corruption'. This was necessary because if Louis Philippe and 'his dynasty come to grief I think it is of the utmost importance that we should be well with the French people'.[17]

On 31 January there was a full-scale debate in the Chamber of Deputies on the government's policy. Both Normanby and Hervey were surprised when the motion of censure against the government was defeated despite Thiers' powerful attack and Guizot's weak defence of his policy. They had both predicted the wholesale desertion of government deputies.[18] Normanby did not, however, think that Guizot's prospects were in any way improved by his victory in the Chamber. On 7 February he informed Palmerston that 'the opinion here is general, I might almost say universal, that the present state of things cannot last long. But the extent and the period of the coming change are very differently estimated.'[19] At one extreme were those who thought that revolution was inevitable unless there was an immediate change of government; others argued that the government ought to cling to office in the hope 'that the

---

[15] Normanby to Palmerston, 27 Jan. 1848. B.P. GC/NO/103.
[16] Palmerston to Normanby, 11 Feb. 1848. Normanby Papers, Box P, bundle 19.
[17] Clarendon to Reeve, 21 Jan. 1848. Clar. Dep. C524.
[18] Normanby to Palmerston, 5 Feb. 1848. B.P. GC/NO/110; Hervey to Reeve, 14 Feb. 1848. Hervey Papers, 941/61/1. The government in fact had a majority of 80; a few days later, however, on the electoral reform question the government majority dropped to 33. See D. Johnson, *Guizot*, 256–7.
[19] Normanby to Palmerston, 7 Feb. 1848. F.O. 27/803.

existing discontent, instead of increasing, may wear itself out before next year'. Normanby thought the latter opinion dangerously optimistic.[20] On 17 February he reported that the French government was itself alarmed at the prospect of serious disturbances arising out of the Banquet which the advocates of electoral reform proposed to hold in the Champs-Elysées. Guizot was said to have received reports from the police which made clear 'the exasperation of the great body of the people and the hatred felt towards the government'.[21] Normanby himself did not anticipate serious consequences from the Banquet: 'It is probably the great object of the Reformers to shew that the French people are capable of an orderly and peaceable popular demonstration. If they can do so it will shew that they have made great progress in the principles of constitutional government.' He added, however, that 'many who have been here longer than me and know the people better, contemplate a revolution as possible'.[22] Hervey was one of those who feared revolution: 'it is impossible to deny that we are in a very important crisis', he wrote to Reeve on 21 February, 'and I cannot answer for the result'.[23]

The Banquet, however, was not the cause of Guizot's fall. It was forbidden by the cabinet. This divided the Banqueteers: the dynastic opposition abandoned their attempts to stage a joint protest with the extra-parliamentary opposition, and returned to the attack in the Chamber. On 22 February the French opposition therefore made two separate protests against Guizot and his government: in the Chamber of Deputies Odilon Barrot and Duvergier de Hauranne, without the support of either Thiers or Molé, tabled a motion accusing the government of having betrayed constitutional liberties, while in the streets of central Paris the 'unrepresented opposition' organised a few small-scale demonstrations. The demonstrators, according to Normanby, were mainly unemployed artisans and students; he was quite unimpressed by them, believing them incapable of organising anything more than 'stupid mischief'. He still

[20] Ibid.
[21] Normanby to Palmerston, 17 Feb. 1848. B.P. GC/NO/113.
[22] Normanby to Palmerston, 19 Feb. 1848. B.P. GC/NO/114.
[23] Hervey to Reeve, 21 Feb. 1848. Hervey Papers, 941/61/1.

thought that 'the desire for change amongst the French people' would be satisfied by Guizot's dismissal.[24] On 23 February the government sought to strengthen its hard-line policy by calling out the National Guard. This decision proved fatal for Guizot as, instead of supporting the government against the demonstrators, the guardsmen did the reverse. Louis Philippe was at last convinced that Guizot must go, and on the afternoon of the 23rd he demanded his resignation and asked Molé to form a new administration.[25] Normanby immediately despatched the news to Palmerston by special messenger:

So Guizot is gone at last! If this was obtained by any other means I cannot say that there would be the slightest mixture in the feeling with which I regard the event. But it says but little for the progress of regular constitutional government that the intervention of armed national guards should be necessary to force a change of ministry from the Sovereign whose reign began behind the barricades.[26]

Palmerston, delighted with Normanby's news, wrote immediately 'to say how much I rejoice and how sincerely I congratulate you on the change of ministry at Paris'.[27] The course of events, however, confirmed his low opinion of the sagacity of Louis Philippe. He wrote to Minto that:

People have long gone on crying up Louis Philippe as the wisest of men. I always have thought him one of the most cunning and therefore not one of the wisest. Recent events have shewn that he must rank among the cunning who out-wit themselves and not among the wise who master events by foresight and prudence.[28]

In Palmerston's view the departure of Guizot undoubtedly improved the prospects for the future; Molé's government would 'be much more liberal than Guizot's both at home and abroad'[29] and Normanby's recent conversation with Molé suggested that the new government might even acquiesce in the

---

[24] Normanby to Palmerston, 22 Feb. 1848. B.P. GC/NO/116.
[25] An excellent account of the fall of Guizot and of the February revolution of 1848 can be found in D. Johnson, *Guizot*, 258–61.
[26] Normanby to Palmerston, 23 Feb. 1848. B.P. GC/NO/117.
[27] Palmerston to Normanby, 24 Feb. 1848. B.P. GC/NO/460.
[28] Palmerston to Minto, 24 Feb. 1848. B.P. GC/MI/591.
[29] Ibid.

removal of the Duchess of Montpensier from the Spanish succession.[30]

Normanby's next report, however, completely dashed Palmerston's hope of fruitful co-operation with Molé. On 24 February he sent another special messenger to London to inform Palmerston that 'there is now little chance of anything but a republic here': the National Guard and the demonstrators were determined that the King as well as Guizot should go.[31] Palmerston's first reaction to these 'extraordinary and marvellous events' was to reflect on their irony:

Strange that a King who owed his Crown to a revolution brought about by royal blindness and obstinacy should have lost it by exactly the same means...and still further that his overthrow should have been assisted by a minister deeply read in the records of history and whose mind was not merely stored with the chronology of historical facts but had extracted from their mass the reasons of events and the philosophy of their causes.[32]

While he did not regret the fall of either Louis Philippe or Guizot, Palmerston lamented that it should have been accompanied by the destruction of the institutions of constitutional monarchy. He had a deep distrust of republican forms of government, and he doubted whether the new French republic would long be able to maintain order in France or peace in Europe.[33] The new government, however, existed; it could not

[30] On 27 Jan. 1848 Molé informed Normanby that if Guizot fell and he were called to power he would make determined efforts to 'be upon a better footing with England'. Normanby then asked 'how were we to get rid of the legacy of discord which this government would leave to its successors?' Molé replied that 'he felt all the embarrassment of the position in this respect and I [Normanby] thus suggested—Suppose the Spanish people were through their representatives themselves to change the present order of the succession. What should you say to that? He at once said that not only would he not oppose it as French minister either directly or indirectly but he would be delighted at such a solution.' Normanby thought that 'this is quite as much as we could ever get and as much as we should have any right to expect from any French minister and in Molé's case it would have the peculiar value of being the assurance of a man who would not break his word but would act loyally up to it'. Normanby to Palmerston, 27 Jan. 1848. B.P. GC/NO/103.
[31] Normanby to Palmerston, 24 Feb. 1848. B.P. GC/NO/118.
[32] Palmerston to Normanby, 26 Feb. 1848. B.P. GC/NO/461.
[33] Palmerston to Normanby, 27 Feb. 1848. B.P. GC/NO/462.

be ignored and should not be offended. Normanby was therefore instructed to inform the new leaders of France that:

> We desire friendship and extended commercial intercourse with France and peace between France and the rest of Europe. We will engage the rest of Europe from meddling with France which indeed we are quite sure they have no intention of doing. The French rulers must engage to prevent France from assailing any part of the rest of Europe: upon such a basis our relations with France may be placed on a footing more friendly than they have been or were likely to be with Louis Philippe and Guizot.[34]

These instructions inaugurated a new chapter in Anglo-French relations. Notwithstanding his dislike of republicanism, Palmerston hoped that a French republic would be a better friend to England than Louis Philippe had been; it could certainly be no worse enemy.[35]

The arrival of Louis Philippe, the Orleans family and Guizot as destitute refugees in London in late February and early March 1848 provoked a good deal of discussion in British government circles on the reasons for their fall and the justice of their fate. 'How quick and terrible', wrote Clarendon with evident satisfaction, 'has been the punishment of the traitors in the Spanish Marriages.'[36] Russell was equally convinced that Louis Philippe had brought calamity upon himself:

> A moderate and constitutional government at home, coupled with an abstinence from ambitious projects for his family, might have laid the foundation of permanent peace, order and freedom in Europe. Selfishness and cunning have destroyed that which honesty and wisdom might have maintained.[37]

The Queen, like her ministers, had no doubts as to the reason for the fall of the Orleans monarchy. To the King of the Belgians she wrote, 'Louis Philippe has brought much of this on by that ill-fated return to a Bourbon Policy.' She thought, however, that 'Guizot is more to blame...he is no Bourbon and he

---

[34] Palmerston to Normanby, 26 Feb. 1848. B.P. GC/NO/461.
[35] Palmerston to Bulwer, 18 Apr. 1848. B.P. GC/BU/579.
[36] Clarendon to Palmerston, 7 Mar. 1848. B.P. GC/CL/483.
[37] Russell to Queen Victoria, 15 Apr. 1848. Q.V.L., 1st series, ii, 200–1.

THE FALL OF THE ORLEANS MONARCHY 331

ought to have behaved differently.'[38] It soon became a settled conviction in England that Louis Philippe and Guizot fell as a direct result of their Spanish marriages policy. It was therefore clear that both King and minister deserved this fate: they had, wrote Prince Albert, offended England by the 'secrecy and violence' of their Spanish policy, and the failure of the *entente* had driven them 'into a line of politics which [France] would not stand'.[39] Palmerston held that they had disgusted Europe by their 'views of international interests' and France by their 'general political principles'.[40] Queen Victoria thought the fate of Louis Philippe 'a great moral'.[41] To Palmerston the moral was obvious; he had, he informed Normanby, no 'political sympathy' for the French exiles, and regarded their presence in England with suspicion. Normanby was instructed to tell Lamartine, the head of the provisional government, that England had only offered asylum to the Orleans family, and would not permit them to organise intrigues against their successors in France.[42] To Stanley, his under secretary at the Foreign Office, Palmerston expressed the view that the Orleans family were 'a bad lot' who, even in their new state of disgrace and penury, continued to try to further their ambitions in Spain.[43] By contrast, Lamartine had assured Normanby that he would 'take an early opportunity of stigmatising' the policy of Guizot and Louis Philippe 'with regard to Spain'. This pleased Palmerston; it would vindicate the good faith and the good name of England, and restore to Spain her independence.[44]

[38] Queen Victoria to the King of the Belgians, 18 Apr. 1848. Ibid., 203-4; Queen Victoria to Russell, 16 Apr. 1848. R.A. C/8/12.
[39] Memorandum by Prince Albert, 7 Mar. 1848. R.A. J/49/62.
[40] Palmerston to Normanby, 4 Apr. 1848. B.P. GC/NO/473.
[41] Queen Victoria to Russell, 16 Apr. 1848. R.A. C/8/12.
[42] Palmerston to Normanby, 7 Mar. 1848. Normanby Papers, Box P, bundle 20.
[43] Stanley to Bulwer, 10 Mar. 1848. Bulwer Papers, S/40.
[44] Normanby to Palmerston, 2 Mar. 1848. Normanby Papers, Box P, bundle 14; Memorandum by Prince Albert, 7 Mar. 1848. R.A. J/49/62.

CHAPTER XII

Conclusion

England's relations with the Orleans monarchy fell into three distinct phases. Firstly there was the decade of the 1830s, the era of the liberal alliance. During the second period, from the autumn of 1841 to the summer of 1846, Aberdeen sought and then claimed to have established an *entente cordiale* with the French government. The third period, from Palmerston's return to the Foreign Office in 1846 to the fall of the Orleans monarchy, was dominated by intense rivalry and witnessed the final abandonment of the idea of a close and special relationship between the two countries. The whole period constitutes a full turn of the circle: suspicion and fear prevailed at the end of the period as they had done at the beginning. In this process Lord Palmerston played a crucial part. He not only dominated the making of British foreign policy for most of the period, but also determined the way in which Anglo-French relations were thought about among both Whigs and Tories.

The idea of the liberal alliance originated with the Foxite Whigs. They believed that the July revolution in France and their reform programme at home had placed the constitutional development of the two countries on parallel lines, and they assumed that similar institutions would give England and France an identity of outlook and would predispose them to understand one another. They hoped that both powers would devote their energies abroad to the defence and propagation of the principles on which their governments rested against the attacks of the eastern autocratic powers. The early 1830s witnessed the addition of yet another unifying factor. Both the British and the French government feared that Russia was intent not only on undermining the European balance of power but also on revising the *status quo* in the near east in her own favour. Both powers regarded the restraint of Russia as a compelling reason for co-operation. In the early 1830s, for the first time in centuries, England and France regarded each other as natural and obvious allies rather than perpetual and implacable enemies. Why then did the liberal alliance prove such a signal failure? It must be admitted that the Whig conception of the alliance was too grandiose and unrealistic. It assumed that both countries would put their common ideals above their national interests. This they never did. Moreover, the alliance was grounded on rigid notions about the behaviour of certain types of state in international society. The Foxite Whigs believed that autocratic states were naturally aggressive and could never co-operate with constitutional states to their mutual benefit. They assumed conversely that constitutional states were naturally and perpetually bound together. The alliance was thus based on political fallacies. These factors explain why the liberal alliance failed to live up to the high ideals with which it was invested rather than why it ended in an almost complete breakdown in Anglo-French relations. The reason for this collapse was that, although conceived as an equal and mutually beneficial relationship, the liberal alliance never was equal in practice. For this Palmerston was largely responsible: he expected the French to follow the British lead and demanded that France should play a secondary rôle to England, especially in western Europe. His was the old policy of Castlereagh and Canning in a new guise. Palmerston saw the liberal alliance as a balance of power policy: he hoped to use it to contain Russia in the east and France in the west. Whereas the Foxite Whigs believed that Orleanist France was essentially peace loving, and that it was wrong to attribute selfish motives of ambition and conquest to French foreign policy, Palmerston believed the exact opposite. Although resistance to French territorial expansion was necessary to defend British interests and the European balance of power, Palmerston never appreciated the difference between French expansionism and their legitimate desire to be an equal member of the community of great powers. The 1815 settlement was bitterly resented in France, not because of any particular losses it entailed but because it had been imposed on her. This seemed to suggest that France was a second-rate power. Her ambition was to appear as the equal of the other powers. This meant playing a part in all great-power negotiations and exercising influence, like the other great powers, over her smaller neighbours. French foreign policy between 1815 and 1848 was thus dominated by the search for status and influence. The liberal alliance was consequently regarded as an unsatisfactory alignment, firstly because it did not afford France equal status with Britain, and secondly because Palmerston was attempting to use it to exclude France from exercising influence in the Iberian peninsula. In so far as it had any value to France, it was as an alternative to isolation. For Palmerston the failure of the French to co-operate with England on the terms he had laid down confirmed all his suspicions and strengthened his fear of France. When the French refused to follow the British lead during the near eastern crisis in 1839 and 1840 Palmerston abandoned the liberal alliance without regret. In his opinion the crisis revealed without any shadow of doubt that France was the major enemy of England and the principal danger to European peace. Whilst Thiers remained in office this was not an unreasonable conviction, although the dangers posed by France stemmed more from drift than from design. The dismissal of Thiers and the appointment of Guizot on a platform of peace completely altered the situation in France, but it in no way altered Palmerston's mind about the character of French foreign policy. He believed that the Foreign Ministers of France were the mere tools of Louis Philippe and the permanent officials of the Quai d'Orsay, that France would always be hostile to England, and that there was therefore no hope of *rapprochement* between the two countries on terms acceptable to England.

The collapse of the liberal alliance had a profound effect on the thinking of British politicians about foreign policy: it divided the Whigs bitterly and it shaped the foreign policy of the Tory government of Peel. There were many in both parties who refused to accept that unrelenting rivalry between England and France was inevitable. On one thing, however, the advocates of good relations with France and Palmerston were agreed: that the liberal alliance could not be revived, the days of ideological and exclusive alignments were past. What Aberdeen sought therefore was to establish an atmosphere of cordiality in which conflicts of interest between the two countries

CONCLUSION 335

could be amicably settled. In fact the *entente cordiale* was as much a failure as the liberal alliance, and for much the same reasons. As the *entente* developed, it became clear that it was an unequal relationship. Guizot expected the British government to accept that his assurances of good intentions indicated the true spirit of his foreign policy, and to overlook his failure to act towards Great Britain in a friendly and conciliatory spirit on many important issues. His constant theme was that 'la politique générale' was more important than 'les questions spéciales'. On practically every issue where the interests of the two countries conflicted Guizot pleaded domestic difficulties to justify either delay or some concession to France. In part Guizot's plea was genuine: until late 1846 he had to work with a slender majority in a predominantly Anglophobe Chamber, and in pursuing good relations with England he had set himself against the main currents of opinion within France on foreign policy. In its way, Guizot's policy was a courageous one, but, as Peel pointed out, too often his courage failed him and he attempted to appease the Anglophobia which he affected to despise at the expense of the *entente* with England which he claimed to cherish. The *entente* also suffered from the severe handicap that it lacked widespread support. In neither England nor France was it a genuinely popular policy. Guizot found it virtually impossible to convert hostility to England into enthusiasm for the *entente*, and Aberdeen did not even try to rouse the English public from its indifference to foreign affairs. Moreover, the rivalry of British and French diplomats remained as fierce in the 1840s as in the late 1830s. Palmerston had encouraged his diplomats to thwart their French counterparts, and Aberdeen did not know how to stop them from doing so. In his attitude to his subordinates, Guizot stood somewhere between Palmerston and Aberdeen. The *entente* of the Foreign Ministers was not paralleled amongst the diplomats; indeed, there was not even an uneasy truce between them. Thus by late 1845 the *entente* rested on nothing more than the personal friendship and mutual confidence of Aberdeen and Guizot.

When it became clear that the days of the Peel government were numbered and that Palmerston would return to the Foreign Office Guizot, not unnaturally, became increasingly anxious for the future. He knew that Palmerston was a consistent and bitter critic of the *entente*, that he had attacked it on the grounds that it was nothing more than a means by which English interests were sacrificed to keep Guizot in office. Guizot also realised that Palmerston's approach to foreign policy, which placed 'les questions spéciales' above 'la politique générale', was the exact opposite of his and Aberdeen's. There was therefore a fundamental difference of perspective between Guizot and Palmerston, and this difference was accentuated by the fact that neither was prepared to compromise; each insisted that the relations of the two countries should be conducted on his own terms. This intransigence was clearly revealed during the negotiations on the Spanish Marriages in July and August 1846: Guizot thought that Palmerston should allow him as free a hand as Aberdeen had done, while Palmerston was determined to reassert British influence at Madrid. The assumptions on which their Spanish policies were based made conflict inevitable. Moreover, both badly miscalculated on the Spanish Marriages question. Despite Bulwer's warnings, Palmerston anticipated no real difficulty in effecting fundamental changes in Spanish politics and in undermining French influence over Spain. Guizot too thought he could have his triumph in Spain without making any sacrifices, that it would be Palmerston, not he, who would suffer. Both were proved wrong. What was surprising about the outcome of the Spanish Marriages negotiations was not the collapse of the *entente*—its maintenance on terms acceptable to both Palmerston and Guizot would have proved impossible—but the fact that rivalry over Spain thereafter dominated the foreign policies of both England and France.

This was all the more surprising in view of the many pressing problems elsewhere in Europe which were of common concern to both powers. Palmerston and Guizot alike exaggerated the importance of the Spanish succession. It was a battle of prestige rather than a clash of vital British and French interests. Palmerston sustained the conflict over the Spanish succession partly to frustrate the French in the wish he attributed to them of subjecting Spain completely to their influence, partly because it was in his character not to admit defeat and to have vengeance on a political opponent. The diplomacy of Palmerston and

CONCLUSION

Bulwer in Spain after the Montpensier marriage was no more than a series of ill-conceived and ambitious schemes which ended in disaster when Bulwer was expelled in May 1848. Palmerston's foreign policy after the autumn of 1846 thus failed where he most wanted it to succeed. His only real successes in this period were at home and in Switzerland: he was able to vindicate his conduct during the negotiations on the Spanish Marriages and to eliminate effective opposition to his strongly anti-French policy, and he outmanœuvred and humiliated Guizot over the *Sonderbund* question. Although Guizot retained the position established in Spain by the marriages, it brought him no appreciable benefits and greatly increased his difficulties. When he negotiated the marriages he had not expected that the whole basis of his policy would be transformed. In 1847 he was caught between Metternich's unbending conservatism and Palmerston's bitter hostility. A middle course was only possible when no action was required; it was impossible in a crisis, as the *Sonderbund* question clearly revealed. Guizot's failure to find an adequate substitute for the *entente* greatly increased both his domestic and his international problems. In 1847 his opponents were able to claim with more justice than ever before that his policy was ineffective and a betrayal of all the July Monarchy stood for. The *entente* collapsed just when Guizot needed it most. Although rivalry in Spain yielded no real results to either Guizot or Palmerston, and only added to their frustrations, neither was prepared to compromise. The position was a complete impasse. The gulf between their policies in Spain was so great that they did not feel it worthwhile to exchange views on them; suspicion and ill-grounded fears thus multiplied. In a sense, therefore, it is true to say that Anglo-French relations in 1847 had reached their lowest point since 1830, as even at the height of the near eastern crisis in 1840 they had continued to discuss their differences.

The fall of the Orleans monarchy brought the impasse to a dramatic end, and both British and French foreign policy immediately lost the false sense of priorities engendered by their Spanish rivalry. By the summer of 1848 the problems that had bedevilled Anglo-French relations in 1847 had been set aside. Tension in Europe shifted from the Iberian peninsula to Italy and Germany, and here Anglo-French relations were on a very different basis. The gravity of the situation in central Europe, particularly in Italy, the ambiguity of the foreign policy of the French Republic, and Palmerston's desire at all costs to avoid a European war, led him to adopt a distinctly more friendly attitude to the Provisional Government than he had to the Orleans monarchy. In part this improvement in Anglo-French relations must be attributed to the changes of personnel which resulted from the February revolution. Palmerston thought Lamartine well-meaning and Cavaignac sensible, whereas he hated Guizot and was convinced that 'England has no bitterer enemies than all the Princes of the House of Orleans from Louis Philippe downwards.' Thus the only positive result of Palmerston's hatred of Orleanist France was to dispose him to be more tactful and understanding towards Republican France. The new situation in Europe and the new régime in France closed a chapter in Anglo-French relations. The *entente* and the bitter rivalry that had followed its failure were forgotten.

SELECT BIBLIOGRAPHY

A. MANUSCRIPT SOURCES

(1) IN GREAT BRITAIN

British Museum
Aberdeen Papers.
Bligh Papers.
Broughton Papers.
Greville–Reeve Correspondence.
Hobhouse Papers.
Holland House Papers.
Howard de Walden Papers.
Napier Papers.
Palmerston Letterbooks.
Peel Papers.
Westmorland Papers
    (British Museum Microfilm).

Public Record Office
Cowley Papers.
Foreign Office Papers. The following series were consulted: F.O. Austria, Belgium, France, Portugal, Prussia, Russia, Spain, Switzerland.
Russell Papers.
Stratford Canning Papers.

Other Libraries, Record Offices and Private Ownership
Beauvale Papers, Royal Archives, Windsor Castle.
Broadlands Papers, Historical Manuscripts Commission.
Bulwer Papers, Heydon Hall, Norwich, Norfolk.
Clarendon Papers, Bodleian Library, Oxford.
Ellice Papers, National Library of Scotland, Edinburgh.
Hervey Papers, Bury St Edmunds and West Suffolk Record Office, 8 Angel Hill, Bury St Edmunds.
Melbourne Papers, Royal Archives, Windsor Castle.
Normanby Papers, Mulgrave Castle, Yorkshire.
Printing House Square MSS., *The Times*, Printing House Square, London.
Royal Archives, Windsor Castle.

(2) IN FRANCE

Archives du Ministère des Affaires Etrangères
Archives du Ministère des Affaires Etrangères. The following series of Correspondance Politique and Mémoires et Documents were consulted: Austria, Belgium, England, Portugal, Prussia, Russia, Spain, Switzerland.
Bourqueney Papers.
Desages Papers.

Archives Nationales
Guizot Papers.

B. PUBLISHED DOCUMENTS

Accounts and Papers, 1847, vols. xxv and lxix.
Discours Prononcé par M. Guizot dans la Discussion du Projet de loi Relatif aux Refugiés Etrangers, 2 July 1846.
Documents Communiqués aux Chambres par le Ministre des Affaires Etrangères: Mariages Espagnols.
Documents Communiqués aux Chambres sur Cracovie.
Hansard's Parliamentary Debates, 3rd series.

C. NEWSPAPERS AND PERIODICALS

(1) ENGLISH

The Edinburgh Review.
The Examiner.
Fraser's Magazine.
The Morning Chronicle.
The Quarterly Review.
The Times.

(2) FRENCH

Le Constitutionnel.
Journal des Débats.
La Presse.
Revue des Deux-Mondes.
Revue Retrospective.
Le Siècle.

(3) SPANISH

(Bulwer frequently sent Palmerston cuttings from the Spanish press. Copies of articles from the Spanish press can be found in the Broadlands Papers, Bulwer Papers and F.O. Spain.)
Clamor Publico.
El Español.
El Faro.
Heraldo.

D. SECONDARY SOURCES

The Correspondence of Lord Aberdeen and Princess Lieven, 1832–1854, ed. E. Jones Parry (Camden Miscellany, 3rd series, lx, London, 1938).
Airlie, Mabell, Countess of, *Lady Palmerston and her times* (2 vols., London, 1922).
Anderson, M. S., *The Eastern Question, 1774–1923* (London, 1966).
—, *The Great Powers and the Near East, 1774–1923* (London, 1970).
Aspinall, A., *Politics and the Press, 1780–1850* (London, 1949).
Bagehot's Historical Essays, ed. N. St John Stevas (New York, 1965).
Baldwin, J. R., 'England and the French Seizure of the Society Islands', *Journal of Modern History*, 1938, x.
Balfour, Lady Frances, *The Life of George, Fourth Earl of Aberdeen* (2 vols., London, 1923).
Bartlett, C. J., *Great Britain and Sea Power, 1815–1853* (Oxford, 1963).
Bell, H. C. F., *Lord Palmerston* (new impression, 2 vols., London, 1966).

SELECT BIBLIOGRAPHY

Bolsover, G. H., 'Nicholas I and the Partition of Turkey', *Slavonic and East European Review*, 1948–9, xxvii.
Bourne, K., *The Foreign Policy of Victorian England, 1830–1902* (Oxford, 1970).
Brougham, Lord, 'Foreign Relations of Great Britain', *Collected Works* (London, 1857).
Bullen, R., 'Guizot and the *Sonderbund* Crisis', *English Historical Review*, July 1971, lxxxvi.
Bulwer, Sir H. (Lord Dalling), *Life of Viscount Palmerston (to 1846)* (3 vols., London, 1870–6).
— and Ashley, Evelyn, *Life of Viscount Palmerston* (2 vols., London, 1879).
Cady, J. F., *Foreign Intervention in the Rio de la Plata, 1835–50* (Philadelphia, 1929).
Carr, Raymond, *Spain, 1808–1939* (Oxford, 1966).
Cecil, Algernon, *British Foreign Secretaries, 1807–1916* (London, 1927).
Chamberlain, Muriel, 'The Character of the Foreign Policy of the Earl of Aberdeen' (unpublished Oxford D.Phil. thesis, Bodleian Library).
Christiansen, E., *The Origins of Military Power in Spain, 1800–1854* (Oxford, 1967).
Conacher, J. B., 'Peel and the Peelites, 1846–1850', *English Historical Review*, July 1958, lxxiv.
Connell, B., *Regina v. Palmerston* (London, 1962).
Cunningham, A. B., 'Peel, Aberdeen and the Entente Cordiale', *Bulletin of the Institute of Historical Research*, November 1957, xxx.
Curato, F. (ed.), *Gran Bretagna e Italia nei Documenti della Missione Minto* (2 vols., Rome, 1970).
Deschamps, H. T., *La Belgique devant la France de Juillet* (Paris, 1956).
Dreyer, F., 'The Whigs and the Political Crisis of 1845', *English Historical Review*, July 1965, lxxx.
Duroselle, J. B. (ed.), *La Politique Etrangère et ses Fondaments* (Paris, 1954).
Eckinger, Carl, *Lord Palmerston und der Sonderbundskrieg* (Berlin, 1938).
Fagan, L., *The Life of Anthony Panizzi* (London, 1880).
Flournoy, F. R., *British Policy towards Morocco in the Age of Palmerston, 1830–1865* (London, 1935).
Gleason, R. H., *The Genesis of Russophobia in Great Britain* (Harvard, 1950).
Greer, D. M., *L'Angleterre, la France et la Révolution de 1848* (Paris, 1925).
The Greville Memoirs, ed. Henry Reeve (new impression, 8 vols., London, 1910).
The Letters of Charles Greville and Henry Reeve, ed. A. H. Johnson (London, 1924).
Guizot, F., *Mémoires pour servir à l'histoire de mon temps* (8 vols., Paris, 1856–67).
—, *Histoire Parlementaire de France* (5 vols., Paris, 1863–4).
Lettres de Monsieur Guizot à sa famille et à ses amis, ed. Madame de Witt (Paris, 1884).
Lettres de François Guizot et de la Princesse de Lieven, ed. Jacques Naville (3 vols., Paris, 1963–4).
Guyot, A., *La Première Entente Cordiale* (Paris, 1926).

Halévy, E., *Victorian Years, 1841–1895* (London, 1951).
Hall, J., *England and the Orleans Monarchy* (London, 1912).
D'Haussonville, A., *Histoire de la Politique Extérieure du Gouvernement Français* (Paris, 1850).
Holbraad, Carsten, *The Concert of Europe* (London, 1970).
Ilchester, the Earl of, *Chronicles of Holland House, 1820–1900* (London, 1937).
Imlah, Ann G., *Britain and Switzerland, 1845–1860* (London, 1966).
Johnson, Douglas, *Guizot: Aspects of French History, 1787–1874* (London, 1963).
—, 'The Foreign Policy of Guizot', *University of Birmingham Historical Journal*, 1959, vi, 1.
Joll, J. (ed.), *Britain and Europe, 1793–1950* (London, 1950).
Jones Parry, E., *The Spanish Marriages, 1841–1846* (London, 1936).
—, 'A Review of the Relations between Guizot and Lord Aberdeen, 1840–52', *History*, 1938, xxiii.
Lamartine, A. de, *Histoire de la Révolution de 1848* (Paris, 1849).
Langer, W. L., *Political and Social Upheaval, 1832–1852* (New York, 1969).
Laughton, J. K., *Memoirs of the Life and Correspondence of Henry Reeve* (2 vols., London, 1898).
Leitao, R. A., *Documentos dos Arquivos de Windsor* (2 vols., Coimbra, 1955).
The Correspondence of Princess Lieven and Lord Grey, ed. G. Le Strange (3 vols., London, 1890).
Livermore, H. V., *A New History of Portugal* (Cambridge, 1969).
Lucas, Sir Reginald, *Lord Glenesk and the Morning Post* (London, 1910).
Macartney, C. A., *The Habsburg Empire, 1790–1918* (London, 1969).
Martin, Sir Theodore, *The Life of the Prince Consort* (5 vols., London, 1876–80).
Mastellone, S., 'Pellegrino Rossi ambasciatore a Roma', *Rivista Storica Italiana*, 1949.
Maxwell, Sir Herbert, *Life of the Fourth Earl of Clarendon* (2 vols., London, 1913).
Merk, Frederick, *The Oregon Question* (Cambridge, Mass., 1967).
Metternich, Prince Clemens, *Mémoires et Documents*, ed. Prince Richard Metternich (7 vols., Paris, 1880–4).
Mitchell, L. G., *Charles James Fox and the Disintegration of the Whig Party, 1782–1794* (Oxford, 1971).
Molares, J. Quero, 'Spain in 1848', *The Opening of an Era: 1848*, ed. F. Fejtö (New York, 1966).
Moseley, Philip E., 'Intervention and Non-Intervention in Spain, 1838–1839', *Journal of Modern History*, 1941, xiii.
Nesselrode, Count, *Lettres et Papiers* (10 vols., Paris, n.d.).
The Letters of Lady Palmerston, ed. Tresham Lever (London, 1957).
Parker, C. S., *Sir Robert Peel from his Private Papers* (3 vols., London, 1891–9).
Pouthas, Charles, 'Sur les Rapports de la France et de l'Angleterre pendant la Monarchie de Juillet', *Revue d'Histoire moderne*, 1927, xii.
—, 'Les ministères de Louis Philippe', *Revue d'Histoire moderne et contemporaine*, June 1954.
Letters of the Prince Consort, 1831–1861, ed. K. Jagow (London, 1938).

SELECT BIBLIOGRAPHY

Rappard, E., *La Constitution Fédérale de la Suisse* (Neuchâtel, 1948).
Rémusat, Charles de, *Mémoires de ma Vie*, ed. Charles H. Pouthas (4 vols., Paris, 1958–62).
Renouvin, P., *Histoire des Relations Internationales: Le XIXe siècle de 1815 à 1871* (Paris, 1954).
Russell, Lord John [Earl Russell], *The Foreign Policy of England, 1570–1870* (London, 1871).
—, *A Letter to the Right Honourable Lord Holland on Foreign Politics* (London, 1819, reprinted with a new introduction, 1831).
—, *Recollections and Suggestions, 1813–1873* (London, 1875).
The Early Correspondence of Lord John Russell, 1805–1840, ed. Rollo Russell (2 vols., London, 1913).
The Later Correspondence of Lord John Russell, ed. G. P. Gooch (2 vols., London, 1925).
Southgate, Donald, '*The Most English Minister*'...*The Policies and Politics of Palmerston* (London, 1966).
Memoirs of Baron Stockmar, ed. E. von Stockmar, trans. Max Müller (2 vols., London, 1872–3).
Taylor, A. J. P., *The Italian Problem in European Diplomacy, 1847–49* (Manchester, 1934).
—, *The Struggle for Mastery in Europe, 1848–1918* (Oxford, 1954).
—, *The Trouble Makers. Dissent over Foreign Policy, 1792–1939* (London, 1957).
Temperley, H. V. W., *The Foreign Policy of Canning, 1822–1827* (new impression, London, 1966).
—, *England and the Near East* (new impression, London, 1964).
Thureau-Dangin, P., *Histoire de la Monarchie de Juillet* (8 vols., Paris, 1880–94).
—, 'La France et l'Europe à la veille de la révolution de 1848', *Revue d'Histoire Diplomatique*, 1892.
History of 'The Times', 1841–1884 (London, 1939).
The Letters of Queen Victoria, 1837–1861, 1st series, ed. A. C. Benson and Viscount Esher (3 vols., London, 1907).
Walpole, Sir Spencer, *The Life of Lord John Russell* (2 vols., London, 1891).
Ward, A. W. and Gooch, G. P., *Cambridge History of British Foreign Policy, 1783–1919* (3 vols., Cambridge, 1923).
Webster, Sir C. K., *The Foreign Policy of Castlereagh, 1815–1822* (2 vols., 2nd edition, London, 1934).
—, *The Foreign Policy of Palmerston, 1830–1841* (2 vols., new impression, London, 1969).
Young, G. M. (ed.), *Early Victorian England* (London, 1936).

INDEX

Abdel Kadir, 39
Aberdeen, George Hamilton Gordon, 4th Earl of, 53, 54, 59, 61, 67, 68, 69, 70, 74, 180, 187; and France, 25, 37, 38, 335–7; and Guizot, 26–7, 28, 30–2, 38–9, 40, 41, 58, 69, 71, 190, 335–7; and Palmerston, 29–33, 35, 59, 89, 91, 184, 190, 194, 200; and principles of foreign policy, 25, 26, 37, 40–1, 55–6; and Spain, 28, 29, 41, 74, 84, 85; and Spanish Marriages, 37, 41, 48–9, 59, 61, 86, 88, 90, 95, 99, 100, 101, 102, 103, 104, 107, 116, 117, 122, 128, 137, 144, 146, 149, 150
Acre, 23
Addington, Henry Unwin, 120
Albert, Prince Consort of England, 66, 68, 87, 94, 95, 112, 128, 189, 197, 228, 229–30, 239, 273, 275, 331
Althorp, Viscount, see Spencer, 3rd Earl
Apponyi, Count Rudolf, 164, 293, 313, 314
Arnim, Heinrich Count von, 206, 313
Auckland, George Eden, 1st Earl of, 62, 199
Austria, 24, 76, 206; and Cracow, 162–5; and France, 205, 210–12, 293–5, 298, 299, 317–21; and the near east, 20, 21; and Spain, 152, 159, 160–1; and Switzerland, 297, 301, 312; see also Eastern Powers
Ayllon, Count, 251, 252, 253, 254, 257, 258, 259

Bagehot, Walter, 52
Baring, Sir Francis, 73
Barrot, Odilon, 327, 129n.
Bayard, Viscount, 257, 258, 260
Beauvale, Frederick Lamb, 1st Baron, 23, 30, 52, 53
Bedford, Francis Russell, 7th Duke of, 33, 34, 35, 45
Belgium, 5–6, 7, 8
Bentinck, Lord George, 190
Bloomfield, John Arthur Douglas, 2nd Baron, 155, 168, 176, 180, 182
Bois-le-Comte, Baron de, 299, 300, 304, 305, 306, 314, 315
Bresson, Count, 46, 48, 62; and Spanish Marriages, 74, 75, 79, 80, 89, 94, 103, 104, 105–10, 113–15, 118, 119, 120, 124, 125, 139, 147, 191, 209; and Spanish politics, 214, 216, 220, 221, 222, 224–5, 238
Broglie, Duke of, 8, 16, 56, 62, 148, 188, 196, 198, 208, 211, 269, 277, 279, 283, 288; and Swiss affairs, 302–3, 306, 307, 308–9, 310, 311–312, 313, 314, 315, 318–19
Brougham and Vaux, Henry Peter, 1st Baron, 204
Brunnow, Ernest Philip, Baron, 19, 152, 155, 179
Buchanan, Sir Andrew, 152
Buller, Charles, 33n.
Bulwer, Sir Henry, 41, 62, 65, 68n., 69, 74, 75n., 79, 197, 199; and Portugal, 217, 218, 219, 227, 231, 238–9, 240, 241, 244–5, 246, 250–251, 253, 254, 256, 257, 261; and the Spanish marriages, 87, 88n., 90, 92–4, 98–105, 109–19, 122,

INDEX

125, 129, 131, 132-6, 139, 140, 142, 143, 147; and Spanish politics, 214, 215, 216, 220-6, 259, 262-5, 266, 267, 270-6, 279-82, 287, 290-1
Bunsen, Christian, Karl Josias, Baron von, 155, 206, 310

Cabralists, 217-19, 232-3, 237, 249, 253, 255, 257, 258, 259, 260
Cadiz, Duke of, see Francisco de Asis
Canada, 34
Canitz, Baron, 152, 154, 164n., 182
Canning, George, 1, 2, 3, 333
Canning, Stratford, 314, 315, 316
Carlists, 14, 15, 82, 160
Carlos, Don, 11, 272
Castlereagh, Robert Stewart, Viscount, 3, 333
Cavaignac, General Eugène, 338
Chambers (French), 121, 150, 175, 185, 186, 188, 190, 192, 256, 323, 326
Charles x, King of France, 4
Christina, Queen Regent of Spain, and the Spanish Marriages, 83, 84, 85, 86, 87, 89, 90, 93, 96, 97, 98, 100, 101, 102, 103, 104-10, 111-18, 120, 124-5, 130, 131, 132; and Spanish politics, 11, 15, 28, 191, 214, 220, 224-5, 261, 266-7, 281, 283-4, 289
Clamor Publico, 132, 133n., 274
Clanricarde, Ulick John, 1st Marquess of, 62
Clarendon, William, Frederick Villiers, 4th Earl of, 15, 16, 21n., 22, 32, 33, 34, 41, 42, 48, 60, 61, 62, 69, 70, 71, 76, 92, 98, 111, 126, 127, 132, 134, 135, 152, 176, 177-178, 194, 196, 197, 198, 199, 204-205, 207, 223, 266, 300, 325, 326
Colettis, 79
Colleredo, Franz, Count, 319, 320, 325
Corn Laws, 41, 44, 46

Cortes (Portuguese), 218, 234, 245, 249, 260
Cortes (Spanish), 83, 114, 117, 125, 133, 134, 136, 139, 216, 223, 262, 263, 264, 270, 273, 276, 279, 284, 291
Cowley, Henry Wellesley, 1st Baron, 70n., 71, 72, 87n., 97
Cowper, Lady, see Palmerston, Lady
Cracow, 64, 162-5, 167-9, 309, 310

Dalmatie, Duke of, 160, 174, 205
Decazes, Duke of, 274
Delane, John Thadeus (ed. *The Times*), 150, 184; see also *The Times*
Desages, Count, 45, 49, 58n., 71, 77, 79, 104n., 106, 107, 208, 209, 243, 256-7, 274
Diet (Swiss), 296, 300, 304, 305, 317, 318, 320, 325
Dietrichstein, Count, 153, 164, 168, 169, 243
Dietz, Baron, 217, 231
Disraeli, Benjamin, 184
Douglas, John Arthur, see Bloomfield
Doyle, Andrew, 43, 318
Duchâtel, Charles Marie, Count, 148, 293, 318, 322, 324, 325
Dumon, 138
Duncannon, Viscount, 22
Dupetit-Thouars, Admiral Abel Aubert, 38

Eastern powers, 6, 7, 8, 9, 10, 11, 12, 15, 21, 23; and Cracow, 162-5, 167-9, 170-2; and the Spanish successions, 137, 138, 141, 142, 143, 147, 149, 150-1, 153, 155-6, 157, 161, 174-5, 272; and Switzerland, 301, 309, 311, 312
Easthope, Sir John, 31, 32, 35, 36, 42, 45, 49, 200
Eden, George, see Auckland, 1st Earl of
Egypt, 9, 17, 18, 20, 21
El Español, 132, 133n.

INDEX

Ellice, Edward, 21, 33, 34, 35, 42, 44, 46, 47, 63, 127
Elliot, Gilbert, see Minto, 2nd Earl
Enrique, Don, Duke of Seville, 96, 97, 98, 99, 100, 101, 102, 103, 105, 106, 108, 109, 110, 111, 112, 115, 116, 117, 122, 135, 136, 216, 220, 222, 270–1
Entente cordiale, Ch. II *passim*, 335–8; and Palmerston's return to office, 58, 59, 67, 71, 73, 76, 78, 81, 93, 108, 109, 112; and the Spanish Marriages, 121, 126, 127, 128, 129, 144–7, 148n., 149, 152, 161, 166, 176, 188, 192, 204–5, 208, 322, 323
Espartero, General Baldomero, Duke of Victory, 26, 32, 84, 85, 95, 96, 97, 102, 109, 134, 215, 264
Examiner, 48

Fane, John, see Westmorland, Earl of
Federal Pact, 295–6, 297, 301, 307, 311, 317, 320
Ferdinand of Saxe-Coburg, King Consort of Portugal, 87, 228–9
Ferdinand VII, King of Spain, 11, 119, 131, 143, 153, 154
Flahaut de la Billardene, Count, 60, 62, 76, 79, 143, 148, 151, 155, 159, 160, 161, 165, 173, 174, 180–1, 183, 208, 209, 211, 212, 297, 307, 319, 320
Fox, Charles James, 2, 3, 4, 36
Fox, Richard Vassal, see Holland, 3rd Baron
Foxite Whigs, 2–3, 4, 8, 20–1, 36, 332–5
France, and Austria, 205, 210–12, 293–5, 298, 299, 317–21; and Belgium, 6–7; and Great Britain, 7, 10, 12–13, 25–9, 38–9, 76–81, 121–2, 166–8, 184–5, 189, 207–12, 293–4, 310–12; and Portugal, 11, 215, 217–20, 232, 236–9, 242–5, 247–51, 254, 255–6, 259–61; and Spain, 10–11, 12, 15, 31, 32, 37–8, Chs. IV, V, VI, VII, VIII, IX *passim*
Francisco de Asis, Duke of Cadiz, King Consort of Spain, marriage of, 100, 105, 106, 107, 108, 109, 112, 113, 115, 116, 119, 120, 124, 130, 135, 143; and Spanish politics, 220, 222, 223, 225n., 262–263, 266, 273, 274, 275, 279, 281
Francisco de Paula, Don, 96n., 100, 104, 108, 112, 116, 123, 131, 177, 215, 216, 223, 266
Fraser's Magazine, 51, 56
Frederick William IV, King of Prussia, 152, 153, 206, 317

Glucksburg, Duke of, 106, 107, 209, 214, 224, 225, 226, 243–4, 251, 255, 259–61, 263, 265, 266–7, 274, 275, 278–81, 283–92
Gordon, George Arthur, see Aberdeen, Earl of
Gordon, Sir Robert, 71, 76, 151–2, 153, 161
Goulburn, Henry, 40
Goyena, 280
Graham, Sir James, 5, 40
Granville, George Leveson-Gower, 1st Earl of, 13, 14, 17, 72
Greece, 17, 28, 55, 75, 79, 206
Greville, Charles, 34, 41, 50, 60, 73, 124, 145, 171, 176, 186n., 325
Grey, Charles, 2nd Earl, 3, 4, 5, 12, 21, 22, 33, 51
Grey, Henry George, 3rd Earl of, see Howick, Viscount
Guizot, Francois Pierre, 22, 23, 69, 73, 74, 79, 80–1, 198, 208; and Aberdeen, 26, 27, 28, 37, 38, 39, 69–70, 71, 78, 80, 335–7; and Cracow, 163, 167–70, 173–4; and the Eastern powers, 160–1, 165–6, 173, 174–5, 205–6, 312–13; and the *entente cordiale*, 26–7, 29, 37, 40, 49, 58, 67, 76, 77, 78, 106, 108, 109, 188, 207–8, 335–8; and Metternich, 157, 159, 161–2, 165–

INDEX

166, 173, 181, 183, 210–12, 293–5, 298, 299, 317–21; and Palmerston, 30–2, 45, 49, 58, 59, 76, 77–8, 79, 80, 81, 87, 106, 107, 113, 120, 121, 125–6, 129, 142–3, 145–6, 148, 166–7, 171, 175, 184–5, 200, 207–209, 212, 214–15, 256, 268, 283, 308, 317; and Portugal, 215, 217–220, 232, 236–9, 242–5, 247–51, 254, 255–6, 259–61; and the Revolution of 1848, 322–31; and Spain, 28, 78–9, 81, 85, 121, 125, 207, 210, 214, 216–17, 223, 226, 237, 261, 262–3, 273, 278–80, 283–92; and the Spanish Marriages, 37, 41, 46, 48, 59, 61, 78–9, 85–6, 87, 88, 89, 90, 94, 103, 104, 105–10, 111, 113–17, 119, 120–3, 124, 125–6, 128, 129–30; and the Spanish Succession, 114, 130–1, 143, 149, 150, 155–7, 165, 173, 180–1, 210, 213, 267–9, 274–5; and Switzerland, 293, 297–9, 301–303, 304, 306–10, 312–15, 316–17, 318–21

Hauranne, Duvergier de, 327
Heraldo, 107
Herbert, Sidney, 1st Baron Herbert of Lea, 46
Hervey, Lord William, 48, 69, 70, 73–4, 76, 78, 87, 91, 111, 118, 134, 140, 152, 190, 197, 204, 220, 275, 300, 315, 318, 320, 322, 324, 326, 327
Holland, Henry Richard Vassal Fox, 3rd Baron, 3n., 4, 5, 6, 16, 20, 21, 22, 23, 52
Howard, Henry Francis, 152
Howden, John Hobart Caradoc, 2nd Baron, 72, 207
Howick, Viscount (later 3rd Earl Grey), 33, 44, 46, 47, 48, 51, 63, 196
Hummelauer, Baron, 180

Isabella II, Queen of Spain, marriage of, 37, 41, 67, 79, 84, 85, 86, 87, 88, 90, 94, 95, 97, 98, 99, 100, 104, 105, 106, 107, 108, 112, 113, 114, 117, 118, 119, 121, 122, 123, 124, 130, 132, 135, 136, 153; and Spanish politics, 215–16, 218, 220, 221, 222–3, 225, 257, 262–92 *passim*
Isturiz, Francisco Javier de, 111, 115, 118, 119, 132, 220, 224, 225, 247, 254, 287, 291
Italy, 164, 165, 173, 181, 182, 183, 206, 207, 211, 293, 295, 320, 337–338

Jarnac, Count Philippe de, 39, 45, 58, 59, 61, 70, 77, 80, 97, 101, 102, 104, 109, 116, 122, 123, 124, 126, 129, 138, 144, 145–6, 149, 155, 160, 166–7, 170, 171, 175, 184, 185, 254, 302
Jesuits, 296, 297, 300, 302, 303, 305, 307, 311, 312, 314, 317
Joinville, Duke of, 38, 323
Journal des Débats, 58, 121, 124, 129, 139, 166, 187, 192

Kaiserfeld, Count, 299, 305, 315
Kisselef, Paul, Count, 313, 314
Klindworth, Chevalier, 183, 205, 206, 210–11, 275, 293, 301

Lamartine, Alphonse de, 166, 331, 338
Lamb, Frederick, *see* Beauvale
Lamb, William, *see* Melbourne, 2nd Viscount
Lansdowne, Henry Petty-Fitzmaurice, 3rd Marquess, 4, 10, 23, 33, 43, 62, 65, 189, 196, 240–1
La Presse, 57n., 166, 192, 194
Le Constitutionnel, 129, 166
Le National, 144
Leopold, Prince of Saxe-Coburg, 67, 87, 89, 90, 93, 94, 95, 97, 98, 100, 102, 103, 104, 106, 108, 110, 111, 112, 115, 116, 117, 122, 187

Leopold I, King of the Belgians, 7, 102, 103, 145, 197, 226n., 231, 330
Leveson-Gower, George, *see* Granville, 1st Earl of
Liberal alliance, 12, 14, 15–17, 19–24, 53, 163, 332–5
Lieven, Princess Dorothea, 26, 27, 50, 73, 78, 111, 192
Louis XIV, King of France, 82, 129, 133, 140, 197
Louis XVIII, King of France, 82
Louis Philippe, King of the French, 4, 14, 20, 31, 47, 49, 55, 127, 128, 152, 155, 161, 207, 213, 322, 324–325, 326, 328, 329, 330–1, 334, 338; and Anglo-French relations, 24, 26, 27, 37, 38, 45, 50, 58, 66–7, 68, 144–5, 146, 148, 174, 186, 195, 197, 334, 338; and Portugal, 244, 248, 253, 259; and Spain, 32, 86–9, 97, 100, 103, 104, 105, 107, 108, 109, 110, 111, 112, 113–16, 119, 123, 125, 126, 137, 142, 151, 186, 210, 224, 244, 268, 269, 277, 282, 286, 287; and Switzerland, 302, 309, 310, 312, 316
Louise, Queen of the Belgians, 144, 145
Luisa, Fernanda, Infanta of Spain, Duchess of Montpensier, marriage of, 41, 55, 67, 79, 86, 90, 98, 105, 106, 112, 115, 116, 117, 119, 120, 125, 130, 131, 132, 140, 153; succession right of, 114, 130–1, 133–4, 137–9, 140, 148, 149, 150–1, 153–154, 155, 157, 161, 165, 169, 174, 176, 210, 213, 215, 222–3, 257, 264, 268, 269, 270, 271, 272, 274, 278, 283–92, 329
Lyons, Sir Edmond, 69, 75, 79

Macaulay, Thomas Babington, 43
Mahmud II, Sultan of Turkey, 18
Maria, Dona, Queen Maria II of Portugal, 10, 217–18, 219, 226, 227, 228–30, 231, 232–3, 235, 236–7, 241, 245, 246, 247, 249–50, 251–2, 254–5, 257, 258, 259–61
Marie Amélie, Queen of the French, 105, 144
Mehemet Ali, ruler of Egypt, 9, 17, 18, 19, 20, 21, 23, 152
Melbourne, William Lamb, 2nd Viscount, 4, 29, 45, 47, 51, 52, 53, 60, 62
Metternich, Prince Clemens, 148, 206–7; and Cracow, 162–5; and France, 23, 153, 206–7, 209; and Guizot, 143, 151–2, 157, 159, 170, 173, 183, 210–12, 293–4, 320; and Spain, 153–4, 155, 160, 161–2, 169, 173, 176, 179–82; and Switzerland, 295–8, 300–1, 303–4, 312–13, 315–16, 318–20
Miguel, Dom, 10, 13, 235, 236, 241, 242
Miguelites, 234, 235, 236–7, 238, 239, 245
Minto, Gilbert Elliott, 2nd Earl, 42, 62, 206, 305, 311, 325, 328
Miraflores, Marquis de, 12, 105
Moderdo party, 28, 83, 84, 85, 93, 96, 97, 100, 101, 107, 109, 111, 113, 114, 122, 132, 134, 135, 142, 199, 210, 214, 215, 216, 217, 218, 219, 220, 221, 227, 250, 257, 258, 259, 262, 263, 264, 265, 266, 268, 273, 279, 286
Molé, Count Louis, 16, 192, 194, 325, 327, 328, 329
Mon, Alejandro, 113, 224, 225
Moncorvo, Baron, 244, 247, 254
Montemolin, Count of, 104, 143, 160, 174, 177n., 181, 223, 271–3, 276, 284, 289
Montpensier, Duke of, 41, 55, 67, 86, 90, 98, 99, 101, 105, 106, 107, 109, 111, 112, 113, 114, 115, 116, 117, 119, 120, 121, 123, 124, 125, 128, 130, 131, 132, 134, 136, 137, 140, 141, 142, 147, 154, 224
Montpensier, Duchess of, *see* Luisa Fernanda, Infanta of Spain

INDEX 349

Morning Chronicle, 29, 30, 31, 33, 35, 36, 43, 50, 57n., 58, 128, 129, 140, 144, 150, 171, 200, 260, 318
Morocco, 39, 40, 199
Münchengrätz, Convention of (1833), 9, 10
Muñoz, Sergeant Fernando, 113

Narvaez, Ramon Maria, 85, 94, 100, 114, 221–2, 226, 257, 269, 275, 276, 279, 280–1, 283–92
Nesselrode, Count Charles Robert de, 19, 152, 159, 162, 165, 176, 182, 320
Nicholas I, Tsar of Russia, 19, 20n., 152
Normanby, Constantine Henry, Phipps, 1st Marquess of, 52–3, 54n., 56n., 64, 65, 70, 226, 320–330; and Anglo-French relations, 71, 72, 73, 170, 173, 176, 186, 187, 188, 190–4, 198, 202, 213, 232, 243, 289; and Spain, 116, 117, 119, 120, 121, 122, 123, 126, 261, 269, 273, 275–7; and Switzerland, 298, 301, 306, 311, 312, 313, 316, 318, 319
Northern Courts, *see* Eastern powers

Ochsenbein, Ulrich, 297, 300, 305, 315n.
Olozaga, Salustiano, 96n., 134, 178, 271–2
Oregon, 50
Orleans, Philippe II, Duke of, 133, 140, 154

Pacheo, J. F., 220, 225–6, 227, 244–245, 250–1, 253, 259, 261–5, 266, 274, 275, 279
Palmerston, Henry John Temple, 3rd Viscount, and Aberdeen, 29, 30, 31, 32, 33, 41, 43, 47, 91–2; and Cracow, 167, 168–72, 174; and the Eastern powers, 143, 150, 151–5, 160–2, 168, 176, 182–3, 205–7, 312; and France, 5, 7, 11, 12–13, 14, 15, 16, 17, 20, 21, 22, 24, 30–1, 32, 49, 54, 66, 127–8, 138–9, 147, 152–3, 170, 194–6, 198–201, 203–4, 207, 229–30, 242–5, 248–9, 254, 269–70, 302–3, 309, 313, 332–8; and Guizot, 23, 31, 32, 45, 47, 49, 77, 129, 136, 148–9, 166–7, 171–2, 176–7, 202–205, 207–8, 269, 303, 309, 313, 330, 335–8; and the near east, 8–9, 17, 18, 19, 20, 21, 22; and opposition, 29, 30, 31, 32, 33–7, 43–7; and principles of policy, 1–2, 5, 32, 35–6, 53–4, 55, 56, 57, 64–5, 66, 68–9, 72–3, 74, 75, 194, 201–3, 333–8; and Portugal, 10–11, 12–13, 198, 213, 217–20, 226–33, 236–46, 246–61, 263–6, 272, 278, 302; and Queen Victoria, 66, 67, 68, 98, 200, 229, 239; and Spain, 11, 15–17, 31, 32, 63, 79, 80, 82, 84, 98–9, 100, 136–138, 198, 213–17, 220, 221, 224, 226, 254–6, 261, 273, 275–8, 282–283, 288–92; and the Spanish Marriages, 91, 92, 94, 95–6, 97, 98, 99, 100–3, 109–13, 115, 116, 117, 118, 120, 122, 123, 124, 126, 127, 136–9, 140, 141, 147; and the Spanish succession, 133, 134, 137–139, 140–1, 147, 148–9, 151–5, 157, 165, 173, 176–83, 194–5, 213, 267–73; and Switzerland, 298, 302–4, 305, 308–9, 310–11, 313–314, 315–16, 317–18; and the Whigs, 1–5, 17–22, 33, 34, 35, 36–37, 41, 42–3, 44, 47–8, 51, 57, 63–64, 128
Palmerston, Lady, 45, 52, 68n., 146
Parker, Admiral Sir William, 219, 227, 258
Parliament, 185, 189
Peel, Sir Robert, 2nd Bt., 25, 28, 29, 39, 40, 41, 44, 47, 50, 51, 59, 68, 76, 80, 87, 89, 90, 104, 144, 146, 150, 197, 200, 201, 323
Peel, Sir Robert, 3rd Bt., 304

INDEX

Petty-Fitzmaurice, Henry, *see* Lansdowne, 3rd Marquess of
Philip v, King of Spain, 11, 37, 85, 98
Phipps, Constantine Henry, *see* Normanby, 1st Marquess of
Piscatory, Theobald-Émile, 75, 79, 286
Poland, 3, 162–3, 171
Polignac, Prince Jules de, 4
Pomare, Queen of Tahiti, 38
Ponsonby, John, Viscount, 71, 67, 153–4, 160, 161, 168, 169, 173, 176, 179, 180, 182–3, 197, 300, 301, 313, 315
Portugal, Prince of (eldest son of Maria II), 272, 278
Portugal, 10–11, 12, 13, 14, 28, 55, 160; and the revolt of 1846–7–68, 217–20, 226–45, 246–61
Pragmatic Sanction, 11, 156, 161, 169, 180
Pritchard, George, 38, 39, 43, 44, 88
Progresista party, and the Spanish Marriages, 92, 93, 95, 96, 97, 98, 99, 100, 101, 106, 113, 117, 118, 125, 132, 133, 134, 135, 140–1; and Spanish politics, 16, 28, 29, 32, 83, 84, 137, 142, 160, 178, 199, 217, 218, 220, 221, 225, 243, 257, 259, 262, 264–5, 266, 273, 274, 275–6, 279, 280
Protectionists, 149, 150
Prussia, 20, 21, 205–6; and Cracow, 162–5; and Spain, 149, 151, 155, 159, 160, 165–6, 168, 174, 176; and Switzerland, 304, 308, 319, 320, 325; *see also* Eastern powers

Quadruple Alliance (1833), 13, 14, 15, 102; in 1847, 235, 236–8, 239, 240–1, 242, 245, 246–7, 254–5

Radowitz, General Joseph Maria von, 317, 319, 320, 325
Rayneval, Count, 158, 159, 165
Reeve, Henry, 76, 150, 171, 184, 196, 197, 199, 204, 205, 317, 324, 325
Revue des Deux-Mondes, 186
Rianzares, Duke of, 105, 106, 113, 114, 115, 118, 119, 132
Right of Search, 28
Rossi, Pellegrino, 274
Rothschild, James, 194
Russell, Francis, *see* Bedford, 7th Duke of
Russell, Lord John, 2, 22, 50, 65, 71, 74, 120, 170, 211; and Anglo-French relations, 4, 59, 60, 61, 115, 121, 124, 127, 128, 145–6, 168–9, 176, 189, 193, 195, 196, 199, 201, 330; and opposition to the government of Peel, 29, 30, 33, 34, 35, 36, 41, 42, 43, 44, 45, 46, 47, 48, 51, 52; and Palmerston, 51, 52, 61, 63–4, 72; and Portugal, 234, 239, 240–2, 245, 246–7, 260; and Spain, 91, 111, 112, 115, 116, 117, 118, 123, 127, 136, 139, 140, 189, 272, 273, 275, 276–8, 279, 283, 287–8, 290; and Switzerland, 299, 306, 310n., 64, 311, 316
Russia, 3, 4, 6, 8–9, 10, 12, 17, 18, 19, 20, 21, 24, 54, 63; and Cracow, 162–5; and Spain, 149, 151, 152–153, 154, 155, 159, 168, 181; and Switzerland, 304, 308, 314; *see also* Eastern powers

Sa da Bandeira, Viscount, 252, 253, 258
Sainte-Aulaire, Count, 70, 80, 88, 90, 91, 92, 122, 148, 149, 175, 184n., 185, 188, 189, 193, 194, 197, 214, 242–3, 248
Salamanca, José de, 262
Saldanha, Duke of, 219, 227, 233, 235, 236, 252
Saxe-Coburg, Ernest II, Duke of, 90, 94, 102, 113
Septembrists, 217–18, 226, 229, 231, 232, 235, 239, 245, 249, 252, 255, 257–8, 259, 260

INDEX

Serrano, General Francisco, 225, 262, 266, 275, 280, 281
Seville, Duke of, *see* Enrique Don
Seymour, George Hamilton, 230n., 242, 249, 251, 252, 253, 256, 257–9
Shiel, Edward, 52n.
Slave Trade, 28
Sonderbund, 297, 298–9, 302, 303, 304, 305, 306, 307, 308, 310, 311, 312, 315, 317
Sotomayor, Duke of, 90, 91, 116, 117, 187, 220, 221, 225, 238, 243–244, 259, 260
Soult, Marshal Nicolas Jean, 21, 22n.
Southern, Henry, 226, 228, 229, 230, 234, 238, 243
Spain, and Anglo-French rivalry, 12–13, 15–17, 24, 28, 31, 32, 37, 74–5, 83, 91, 92–3, 103, 104, 109, 112, 125, 130, 198–9, 213–14, 248–9; and constitutional government, 12, 55, 92, 99, 100–1, 113, 214; and Portugal, 11, 215–20, 231, 236–44, 246–7, 247–61; *see also* Spanish Marriages *and* Spanish Succession
Spanish Marriages, and British policy towards, 37, 41, 48–9, 67, Ch. IV *passim*; and French policy towards, 37, 41, 46, 48–9, 67, 79–80, Ch. IV *passim*; arrangement of, 105–9, 118–19; reactions to, 120, 121, 122–3, 124–6, 127–8, 134, 136, 147, 173
Spanish Succession, French policy towards, 114, 130–1, 143, 155–7, 173, 180–2, 214, 222, 263, 276–70, 274–5; British policy towards, 133–4, 137–9, 140, 141, 147, 148, 150, 151–4, 157, 171, 173, 176, 180–3, 213–14, 222, 264, 267–73, 289–92; Eastern powers and, 137, 138, 141, 143, 147, 151, 153, 159–160, 168, 169, 174, 179–82, 271
Spencer, John Charles Spencer, 3rd Earl, 4, 22, 34

Stanley, Edward Lord, 184, 189
Stanley, E. J., 110, 111, 240, 331
Stockmar, Baron, 179
Stewart, Robert, *see* Castlereagh
Switzerland, 157, 173, 181, 182, 183, 211, Ch. x *passim*

Tacon, 244
Tahiti, 38, 39, 40, 41, 42, 43, 88
Talleyrand, Perigord Charles Marie de, Prince, 13
Temple, Henry John, *see* Palmerston, 3rd Viscount
The Globe, 11n., 12n., 23n., 33n., 254, 260
The Times, 30, 33, 39, 76, 124, 127, 128, 129, 135, 139, 144, 146, 150, 184, 187, 190, 194, 205, 317, 318, 326
Thiers, Louis Adolphe, 16n., 21, 22, 29, 44n., 49, 61, 77, 129, 149, 152, 176, 185, 188, 190, 191, 192, 203n., 212, 237, 294, 323, 326, 327
Thomar, Count, 236, 238, 257
Tory party, 4, 25
Trapani, Count of, 86, 87, 93, 105
Turkey, 9–10, 17, 18

United States of America, 31, 34
Unkiar Skelessi, Treaty of (1833), 9, 10, 19, 20
Utrecht, Treaty of (1713), 133, 140, 160, 165, 174, 178, 180, 183, 205, 264; British interpretation of, 140, 141, 149, 150–1, 154, 157, 178–9; French interpretation of, 155–7

Varenne, Count, 243, 248, 252, 253, 254, 256, 257, 258, 259
Victoria, Queen of England, 44, 45, 47, 50, 55, 59, 66, 123, 124, 126, 127, 168, 282; and Anglo-French relations, 27, 37, 41, 66, 67, 68, 98, 112, 119, 128, 144–5, 147, 149, 197, 200, 330–1; and Palmerston, 66, 67, 68; and Portugal, 229–30, 231, 234, 235, 239, 260–1; and

Victoria, Queen of England—*cont.*
  Spain, 87, 94–5, 97–8, 102, 112, 116, 137, 139, 140, 144–5, 283
Vienna, Treaty of (1815), 5, 163, 165, 171n., 297
Villiers, William Frederick, *see* Clarendon, 4th Earl of

Webster-Ashburton, Treaty of (1842), 31, 34
Wellesley, Arthur, *see* Wellington, 1st Duke of
Wellesley, Henry, *see* Cowley, 1st Baron
Wellesley, Henry Richard Charles, 197
Wellington, Arthur Wellesley, 1st Duke of, 1, 2, 3, 40, 41, 201
Westmorland, John Fane, Earl of, 155, 168, 178, 180, 206
Wood, Sir Charles, 33, 60, 63, 149, 196, 201
Wylde, Colonel, 95, 228, 230, 231, 232, 234, 236, 249, 252

Soc
DA
47.1
B77